7.00

7-17-07

U.C. BERKELEY
ENGINEERING LIBRARY

ENVIRONMENTAL SYSTEMS OPTIMIZATION

ENVIRONMENTAL SYSTEMS OPTIMIZATION

Douglas A. Haith
Cornell University

John Wiley & Sons
New York   Chichester   Brisbane   Toronto   Singapore

Copyright © 1982, by John Wiley & Sons, Inc.

All rights reserved. Published simultaneously in Canada.

Reproduction or translation of any part of
this work beyond that permitted by Sections
107 and 108 of the 1976 United States Copyright
Act without the permission of the copyright
owner is unlawful. Requests for permission
or further information should be addressed to
the Permissions Department, John Wiley & Sons.

Library of Congress Cataloging in Publication Data

Haith, Douglas A.
  Environmental systems optimization.

  Includes bibliographies and index.
  1. Environmental protection—Mathematical
models.   I. Title.

TD170.2.H34   363.7'00724   81-3050
ISBN 0-471-08287-2   AACR2

Printed in the United States of America

10 9 8 7 6 5 4 3 2 1

To Charles R. Scherer, Ph.D. (May 13, 1943–January 1, 1979)

Near the snow, near the sun, in the highest fields,
See how these names are fêted by the waving grass
And by the streamers of white cloud
And whispers of wind in the listening sky.
The names of those who in their lives fought for life,
Who wore at their hearts the fire's centre.
Born of the sun, they travelled a short while toward the sun,
And left the vivid air signed with their honour.

From "I think continually of those . . ." by Stephen Spender. Reprinted by permission from Stephen Spender, *Collected Poems 1928–1953,* Random House, New York, 1955.

PREFACE

The problems associated with managing land, water, air, and energy resources have never been simple. It often seems that the complexities of environmental management, which includes the control of pollution and the allocation of resources, are so intimidating that rational analysis is futile. This is partially because of the political nature of environmental decisions. However, a substantial source of complexity is the intricate physical interactions within environmental systems. Wastes are transported by water or air from one location to another with attendant chemical transformations. Land used for one purpose may limit other uses, and energy planning must consider a bewildering array of competing sources and consumers. It can be difficult to trace the impacts of pollution control and resource management decisions, and it often seems impossible to determine which of several alternatives best meet management objectives.

Fortunately, there is an analytical process that promises to reduce the complexities of environmental problems to manageable levels. During and after World War II a problem-solving approach known as systems analysis evolved that has proved very useful in the resolution of complex management problems. Systems analysis has been applied recently with considerable success to environmental management. The applications that have been most fruitful are based on the mathematical modeling of environmental systems and the use of optimization techniques to identify promising management decisions.

This book provides students and practicing professionals with an introduction to the application of systems analysis and, most particularly, mathematical modeling and optimization techniques to environmental management. It is intended for engineers, biologists, economists, and planners who are interested in solving pollution control and resource allocation problems.

Two principal topics are emphasized. The first is the use of mathematical models that reduce environmental problems to mathematical relationships that can be manipulated to evaluate the effects of management alternatives. The second is the application of optimization methods such as search techniques, linear programming, dynamic programming, and integer programming to determine which management alternatives are better than others. Many examples are offered in the text; even though the standard applications of water and air pollution control and solid waste management are discussed fully, the examples include more recent applications such as land disposal of wastes, nonpoint source pollution, land use management, energy planning, and multiobjective planning. Artificial problems have been avoided; two chapters are devoted to extensive analyses of environmental problems based on "real-world" data.

The basic concepts of systems analysis are relatively simple and require only a year of college calculus to interpret. Mathematical proofs are based on intuition, graphical methods, and simple algebra. Computer programming capability is not a prerequisite for understanding the material in the book, but it is required for many of the exercises. Previous experience or coursework in environmental management is not necessary, but would be useful in understanding some of the examples.

The book is based on material presented in a one-semester, upper-class course at Cornell University. Although the course is required or recommended for environmental majors in several fields, it has attracted many other students who desire an introductory systems analysis course. All or portions of the book will serve similar purposes elsewhere. To the extent possible, the chapters are self-contained, thereby facilitating its use as a reference source.

Many individuals have contributed to this book. Early versions were reviewed by J. Robert Cooke, Ronald B. Furry, Charles D. Gates, Daniel P. Loucks, Jery R. Stedinger, and Michael F. Walter. They corrected my logic and mathematics, and made many substantial suggestions for improvement. My students suffered through early drafts; their reactions forced me to revise and clarify continually, my ideas and writing. Carol L. Beasley, Merrill G. Floyd, Vivian Kahane, Linda Indig, Kevin J. Murphy, and their colleagues at Wiley provided the steady level of encouragement and competence that transform manuscripts into published books. Karen E. Rizzo typed the manuscript and its several revisions with great efficiency, and she also prepared preliminary drawings for many of the figures. My deepest gratitude is reserved for Ellen, Robert, and Benjamin, who have given me more encouragement and love than any husband and father deserves.

Douglas A. Haith

CONTENTS

CHAPTER 1 ENVIRONMENTAL SYSTEMS ANALYSIS

Elements of Benefit/Cost Analysis	2
An Example of the Systems Approach	6
Definition of Objectives and System	8
Generation and Evaluation of Alternatives	9
Selection of an Alternative	11
Summary	11
Selected References	12

CHAPTER 2 MATHEMATICAL MODELING AND OPTIMIZATION   13

Modeling of a Wastewater Management Example	13
Model Construction	13
Model Solution	16
Generalization of the Systems Approach	20
Steps of the Systems Approach	21
General Form of an Optimization Model	22
Characteristics of Problems Amenable to Systems Analysis	22
Mathematical Modeling of a Pesticide Management Problem	23
Definition of System and Objectives	25
Model Construction	26
Solution	28
Summary	31
Selected References	33
Exercises	33

CHAPTER 3 APPLICATION: OPTIMIZATION MODEL FOR THE PLANNING OF MUNICIPAL WASTEWATER TREATMENT   41

Problem Description	41
Technical Background	42
Treatment and Discharge to Receiving Waters	42
Land Application of Municipal Wastewater	47
Wastewater Treatment Costs	50
Systems Analysis	51
Definition of System and Objectives	51

x CONTENTS

Generation of Alternatives—Construction of a Mathematical Model	51
Evaluation of Alternatives—Model Solutions	55
Selection of Alternative	59
Summary	61
Selected References	61
Exercises	62

CHAPTER 4 INTRODUCTION TO OPTIMIZATION ALGORITHMS 67

Method of Lagrange Multipliers	68
Unconstrained Optimization	68
Constrained Optimization	69
Limitations of Lagrange Multipliers	72
Sequential Search Algorithms	74
Box's Algorithm	75
Application	77
Limitations of General Search Algorithms	82
Summary	83
Selected References	83
Exercises	83

CHAPTER 5 LINEAR PROGRAMMING MODELS 85

A Two-Dimensional Linear Programming Example	86
Linear Programming Solution	88
Sensitivity Analysis	88
The Simplex Method	90
General Characteristics of Linear Programming Problems	94
Standard Form	94
Transforming to the Standard Form	96
Properties of Linear Programming Solutions	100
Dual Linear Programming Models	102
Generalization of Primal/Dual Linear Programming Models	106
Application of Linear Programming to Air Pollution Control	110
Application of Duality	118
General Linear Programming Models for Air Quality Management	121
Proportional Rollback Models	121
Air Pollution Transport Models	122
Summary	127
Selected References	127
Exercises	128

CHAPTER 6 APPLICATION: MANAGEMENT OF AGRICULTURAL NONPOINT SOURCE POLUTION 135

Nonpoint Source Water Pollution	135

General Description	135
Control of Agricultural Nonpoint Source Pollution	135
Problem Description	136
Dairy Farm Activities	137
Nonpoint Source Pollution from Dairy Farms	138
Limitations of the Systems Approach	138
Systems Analysis	139
Definition of System and Objectives	139
Model Construction	141
Implementation	146
Data	146
Model Summary	151
Model Solution: Impacts of Constraints on Nonpoint Source Pollutants	151
Regulatory Implications	155
Summary	156
Selected References	156
Exercises	157

CHAPTER 7   SEPARABLE AND INTEGER PROGRAMMING   161

Separable Programming	161
Separable Objective Functions	161
Generalized Separable Programming for Nonlinear Objective Functions	169
An Example of Separable Programming Applied to Multiobjective Planning	173
Generalized Separable Programming	179
Integer Linear Programming	179
Integer Programming Algorithms	181
Municipal Solid Wastes Management Example—A Fixed Charge Problem	187
Linearization by Mixed Integer Methods	196
Summary	198
Selected References	199
Exercises	200

CHAPTER 8   TRANSPORTATION MODELS   205

Allocation of Energy Resources Using a Transportation Model	207
Model Construction	208
Solution Algorithm	210
Degeneracy	218
The Assignment Problem	218
Recreation Planning Problem	220
A General Assignment Model Algorithm	221
Summary	223
Selected References	225
Exercises	225

xii CONTENTS

CHAPTER 9   DYNAMIC PROGRAMMING MODELS 229

   Application of Dynamic Programming to Land Use Planning 230
   Dynamic Programming Notation 237
      Characteristics of Dynamic Programming Problems 241
   Example of Phosphorus Removal from Municipal Wastewaters 242
      Construction of an Optimization Model 243
      Reformulation of Model 245
      Dynamic Programming Solution 247
      Sensitivity Analysis 252
   Generalized One-Dimensional Dynamic Programming 253
      Optimization Model 254
      Recursive Equations 255
   Inventory Problems 255
      Optimization Model 257
      Dynamic Programming Solution 258
      Overview 261
   Application of Dynamic Programming to Air Pollutant Emissions Control 262
      Dynamic Programming Formulation 263
      Computational Tables 265
      Extension to Multiple Pollutants 266
   Forward Dynamic Programming 268
      Forward Dynamic Programming Computations 270
      Summary of Forward Dynamic Programming 273
   Summary 273
   Selected References 274
   Exercises 274

CHAPTER 10   OPTIMIZATION OVER TIME 281

   Discounting of Future Objectives 281
   Evaluation of Future Monetary Benefits and Costs 284
      Present Value Computations 285
      Equivalent Annual Value 286
      Effects of Inflation 288
   Selection of Discount Rates for Public Investments 289
   Capacity Expansion Problems 291
   Summary 297
   Selected References 298
   Exercises 298
INDEX 301

ENVIRONMENTAL SYSTEMS OPTIMIZATION

CHAPTER 1
ENVIRONMENTAL SYSTEMS ANALYSIS

The management of environmental problems is a challenging venture. These problems involve land, water, air, and energy resources that significantly affect human activities and attitudes. A major difficulty is that individual parts of environmental problems function together to produce unwanted results. For example, the water pollution associated with a wastewater discharge to a stream is related to many factors: waste sources and properties, waste collection, treatment processes, method and location of discharge, transport of the wastes in the stream, and the effects of the wastes on biota and human use. Each component can be and often is analyzed separately, but a water pollution problem results from the interactions and collective effects of a water pollution *system*.

There are obvious advantages in treating environmental problems as systems. Problems can be considered in their totality, and the most effective points of control can be sought. In a wastewater discharge example this might produce combinations of source reductions, treatment methods, and discharge locations that are more effective and possibly less costly than improved treatment alone. A consequence of a systems perspective on environmental quality is the broadening of possible control options and subsequent opportunities for efficient, integrated management strategies.

Systems are collections of things that function together; the study of these collections is called *systems analysis*. This is a general definition that includes many professional disciplines and applications, from computer science to sociology. Common to many applications involving problem solving is a *systems approach* involving three steps:

1. Definition of the relevant system and objectives.
2. Generation and evaluation of alternatives for meeting the objectives.
3. Selection of an alternative.

These steps are an obvious (if somewhat optimistic) prescription of logic. However, several refinements can lend a unique and powerful character to the approach. The first is an emphasis on quantitative analysis. Although the systems approach can be carried out in a qualitative, descriptive fashion, its most impressive results are produced with numbers. When system components, objectives, and management alternatives are described numerically, it is easier for analysts to communicate their results; the ultimate users of the analyses can interpret problem solutions more readily. Quantification does not eliminate subjectivity, but it discourages vagueness.

A second refinement follows from the decision to quantify. In any but the very simplest system there are usually many combinations of management options for the various components. The numerical accounting of all resulting system interactions is a tedious bookkeeping process that can be accomplished efficiently by using mathematical models. Models are approximations or abstractions of the actual system and include mathematical descriptions of objectives, component interactions, and management methods. Mathematical models are essentially experimental tools. The analyst can vary parameters of the models and use model outputs as predictions of the performance of the real system. Thus mathematical models help to generate and evaluate rapidly alternative solutions to a problem.

A final refinement to the systems approach is to impose conditions on the types of solutions we wish to obtain from models. These conditions are dictated by efficiency needs. Most mathematical models are capable of evaluating an infinite number of alternatives, and it is clearly desirable to discover alternatives that most closely meet the objectives of the problem being analyzed. Such alternatives can be found through the use of optimization techniques. When these techniques are combined with a mathematical model of a system, an *optimization model* results.

This book is about environmental systems analysis, or the application of the systems approach to environmental management. However, emphasis is on the quantitative aspects of systems analysis, especially the use of optimization models to aid in the development of solutions to environmental problems. This does not imply that other forms of systems analysis are not useful in environmental management nor does it mean that optimization models will always produce ideal solutions to environmental problems. Nevertheless, successful applications of optimization have indicated that the procedures promise to improve the analytical capability of environmental engineers, planners, and scientists.

ELEMENTS OF BENEFIT/COST ANALYSIS

Management of an environmental problem requires objectives or criteria against which alternative solutions can be measured. One general objective is the maximization of net social benefits. The quantification of these benefits in monetary terms is a major interest of benefit/cost analysis. The analysis has two key components, one of which is the idea of resource allocation. The environment (water, air, land, energy) can be viewed as a resource that should be used to improve social welfare. The second component is the concept of social accounting, which requires that the benefits and costs to *all* users of a resource affected by an environmental problem should be determined. Benefit/cost analysis can be illustrated by the water pollution situation in Figure 1-1.[1]

A factory is discharging into a river a toxic waste that affects the catch by a downstream commercial fishery. It is assumed that the factory and fishery are the river's

---

[1]This example has its genesis in a comparable problem presented in A. V. Kneese, *The Economics of Regional Water Quality Management*, Johns Hopkins Press, Baltimore, 1964.

ELEMENTS OF BENEFIT/COST ANALYSIS   3

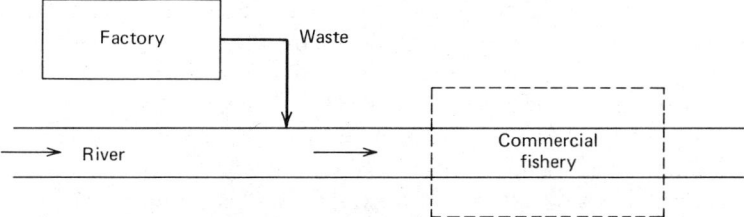

Figure 1-1 Water pollution problem used to illustrate benefit/cost analysis.

only users. The discharge, with its resulting effect, is an example of an economic *externality*, which is defined as a cost or benefit produced by one economic unit that is incurred by other economic units. Thus the factory's waste disposal has an associated cost, but that cost is borne by the fishery, not the factory. The cost is "external" to the factory's accounting of income and costs. Implicit in the concept of externality is the idea of unfairness. It does not seem just that the fishery should pay for the factory's waste disposal. However, justice and fairness are often ambiguous. Consider the example of an estate maintained by a wealthy family near a large metropolitan area. Parts of the estate might consist of forests and rolling fields that lie along public roads. The result for travelers (by car, by bicycle, or on foot) is a scenic rural vista within an otherwise highly developed area. Many, if not most, travelers derive pleasure from this scenery. The fields are an externality in that they produce uncompensated benefits incurred by the traveling public. Fairness would dictate that the estate owners be compensated for the benefits they are providing. This externality may not seem as obvious as the waste discharge, yet it is clearly comparable. In the waste discharge case the environmental resource is being degraded by one party without subsequent compensation to other users. Conversely, the scenic externality involves the uncompensated improvement of an environmental resource by one party that provides benefits for many others.

Returning to the example in Figure 1-1, what are the possible solutions to this problem? The two extreme solutions are to do nothing or to ban the discharge entirely. Although both solutions are defective, they are not without merit. The "do-nothing" approach is based partly on the realization that waste products are an unavoidable consequence of human activity. Something must be done with them, and river discharge is a logical disposal means. Moreover, it has long been known that the environment has an impressive ability to assimilate wastes. For example, given a sufficient supply of oxygen, much of the organic matter in wastes can be fairly rapidly oxidized to carbon dioxide and water by microbes in streams and rivers. Waste assimilation can thus be considered a valuable use of the environmental resource. The difficulty with this approach is that the waste *assimilation capacity* of an environmental resource (in this case, a river) is finite. Excessive waste discharges may not be assimilated, or at least not in a desirable fashion. When the river oxygen is depleted, the river will become a septic, vile-smelling sewer. In this case the organic wastes may still be assimilated (degraded), but most people would not be pleased with the results. Similarly, toxic substances may be assimilated by cycling through aquatic food chains and ultimately destroying fish and other wildlife or endangering human food sources.

Juxtaposed to the do-nothing solution is the banning of waste discharge, presumably on the grounds that this would return the river to a natural (unpolluted) condition. The merits of this solution are less obvious, but it certainly appeals to real social preferences for cleanliness, pure water, protection of wildlife, and the like. However, banning the waste discharge in this case carries the implicit assumption that commercial fishing is a better or more valuable use of the river than waste assimilation. Of course, fishing is a disturbance of the river's natural condition, and it might also be consistent to ban the fishery. In this case, there would be no users of the environmental resource. Other users, such as people fishing for sport, boaters, and swimmers, may subsequently appear. The new users are similar to the fishery in that they interfere (if only in a minor way) with the river's natural condition. The approach of prohibiting waste discharges leads either to the prevention of all uses of the river or the favoring of certain uses over others. The latter implies a judgment concerning the relative value of uses and leads to a third approach to resolving the water pollution problem, the application of benefit/cost analysis.

The benefit/cost approach is based on the concept that the river is a resource that should be used in the most beneficial way. This requires an examination of the monetary consequences of the waste discharge to both users of the river. Let us assume that the factory is presently incurring no waste disposal cost and that its cheapest alternative to river waste disposal would cost $50,000. The fishery's current profits are $10,000, but it is estimated that elimination of the waste discharge would increase catches sufficiently to raise profits to $30,000. Thus the present (do-nothing) alternative provides the factory with $50,000 in benefits at a cost of $20,000 to the fishery, for a net benefit of $30,000. Conversely, prohibiting the waste discharge eliminates both factory benefits and fishery costs, producing no net benefits. The conclusion of the analysis is that the present use of the river for both waste discharge and fishing is more valuable than its use for fishing alone. Of course, better alternatives may exist. For example, diversion of a portion of the waste from the river for $10,000 might increase the fishery profits to $25,000, for a net benefit of ($50,000 − 10,000) − ($30,000 − 25,000) = $35,000. Each possible alternative could be evaluated similarly and the alternative yielding the greatest net benefit (most valuable use of the resource) selected.

Benefit/cost analysis is the aggregation of the monetary cost and benefits to all economic units affected by the various solutions to an environmental problem. This is an indication of the value of the environmental resource to society. The indicator is imperfect for many reasons, the most important of which is that it ignores social preferences for the *distribution* of costs and benefits. For example, if the fishery is owned by a native or minority group whose economic development is being encouraged by government action, the loss of $20,000 profits may be more important than a $50,000 waste disposal cost incurred by the factory. Clearly, there are social goals that are inadequately accounted for in benefit/cost analysis, and the net benefit criterion is seldom used as an exclusive method for selecting solutions to environmental problems. Nevertheless, it is an essential tool for environmental management, primarily because it forces the explicit accounting, in quantitative (monetary) terms, of the beneficial and adverse effects of environmental pollution. In addition, it requires a determination of the economic impact of pollution control alternatives.

Benefit/cost analysis provides the rationale for *effluent charges*, which are imposed on waste discharges. Effluent charges are in essence a "price" or "user fee" that a waste discharger pays for using the environment for waste assimilation. The charge should be equal to an opportunity cost, or the value of the environmental resource in its most productive alternative use. In the factory/fishery example, this opportunity cost is $20,000, or the lost profits of the fishery. Note that effluent charges do not necessarily reduce pollution. In the example, the factory would discharge as long as the effluent charge was less than $50,000. The objective of an effluent charge is to internalize the externalities associated with environmental pollution; that is, the waste discharger is forced to include the off-site costs of resulting pollution in cost and revenue accounting.

There are several other difficulties in applying benefit/cost analysis (with or without effluent charges) to real-world problems. Suppose, for example, that instead of a fishery, the second use of the river is as part of a public park that provides boating, swimming, sport fishing, scenic beauty, and the like. Furthermore, assume that the waste discharge interferes with these uses. In order to apply benefit/cost analysis, the monetary costs (or lost benefits) incurred by the users as a result of the waste discharge must be determined. Since the individual users generally would not maintain a revenue and cost accounting of their recreational activities, the estimation of the river's value to the park users could be exceedingly difficult. Without such an estimate, the net benefits of waste management alternatives could not be computed.

This type of situation can be dealt with by the imposition of an *environmental quality standard*, which is a law or regulation specifying a minimum allowable quality level, in measureable parameters, for an environmental resource. In this case the standard might be a maximum concentration of a toxic chemical in the river at the park. The standard would imply that the factory must reduce toxic waste discharges to the point where the resulting river levels meet the standard. Environmental standards are set by political processes that implicitly consider trade-offs between competing uses of the environmental resource.

Quality standards can also be a mechanism for handling social preferences for benefit and cost distributions. For example, in the factory/fishery situation, if commercial fishing is considered by government to be a favored activity, a water quality standard might be set in terms of parameters affecting fish mortality. Once the standard has been set, the net benefits of alternatives that meet the standard can be determined and the alternative selected that maximizes net benefits. Thus environmental standards can be a means of dealing with the imperfections of benefit/cost analysis.

Environmental quality standards can be implemented when the cause-and-effect relationships between a waste discharge and environmental quality parameters can be determined. This is not always easy, since most potential pollutants undergo physical, chemical, and biological changes when introduced into the environment. If there were many waste discharges to the river upstream of the park, it could be difficult to determine how much each of these discharges should be controlled to meet the quality standard. In this case it might be advisable to impose *effluent standards*, which would limit the amount and characteristics of each waste discharge more or less equally. If these standards are met, water quality presumably will improve, although the improvement is not necessarily obtained in an economically efficient manner. For example, the control of just the major discharges closest to the park might be less expensive than control of all upstream discharges, and water quality improvements may be comparable.

Effluent standards have two major advantages, administrative convenience and equity. The administration of water pollution control programs can be costly and difficult. Effluent standard compliance can be readily monitored by sampling and analysis of waste discharges. Violations are eliminated by additional removal of the offending substances. Although environmental quality standards can also be monitored, violations are not readily corrected, since the relative contribution of each discharge to the violation must be determined. Effluent standards also have an element of fairness to them, particularly when they are set on a uniform basis for each category of waste discharge.

Environmental quality and effluent standards are common environmental management tools. Standards tend to disaggregate benefit/cost analysis. In the case of effluent standards, the decomposition is complete, with each waste discharger able to maximize his or her own net benefits (minimize net costs) of meeting the standard. Application of benefit/cost analysis results in three different types of environmental management problems.

1. Maximization of the total net monetary benefits (minimization of the total monetary costs) to all users of an environmental resource.
2. Maximization of the total net monetary benefits (minimization of the total net monetary costs) to all waste dischargers of meeting an environmental quality standard.
3. Maximization of the total net monetary benefits (minimization of the total net monetary costs) to each discharger of meeting an effluent standard.

Most environmental problems are variations of, or a combination of, types two and three. The basic concepts of benefit/cost analysis are preserved, but constraints (in the form of standards) are imposed on the analysis. Such constraints imply that the values of certain resource uses either cannot be evaluated monetarily or that the monetary values that can be obtained do not reflect social preferences.

As a final note *cost-effectiveness* refers to a search for the least expensive way to meet an objective. The determination of an environmental management alternative that satisfies standards at minimum cost is a cost-effectiveness problem.

AN EXAMPLE OF THE SYSTEMS APPROACH

Although the mathematical modeling of environmental problems is emphasized in this book, we have observed that systems analysis can be applied without resorting to models. The basic ideas of systems analysis are illustrated in the following water quality problem.[2] This same problem is analyzed in Chapter 2, using a mathematical model.

EXAMPLE 1-1 Wastewater Management
A metal refining factory has a waste disposal problem. For 1 kg of metal produced, 3 kg of waste are created. The waste is contained in wastewater at a concentration of 2 kg/m^3. Wastewater has been discharged to a nearby river with partial treatment. The government has imposed an effluent standard of 100,000 kg/wk on the factory's waste discharge. The factory has a production capacity of 55,000 kg of metal per week. Metal is sold at a price of $1.30/kg and production costs are $0.90/kg. The factory's wastewater treatment facility has a capacity of 70,000 m^3/wk. However, the facility's efficiency (fraction of waste removed) varies with waste loading. If W is the wastewater inflow to treatment in 10^4 m^3/wk then, for W between 0 and 70,000 m^3/wk, treatment efficiency is given by $1 - 0.06W$. Thus the more heavily the plant is loaded, the less efficient it is at removing the waste from the wastewater. Wastewater treatment costs are $0.20/m^3. □

This wastewater management problem, which is illustrated in Figure 1-2, involves the determination of an efficient way for the factory to meet its effluent standard. Although the example is deceptively simple, it has similarities to other environmental pollution problems.

1. Waste output is related to production level. It is a direct function of factory's output of a useful product (refined metal).
2. The waste material or pollutant is flushed from the factory in water. This is known as *wastewater*, the strength of which is measured by its concentration of pollutant (2 kg/m^3).

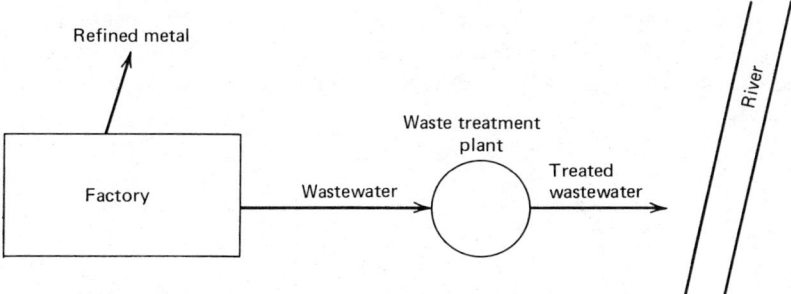

Figure 1-2 Wastewater management example.

---

[2]This example was suggested by a comparable problem in M. B., Fiering, J. J. Harrington, and R. J. deLucia, "Water Resources Systems Analysis," Information Canada, Ottawa, 1971.

8 ENVIRONMENTAL SYSTEMS ANALYSIS

3. An effluent standard is set in terms of the *contents* of the wastewater (kg of pollutant), not the quantity or volume of wastewater.
4. Waste treatment facilities seldom remove all pollutants. Furthermore, removal efficiency, e = pollutant mass removed/pollutant mass treated, is often a function of waste loading. Removal efficiency for this problem is shown in Figure 1-3. For example, with a wastewater flow of 25,000 m^3/wk, the fraction of pollutant mass removed is 0.85, but at 50,000 m^3/wk, efficiency drops to 0.70.

Each factor complicates the problem, and it does not seem to have an obvious solution. The three steps of the systems approach are described in the following discussion.

Definition of Objectives and System

Objectives Without clear objectives it can be very difficult to solve a problem. Some possible objectives for the example are to (1) reduce pollution, (2) protect the environment, (3) treat wastes, and (4) save money. These goals are all desirable and may result from the solution to this water pollution problem. However, they are not sufficient for systems analysis. *An objective must be specific enough so that we can measure how well it has been achieved*. Since systems analysis involves evaluations of many possible solutions, objectives must provide criteria by which alternative solutions can be compared. Two alternatives may protect the environment, treat wastes, and so forth but, for comparison, we must know which alternative does these things better.

Objectives must also be relevant to the problem's *decision makers*. A decision maker is an individual or group that can implement or reject a solution to the problem. Thus, if the factory's plant manager decides whether or not to implement a solution, the manager's objectives may be more relevant than those of a citizens' environmental group. Of course, if the citizens' group is planning a lawsuit against the factory, the group's objectives could be very important to the manager. Assuming that the plant manager is the appropriate decision maker, one of the objectives obviously must be to meet the effluent standard (because it is a legal requirement). The effect of this standard on the environment may be irrelevant to the manager. A specific quantitative objective is as follows.

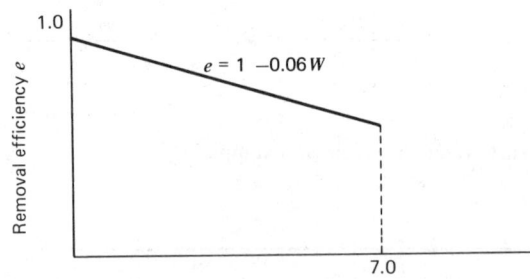

Figure 1-3 Treatment efficiency as a function of wastewater loading.

Objective One Discharge no more than 100,000 kg/wk of waste into the river.

The financial implications of achieving the effluent standard are also important. There is likely to be more than one way to meet the standard, and the manager would doubtless want to examine the costs of the alternatives. A second objective could be the minimization of treatment costs. However, this would be a fairly narrow financial viewpoint. Presumably the factory's profits are the manager's overriding concern, and a more appropriate objective is offered next.

Objective Two Maximize the factory's profits ($/wk).

The difference between this objective and the minimization of treatment costs is great. The latter implies that waste production level cannot be changed or, conversely, that the effects of waste treatment on production (and hence revenues) can be ignored. These are questionable assumptions that preclude problem solutions involving production changes. Treatment cost minimization limits the systems analysis to treatment alternatives only, while the maximization of profits permits exploration of a wider range of possible management options.

Most environmental problems are multiobjective. There is usually more than one goal or criterion by which alternatives must be evaluated. Moreover, objectives often conflict with one another. In this example, the effluent objective may tend to reduce profits; therefore the profit maximization objective will be constrained by the first objective. Sometimes objectives may conflict to such a degree that no solution to the problem is possible. If, for example, the first objective was to minimize the amount of waste discharged, the two objectives (waste minimization and profit maximization) would be absolutely inconsistent. Waste discharge is minimized when the factory is closed down; profits are maximized by production at full capacity.

Although this observation may be obvious, it is hardly trivial. Unrealistic objectives are often proposed for environmental quality management. Unfortunately, the idealistic "minimize pollution at maximum profits" is seldom possible. It is usually necessary to select one objective for maximization or minimization and to define the remaining objectives in terms of upper or lower limits.

System This discussion leads to the definition of the environmental system, or the collection of things to be studied. With the two given objectives, the boundaries of the system should include the factory and waste treatment facility and should exclude the river. The factory and treatment facility are *components* of the system. Other objectives could lead to a different system identification. For example, if the objectives were to meet a water quality standard with minimum treatment costs, the system would consist of the river and the treatment plant.

Generation and Evaluation of Alternatives

Generating Alternatives The generation of alternatives is a search for various ways of solving the problem and is the part of the systems approach that demands the most creativity. A useful starting point is a delineation of the problem factors that can be controlled and hence changed. For example, as implied by Objective One, the effluent standard cannot be tampered with. However, if the standard is subject to further public review and hearings, it could be considered at least partially controllable. This would lead to a redefinition of objectives, perhaps adding the new objective of raising the discharge limitation of the effluent standard.

Assuming that the effluent standard is fixed, what else can be controlled? A logical candidate is the operation of the waste treatment facility. Since treatment efficiency improves with decreasing wastewater flows, it may be desirable to reduce the amount of wastewater treated in order to lower treatment costs. This implies that some wastewater may be discharged without treatment, as indicated by the bypass in Figure 1-4. A second control option is to vary levels of metal production, hereby changing waste quantities.

The bypassing of treatment and the variation of factory production levels are not obvious wastewater control measures, and they are often ignored in otherwise excellent engineering studies of wastewater treatment. Their consideration in this example is a consequence of a systems approach that encourages a broad definition of objectives. Thus the objectives do not exclude the discharge of untreated wastewater, provided the effluent standard is met. In summary, the two factors that can be controlled in the problem are production levels and amount of wastewater treated. An alternative or possible solution to the water pollution problem consists of two decisions, selection of production and wastewater treatment levels. Alternatives are generated by selecting feasible values for these decisions.

Evaluating Alternatives   Each generated alternative must be evaluated with respect to the objectives. We must determine if an alternative meets the effluent standard and what the factory's profits would be upon implementation. This evaluation consists of little more than some accounting of revenues and costs and the computation of mass balances. For example, consider an alternative of producing 50,000 kg/wk of metal. This yields 150,000 kg/wk of waste, and the second decision might be to treat 100,000 kg/wk of the waste. Therefore the alternative is to produce 50,000 kg/wk of metal and treat 100,000 kg/wk of waste.

To evaluate the alternative, the effluent objective is considered first. The total

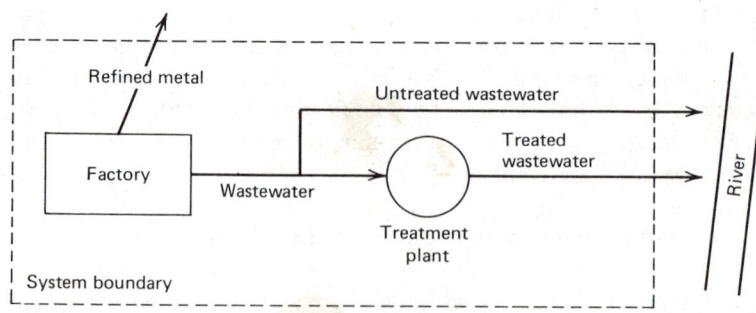

Figure 1-4 System definition for Example 1-1.

waste discharge is the 50,000 kg/wk of untreated waste plus the waste remaining in the discharge from the treatment plant. Since the waste concentration is 2 kg/m^3, the 100,000 kg/wk of wastewater is contained in a wastewater flow of 100,000 kg/wk ÷ 2 kg/m^3 = 50,000 m^3/wk to the treatment plant. The resulting efficiency is $e = 1 - 0.06(5) = 0.70$. Seventy percent of the influent waste is removed, and the treatment plant discharge is 30,000 kg/wk. The total effluent of 80,000 kg/wk satisfies Objective One, since it meets the effluent standard of 100,000 kg/wk. Evaluation with respect to the second objective (profits) is as follows.

Profits = sales − production costs − waste treatment costs
Sales revenue   = 50,000 kg/wk(1.3\$/kg)   = +\$65,000/wk
Production costs   = 50,000 kg/wk(0.9\$/kg)   = −\$45,000/wk
Waste treatment costs = 50,000 m^3/wk(0.20\$/m^3) = −\$10,000/wk

The evaluation of the alternative indicates an effluent of 80,000 kg/wk (Objective One) and a profit of \$10,000/wk (Objective Two).

Additional alternatives can be evaluated in the same straightforward manner. The procedure is essentially mechanical and, given that many alternatives are possible, the only shortcoming of the evaluation procedures is the tedium of the many repetitive computations.

Selection of an Alternative

The final step of the systems approach is the designation of one of the problem solutions for implementation. This selection is properly the function of the decision maker(s), and the determination of what is best is frequently not obvious. In the present example, however, the objectives are defined so that selection is obvious. From the set of generated solutions, any alternatives that fail to meet the effluent standard are eliminated. Within the subset alternatives that meet the standard, the one with the greatest profit is selected.

Summary

This chapter has introduced quantitative applications of the systems approach to environmental management. The discussions of benefit/cost analysis and the systems analysis example are the most important aspects of the chapter.

Benefit/cost analysis, with its limitations, establishes a rational framework for environmental management. The consideration of monetary benefits and costs to all users of a water, land, air, or energy resource results in a data base for the evaluation of management alternatives and provides the conceptual basis for effluent charges. The use of environmental quality and effluent standards offers a way of dealing with the limitations of benefit/cost analysis.

The systems approach consists of a logical series of steps that can lead to the solution of an environmental problem. The approach may appear mechanical but, as applied to the wastewater management example, it should be clear that the approach requires a good deal of judgment. The definition of objectives, the determination of what factors are controllable, and the development of alternative solutions to a problem follow logically from the steps of the systems approach, but each requires substantial creativity. For this reason systems analysis is sometimes considered to be both art and science. The systems approach provides a framework for problem solution, but the quality of the solution obtained is determined by the analyst's originality and attention to detail. It is unlikely that any two individuals will apply the approach in exactly the same way.

SELECTED REFERENCES

1. Aguilar, R. J., *Systems Analysis and Design*, Prentice-Hall, Englewood Cliffs, N. J., 1973.
2. Brebbia, C. A., (editor), *Mathematical Models for Environmental Problems*, Wiley, New York, 1976.
3. Churchman, C. W., *The Systems Approach*, Dell, New York, 1968.
4. Deininger, R. A. (editor), *Models for Environmental Pollution Control*, Ann Arbor Science Publishers, Ann Arbor, Mich., 1973.
5. deNeufville, R., and D. Marks (editors), *Systems Planning and Design*, Prentice-Hall, Englewood Cliffs, N. J., 1974.
6. deNeufville, R., and J. H. Stafford, *Systems Analysis for Engineers and Managers*, McGraw-Hill, New York, 1971.
7. Herfindahl, O. C., and A. V. Kneese, *Quality of the Environment*, The Johns Hopkins Press, Baltimore, 1965.
8. Holcomb Research Institute, *Environmental Modeling and Decision Making*, Praeger, New York, 1976.
9. Kneese, A. V., and B. T. Bower (editors), *Environmental Quality Analysis*, The Johns Hopkins Press, Baltimore, 1972.
10. Pantell, R. H., *Techniques of Environmental Systems Analysis*, Wiley, New York, 1976.

CHAPTER 2
MATHEMATICAL MODELING AND OPTIMIZATION

Systems analysis does not require mathematical models. However, nonmodeling applications can be very inefficient, since the repeated evaluation of a large number of alternatives is tedious and time consuming. The primary advantage of mathematical models is that they permit rapid, systematic generation and evaluation of alternatives. The use of models for these purposes is demonstrated in this chapter. The modeling process will be seen to have two components. The first is the construction of an optimization model that provides a mathematical description of the environmental problem being studied; the second is the manipulation or *solution* of the model.

There are no "best ways" to build mathematical models. Models are abstractions or copies of prototype (real-world) situations, and the best criterion of model quality is the extent to which a model captures the essential features of its prototype. If these features are modeled solutions to the model presumably are indicative of solutions to the problem under study. Modeling skills are acquired by practice with different problems. There are few principles or rules to be learned. Accordingly, the remainder of this chapter discusses two different environmental modeling examples. After completing the chapter, readers should know how models can be used to generate and evaluate alternative solutions to environmental problems.

MODELING OF A WASTEWATER MANAGEMENT EXAMPLE

Example 1-1 was described and analyzed in the previous chapter without the use of a mathematical model. In the following discussion, a mathematical model is developed for the problem, and the model is subsequently solved to identify the best solution to the example.

Model Construction

Model building begins after the definition of the objectives and system (step one of the systems approach in Chapter 1). Although there are many ways to start, a reasonable beginning is the *definition of variables*. The number and types of variables differ with the problem being modeled, but a general guideline is that the factors that can be controlled should have associated variables. In this example, two variables should be defined.

$$X = \text{factory metal production level } (10^4 \text{ kg/wk})$$
$$Y = \text{quantity of waste being treated } (10^4 \text{ kg/wk})$$

The variables can then be combined in mathematical expressions that describe the parts of the problem.

The relationships between variables that are important in environmental problems are often based on mass balance or conservation. These functions are most easily developed with the aid of a diagram such as Figure 2-1, which shows the various mass fluxes in terms of the variables X and Y. Thus the waste produced in 10^4 kg/wk is $3X$, and the quantity of waste discharged without treatment is $3X - Y$. To determine the quantity of waste discharged after treatment, the efficiency e of the treatment must be considered. As shown in Figure 1-3, this efficiency is given by $e = 1 - 0.06W$, where W is the wastewater flow to the plant in 10^4m^3/wk. Wastewater flow W can be expressed in terms of Y, the waste mass treated, by observing that:

$$\text{Mass flux } (10^4 \text{ kg/wk}) = \text{flow } (10^4 \text{m}^3/\text{wk}) \cdot \text{concentration } (\text{kg/m}^3)$$

Since the waste concentration is 2 kg/m³, the wastewater flow is $W = Y/2$ and treatment plant efficiency is $e = 1 - 0.03Y$. This defines the fraction of waste mass removed by treatment. The fraction that is *not* removed is $1 - e = 0.03Y$, and the waste mass leaving the plant is $Y(1 - e) = 0.03Y^2$, as shown in Figure 2-1.

To evaluate alternatives, the objectives of profit maximization and meeting the effluent standard must be expressed in terms of the variables X and Y. The total waste effluent is readily seen from Figure 2-1 to be $3X - Y + 0.03Y^2$. Profits are equal to sales revenue minus production and waste treatment costs. Designating weekly profits by Z in \$/wk and recalling that the dimensions of X and Y are in 10^4 kg/wk, we have

$$Z = (1.3)10^4 X - (0.9)10^4 X - (0.20)10^4 \frac{Y}{2}$$

or

$$Z = 4000X - 1000Y \qquad (2.1)$$

The objectives can now be stated mathematically as

$$\text{Max } Z = 4000X - 1000Y \qquad (2.2)$$
$$\text{s.t.} \qquad 3X - Y + 0.03Y^2 \leq 10 \qquad (2.3)$$

Expression 2.2 states that profits Z are to be maximized. The "s.t." in Expression 2.3 is shorthand for "subject to" or "such that" and indicates that profits are to be maximized subject to waste effluent being less than or equal to $(10)10^4$ kg/wk. In other words, the

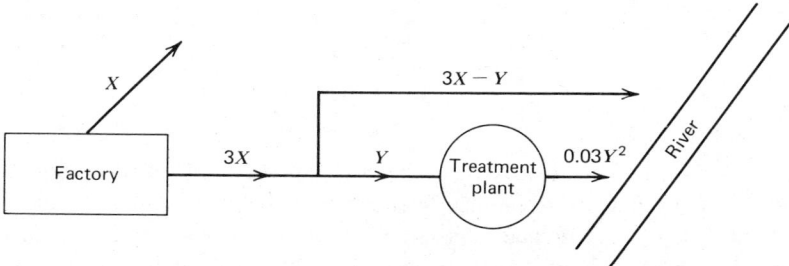

Figure 2-1 Mass fluxes in terms of variables for Example 1-1.

values of X and Y that are chosen to maximize profits must also result in a waste discharge $(3x - Y + 0.03Y^2)$ that is no more than the effluent standard.

The mathematical relationships in Expressions 2.2 and 2.3 form the basis of an optimization model, which specifies how variables can be chosen to meet the objectives of the problem. The model is not complete, however, since there are other restrictions on X and Y. One trivial restriction is nonnegativity. Neither X nor Y can be less than zero.

$$X \geq 0 \qquad (2.4)$$

$$Y \geq 0 \qquad (2.5)$$

Similarly, none of the mass fluxes can be negative. For example,

$$3X - Y \geq 0 \qquad (2.6)$$

From Figure 2-1, the additional mass fluxes are waste quantity $(3X)$ and discharge of treated waste $(0.03Y^2)$. However, requiring both X and Y to be nonnegative (Expressions 2.4 and 2.5) will also prevent negative values for $3X$ and $0.03Y^2$.

The remaining restrictions are on factory production capacity ($5.5 \; 10^4$ kg/wk) and treatment plant capacity ($7 \; 10^4$ m³/wk or $14 \; 10^4$ kg/wk). These capacity limitations are stated mathematically as

$$X \leq 5.5 \qquad (2.7)$$

$$Y \leq 14.0 \qquad (2.8)$$

A complete optimization model can now be written.

$$\text{Max } Z = 4000X - 1000Y \qquad (2.2)$$

s.t.
$$3X - Y + 0.03Y^2 \leq 10 \qquad (2.3)$$

$$X \leq 5.5 \qquad (2.7)$$

$$Y \leq 14.0 \qquad (2.8)$$

$$3X - Y \geq 0 \qquad (2.6)$$

$$X \geq 0 \qquad (2.4)$$

$$Y \geq 0 \qquad (2.5)$$

The model is a mathematical way of saying "find the combination of production and treatment decisions that will meet the effluent standard in a physically possible way and maximize profits." The reference to physical possibility means that the physical limits to the problem (capacity limits, nonnegative mass fluxes) must be met.

In mathematical terms the model is a *constrained optimization problem*. The quantity to be maximized (Z) is an *objective function*, and Expressions 2.3 to 2.8 are *constraints*. Note that the objective function contains only one of our two objectives (profit maximization) and the other objective (effluent limit) is a constraint. In the context of an optimization model "objective function" refers only to the mathematical expression that is to be optimized. It is seldom possible to describe all of a problem's multiple objectives with a single mathematical function. The *decision variables* in the model are X and Y. A *feasible solution* to the model is a pair of values for X and Y that satisfies all constraints. A feasible solution that maximizes the objective function is an *optimal solution*.

The optimization model is a concise mathematical statement of the environmental problem described in the wastewater management example. If the model includes all relevant factors a solution to the model should approximate a solution to the environmental problem. As a tool for generating and evaluating alternatives, the model is clearly superior to the *ad hoc* procedure outlined in Chapter 1. An alternative is generated by selecting values of X and Y that are nonnegative and physically realistic (i.e., $X \leq 5.5$, $Y \leq 14.0$, $3X - Y \geq 0$). The alternative is evaluated by computing profits, $Z = 4000X - 1000Y$, and determining if the effluent, $3X - Y + 0.03Y^2$, meets the standard.

Model Solution

Although the mathematical model described by Expressions 2.2 to 2.8 provides an efficient means of generating and evaluating alternatives, we will extract the most value from the model by actually obtaining an optimal solution (that is, a solution that meets the constraints and achieves profits equal to or better than those of any other alternative). Solving an optimization model is seldom easy and is frequently more difficult than model construction. Optimization models are solved by iterative procedures that evaluate successive solutions in an attempt to find the best solution. Optimization methods differ chiefly in their efficiency and degree of structure. The simplest methods are *informal search* procedures, which rely on intuitive examination of a model's feasible region and a more-or-less rational elimination process that successively discards inferior alternatives. The approach may lead to only an approximate solution to an optimization model, and its efficiency, as indicated by the number of alternatives that need to be evaluated in order to converge on the approximate solution, is determined largely by the cleverness of the analyst.

A number of more structured techniques are available for solving optimization models. These methods, which include Lagrange multipliers, search algorithms, and mathematical programming, are often both more exact and efficient than informal search. However, each of the procedures is limited to certain types of optimization models, and their presentation is deferred to later chapters. The optimization models developed in this chapter are solved using informal search, thus demonstrating that optimization models can sometimes be solved by commonsense trial-and-error methods. The emphasis on informal search is important, since it illustrates an approach that is useful for a broad range of optimization models. Although trial-and-error methods are often proposed when "all else fails," the unfortunate truth is that all else often *does* fail, and the ability to obtain a good solution to an optimization model by search methods is an essential skill for the systems analyst.

The central difficulty in solving optimization models is the large number of feasible solutions. Since the wastewater management example is two dimensional (there are only two variables, X and Y), the feasible solutions can be shown graphically, as in Figure 2-2. The model constraints are shown as equations in the figure. For

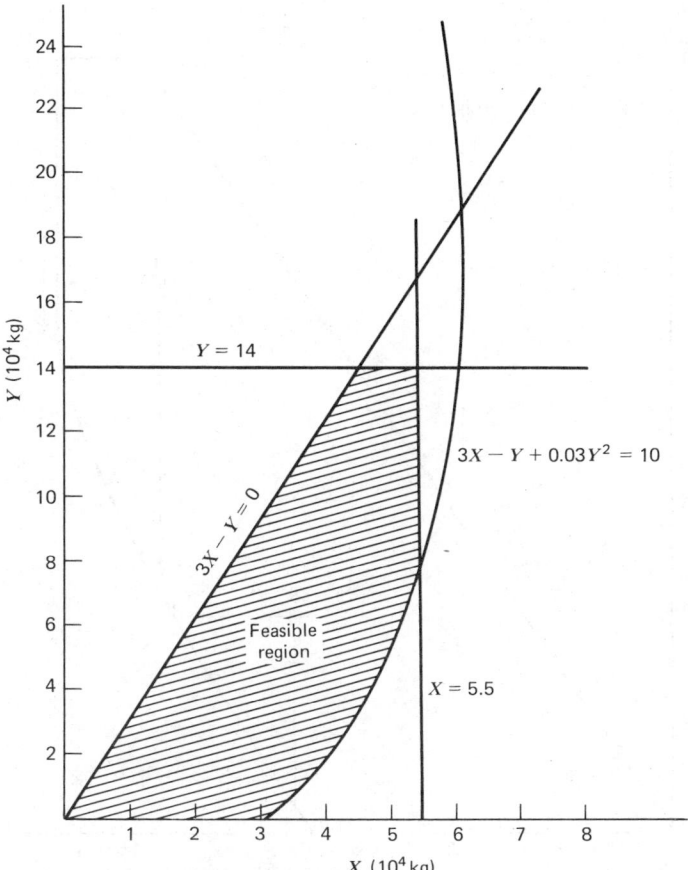

Figure 2-2 Graphical representation of constraints for wastewater management example.

18 MATHEMATICAL MODELING AND OPTIMIZATION

example, the constraint $X \leq 5.5$ is drawn as the line $X = 5.5$. Any point on or to the left of the line satisfies the constraint. The constraint $3X - Y \geq 0$ is plotted as $3X - Y = 0$, and any combination of X and Y that falls below or on the line $3X - Y = 0$ will satisfy the constraint. Solutions that satisfy the remaining constraints can be similarly determined.

Taken together, the constraints in Figure 2-2 define the optimization model's *feasible region*. This is shown in an enlarged form in Figure 2-3. Any combination of values for X and Y that lies within the solid boundaries satisfies all constraints and, hence, is a feasible solution to the model. As is the case with most optimization models, the feasible region is large; in fact, the number of feasible solutions to the model is infinite. If the optimal solution to the model is to be arrived at by trial and error, we must have some method for selecting the alternatives to "try." A random selection of alternatives within the feasible region is not likely to be adequate. It would be highly desirable to examine some subset of alternatives within the feasible region that are better than others. Since no more than a limited number of alternatives can be evalu-

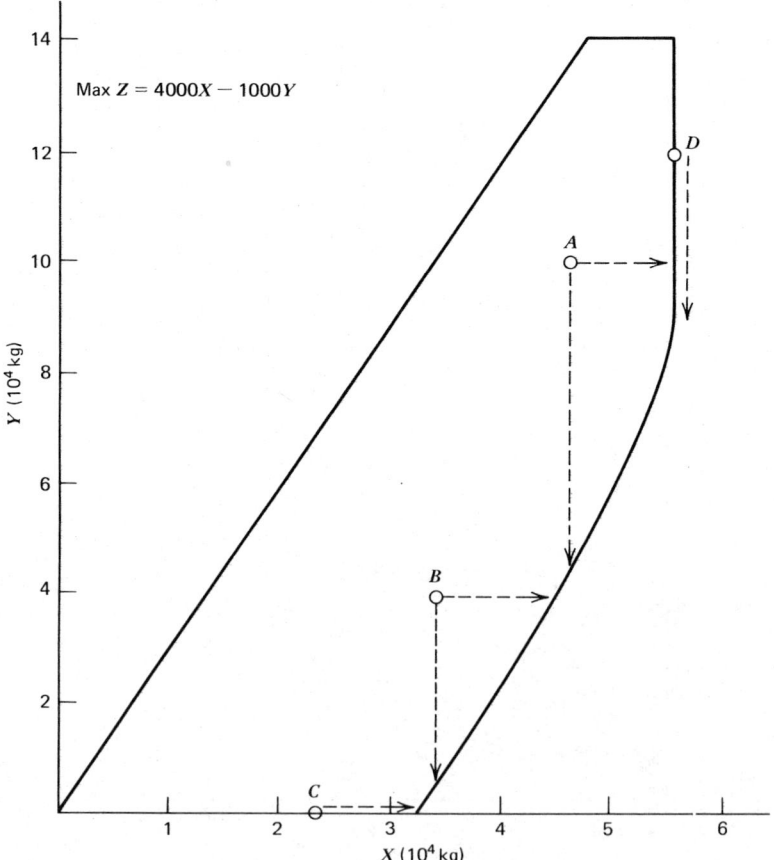

Figure 2-3 Examination of feasible solutions for wastewater management example.

MODELING OF A WASTEWATER MANAGEMENT EXAMPLE

ated, the quality of the approximate solution that is obtained is highly dependent on the selection of alternatives for trial-and-error examination. If, for example, there is reason to believe that the true optimum solution is in one part of the feasible region, there would be little point in examining other portions of the region.

The procedure of making a judicious selection of alternatives to evaluate can be considered a *search strategy*. Given that only a finite number of alternatives can be examined, success of the search procedure is dictated by the quality of the strategy. The development of a strategy is an intellectual and creative challenge. There is no one way to do this, since it depends on personal ingenuity. A strategy will be outlined for the current optimization model, but it is only indicative of the possible approaches that could be taken. There may be better or more efficient strategies that could be developed. Moreover, since each model is somewhat unique, it is unlikely that an identical search strategy would work for another model.

A starting point for most strategies is an examination of the optimization model's objective function. For the present case this is

$$Z = 4000X - 1000Y \tag{2.1}$$

Since the coefficient of X is positive and the coefficient of Y is negative, it is desirable to make X as large as possible and Y as small as possible. With this in mind, we can determine which of the feasible solutions or alternatives are dominated by, or inferior to, others. For example, consider point A in Figure 2-3 ($X = 4.6$, $Y = 10$). If we move horizontally to the right, Y remains the same, but X increases, hence increasing Z. Conversely, if we move vertically downward, X does not change but Y is decreased and, as a result, the objective function is again increased. The conclusion is that point A is dominated by solutions on the right boundary of the feasible region.

Similarly, it can be seen that points B and C are likewise dominated by solutions on the right boundary. In fact, *any* alternative within the feasible region is inferior to points on the right boundary. Moreover, one portion of that boundary is inferior. Consider point D on the vertical boundary. Since Y is decreased by moving vertically downward, any alternative on the vertical boundary is dominated by the intersection with the curved portion (approximately $X = 5.5$, $Y = 8.9$).

The search strategy indicates that only alternatives on the right curved portion of the boundary to the feasible region need be considered. Since such alternatives dominate the remaining points of the feasible region, we know that the curved boundary contains the optimal solution to the model. This boundary is the effluent equation $3X - Y + 0.03Y^2 = 10$, and the physical meaning of the strategy is that the factory should not discharge less than the maximum allowable waste effluent (10 10^4 kg/wk).

The remaining step is to evaluate some solutions on the boundary. This is easily done by selecting values of Y between 0 and 8.9 and solving the effluent equation for X.

$$X = \frac{10 + Y - 0.03Y^2}{3} \tag{2.9}$$

Solutions to Equation 2.9 are given in Table 2-1. Since the mathematical relationships

TABLE 2-1 Solutions to Equation 2.9

Y (10^4 kg/wk)	X (10^4 kg/wk)
0	3.33
1	3.66
2	3.96
3	4.24
4	4.51
5	4.75
6	4.97
7	5.18
8	5.36
8.9	5.51

used in the model are unlikely to be accurate to the two decimal places given in the table, the last decimal value can be dropped from the metal production variable, X. Note that values of X should not just be rounded off because this might lead to violation of the effluent standard. For example, from Table 2-1, when $Y = 5$, then $X = 4.75$. If X is rounded to 4.8, the resulting waste effluent is $3X - Y + 0.03Y^2 = 10.15$, which exceeds the effluent standard of 10.

The resulting alternatives are summarized in Table 2-2. Of the 10 alternatives evaluated in the table, the best is number 5, which is $X^* = 4.5$ (produce 45,000 kg/wk of metal) and $Y^* = 4$ (treat 40,000 kg/wk of waste), producing a total profit of $Z^* = \$14,000$/wk.[1] The mass balances for this optimal solution are shown in Figure 2-4.

Perhaps the most interesting aspect of this exercise is that several alternatives are almost as good as the approximate optimal solution. Referring to Table 2-2, the worst alternative (number 10) would only decrease profits 6% compared to the optimum. This suggests that the factory has considerable flexibility in meeting the effluent standard. It could, for example, shut down the treatment facility completely (alternative 1, $X = 3.3$, $Y = 0$) with relatively little profit loss.

GENERALIZATION OF THE SYSTEMS APPROACH

Having finally solved an environmental (albeit hypothetical) problem using systems analysis, it is appropriate to summarize the main features of the systems approach. This summary has three principal aspects: the steps of the system approach, a general description of optimization models, and a discussion of the types of problems for which systems analysis can be used.

---

[1] An asterisk (*) is often used to designate the optimal solution to an optimization model.

TABLE 2-2 Evaluation of Alternatives Selected by the Search Strategy

Alternative	Metal Production X (10^4 kg/wk)	Waste Treated Y (10^4 kg/wk)	Waste Effluent $3X - Y + 0.03Y^2$ (10^4 kg/wk)	Profits $Z = 4000X - 1000Y$ ($/wk)
1	3.3	0	9.9	13,200
2	3.6	1	9.8	13,400
3	3.9	2	9.8	13,600
4	4.2	3	9.9	13,800
5	4.5	4	10.0	14,000
6	4.7	5	9.9	13,800
7	4.9	6	9.8	13,600
8	5.1	7	9.8	13,400
9	5.3	8	9.8	13,200
10	5.5	8.9	10.0	13,100

Steps of the Systems Approach

These steps were outlined in Chapter 1 and are repeated here in expanded form.

- **A.** Definition of system and objectives
  1. Identification of decision maker(s)
  2. Definition of system boundaries and components
  3. Quantification of objectives
- **B.** Generation and evaluation of alternatives
  1. Construction of an optimization model
     a. Definition of variables
     b. Relationships between variables
  2. Solution of the optimization model
- **C.** Selection of an alternative

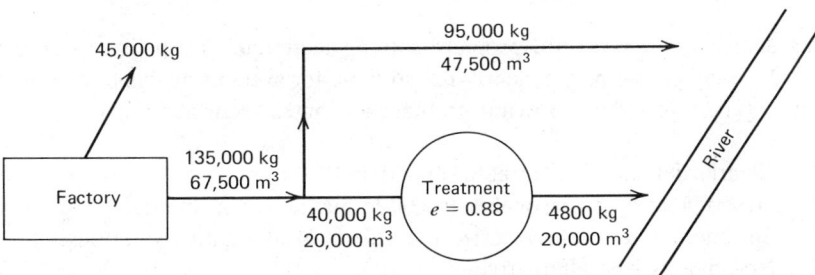

Figure 2-4 Mass balances for optimal solution.

These steps are not as mechanical as may be suggested by this simple list, nor are they necessarily sequential. The objectives of decision makers are not often obvious, and it may even be difficult to identify the individuals (decision makers) who have the power to select an alternative. The evaluation of alternatives sometimes indicates that none of the generated alternatives seem reasonable. This frequently indicates that either the problem has been modeled incorrectly or the wrong objectives have been chosen. Solving the optimization model often implies the selection of an alternative, particularly if the objectives of decision makers have been well accounted for in the model. However, the selection of an alternative is properly the role of decision makers, and the systems analyst generally can only recommend a "best" solution to the problem under study.

General Form of an Optimization Model

An optimization model is a concise mathematical description of the decisions that can be made to solve a problem. The general form is

$$\text{Max (Min) } Z = F(X_1, X_2, \ldots, X_n) \tag{2.10}$$

s.t
$$g_1(X_1, X_2, \ldots, X_n) \leq, =, \text{ or } \geq b_1$$
$$g_2(X_1, X_2, \ldots, X_n) \leq, =, \text{ or } \geq b_2 \tag{2.11}$$
$$\vdots$$
$$g_m(X_1, X_2, \ldots, X_n) \leq, =, \text{ or } \geq b_m$$

An optimization model consists of *decision variables* $(X_1, X_2, \ldots, X_n)$ an *objective function* $Z = F(X_1, X_2, \ldots, X_n)$ that is to be maximized or minimized, and *constraints* $g_1(X_1, X_2, \ldots, X_n), \ldots, g_m(X_1, X_2, \ldots, X_n)$ that define *feasible* values of the decision variables. Constraints are in the form of equations (=) or inequalities ($\leq$, $\geq$). The quantities $b_1, b_2, \ldots, b_m$ on the right side of Constraints 2.11 are constants. Any combination of values for $X_1, X_2, \ldots, X_n$ that satisfies Constraints 2.11 is a *feasible solution* to the optimization model. The feasible solution that maximizes or minimizes Z is the *optimal solution* to the model.

Characteristics of Problems Amenable to Systems Analysis

Systems analysis is a powerful problem-solving technique, but it is not universally applicable. Many problems are clearly not suitable for systems analysis. Although it is difficult to generalize, the following problem attributes seem necessary.

1. Clearly defined, quantifiable objectives;
2. Describable by a reasonably tractable mathematical model.
3. Sufficient data to characterize the effects of alternative solutions.
4. No obvious best alternative.

The list is self-explanatory. At the national level in the United States, the Apollo program to land a man on the moon in the 1960s was an example of a suitable problem for systems analysis. President Johnson's "War on Poverty," carried out during the same decade, is an example of a problem that could not be successfully dealt with using systems analysis, since none of the first three attributes could be met.

MATHEMATICAL MODELING OF A PESTICIDE MANAGEMENT PROBLEM

EXAMPLE 2-1 Pesticide Management

A 100,000 m³ lake is surrounded by 1000 ha of agricultural crop land. A portion of the pesticide used on crops reaches the lake and is having harmful effects on hawks that feed on the fish from the lake. A state environmental agency is trying to determine how the agricultural land can be managed without damaging the hawks. Agency biologists have determined that pesticide in the lake water is magnified in the food chain. Based on their studies, it has been found that the pesticide concentrations increase geometrically with steps in the food chain. If C is the pesticide concentration (ppm)[2] in the lake water, the concentration in the phytoplankton (algae) floating in the water is C^2. Pesticide concentration in the fish that feed on the phytoplankton is C^3. The hawks eat the fish, and the resulting pesticide concentration in their body tissue is C^4. These concentration relationships assume that pesticide concentration C is not less than 1 ppm. Hawks can tolerate a maximum concentration in their bodies of 100 ppm.

The two crops grown on the 1000 ha have different pesticide application and loss rates, returns, and costs as follows.

Crop	Pesticide Application (kg/ha)	Rate of Pesticide Loss to lake (%)	Crop Return ($/ha)	Crop Costs ($)
1	6	15	300	$1500\sqrt{\text{area}}$
2	2.5	20	150	$600\sqrt{\text{area}}$

For example, if 30 ha of crop 1 is grown, $6(30) = 180$ kg of pesticide is applied, of which 15%, or 27 kg, is lost to the lake. The net return to the farmers is $300(30) - 1500\sqrt{30} = \$784$/yr. The lake's flushing time is 6 months; that is, 200,000 m³ of water flows through the lake each year. □

---

[2]ppm = Parts per million, by mass; and is equivalent to mg/kg. In dilute solutions, 1 ppm is approximately equal to 1 mg/liter, since 1 liter of water has a mass of 1 kg.

The contamination of the lake with pesticides is an example of nonpoint source water pollution. Such pollution occurs not as a result of the direct discharge of waste from a pipe into a stream but because of the natural process of precipitation washing substances from the landscape and carrying them away in drainage waters. In the present situation, farmers place pesticides on their fields, not in the lake, and it is the subsequent precipitation that washes pesticides into creeks and other drainage channels that eventually reach the lake. Other examples of potential nonpoint sources are fertilizers, eroded soil and animal wastes in agricultural areas and road salts, street litter, and toxic chemicals in urban areas.

Nonpoint source pollutants are a specialized water quality problem. Since they are seldom the result of deliberate attempts to pollute water bodies, it is difficult to develop legal control remedies. Nonpoint sources do not reach streams through obvious and visible discharge pipes (as with point sources), so they are difficult to measure and even harder to control. It is obviously infeasible to install a waste treatment plant to treat the runoff from a farmer's field. Instead, control options for nonpoint sources often imply the management of potential pollutants on the land surface. For example, in the pesticide problem, it is possible to select crops that require less pesticides or have less associated pesticide loss. Crops vary in their ability to retain pesticides on the field because different crops result in different amounts of runoff and soil erosion. Runoff and eroded soil are the carriers of pesticides to streams.[3]

The impacts of pollutants are usually determined by their concentrations in the environment. For example, most water quality standards are expressed in milligrams of pollutant per liter of water. Such standards explicitly account for a water body's ability to dilute waste. For example, consider a stream with a water flow of 1000 m^3/day. If 10 kg of waste is discharged into the stream each day the resulting waste concentration is 0.01 kg/m^3, or 10 mg/liter in the stream.[4] If the streamflow is 10,000 m^3/day, the waste concentration would be only 1 mg/liter, and this would presumably have less adverse effects on the stream than the higher concentration. Considering the present lake problem, if 500 kg of pesticide enter the lake annually, it would be diluted by 200,000 m^3, the total quantity of water that flows through the lake in a year. The average pesticide concentration in the lake would thus be (500/200,000) 1000 = 2.5 mg/liter.

This example also illustrates one of the ways in which the environment often assimilates toxic wastes: by a concentrating or magnifying effect in the food chain. in this problem a pesticide concentration of 2.5 ppm in lakewater results in concentrations of 6.25, 15.63, and 39.06 ppm in phytoplankton, fish, and hawks, respectively.

Another aspect of the example that is common in environmental problems is the presence of *economies of scale*. Thus the costs per hectare of growing a crop decrease as the area under cultivation increases. For example, when only 10 ha of crop 1 are grown, the costs are $1500\sqrt{10}$ = \$4743, or \$474.30/ha. With 100 ha, the cost drops

---

[3]The management of nonpoint source water pollution is discussed in more detail in Chapter 6.
[4]1 kg/m^3 = 1000 mg/liter.

to $1500\sqrt{100}/100 = \$150$/ha. Economies of scale are often associated with fixed costs that must be incurred regardless of size. A farmer will need a tractor to crop 10 ha or 30 ha. With the larger area, the fixed cost of the tractor per hectare is much less (one-third).

Definition of System and Objectives

This problem is substantially different from the wastewater management example. One notable difference is the type of decision-making procedures that could lead to implementation of a problem solution. In the previous example, the relevant decision maker was in the private sector; in this case decision making rests with a public agency. Moreover, the identity of the decision maker(s) is not necessarily obvious. Presumably there is an individual, say a department head within the environmental agency, who will have the authority to select a plan. However, in making a selection, the decision maker will not be able to ignore the interests of other individuals. In particular, the farmers who own the 1000 ha of cropland must be considered. If the department head selects an alternative that forces the farmers out of business, there is reason to believe that the alternative would not be implemented. The maintenance or protection of agriculture is usually an explicit government policy. Although the agency's primary role may be environmental management, the decision maker will have to be responsive to the government's concern for agriculture if the selection is to be politically feasible. The decision maker must realistically consider both environmental and agricultural objectives. The systems analyst must recognize these dual concerns and define objectives that meet environmental goals and are sensitive to the implied decision-making power of the farmers.

The environmental objective is reasonably clear. Since the pesticide problem is manifest in the effects on hawks, the protection of these predators is important. This objective is defined and quantified as follows.

Objective One Limit pesticide concentrations in the hawks to no more than 100 ppm.

Agricultural objectives are less obvious. As in the wastewater management example, one objective that is logical is profit maximization.

Objective Two Maximize the profits (\$/yr) to farmers from crops grown on the 1000 ha.

This is not necessarily the only agricultural objective, however. An additional, or perhaps alternative, objective could be to maintain the land in agriculture. This goal may not be equivalent to (and, in fact, can be in conflict with) profit maximization. In order to meet the pesticide standard (Objective One), it may be possible for the farmers to leave part of the 1000 ha idle and plant the remainder to the more profitable crop. If the entire land area must remain in production, this might force the less profitable crop to be planted.

The nature of the agricultural objective will depend somewhat on the goals of government policy. If, for example, the lake and its surrounding farmland are in an area that is experiencing suburban development, the purpose of protecting farmland may be to provide greenbelts of undeveloped land. In this case farmer profits could be a secondary concern.

For now we will assume that profits are most important, and Objectives One and Two as defined previously will be used in the systems analysis. We will subsequently return to the proposed third objective to see how it changes the nature of the solutions to the problem that can be generated. The system that is consistent with these objectives includes the farmland, lake, and hawks.

Model Construction

The first step to the generation of alternatives and the construction of an optimization model is usually to determine what can be controlled or managed in the problem. The selection of crops or, more precisely, the amount of land that will be planted to each crop, seems to be the only aspect to the problem that can be changed and hence controlled. However, other controls may be possible, including changes in pesticide compounds and application rates and soil and water conservation practices that would reduce erosion and runoff from croplands. None of these options is suggested by the description of the example, and the implication is that crop changes are the only controls to be considered in the analysis.

This may seem a puzzling conclusion. In Chapter 1 the importance of looking at a full range of alternatives was discussed, and yet in the current example several possibly promising options are essentially ignored. There could be several reasons for limiting controls to crop selections. Foremost is the fact that such "standard" alternatives may be the only options for which data exist. For example, in order to study changes in pesticide application rates, the effects of various application rates on pesticide losses and crop yields (and hence returns) must be known. This information may not be available, so these alternatives could not be evaluated with respect to the problem's objectives.

This difficulty suggests a serious limitation to systems analysis. It is seldom possible to consider all reasonable (or unreasonable) alternatives in an analysis. Instead, study must be restricted to the control options for which data can be obtained.

There are three basic ways in which data limitations can be dealt with.

1. The systems analyst may go forward with the data at hand and attempt to obtain a best solution for the problem. This approach may be justified by the fact that a problem exists that must be solved. It cannot be ignored, and it is therefore desirable to proceed using the available information.
2. A second option is to make some "informed guesses" about the missing data. This is risky, of course, and the analyst may have difficulty in defending the credibility of the problem solutions that are generated.
3. A stalling tactic can sometimes be a viable third approach. If there is reason to believe that the undocumented control options may be of

value, the analysis can be deferred until the necessary data are produced by field or experimental research studies.

These approaches are not always correct. The systems analyst must use judgment in deciding which is to be taken. It should be apparent that a problem solution based on meager data may be very misleading. Conversely, if the problem is important, delays in solving it may have serious results (the hawks may all die before we are finished).
In the pesticide management example, the analyst's judgment might indicate that a selection between the two crops is the only reasonable option that could be taken. Suppose that the two crops are the only ones suitable for the farmers' operations (e.g., a vegetable farmer cannot be expected to grow hay). Furthermore, if the farmers have obtained good yields using their present practices, including pesticide applications, it may be pointless to propose "unconventional" alternatives, even if data were available for their evaluation. In this case the analyst might do well to limit the study to these two crops, even if practices such as pesticide changes and soil and water conservation have certain advantages. If sufficient data, time, and money are available, a second study could explore a broader range of alternatives.
Assuming that such judgment is acceptable, decision variables for the pesticide example are

X_1 = number of hectares planted with crop 1

X_2 = number of hectares planted with crop 2

The optimization model for the example will provide a mathematical description of the ways in which these variables can be chosen to accomplish the objectives. As with previous examples, the bases for the model are algebraic relationships describing the objectives and mass conservation. Profits, Z in \$/yr, are

$$Z = 300X_1 - 1500\sqrt{X_1} + 150X_2 - 600\sqrt{X_2} \tag{2.12}$$

To determine the pesticide concentrations in the hawks' bodies, the quantity of pesticide entering the lake must first be calculated. Each hectare of crop 1 requires 6 kg of pesticide, of which 15% is lost to the lake. The total loss from crop 1 is $6(0.15)X_1 = 0.9X_1$ kg. Similarly, the pesticide entering the lake from crop 2 is $2.5(0.20)X_2 = 0.5X_2$ kg. The average pesticide concentration (kg/m^3) in the lake is $(0.9X_1 + 0.5X_2)/200{,}000$. Converting to mg/liter (ppm),

$$C = \frac{0.9X_1 + 0.5X_2}{200} \tag{2.13}$$

The concentration in the hawks is C^4, and Objective One requires the concentration to be no more than 100 ppm.

$$\left(\frac{0.9X_1 + 0.5X_2}{200}\right)^4 \leq 100 \tag{2.14}$$

28 MATHEMATICAL MODELING AND OPTIMIZATION

The remaining mass balance relationship places a limitation on total cropland.

$$X_1 + X_2 \leq 1000 \tag{2.15}$$

The complete model is

$$\text{Max } Z = 300X_1 - 1500\sqrt{X_1} + 150X_2 - 600\sqrt{X_2} \tag{2.12}$$

$$\text{s.t.} \quad \left(\frac{0.9X_1 + 0.5X_2}{200}\right)^4 \leq 100 \tag{2.14}$$

$$X_1 + X_2 \leq 1000 \tag{2.15}$$

$$X_1, X_2 \geq 0 \tag{2.16}$$

The objective function in Expression 2.12 and Constraints 2.14 to 2.16 are a mathematical way of saying "determine the amounts of land that should be planted to each of two crops in order that a pesticide standard for hawks may be met in a way that maximizes farmer profits."

Solution

In developing a search strategy, it is usually worthwhile to see if any of the relationships in the optimization model can be simplified. For example, it is sometimes possible to replace inequality constraints with equations. While it may not be clear that any constraints in the present model can be reduced to equations, the pesticide concentration in Constraint 2.14 can be written in a simpler form as

$$\frac{0.9X_1 + 0.5X_2}{200} \leq (100)^{1/4} \tag{2.14a}$$

or, equivalently,

$$0.9X_1 + 0.5X_2 \leq 632.5 \tag{2.14b}$$

Constraints 2.14b and 2.15 are plotted in Figure 2-5, showing the feasible region for the optimization model.[5]

The objective function for this model is not as simple as it was for the wastewater management example. To examine the function, we can divide it into two parts.

---

[5] As with the wastewater management example, we are again dealing with a two-dimensional problem. This leads to a convenient graphical presentation, but it is also misleading. Many, if not most, optimization models have more than two decision variables and do not lend themselves to the graphical devices used in these two examples.

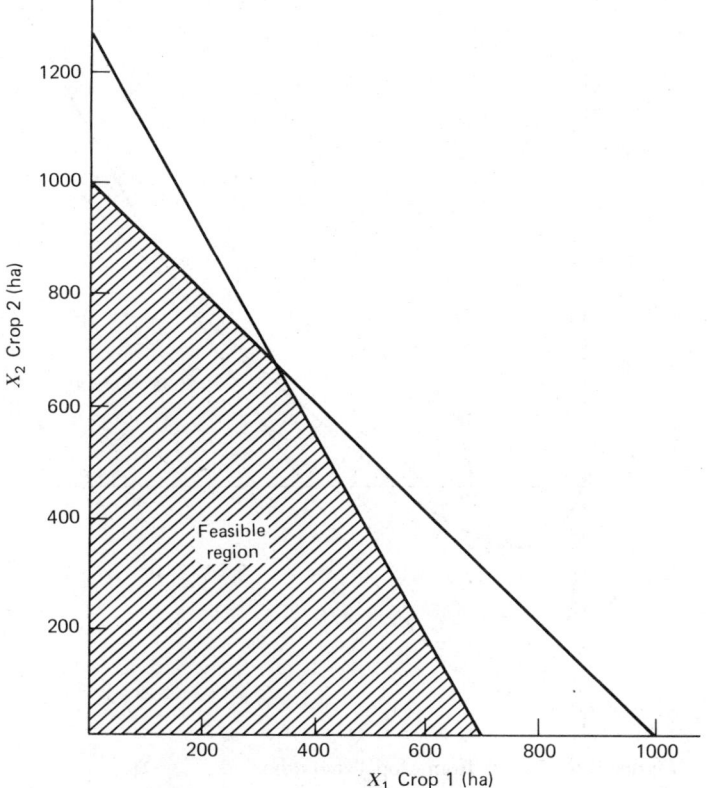

Figure 2-5 Feasible region for pesticide example.

$$Z = (300X_1 - 1500\sqrt{X_1}) + (150X_2 - 600\sqrt{X_2}) \quad (2.12)$$

The quantities in parentheses are the profits from crops 1 and 2, respectively. These are plotted in Figure 2-6. It can be seen that profits are negative for $X_1 < 25$ ha and $X_2 < 16$ ha. For larger areas (X_1 and $X_2 > 36$ ha), crop 1 is relatively more profitable than crop 2. When this result is combined with Constraint 2.14b, the essential nature of the pesticide problem becomes apparent. Since crop 1 is the more profitable, it would be to the farmer's advantage to plant the entire 1000 ha to the crop. However, from Constraint 2.14b, each hectare of crop 1 results in almost twice as much pesticide loss to the lake as a hectare of the second crop (0.9 kg/ha versus 0.5 kg/ha). Thus Objective One (pesticide control) is favored by crop 2, while Objective Two (profits) is enhanced by crop 1.

The feasible region is enlarged in Figure 2-7. As with the previous example, certain alternatives are inferior to others. Since profits are negative, any solution with either $0 < X_1 < 25$ or $0 < X_2 < 16$ is dominated by other feasible solutions, and the shaded region can be ignored. Any solution along the vertical and horizontal boundaries

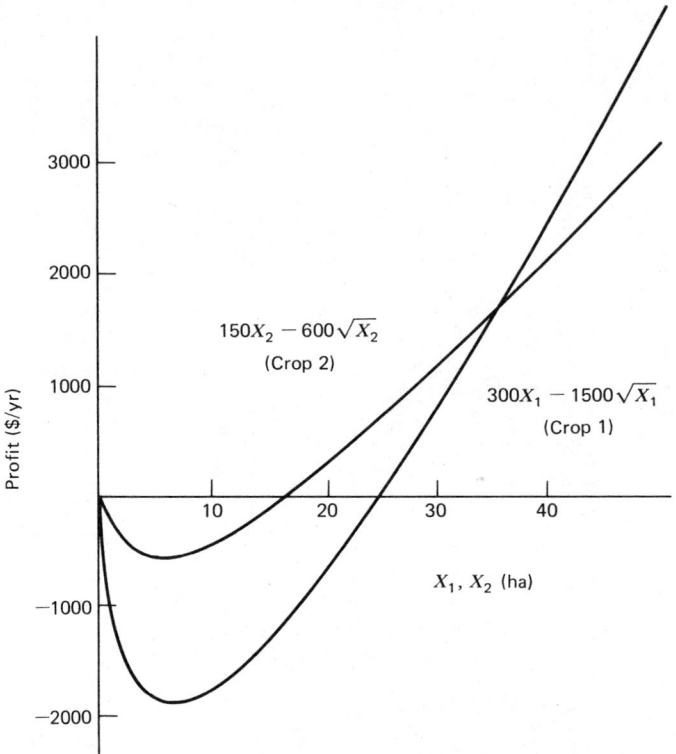

Figure 2-6 Profits from crop 1 and crop 2.

is inferior to the end point solutions (e.g., A' is dominated by A and B' by B). Similarly, interior alternatives such as C are dominated by boundary points (D or E). The search strategy indicates that the only alternatives that could be optimal are A, B, and the remaining portions of the right boundary with $X_1 \geq 25$ and $X_2 \geq 16$.

Twelve of these alternatives are evaluated in Table 2-3. Alternatives 2 to 6 are on the upper right boundary of the feasible region ($X_1 + X_2 = 1000$) and alternatives 8 to 11 are on the lower right boundary ($0.9X_1 + 0.5X_2 = 632.5$).

The seventh alternative (F) is at the intersection of the two boundary portions. As might be suspected from Figure 2-6, the table indicates the value of making X_1 as large as possible. The optimal solution to the problem is to plant only crop 1 (703 ha) for a total profit of $171,000/yr. The resulting pesticide concentration in the lake is $0.9(703)/200 = 3.16$ ppm, which produces a concentration of 100 ppm in the hawks.

In the earlier discussion of objectives a possible third objective, the maintenance of the 1000 ha in agriculture, was mentioned. If this objective is included in the systems analysis, Constraint 2.15 in the optimization model becomes the equation

$$X_1 + X_2 = 1000 \tag{2.15a}$$

Equation 2.15a restricts the feasible region in Figure 2-7 to the line AF. From Table

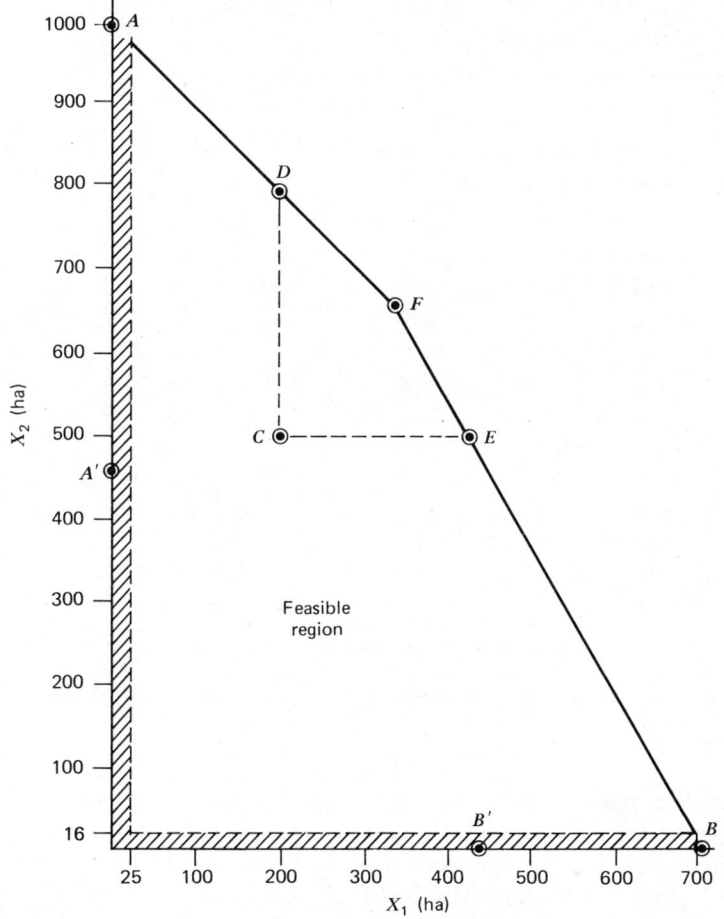

Figure 2-7 Determination of inferior alternatives.

2-3, the optimal alternative is point F, $X_1^* = 331$ ha, $X_2^* = 669$ ha, which produces profits of $Z^* = \$157,000$. The addition of this objective would thus reduce profits by $\$171,000 - \$157,000 = \$14,000$.

Summary

Mathematical models can be efficient tools for generation and evaluation of alternative solutions to environmental problems. Model construction requires definition of variables and construction of mathematical functions of these variables, which describe a problem of interest. These functions include mathematical descriptions of objectives, mass balance relationships, and physical limitations on the values the variables can have. The result is a constrained optimization model consisting of an objective function and constraints. The objective function usually consists of at least one of the defined objectives in the problem being modeled. For example, in both examples studied in this

TABLE 2-3 Alternative Feasible Solutions to the Pesticide Optimization Model

Alternative	X_1 Area of Crop 1 (ha)[a]	X_2 Area of Crop 2 (ha)[a]	Z Profits ($/yr)[b]
1(A)	0	1000	131,000
2	25	975	128,000
3	40	960	128,000
4	100	900	132,000
5	200	800	142,000
6	300	700	153,000
7(F)	331	669	157,000
8	600	185	163,000
9	650	95	165,000
10	680	41	167,000
11	694	16	169,000
12(B)	703	0	171,000

[a] Solutions 7 to 12 are rounded to the nearest hectare.
[b] Rounded to nearest thousand.

chapter, the objective of profit maximization became the objective function. Remaining objectives are stated as constraints in the optimization model.

Optimization models must be solved in order to select alternatives to recommend to decision makers. Although models can be solved by various means, the most general procedure is an informal search, or trial-and-error exploration, of feasible combinations of decision variables. Optimal solutions produced by informal search are often approximate, since no more than a small fraction of possible solutions can be evaluated and it can seldom be proven that the best of these alternatives is superior to all other possibilities. The success of the approach depends on the selection of a search strategy. As applied to the examples in this chapter, a strategy usually involves examination of the objective function and manipulation of constraints to eliminate inferior model solutions.

Although the modeling illustrations were the central focus of the chapter, other factors of general interest to environmental management were introduced, including waste treatment efficiency, the use of different means of describing pollutant quantities (mass fluxes, concentrations, and wastewater flows), nonpoint source pollution, and economies of scale. Certain difficulties in applying systems analysis were observed, particularly with the pesticide management example. It is sometimes difficult to identify decision makers and their associated objectives. In addition, data for evaluation of alternatives are often not readily available. It is not surprising that many problems, particularly those involving social problems, are not suitable for systems analysis.

SELECTED REFERENCES

1. Chacko, G. K. (editor), *Systems Approach to Environmental Pollution,* Operations Research Society of America, Arlington, Va., 1972.
2. Daetz, D., and R. H. Pantell (editors), *Environmental Modeling: Analysis and Management,* Dowden, Hutchinson and Ross, Stroudsburg, Pa., 1974.
3. Ott, W. R. (editor), *Environmental Modeling and Simulation,* U.S. Environmental Protection Agency, Washington, D.C., 1976.
4. Shannon, R. E., *Systems Simulation: The Art and Science,* Prentice-Hall, Englewood Cliffs, N.J., 1975.
5. Toebes, G. H. (editor), *Natural Resource Systems Models in Decision Making,* Water Resources Research Center, Purdue University, Lafayette, Ind., 1970.

EXERCISES

2-1.

One of the simplest and most useful relationships in environmental modeling is the basic mass balance or continuity equation for a conservative substance in a storage unit; that is, input - output = change in amount in storage. For example, if S_o is the original quantity in storage, I is the input to storage, R is the release or output from storage, and S is the quantity remaining in storage after inputs and outputs are made then $I - R = S - S_o,$ or $S = S_o + I - R.$

Consider the following. In the western United States, irrigation water draining from cropland often contains high salt concentrations (dissolved solids, or DS). The salt in these irrigation return flows can, when it reaches a river, contaminate the river unless diluted by cleaner water. A reservoir has been constructed to store water and release it to dilute the salt level in a river below an irrigated area during the month of July.

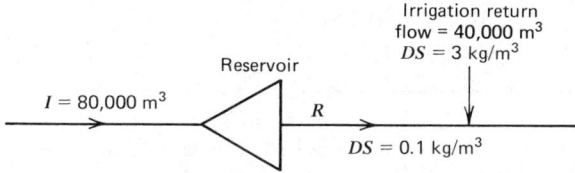

Irrigation water is supplied from other sources. It is not withdrawn from the river during July. Return flows and reservoir inflows during July are as shown in the figure. The reservoir has a capacity of 140,000 m³ and contains 100,000 m³ on July 1. Maximum allowable DS concentration in the river is 1 kg/m³ (an environmental quality standard). The reservoir is also used for recreation. If S is the amount of water in the reservoir (m³) at the end of July, recreation benefits ($) are given by $4S - 0.00004S^2$.

(a) Construct an optimization model that can be used to determine how the reservoir should be operated during July.

34 MATHEMATICAL MODELING AND OPTIMIZATION

(b) Obtain the optimal solution to the model.

2-2.

Consider the following modifications to Example 1-1: (1) waste production (10^4 kg/wk) is given by $0.6 X^2$ instead of $3X$, where X is in units of 10^4 kg/wk; and (2) in addition to the effluent standard, there is an effluent *charge* of \$0.08/kg of waste discharged to the river. All other aspects of the example (capacities, efficiency, sale price, production and treatment costs) remain the same.
  (a) Construct a new optimization model for the example.
  (b) Show the feasible region on a graph.
  (c) Solve the model using informal search.

2-3.

It has been determined that runoff from 100 ha of cropland is carrying phosphorus into a small lake and contributing to the lake's eutrophication. Three crops are grown on the 100 ha. Let p_i = kg/ha/yr of phosphorus that enters the lake in runoff from crop i. Thus, if there are 30 ha of each crop, the total phosphorus entering the lake from cropland in one year would be $p_1 30 + p_2 30 + p_3 30$. An environmental agency has determined that the total input of phosphorus to the lake from cropland runoff must not exceed 800 kg/yr.

The farmers using the 100 ha require minimum quantities of each crop (L_i = minimum number of ha of crop i) and obtain net returns of $R_i(X_i)$ from crop i (\$/yr), where X_i = ha of crop i. These data are summarized here.

Crop i	p_i (kg/ha)	L_i (ha)	$R_i(X_i)$ (\$/yr)
1	10	30	$1000 X_1^{1/2}$
2	12	20	$3000 X_2^{1/3}$
3	9	10	$1200 X_3^{1/2}$

(a) Construct an optimization model for this problem.
(b) Solve the model using informal search.

2-4.

A municipal sewage authority operates three secondary sewage treatment plants that are presently discharging into a lake. These plants are the only waste discharges into the lake. In order to meet an environmental standard for lake phosphorus levels, additional treatment is required to remove phosphorus from the wastewater. The annual cost of such treatment is $e(aQ^b)$, where e is phosphorus removal efficiency as a fraction, Q

is the wastewater flow in $10^3 \text{m}^3/\text{day}$, and a and b are constants. The maximum possible value of e is 0.90 (maximum removal of 90% of the phosphorus).

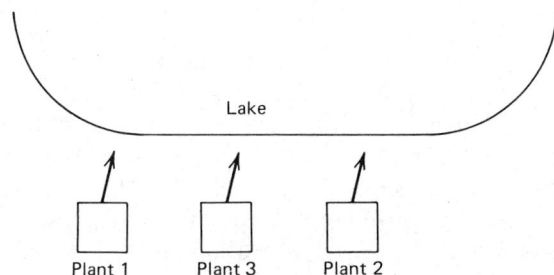

The sewage authority can install additional phosphorus removal treatment at each plant and place a large phosphorus treatment facility at plant 3, which could then treat wastewater from plant 3 and some or all of the wastewater from plants 1 and 2. The annual cost of transmission lines is cQ^d/km, where Q is the transmitted wastewater flow in $10^3 \text{m}^3/\text{day}$ and c and d are constants. Plant 3 is 2 km from plant 1 and 3 km from plant 2.

The total phosphorus input to the lake is the sum of the wastewater phosphorus and an uncontrollable input of phosphorus from land drainage equal to p_L (kg/yr). The average annual concentration of phosphorus in the lake cannot exceed a maximum level. That is, the total yearly input of phosphorus divided by the water volume flowing through the lake each year must be less than a specified value, which in this case is 0.1 mg/liter. The water volume is V million m^3. The flows of wastewater from the secondary treatment plants are constant and are given by 15, 30, and 20 ($10^3 \text{m}^3/\text{day}$), respectively, for plants 1, 2, and 3. Phosphorus concentrations in the wastewaters from the secondary plants are all 10 mg/liter. Construct an optimization model that can be used by the authority to determine the additional treatment needed at each treatment plant.

2-5.

Old Nasty Products, Inc. is presently operating a plant that produces 100 m^3/day of wastewater that is discharged into Pristine Brook. The wastewater contains 1 kg/m^3 of YUK, a toxic substance. The Environmental Protection Agency has imposed an effluent standard on the plant prohibiting discharge of more than 20 kg/day of YUK.

Old Nasty Products has analyzed two methods for reducing its discharges of YUK. Method 1 is land disposal, which costs $X_1^2/20$ in $/day, where X_1 is the amount of wastewater (m^3/day) disposed of on the land. With this method, 20% of the YUK applied to the land will eventually drain into the stream (i.e., 80% of the YUK is removed). Method 2 is a chemical treatment system that costs $1.50/\text{m}^3$ of wastewater treated. The chemical treatment has an efficiency of $e = 1.0 - 0.005X_2$, where X_2 is the amount of wastewater (m^3/day) treated. For example, if $X_2 = 50$ m^3/day, then $e = 1.0 - 0.005(50) = 0.75$; that is 75% of the YUK in X_2 is removed.

(a) Construct an optimization model that can be used by the plant to determine how best to meet the effluent standard.

(b) Solve the model using informal search.

2-6.

The president of the Wildcat Oil Co. has read of the impressive accomplishments of systems analysis and has hired you to perform a study. Wildcat has two oil wells and three refineries. Well 1 is an older well that can produce up to 10,000 bpd (barrels per day). Well 2 is a new well capable of 13,000 bpd. Refinery 1, which is 10 km from well 1 and 22 km from well 2, converts crude oil to gasoline at an efficiency of 90% (90% of the crude oil becomes gasoline) and a profit of $3/barrel of gasoline produced (not including costs of well pumping and oil transport to the refinery). Refinery 2 is 12 km from well 1 and 16 km from well 2 and converts crude oil to heating oil with an efficiency of $[95 - (V/300)]\%$ where V is the amount of crude oil that goes into the refinery (bpd). Profit is $4/barrel of fuel oil produced. Refinery 3, which is 15 km from refinery 1 and 7 km from refinery 2, converts the leftover or waste oil from refineries 1 and 2 into petroleum products at a profit of $1/barrel of waste oil.

Capacities of refineries 1, 2, and 3 are 10,000, 8000, and 6000 bpd, respectively. Pumping costs at well 1 are $0.10/barrel and at well 2 are $0.20/barrel. Transport costs are $0.05/barrel/km.

(a) Construct an optimization model for Wildcat that will tell the company how to run its wells and refineries; that is, how much to pump from each well, how much oil should go from each well to each of the two refineries, and so forth.

(b) Having modeled this problem, you are now faced with the following situation. As part of its oil allocation program, the federal government has ruled that 50% of the company's daily well production must be used for fuel oil. Also, the company may charge a $2/barrel surcharge on all gasoline and fuel oil refined from crude oil pumped from the *new* well (well 2); that is, profits for such gasoline and oil will increase by $2/barrel. Construct an optimization model for this new situation.

(c) Solve the optimization model developed in part a.

2-7.

Recent college graduate I. M. Forbirds has acquired 100 ha of good agricultural land on which he wishes to raise two crops. Mr. Forbirds has been very impressed by several environmental quality courses that he took at college and is convinced that farmers use excessive amounts of pesticides. He has also heard that systems analysis may be a useful technique for dealing with environmental problems. Mr. Forbirds has learned that you are an expert in this area and has hired you to develop a production plan for his 100 ha. His basic premise is that economic considerations would result in reduced pesticide use. That is, the goal of maximizing farm income would result in efficient pesticide use. Although you may not be convinced of this, you have agreed to perform a systems analysis of the problem. In your preliminary analysis you have learned the following.

For the two crops to be considered, there are two possible pesticides that could be used. Pesticide A is generally quite effective and relatively expensive at $10/kg applied. Pesticide B is less effective but cheaper at $5/kg applied. Application of the pesticides to the two crops results in the following crop yields.

Crop 1

If pesticide A is used at rate P_{1A} (kg/ha) crop yield in t/ha is

$$4 + 6[1 - \exp(-0.18P_{1A})]$$

If pesticide B is used at rate P_{1B} (kg/ha) crop yield in t/ha is

$$4 + 0.4P_{1B} \quad \text{if} \quad P_{1B} \leq 10$$
$$8 \quad \text{if} \quad P_{1B} > 10$$

Crop 2

If pesticide A is used at rate P_{2A} (kg/ha) crop yield in t/ha is

$$5 + 7[1 - \exp(-0.12P_{2A})]$$

If pesticide B is used at rate P_{2B} crop yield in t/ha is

$$5 + 0.25P_{2B} \quad \text{if} \quad P_{2B} \leq 12$$
$$8 \quad \text{if} \quad P_{2B} > 12$$

Costs of raising the two crops exclusive of pesticide costs are $200/ha and $130/ha for crops 1 and 2, respectively. The crops are sold at prices of $40/t and $30/t for crops 1 and 2, respectively.
    (a)   Construct an optimization model that can be used to maximize Mr. Forbirds' income from his 100 ha.
    (b)   Solve the model using informal search.

2-8.

A toxic waste chemical ZAP is to be disposed of by conversion to a concretelike capsule and subsequent burial. The waste is handled in 20 kg units, and each 20 kg of ZAP is combined with three materials. The first two are chemicals designed to speed the waste's degradation or decay. The yearly decay rate is given by

$$D = 0.003 \text{ (kg of chemical 1)} + 0.005 \text{ (kg of chemical 2)}$$

Thus, if 10 kg and 40 kg of chemicals 1 and 2 are mixed with the 20 kg of ZAP, the fraction of ZAP that decays in any year is $D = 0.003(10) + 0.005(40) = 0.23$. By "decay" we mean that ZAP is degraded into inert (harmless) substances.

The third material added is a type of concrete and must constitute at least 50% (by mass) of the capsule mixture (20 kg waste + chemicals + concrete). To minimize opportunities for contamination, *it is desirable to keep the capsule size (volume) as small as possible.* The capsule's initial density (ρ, kg/m^3) is affected by the mixture and is given by

$$\rho = 2000\left(1 - \frac{\text{mass of chemicals 1 and 2}}{\text{total mass of capsule}}\right)$$

Two types of environmental objectives are relevant. The first is that no more than 1% of the original 20 kg of ZAP can remain active (undecayed) in the capsule at the end of 20 years. The second objective concerns the leakage of the ZAP from the capsule. Leakage is impossible to prevent and is affected by the amount of concrete in the capsule mixture. The fraction of undecayed ZAP that escapes each year from the capsule, L, is

$$L = 0.02, \text{ when the capsule is } < 60\% \text{ concrete (by mass)}$$

$$L = 0.01, \text{ when the capsule is } \geq 60\% \text{ concrete (by mass)}$$

The leakage standard requires that the *average* leakage of ZAP from the capsule over 20 years not exceed 0.05 kg/yr.
  (a) Formulate an optimization model (or models) that can be used to design the ZAP disposal capsules.
  (b) Develop an efficient procedure for solving the optimization model (models).
  (c) Obtain the optimal mixture for the capsules.

Note. As an example of the calculations needed in this problem, suppose the following mixture is proposed.

Chemical 1: 20 kg
Chemical 2: 50 kg
Concrete (material 3): 100 kg

This produces a decay rate of

$$D = 0.003(20) + 0.005(50) = 0.31$$

The total mass of the capsule is $20 + 20 + 50 + 100 = 190$ kg. Hence the concrete is $100/190 = 0.526$ of the capsule, and the leakage rate is $L = 0.02$.

During the first year of storage, $0.02(20) = 0.4$ kg of ZAP leaks from the capsule, and $0.31(20) = 6.2$ kg of ZAP is decayed. At the end of the year, $20 - 0.4 - 6.2 = 13.4$ kg of ZAP remains. During the second year, leakage is $0.02(13.4) = 0.268$ kg and decay is $0.31(13.4) = 4.154$ kg, leaving $13.4 - 0.268 - 4.154 = 8.978$ kg of ZAP at the end of year 2.

In solving the problem, the following relationship may be useful.

$$1 + x + x^2 + \ldots + x^n \simeq \frac{1}{1-x}$$

for $x^2 < 1$ and $n > 10$.

CHAPTER 3
APPLICATION: OPTIMIZATION MODEL FOR THE PLANNING OF MUNICIPAL WASTEWATER TREATMENT

This chapter is an analysis of a water pollution example. Unlike the problems in the previous chapter, this is a realistic demonstration of an actual water quality problem. Although the specific problem setting is hypothetical, the descriptions of treatment processes, costs, water quality impacts, and other characteristics are based on real-world phenomena and data. As a result the analysis and resulting optimization model are more complicated than preceding ones. The solution of the model is correspondingly difficult and, like most realistic problems, a computer or programmable calculator is necessary to evaluate alternative problem solutions. This chapter illustrates the level of detail required to apply systems analysis to actual environmental problems and demonstrates general modeling approaches for wastewater management studies.

PROBLEM DESCRIPTION

EXAMPLE 3-1
A city of 100,000 people discharges sewage or wastewater into a river. This wastewater flow of 40,000 m^3/day receives secondary treatment, which is a combination of settling and biological oxidation designed to remove organic matter from the sewage. However, the treatment does not eliminate water quality problems in the river. The treatment plant effluent produces a summertime dissolved oxygen (DO) level in the river that is below the water quality standard of 5 mg/liter. This standard has been set by regulatory agencies to maintain aquatic life. The city is thus forced to evaluate additional treatment methods that would produce a higher-quality effluent.

The city is considering two general strategies. The first is installation of additional treatment processes prior to effluent discharge to the river. The second is to reduce or eliminate the river discharge by diverting the secondary effluent to a land application site 3 km from the secondary treatment plant where a corn (maize) crop would be irrigated with the wastewater. The city would like these strategies evaluated to obtain a cost-effective plan for meeting environmental standards. □

This example typifies several aspects of municipal wastewater management. Sewage disposal for cities has often been by discharge to surface receiving waters. Concern for public health and environmental quality leads to progressive tightening of water quality and effluent standards requiring upgrading of treatment works. Since wastewater treatment is costly, municipal engineers are motivated to evaluate a variety of alternatives, including those that involve productive reuse of the wastewater. Irrigation of agricultural crops or "sewage farming" is a classic means of reuse and has long been considered a viable option to the direct discharge of sewage to receiving waters.

Municipal wastewater management is a problem that is well-suited to systems analysis and, although different words have been used, the systems approach has long been part of such management. For example, in an 1886 report (6), a Massachusetts commission presented its evaluation of four wastewater treatment and disposal options for cities in the eastern part of that state: (1) ocean discharge without treatment; (2) sewage farming; (3) "intermittent downward filtration" (through layers of porous soil); and (4) chemical precipitation. The commission was obliged to "approach all proposals from the pecuniary point of view"; it recommended cost-effective mixtures of management options that placed heavy emphasis on land application for the various cities.

The implementation of wastewater treatment proceeds in four steps: planning, design, construction, and operation. As with the 1886 Massachusetts study, the present example involves only the first, or planning stage. Wastewater management planning is a general analysis of the costs and environmental impacts of treatment options, with the goal of identifying the treatment method or combination of methods that seems to be cost-effective. The subsequent design stage is a detailed engineering analysis that (hopefully) produces accurate cost estimates, specifications for the treatment processes, and evaluation of financial and operating procedures required during construction and subsequent plant operation. Treatment works design is time consuming and expensive; therefore a preliminary or planning step is necessary to screen possible treatment methods in order to eliminate all but one or, at most, several that can be carried into the design phase. Since generation and evaluation of alternatives occur at the planning stage, that aspect of wastewater management is most amenable to systems analysis.

TECHNICAL BACKGROUND

Treatment and Discharge to Receiving Waters

Sewage discharges have a variety of effects on water bodies; one of the most severe is the impact on dissolved oxygen (DO). Oxygen is essential to aquatic animals; however, its supply is limited in all waters since, even at saturation levels, DO concentrations are seldom more than 10 mg/liter in fresh waters (and even lower in saline waters). Dissolved oxygen is depleted by microbial oxidation of organic matter. This is a natural process that occurs in all water bodies, but it is intensified by organic wastes. Oxygen consumed in organic matter oxidation is termed biochemical oxygen demand (BOD). The two principal forms of oxidation are the decomposition of carbonaceous and of nitrogenous compounds. The corresponding oxygen demands are carbonaceous BOD (CBOD) and nitrogenous BOD (NBOD). Carbonaceous BOD is associated with a variety of microorganisms and biochemical processes, but NBOD is due principally to the oxidation of ammonium to nitrate by two distinct bacterial groups (*Nitrosomonas* and *Nitrobacter*).

Because of the importance of DO in the maintenance of aquatic life, the pollution potential of wastewaters is often described in terms of CBOD and NBOD. Figure 3-1 indicates the general effect of wastewater CBOD and NBOD on DO of a river or stream. Immediately after an effluent is discharged, river DO drops sharply, since it mixes with the wastewater, which usually has very low DO concentrations. Downstream of the discharge, DO continues to fall because of the oxidation of carbonaceous and nitrogenous compounds. This "DO sag" recovers, since oxygen is absorbed from the atmosphere. In the absence of further waste inputs, the river DO concentration can eventually recover to saturation.

Steady-state river dissolved oxygen $C(x)$ in mg/liter at a distance x km downstream of a single wastewater discharge can be determined from the differential equation

$$u \frac{dC}{dx} = k_2(C_s - C) - k_1 B - k_n N \qquad (3.1)$$

in which u is the river velocity (km/day), k_2 is a reaeration rate (day^{-1}), C_s is saturation DO (mg/liter), B and N are remaining CBOD and NBOD (mg/liter) in the river at distance x, and k_1 and k_n are rate constants (day^{-1}) indicating the fractions of CBOD and NBOD exerted per day. The first term on the right of equation 3.1 is an oxygen increase caused by reaeration; it is proportional to the oxygen deficit below saturation,

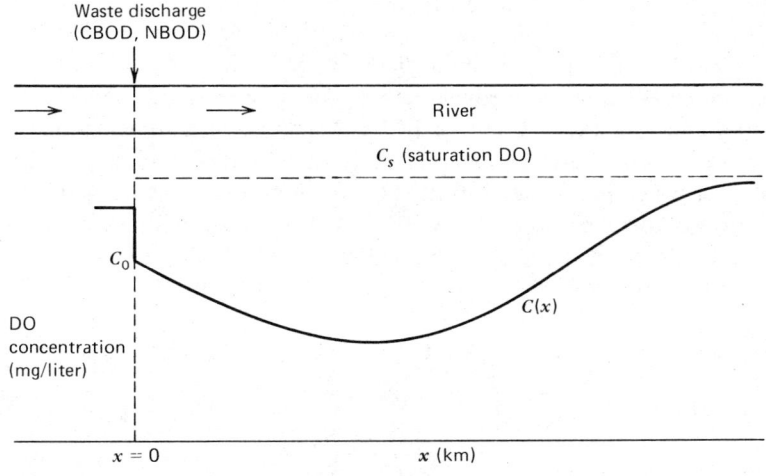

Figure 3-1 Effect of a waste discharge on river dissolved oxygen concentration.

$C_s - C$. The two remaining terms describe the removal of DO through the oxidation of carbonaceous and nitrogenous matter.

Both BOD quantities will decrease with downstream distance as the waste is degraded in the river. This is often described by first-order decay mechanisms of the following form.

$$u\frac{dB}{dx} = -k_1 B \tag{3.2}$$

$$u\frac{dN}{dx} = -k_n N \tag{3.3}$$

These equations can be solved for B and N to obtain

$$B = B_0 e^{-k_1 x/u} \tag{3.4}$$

$$N = N_0 e^{-k_n x/u} \tag{3.5}$$

where B_0 and N_0 are initial CBOD and NBOD in the river immediately after discharge.

When Equations 3.4 and 3.5 are substituted into Equation 3.1, that equation can be solved for river DO, $C(x)$.

$$\begin{aligned}C(x) = {} & C_s(1 - e^{-k_2 x/u}) + C_0 e^{-k_2 x/u} \\ & - \frac{B_0 k_1}{k_2 - k_1}(e^{-k_1 x/u} - e^{-k_2 x/u}) \\ & - \frac{N_0 k_n}{k_2 - k_n}(e^{-k_n x/u} - e^{-k_2 x/u})\end{aligned} \tag{3.6}$$

In Equation 3.6 C_0 is the river DO immediately after discharge. Additional factors that are sometimes included in these equations are oxidation of sludge deposits, plant and algal photosynthesis and respiration, and CBOD removal by sedimentation (1, 8, 13).

Initial values C_0, B_0, and N_0 are generally based on the assumption of complete mixing of river water and waste effluent at the point of discharge. Thus, if Q_r, C_r, B_r, and N_r are river flow (m³/day), DO, CBOD, and NBOD (mg/liter) immediately upstream of the effluent, and Q_w, C_w, B_w, and N_w are the analogous waste parameters, initial values are given by

$$C_0 = \frac{C_r Q_r + C_w Q_w}{Q_r + Q_w} \tag{3.7}$$

$$B_0 = \frac{B_r Q_r + B_w Q_w}{Q_r + Q_w} \tag{3.8}$$

$$N_0 = \frac{N_r Q_r + N_w Q_w}{Q_r + Q_w} \tag{3.9}$$

Equations 3.6 to 3.9 establish a cause-and-effect relationship between wastewater characteristics and water quality (DO in the river). In their most general form, such equations are pollutant transport or assimilation relationships that estimate environmental quality at one point in space or time as functions of waste discharges to the environment at another point in space or time. Whenever problems involve environmental instead of effluent standards, transport equations are necessary, since they provide the quantitative means of determining whether or not environmental standards such as the 5 mg/liter DO limit are met by alternative control methods.

Prediction of river DO requires knowledge of the parameters in Equation 3.6. This is accomplished by direct field and laboratory measurements, past experience, and empirical formulas. Carbonaceous and nitrogenous BOD rates (k_1, k_n) are functions of waste and river characteristics and increase with temperature. Reaeration rate (k_2) is a function of temperature and river turbulence. Saturation DO (C_s) is primarily determined by temperature. River DO, CBOD, and NBOD (C_r, B_r, and N_r) are often estimated or measured directly and are largely determined by upstream inputs of organic matter. Since downstream DO, $C(x)$, will vary with both temperature and river flow, "critical" flow and temperature conditions are assumed for Equations 3.6 to 3.9. In many parts of the world, these conditions are reached in late summer, when high water temperatures increase reaction rates and decrease saturation DO and low river flows decrease waste dilution and river turbulence. Parameter values for the current example are given in Table 3-1.

Wastewater treatment processes reduce the CBOD and NBOD of wastewater. Effluent CBOD, NBOD, and DO from treatment options considered in the example are given in Table 3-2. Secondary treatment, which is the existing process in the example, includes a controlled oxidation process in which microorganisms decompose much of the carbonaceous organic material in the sewage, usually reducing the CBOD of the effluent by 80 to 90%. Removal of NBOD is only partially achieved by secondary

TABLE 3-1 Water Quality Parameters for Example 3-1

Parameter	Value
River flow, Q_r	110 $10^3 m^3$/day
River velocity, u	7.9 km/day
CBOD rate, k_1	0.35 day^{-1}
Reaeration rate, k_2	0.50 day^{-1}
NBOD rate, k_n	0.20 day^{-1}
River DO, C_r	8.0 mg/liter
River CBOD, B_r	2.0 mg/liter
River NBOD, N_r	5.0 mg/liter
Saturation DO, C_s	8.0 mg/liter

TABLE 3-2 Effluent Quality from Treatment Options for Municipal Wastewater

Treatment Processes	Effluent Quality (mg/liter)		
	CBOD	NBOD	DO
Secondary (settling + biological oxidation)	25	54	2
Secondary + filtration (microscreening)	13	50	2
Secondary + nitrification	13	10	2
Secondary + nitrification + filtration	7	10	2

treatment, and an additional biological process (nitrification) is required to reduce wastewater NBOD substantially. Filtration is a physical process that removes portions of the undissolved carbonaceous and nitrogenous waste.

As noted in the description of the example, secondary treatment is not sufficient to meet the river DO standard of 5 mg/liter. This can be seen by solving Equations 3.6 to 3.9 using the parameters from Table 3-1 and the secondary effluent quality in Table 3-2. Resulting downstream DO concentrations are given in Table 3-3.

TABLE 3-3 Present River DO Predicted from Equation 3.6 (Secondary Treatment) for Example 3-1

Distance Downstream x (km)	Dissolved Oxygen $C(x)$ (mg/liter)
5	3.6
10	2.1
15	1.4
20	1.2
25	1.4
30	1.7
40	2.7
50	3.8

Land Application of Municipal Wastewater

Although a variety of land application methods are sometimes feasible, one of the most popular is the irrigation of agricultural crops with wastewater effluent. The crops can use both the water and wastewater nutrients for growth, and the sale of crops can recover some of the treatment costs for the municipality. Alternatively, cities can sometimes sell sewage effluent directly to farmers. Irrigation is a beneficial recycling of municipal wastewater, and it is not surprising that this practical means of sewage disposal has been used for decades in most parts of the world.

A common configuration for land application is shown in Figure 3-2. Since farmland is not often adjacent to the sewage treatment plant, a pipeline or canal is usually needed to transport effluent to the land application site. Although irrigation is alternated among various fields, weather conditions will not allow continuous irrigation, so storage lagoons are required at the application site. After application to the crop, a portion of the irrigated effluent will be utilized to meet crop evapotranspiration requirements. In arid climates evapotranspiration can consume much, if not all, of the applied wastewater. However, in wetter regions substantial portions of the water will percolate downward through the soil profile. In land application sites with poor soil drainage percolation is collected by tile drainage networks in the soil. In the present example it is assumed that percolation enters a groundwater aquifer beneath the soil.

The planning of land application systems requires consideration of a different set of factors from those that are important with sewage discharge to surface waters. DO and BOD are relatively unimportant with wastewater irrigation because of the soil's

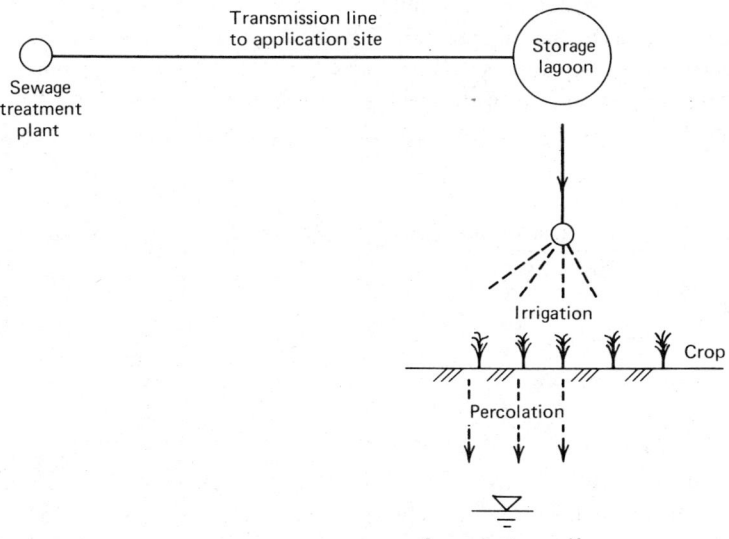

Figure 3-2 Components of a wastewater land application system.

ability to rapidly assimilate waste organics. Irrigation rates must be balanced with precipitation, evapotranspiration, and soil drainage capacity so as not to waterlog or flood the site. Although several parameters can be of environmental concern, wastewater pathogens and nitrogen are often the critical pollution parameters. Pathogens are important if the wastewater effluent has not been disinfected or if crops are grown for human consumption. Assuming that in the present example neither situation occurs, nitrogen remains the major source of environmental impact.

Nitrogen is a significant problem in land application sites, since the wastewater nitrogen that is unused by the crop can be transported, in the form of nitrate, to groundwater by percolation. Aquifers are often used as sources of drinking water, and nitrate can be toxic to both infants and livestock. Standards for drinking water nitrate content are set by public health authorities in most countries and, in this example, this standard is 10 mg/liter of nitrate-nitrogen.[1]

This overview of wastewater irrigation provides the basis for a simple model of land application that can be used for the wastewater management example. The model is based on mass balances for water and nitrogen at the application site during the irrigation season. At an irrigation rate of r cm/wk for an irrigation season of T weeks, the total water input (cm) to the site is $rT + P$, where P is the precipitation (cm) during T weeks. Since land application sites are designed to prevent runoff, the only water outputs from the site are evapotranspiration ET (cm) in the irrigation season and percolation. Percolation (cm) is thus

$$\text{Percolation} = rT + P - ET \tag{3.10}$$

A nitrogen balance is required to estimate the nitrogen loss in percolation to groundwater. If the nitrogen concentration in the wastewater is n (mg/liter), the total nitrogen input to the irrigation site is $0.1Trn$ (kg/ha).[2] The unused or excess nitrogen from the wastewater irrigation is $0.1Trn - NC$, where NC is the crop nitrogen uptake. Assuming that this excess nitrogen is in the form of nitrate and is leached from the soil by percolation, the average concentration c_n (mg/liter) of nitrate-nitrogen in the percolation is

$$c_n = \frac{\text{nitrogen loss in mg/ha}}{\text{percolation in liters/ha}}$$

$$= \frac{(0.1Trn - NC)(\text{kg/ha})\, 10^6(\text{mg/kg})}{(rT + P - ET)(\text{cm})\, 10^{-2}(\text{m/cm})\, 10^4(\text{m}^2/\text{ha})\, 10^3(\text{liters/m}^3)}$$

---

[1] The molecular weight of nitrate (NO_3^-) is 62, of which $(14/62)100 = 22.58\%$ is nitrogen. 10 mg/liter of nitrate-nitrogen is approximately equal to an NO_3 concentration of 45 mg/liter.

[2] The "0.1" in $0.1Trn$ is a conversion factor based on the following: 1 ha = 10^4m^2, 1 m = 10^2 cm, 1 m³ = 10^3 liters, 1 kg = 10^6 mg.

or

$$c_n = \frac{Trn - 10NC}{rT + P - ET} \qquad (3.11)$$

Equation 3.11 provides a means for determining nitrate-nitrogen concentrations in percolation water from the land application site as a function of irrigation rate. However, the environmental standard for nitrate-nitrogen of 10 mg/liter applies to drinking water supplies. In principle, mathematical relationships describing the transport of nitrogen through the groundwater aquifer to water supply wells are necessary to evaluate alternative irrigation rates. However, such relationships are difficult to obtain and, in the absence of extensive testing using field measurements, they are of questionable accuracy. Moreover, nitrate contamination is a long-term problem. Nitrate is essentially conserved in aquifers and is subject to progressive buildup that can threaten future water supply sources. For these reasons a conservative approach to nitrate pollution seems justified that limits the nitrate-nitrogen concentrations of aquifer input waters to the public health standard of 10 mg/liter. This insures that at no time in the future will water supplies taken from the aquifer exceed the nitrate standard. As applied to land application, this restricts the nitrate-nitrogen concentration of percolation water as determined from Equation 3.11 to be no more than 10 mg/liter.

Several parameters of the land application site must be known to apply Equation 3.11. Parameter values for the example are given in Table 3-4. These values are based on a well-drained soil and a 13-wk irrigation season for corn in a climate that is sufficiently wet so that crop evapotranspiration needs are approximately met by precipitation.

TABLE 3-4 Land Application Parameters for Example

Parameter	Value
Irrigation season, T	13 wk
Nitrogen concentration of wastewater, n	20 mg/liter
Crop nitrogen uptake, NC	170 kg/ha
Precipitation − evapotranspiration, $P - ET$	0
Maximum soil drainage, $\bar{r}$	14 cm/wk

Wastewater Treatment Costs

The costs of wastewater treatment include construction, operation and maintenance costs, engineering fees and a general category of "contingency" costs. Cost estimating is an exacting process and is a major aspect of engineering design. In the planning stage, however, time and resources seldom permit a thorough analysis of wastewater treatment costs. Instead, cost estimates are usually based on experience with similar treatment processes elsewhere. Such data, adjusted for possible inflation, are often summarized in the form of general cost curves. These curves can be fitted by mathematical functions such as those given in Table 3-5. Costs are divided into capital costs, which are incurred in constructing the treatment plant (including contingencies and engineering fees), and operation and maintenance (O&M) costs that are required for the future running of the plant. Capital costs are usually met by borrowing through municipal bonds that are paid off during the useful life of the treatment works. Capital costs are amortized[3] as fixed payments per year, and both capital and O&M costs can be expressed as annual payments.

Cost curves are available for land application of wastewater, but their mathematical description generally is more complicated than those in Table 3-5. Separate cost functions are required for wastewater transmission, storage, irrigation, land purchase or rent, and cropping. These functions are given in Table 3-6 for this example. Transmission costs are for a gravity pipeline from the sewage treatment plant to the land application site. Storage costs are based on a lagoon for storage of one week's wastewater flow. Irrigation costs are functions of both average wastewater flow and irrigation rate and include the costs of growing corn on the site. Land and cropping costs include land rent and income from crop sales. This income is reported as a negative O&M cost ($-0.87A$).

TABLE 3-5 Cost Functions for Filtration and Nitrification

Treatment Process[a]	Costs ($10³/yr)	
	Capital	Operation and Maintenance
Filtration	$3.0Q^{0.93}$	$20.1Q^{0.55}$
Nitrification	$13.8Q^{0.68}$	$31.8Q^{0.42}$

[a] Q is the average wastewater flow treated by the process ($10^3 m^3$/day).

---

[3] The computation of annual costs is discussed in more detail in Chapter 10.

TABLE 3-6 Cost Functions for Land Application

Component[a]	Costs ($10³/yr) Capital	Operation and Maintenance
Transmission	$7.3LQ^{0.28}$	—
Storage	$1.2Q^{0.78}$	$0.6Q^{0.54}$
Irrigation	$(13.1 + 48/r)Q^{(0.74+0.32/r)}$	$(15.3 + 57/r)Q^{(0.79+0.28/r)}$
Land and cropping	$0.19A$	$-0.87A$

[a] Q = average wastewater flow (10^3m³/day), L = length of transmission line (km), r = irrigation rate (cm/wk), and A = area of irrigated land (ha).

SYSTEMS ANALYSIS

Definition of System and Objectives

Based on the description of the example and the technical background discussion, three objectives can be given and quantified.

1. Minimize the costs ($/yr) of additional wastewater treatment.
2. Raise the DO concentrations in the river downstream of the wastewater discharge to at least 5.0 mg/liter.
3. Limit nitrate-nitrogen concentrations in percolation water from the land application site to a maximum of 10 mg/liter.

The system consistent with these objectives is shown in Figure 3-3. Components include processes for additional treatment before discharge to the river (nitrification, filtration), a transmission line to the land application site, a storage lagoon, irrigated land, and river. Note that the present secondary treatment plant is excluded from the system. Although it is a critical part of the total wastewater management process, its only role in this analysis is to supply a fixed input to the system. Similarly, the groundwater aquifer is important in the planning of land application, but impacts on the aquifer are quantified by an effluent standard for percolation water. Therefore the aquifer is not a necessary system component.

Generation of Alternatives—Construction of a Mathematical Model

The example contains several variables that are subject to control. The basic decisions are the divisions of wastewater flow among the various treatment options. As indicated

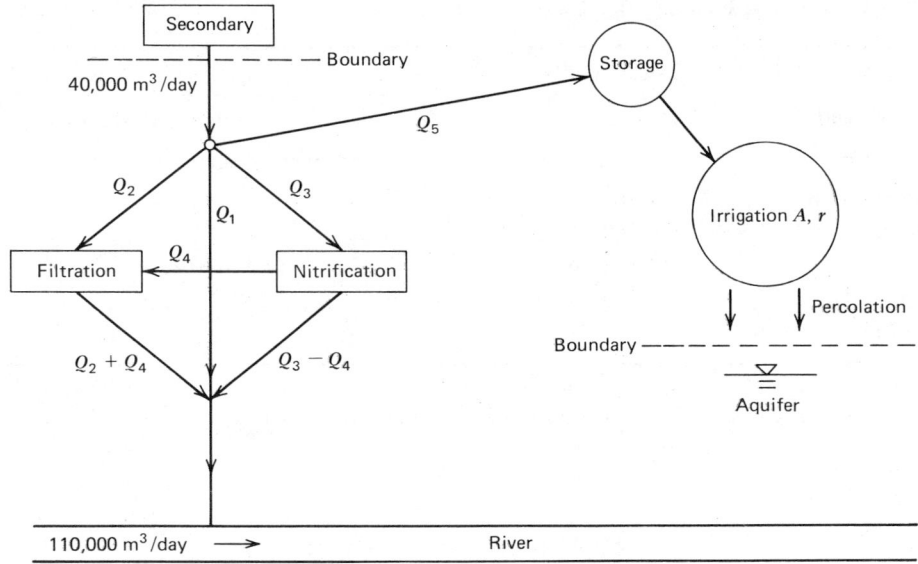

Figure 3-3 System definition for Example 3-1.

in Figure 3-3, wastewater can be filtered, nitrified (or both), or transported to land application. The decision variables defining these flows are

Q_1 = wastewater discharged without additional treatment ($10^3 m^3$/day)
Q_2 = wastewater receiving only filtration as additional treatment ($10^3 m^3$/day)
Q_3 = wastewater receiving nitrification ($10^3 m^3$/day)
Q_4 = wastewater receiving nitrification and filtration ($10^3 m^3$/day)
Q_5 = wastewater receiving land application ($10^3 m^3$/day)

Additional control variables at the land application site are

r = irrigation rate (cm/wk)
A = irrigated area (ha)

The three variables Q_5, r, and A are not independent, since

$$r = \frac{70 Q_5}{A} \qquad (3.12)$$

Since the additional wastewater treatment is required only during the low-flow summer months (when the DO standard is violated), the preceding variables are in terms of summer wastewater flows; for example, Q_5 = average daily wastewater flow to the land application site during the summer. The configurations of filtration and nitrification in Figure 3-3 follow the definitions of the processes given in Table 3-2. Thus a filtration unit should follow a biological treatment process such as a secondary treatment or nitrification and not precede the processes. Wastewater discharge to the river consists of a mixture of secondary, filtered, and nitrified effluents.

Relationships between variables are determined from mass balances, capacity limits, and mathematical descriptions of objectives. A water balance at the land application site is given by Equation 3.12. There are two operational limits on irrigation rates. The first is an upper limit $\bar{r}$ (cm/wk) dictated by soil drainage rate. Thus, for $\bar{r} = 14$ cm/wk (Table 3-4), we have

$$r \leq 14 \tag{3.13}$$

The irrigation rate should also be sufficient to satisfy the corn crop's nitrogen requirements of $NC = 170$ kg/ha. Since the total nitrogen in the wastewater is $0.1Trn$, the data from Table 3-4 indicate that $0.1(13)r(20) \geq 170$, or

$$26r \geq 170 \tag{3.14}$$

The nitrate-nitrogen concentration in percolation is computed from Equation 3.11, and the effluent standard for percolation is

$$\frac{260r - 1700}{13r} \leq 10 \tag{3.15}$$

Mass balances for the treatment options that discharge to the river are conservation of water, DO, CBOD, and NBOD. Since all wastewater must be disposed of,[4]

$$Q_1 + Q_2 + Q_3 + Q_5 = 40 \tag{3.16}$$

The total discharge to the river is $Q_1 + Q_2 + Q_3$, and the river flow after discharge is $110 + Q_1 + Q_2 + Q_3$.

Equation 3.6 is used to determine DO concentrations, $C(x)$ at any point downstream. The DO constraint is given as

$$C(x) \geq 5.0 \, \forall x \tag{3.17}$$

The symbol "$\forall$" is read "for all," and Constraint 3.17 states that DO concentrations must be no less than 5.0 mg/liter at any point downstream of the waste discharge. From a modeling viewpoint, the constraint is too comprehensive to be useful. It is impractical to determine $C(x)$ at every possible location, and the constraint generally would be checked only at fixed intervals (say every 5 or 10 km). Furthermore, some upper limit that is applicable to the problem must be placed on the downstream distance. This might be determined by the location of the next wastewater discharge or the location of the recovery portion of the DO sag (Figure 3-1). Clearly, the concentrations should be checked at least until it is observed that $C(x)$ has passed the minimum. In the present example this is done at 5-km intervals.

$$C(x) \geq 5 \quad x = 5, 10, 15, \cdots \tag{3.17a}$$

Initial DO, CBOD, and NBOD (C_0, B_0, N_0) for Equation 3.6 can be determined

---

[4] A fourth objective in the example could have been stated as "dispose of 40,000 m³/day of wastewater." The distinction between an explicit objective and a physical limitation is often arbitrary. Both are described by Equation 3.16.

based on effluent quality characteristics in Table 3-2 and effluent quantities in Figure 3-3. These initial values are computed from mass balances identical to Equations 3.7, 3.8, and 3.9. River quality data is taken from Table 3-1.

$$C_0 = \frac{8(110) + 2(Q_1 + Q_2 + Q_3)}{110 + Q_1 + Q_2 + Q_3} \quad (3.18)$$

$$B_0 = \frac{2(110) + 25Q_1 + 13Q_2 + 13(Q_3 - Q_4) + 7Q_4}{110 + Q_1 + Q_2 + Q_3} \quad (3.19)$$

$$N_0 = \frac{5(110) + 54Q_1 + 50Q_2 + 10(Q_3 - Q_4) + 10Q_4}{110 + Q_1 + Q_2 + Q_3} \quad (3.20)$$

The only remaining portion of the problem to be described mathematically is the objective of cost minimization. This is given by an objective function, $Z(\$10^3/\text{yr})$, which is the sum of treatment costs given in Tables 3-5 and 3-6. All O&M costs in Table 3-5 and 3-6, except for the crop return ($-0.87A$), are based on continuous year-round operation. To estimate the O&M costs of summertime operation only, the costs are divided by 3. From the problem statements, the transmission line length is $L = 3$ km.

The complete optimization model is

$$\text{Min } Z = 3(Q_2 + Q_4)^{0.93} + 6.7(Q_2 + Q_4)^{0.55} + 13.8Q_3^{0.68}$$
$$+ 10.6Q_3^{0.42} + 21.9Q_5^{0.28} + 1.2Q_5^{0.78} + 0.2Q_5^{0.54}$$
$$+ \left(13.1 + \frac{48}{r}\right)Q_5^{(0.74 + 0.32/r)}$$
$$+ \left(5.1 + \frac{19}{r}\right)Q_5^{(0.79 + 0.28/r)} - 0.68A \quad (3.21)$$

s.t.
$$Q_1 + Q_2 + Q_3 + Q_5 = 40 \quad (3.16)$$

$$C_0 - \frac{880 + 2Q_1 + 2Q_2 + 2Q_3}{110 + Q_1 + Q_2 + Q_3} = 0 \quad (3.18)$$

$$B_0 - \frac{220 + 25Q_1 + 13Q_2 + 13Q_3 - 6Q_4}{110 + Q_1 + Q_2 + Q_3} = 0 \quad (3.19)$$

$$N_0 - \frac{550 + 54Q_1 + 50Q_2 + 10Q_3}{110 + Q_1 + Q_2 + Q_3} = 0 \quad (3.20)$$

$$C_0 e^{-0.063x} - 2.33B_0(e^{-0.044x} - e^{-0.063x})$$
$$- 0.67N_0(e^{-0.025x} - e^{-0.063x})$$
$$+ 8(1 - e^{-0.063x}) \geq 5 \qquad x = 5, 10, \ldots \quad (3.22)$$

$$r - \frac{70Q_5}{A} = 0 \qquad (3.12)$$

$$r \leq 14 \qquad (3.13)$$

$$26r \geq 170 \qquad (3.14)$$

$$\frac{260r - 1700}{13r} \leq 10 \qquad (3.15)$$

$$Q_3 - Q_4 \geq 0 \qquad (3.23)$$

$$Q_j \geq 0 \; \forall j \qquad (3.24)$$

The model contains 10 decision variables (Q_1, Q_2, Q_3, Q_4, Q_5, r, A, C_0, B_0, N_0), although many of these are not independent. Thus C_0, B_0, N_0 are all functions of the various Q_j, and A is determined by r and Q_5. Constraints 3.23 and 3.24 are necessary to prevent negative mass fluxes. Constraint 3.24 will also prevent C_0, B_0, and N_0 from being negative. Constraint 3.14 prevents negative irrigation rates r; since both r and Q_5 are nonnegative, irrigated area A cannot be negative because of Equation 3.12.

Evaluation of Alternatives—Model Solutions

The optimization model has a complicated structure that does not meet mathematical programming requirements, and search methods are the only viable means of evaluating alternative treatment plans. Since the model consists of more than several variables and constraints, it is difficult to devise a search strategy. Obviously, the graphical artifices used for the examples in Chapter 2 are not feasible with this larger problem. Nevertheless, the same general principles used for deriving search strategies for simple examples apply also to this more complicated model. A feasible region must be found, the effects of decision variables on the objective function examined, and alternatives screened by observing which are inferior to or dominate others.

The feasible region for the decision variables can be partially determined by decomposing the optimization model into two parts corresponding to the land application and river discharge options. This is possible, since the costs of these two sets of options are independent of each other (river discharge costs depend on Q_2, Q_3 and Q_4, while land application costs are functions of Q_5, r, and A) and each has an independent constraint set (Expressions 3.18 to 3.20 and 3.22 for river discharge and Expressions 3.12 to 3.15 for land application). The two decomposed problems are linked by Equation 3.16.

The decomposition permits a straightforward determination of feasible land application variables (Q_5, r, A). The crop nitrogen constraint in Expression 3.14 and the nitrate constraint in Expression 3.15 reduce to

$$r \geq 6.5 \qquad (3.14a)$$

$$r \leq 13.1 \qquad (3.15a)$$

Since any value of irrigation rate r that satisfies Constraint 3.15a will also meet Constraint 3.13, the latter is redundant (unnecessary), and feasible values of r are

$$6.5 \leq r \leq 13.1 \tag{3.25}$$

The lower and upper bounds in Constraint 3.25 are the minimum irrigation rate, which supplies crop nitrogen needs, and the maximum irrigation rate, which meets the nitrate standard. Assuming that it is possible to meet stream DO requirements with $Q_5 = 0$ (this will subsequently be confirmed), feasible values of r, Q_5, and A are given by Constraint 3.25 and the following.

$$0 \leq Q_5 \leq 40 \tag{3.26}$$

$$A = 70 Q_5 / r \tag{3.12a}$$

Costs associated with land application,

$$Z_1 = 21.9 Q_5^{0.28} + 1.2 Q_5^{0.78} + 0.2 Q_5^{0.54} + \left(13.1 + \frac{48}{r}\right) Q_5^{(0.74 + 0.32/r)}$$

$$+ \left(5.1 + \frac{19}{r}\right) Q_5^{(0.79 + 0.28/r)} - 0.68 A \tag{3.27}$$

can be computed for a range of feasible Q_5, r, and A, as shown in Table 3-7. It can be seen from the results that land application costs are insensitive to irrigation rates (and hence irrigated land area). As long as the irrigation rate is within the feasible limits ($6.5 \leq r \leq 13.1$), it can be selected arbitrarily with little effect on treatment costs.

The feasible region for the variables associated with river discharge (Q_1, Q_2, Q_3, Q_4) cannot be easily determined because of the complicated form of the DO constraint. To get a general feel for the feasible region, several single-treatment options (all wastewater filtered or nitrified, etc.) can be evaluated. This evaluation requires a computer program to calculate relevant mass fluxes, concentrations, and costs. Instead of programming just the river discharge portion of the model, it is more efficient to construct a general computer program for evaluation of all combinations of decision variables. A flowchart for this general program is shown in Figure 3-4. Program inputs are flows to the various treatment options (Q_2—filtration; Q_3—nitrification; Q_4—nitrification and filtration; and Q_5—land application) and the irrigation rate r. Program output corresponds to the three objectives in the problem: nitrate-nitrogen concentrations in percolation, DO concentrations in the river, and total annual costs.

Five single-option alternatives are given in Table 3-8. Costs, nitrate-nitrogen concentrations, and DO concentrations for these alternatives are given in Table 3-9. Since land application costs are not sensitive to irrigation rate, an arbitrary feasible value of $r = 10$ cm/wk was selected. It can be seen that neither filtration nor nitrification alone will meet the 5 mg/liter DO standard. Combined nitrification and filtration is the most expensive option, but it does satisfy the DO standard. Land application is somewhat less expensive and, since all wastewater is diverted from river discharge, DO levels easily exceed 5.0 mg/liter. Note that an oxygen sag results even from this total diversion, because of the BOD already in the river upstream of the discharge point.

TABLE 3-7 Costs of Feasible Land Application Alternatives

Flow to Land Application, Q_s (10^3/day)	Irrigation Rate, r (cm/wk)	Irrigated Area, A (ha)[a]	Land Application Cost, Z_1 ($\$10^3$/yr)
40	6.5	431	341
	8.0	350	342
	10.0	280	346
	12.0	233	346
	13.1	214	351
30	6.5	323	292
	8.0	263	291
	10.0	210	293
	12.0	175	293
	13.1	160	295
20	6.5	215	233
	8.0	175	231
	10.0	140	231
	12.0	117	231
	13.1	107	231
10	6.5	108	157
	8.0	88	155
	10.0	70	154
	12.0	58	154
	13.1	53	153

[a]From Equation 3.12a, rounded to nearest ha.

The results of these preliminary simulations indicate the general nature of the feasible region for the optimization model. Since land application and combined nitrification/filtration are the only options that meet the DO standard, feasible alternatives must incorporate at least one of the options. Several treatment combinations with nitrification/filtration are shown in Table 3-10. The alternatives are divided into three groups that pair nitrification/filtration with no additional treatment (i.e., secondary, Q_1), filtration (Q_2), or nitrification alone ($Q_3 - Q_4$). Within each group, an attempt is made to find the least expensive alternative that meets the DO standard. A feasible filtration alternative was not determined, since even the unfeasible alternative 9 is as expensive as land application alone (alternative 5). Alternatives 10 and 11, which nitrify all the effluent ($Q_3 = 40$) but filter only portions, are each less expensive than land application, and alternative 11 at \$319,000 dominates all feasible alternatives in Tables 3-9 and 3-10.

58 PLANNING OF MUNICIPAL WASTEWATER TREATMENT

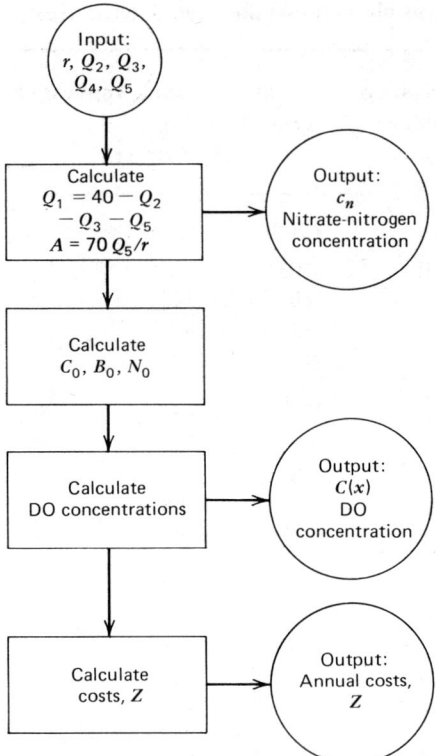

Figure 3-4 Computer program flowchart for optimization model.

TABLE 3-8 Single-Option Treatment Alternatives

Alternative	Option	Wastewater Flows (10^3 m³/day)					Irrigation Rate r (cm/wk)	Irrigated Area A (ha)
		Q_1	Q_2	Q_3	Q_4	Q_5		
1	Secondary	40	0	0	0	0	—	—
2	Filtration	0	40	0	0	0	—	—
3	Nitrification	0	0	40	0	0	—	—
4	Nitrification + filtration	0	0	40	40	0	—	—
5	Land application	0	0	0	0	40	10.0	280

TABLE 3-9 Evaluation of Single Option Treatment Alternatives Defined in Table 3-8

Alternative	Option	Nitrate- in Percolation (mg/liter)	River Dissolved Oxygen (mg/liter) at $x =$							Annual Cost (10^3/yr)
			5	10	15	20	25	30	40	50km	
1	Secondary	—	3.6	2.1	1.4	1.2	1.4	1.7	2.7	3.8	0
2	Filtration	—	4.3	3.1	2.6	2.4	2.6	2.8	3.6	4.4	144
3	Nitrification	—	5.4	4.8	4.7	4.7	4.9	5.1	5.6	6.1	219
4	Nitrification + filtration	—	5.6	5.3	5.1	5.2	5.3	5.5	6.0	6.4	363
5	Land application	6.9	7.2	6.7	6.4	6.3	6.3	6.4	6.6	6.9	346

Treatment combinations with land application are listed in Table 3-11, with the same groupings (secondary, filtration, nitrification) used in Table 3-10. Alternative 13, which discharges 8000 m^3/day without additional treatment and diverts 32,000 m^3/day to land application, is the least expensive of all the feasible alternatives that have been generated; it is therefore an approximate solution to the optimization model.

Selection of Alternatives

Manipulation of the mathematical model has indicated that the land application/direct discharge alternative 13 is the least expensive solution to this planning problem. However, as indicated earlier, the information used in developing cost functions is approximate, and the actual costs of treatment may be substantially different than those given by the cost functions. The nitrification alternative 11 is nearly as cheap as the

TABLE 3-10 Treatment Combinations with Nitrification/Filtration

Alternative	Flows (10^3m^3/day)					Dissolved Oxygen (mg/liter) at $x =$				Annual Cost (10^3/yr)
	Q_1	Q_2	Q_3	Q_4	Q_5	10	20	30	40	50km	
6	5	0	35	35	0	4.9	4.7	5.1	5.6	6.1	331
7	2	0	38	38	0	5.1	5.0	5.3	5.8	6.3	350
8	0	10	30	30	0	4.7	4.5	4.9	5.4	5.9	327
9	0	5	35	35	0	5.0	4.8	5.2	5.7	6.2	346
10	0	0	40	30	0	5.2	5.1	5.4	5.9	6.3	334
11	0	0	40	25	0	5.1	5.0	5.4	5.8	6.3	319

TABLE 3-11 Treatment Combinations with Land Application

Alternative[a]	Flows ($10^3 m^3$/day)					Dissolved Oxygen (mg/liter) at $x =$					Annual Cost ($\$10^3$/yr)
	Q_1	Q_2	Q_3	Q_4	Q_5	10	20	30	40	50km	
12	5	0	0	0	35	5.9	5.5	5.6	6.0	6.4	320
13	8	0	0	0	32	5.5	5.0	5.2	5.6	6.1	304
14	9	0	0	0	31	5.4	4.9	5.1	5.5	6.0	298
15	0	10	0	0	30	5.6	5.1	5.3	5.7	6.1	342
16	0	12	0	0	28	5.4	4.9	5.1	5.5	6.0	338
17	0	0	10	0	30	6.1	5.8	6.0	6.3	6.7	387
18	0	0	20	0	20	5.6	5.4	5.6	6.1	6.5	374
19	0	0	30	0	10	5.2	5.0	5.3	5.8	6.3	338

[a]Irrigation rate $r = 10$ cm/wk.

optimal solution and, given the approximate costs, the difference cannot be considered significant. Moreover, this alternative is very different from land application; if additional factors are uncovered in the design process that are unfavorable to land application it would be advisable to have an economical second alternative. The planning process output is thus the selection of the two alternatives in Table 3-12. Both options

TABLE 3-12 Wastewater Management Alternatives Selected by the Planning Process

Alternative	Description	Nitrate-Nitrogen Concentration in Percolation (mg/liter)	Minimun River DO Concentration (mg/liter)	Annual Cost ($\$10^3$/yr)
11	Entire wastewater flow is nitrified ($Q_3 = 40,000$ m^3/day), and $Q_4 = 25,000$ m^3/day is filtered after nitrification. All effluent is discharged into river	—	5.0	319
13	Most wastewater ($Q_5 = 32,000$ m^3/day) is diverted to land application and the remainder ($Q_1 = 8,000$ m^3/day) is discharged to the river without additional treatment. An area of $A = 224$ ha is irrigated at a rate of $r = 10$ cm/wk	6.9	5.0	304

are potentially cost-effective and, based on available data, are equally effective at meeting the wastewater management objectives.

Summary

The environmental quality problem just analyzed is an example of the level of detail required in solving real-world problems. The development and solution of the appropriate optimization model required more thought and effort than the examples in Chapter 2. However, the mechanics of the systems analysis did not change. The same general concepts (the steps of the systems approach, definition of variables, relationships between variables based on mathematical descriptions of mass fluxes and objectives, and search strategies for solving the models) apply to both simple and complex models.

As with most search applications, the approximate solution obtained for the optimization model is only an estimate of the true optimum. Intuitively, it seems to be a good estimate, but it is likely that evaluating other alternatives might produce an even better solution. This inherent uncertainty is unavoidable when informal search methods are used. True optimal solutions can be produced only by more formal optimization techniques. The next chapter introduces several of these methods.

SELECTED REFERENCES

1. Eckenfelder, W. W., Jr., *Water Quality Engineering for Practicing Engineers*, Barnes & Noble, New York, 1970
2. Environmental Quality Systems, "Technical and Economic Review of Advanced Waste Treatment Processes," Report to U. S. Army Corps of Engineers, Washington, D.C. 1973
3. Haith, D. A., and D. C. Chapman, "Best Practicable Waste Treatment Screening Model," American Society of Civil Engineers, *Journal of the Environmental Engineering Division*, Vol. 103, No. EE3, 1977, pp. 397–412
4. Loehr, R. C., W. J. Jewell, J. D. Novak, W. C. Clarkson, and G. S. Friedman, *Land Application of Wastes*, Van Nostrand Reinhold, New York, 1979
5. Loucks, D. P., "Surface-Water Quality Management Models," in A. K. Biswas (editor), *Systems Approach to Water Management*, McGraw-Hill, New York, 1976, pp. 219–252
6. Massachusetts Drainage Commission, *Report of a Commission Appointed to Consider a General System of Drainage for the Valleys of the Mystic, Blackstone and Charles Rivers*, Wright and Potter Printing, Boston, 1886
7. Metcalf & Eddy, Inc., *Wastewater Engineering: Treatment, Disposal and Reuse*, 2nd ed., McGraw-Hill, New York, 1979
8. O'Connor, D. J., "The Temporal and Spatial Distribution of Dissolved Oxygen in Streams," *Water Resources Research*, Vol. 3, No. 1, 1967, pp. 65–79

9. Pound, C.E., R. W. Crites, and D. A. Griffes, "Costs of Wastewater Treatment by Land Application," Report EPA-430/9-75-003, U. S. Environmental Protection Agency, Washington, D.C. 1975.
10. "Process Design Manual for Land Application of Municipal Wastewater," Report EPA-625/1-77-008, U. S. Environmental Protection Agency, Washington, D.C. 1977
11. "Quality Criteria for Water," U. S. Environmental Protection Agency, Washington, 1976
12. Rideal, S., *Sewage and Bacterial Purification of Sewage*, 3rd ed., Sanitary Publishing, London, 1906.
13. Thomann, R. V., *Systems Analysis and Water Quality Control*, McGraw-Hill, New York, 1972.
14. VanNote, R. H., P. V. Hebert, R. M. Patel, C. Chupek, and L. Feldman, "A Guide to the Selection of Cost-Effective Wastewater Treatment Systems," Report EPA-430/9-75-002, U. S. Environmental Protection Agency, Washington, D.C., 1975.

EXERCISES

NOTE. Exercises 3-1 and 3-4 require a computer or programmable calculator.

3-1.

Subsequent consideration of Example 3-1 has resulted in several planning modifications. Because of reduced population growth, the anticipated daily wastewater flow is 30,000 m³/day instead of 40,000 m³/day. In addition, the proposed land application site is no longer available. A new site has been located 5 km from the sewage treatment plant. Soil on the site has a drainage capacity of 9.5 cm/wk. Repeat the planning analysis using these new data to determine cost-effective alternatives.

3-2.

Two cities are exploring the possibility of regional (joint) wastewater management. In this way they may be able to take advantage of economies of scale. Thus it might be economical to build a treatment plant in only one city and to pump the sewage from the other city to this plant. Only two treatment plant sites are available, one in each city. The cities (and the plant sites) are 5 km apart. Wastewater production is 40,000 m³/day and 60,000 m³/day for cities 1 and 2, respectively. State and federal environmental agencies require secondary treatment of all wastewater.

The annual cost ($/yr) of secondary treatment at site j is

$$35Q_j^{0.8} + 25Q_j^{0.7}$$

where Q_j is the wastewater treated at site j (m³/day). Wastewater transmission costs include costs of a pipeline plus pumping.

Pipeline: $15Q^{0.6}$ ($/km/yr)
Pumping: $30Q^{0.7}$ ($/yr)
Q is the wastewater transmitted (m³/day)

Regionalization is also possible for sludge disposal. Sludge, consisting of solids and other materials removed from the sewage, is a by-product of secondary treatment. After being dewatered, such sludges amount to about 0.8 kg/m³ of wastewater treated and must be disposed of, usually by incineration, sanitary landfills, or land application to agricultural crops. Incinerators can be constructed at either or both wastewater treatment sites, and associated costs ($/yr) are $1600S^{0.8}$ at city 1 and $1400S^{0.8}$ at city 2, where S is the amount of sludge incinerated in t/day.

In addition, landfill and land application alternatives are available at some distance from each city. The land application area is 5 km from city 1 and 10 km from city 2. If this alternative is used, the associated annual cost is $7,000 plus $15/ha. Sludge can be applied at a maximum rate of 20 t/ha/yr. Available cropland is limited to 1000 ha. The sanitary landfill is 10 km from city 1 and 3 km from city 2. Disposal costs are $1.60/t, and the landfill can accommodate up to 50 t/day of sludge. Sludge transportation costs to either the landfill or land application area are $0.30/t/km. Since the incinerators are located at the wastewater treatment sites, there are no transportation costs with incineration (assume that sludge would not be transported from a city's treatment plant to an incinerator in another city).

(a) Construct an optimization model that can be used to develop a wastewater and sludge management plan for the cities.
(b) Solve the optimization model; that is, obtain an "approximate" optimal solution using informal search.

3-3.

We have seen that stream flows can have a pronounced effect on water quality. Taking advantage of this fact, a community has constructed a reservoir to increase summer flows in the stream into which it disposes of its sewage. With a combination of sewage treatment and reservoir releases, the community hopes to bring the minimum DO level in the stream to a stream standard, $\overline{C}$ (mg/liter) in both winter and summer. It is also planned for the reservoir to provide the community's water supply. The entire system is shown in the following figure.

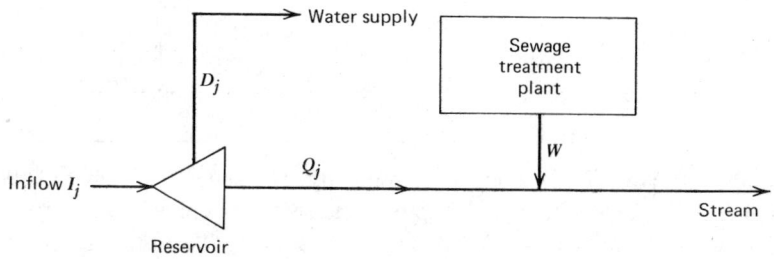

During the winter (October to March), inflow to the reservoir is I_1 (m³/day); during the summer (April to September), it is I_2 (m³/day). Reservoir capacity is K (m³). If the water supply diversion does not reach R_j, the remainder is purchased from a neighboring community at a cost of $\$b/m^3$. Reservoir decision variables are D_j, the water supply diversion, and the reservoir release Q_j in season j (m³/day). Water in the reservoir is at saturation DO and has zero CBOD and NBOD.

The daily sewage production is W (m³/day) and, before treatment, has a CBOD of B_W (mg/liter) and an NBOD of N_W (mg/liter). The sewage treatment plant removes both CBOD and NBOD at efficiencies between 0.35 and 0.85. However, for each 0.01 increase above 0.35, a cost of $\$c/m^3$ is incurred. (e.g., 40% removal costs $\$5c/m^3$). The removal efficiencies for both CBOD and NBOD are the same. The DO of the sewage discharge is zero.

Construct a two-season cost-effectiveness optimization model for meeting the minimum DO standard, $\overline{C}$. Read this problem carefully; of the quantities defined in the discussion, only $\overline{C}, I_j, K, R_j, b, c, W, B_W$, and N_W are fixed (i.e., known data). I_1 and I_2 are known and assumed to be the same year after year. Does this imply a relationship between the volumes of water in the reservoir at the beginning and end of the year?

3-4.

Two communities are presently discharging untreated wastewater into a river. City 1 discharges 10,000 m³/day and city 2, which is 10 km downstream, discharges 5000 m³/day. These discharges result in violation of the river DO standard (5 mg/liter). The communities are considering the joint treatment possibilities shown in the following figure. Each community can install secondary and tertiary treatment to remove CBOD and NBOD. In addition, untreated wastewater can be piped, by means of a 10-km transmission line, from the first to the second community. The untreated wastewater has CBOD = 200 mg/liter and NBOD = 100 mg/liter.

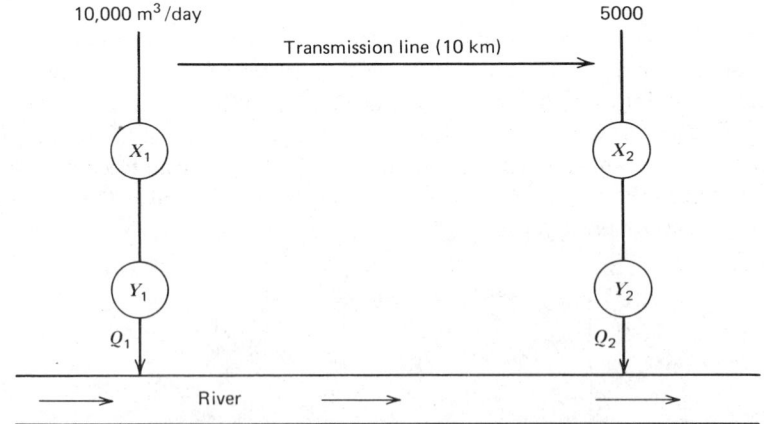

Secondary treatment can operate at removal efficiencies (X_j) up to 0.90. The fractions of CBOD and NBOD removed by secondary treatment at location j are X_j and $X_j/2$. Tertiary treatment removes Y_j of the *remaining* NBOD (after secondary treatment), and the maximum value of Y_j is 0.95. Effluent DO from all treatments is 2.0 mg/liter. The costs of treatment at plant j ($\$10^3$/yr) are

Secondary: $40Q_j^{0.6}(X_j/0.9)$
Tertiary: $30Q_j^{0.7}(Y_j/0.95)$

where Q_j is the flow through the two treatment processes at location j (10^3m^3/day). The cost of wastewater transmission in $\$10^3$/yr/km is $2.0Q^{0.3}$, where Q is the wastewater transmitted, $10 - Q_1$, in 10^3m^3/day.

River parameters upstream of site 1 are $Q_r = 110{,}000$ m^3/day, $C_r = 8.0$ mg/liter, $B_r = 2.0$ mg/liter, $N_r = 5.0$ mg/liter. Reaction rates in the river are $k_1 = 0.35$ day^{-1}, $k_2 = 0.50$ day^{-1}, and $k_n = 0.20$ day^{-1}. Saturation DO is $C_s = 8.0$ mg/liter, and the river velocity is 7.9 km/day.

(a) Construct an optimization model that can be used to determine a cost-effective wastewater treatment plan for the two communities.
(b) Subsequent analyses have indicated that environmental regulatory authorities require a minimum treatment level of secondary treatment at 90% removal efficiency ($X_j = 0.90$). Construct a new model for this situation.
(c) Solve the optimization model developed in part b.

CHAPTER 4
INTRODUCTION TO OPTIMIZATION ALGORITHMS

The primary advantage of informal trial-and-error procedures for solving optimization models is their applicability to many types of models. However, the methods are limited by the ingenuity of the systems analyst. It is possible, and even likely, that two analysts will obtain different solutions to the same optimization model; since solutions are only approximate, neither result may be close to the true or exact optimal solution. Furthermore, with large models involving many constraints and variables, it can be exceeding difficult to formulate plausible search strategies. More structured approaches, or *algorithms*, can often be used to make optimization less subjective. An algorithm is a well-defined computational procedure designed to produce a desired result. Analogies can be made to a circuit diagram or cake recipe. If the directions are followed, current will flow or the cake will be edible. Similarly, an optimization algorithm is a set of directions for computations which, if carried out, should produce an optimal solution.

Given the *ad hoc* nature of informal search strategies and the approximate solutions they produce, it is not surprising that systems analysts use optimization algorithms whenever possible. However, the mathematical structures of many models can prevent the use of available algorithms. No one has ever designed a general algorithm that can efficiently solve all types of optimization models. The most efficient algorithms, such as those used with the mathematical programming models discussed in the remaining chapters of this book, can often produce optimal solutions with minimal computations. Unfortunately, these algorithms are restricted to certain classes of optimization models. For example, linear programming algorithms are used with models having a linear objective function and linear constraints. More general algorithms, such as the ones in this chapter, are suitable for a wider variety of mathematical structures but often require so many calculations that they are impractical even with large computers.

This chapter introduces the algorithms that can be used to solve optimization models. Two specific approaches are presented—the methods of Lagrange multipliers and sequential search. When an optimization model has the appropriate structure, mathematical programming is usually more efficient than either approach. However, when this is not the case and informal search procedures cannot be applied with confidence, Lagrange multiplier or sequential search algorithms may be viable alternatives.

METHOD OF LAGRANGE MULTIPLIERS

Unconstrained Optimization

The Lagrange multiplier method uses calculus to identify *stationary points* of an objective function. The function $Z = F(X)$ shown in Figure 4-1 has six of these points, which occur when the slope of $F(X)$ is zero. Stationary points are thus identified by solutions to the equation

$$\frac{dF}{dX} = 0 \qquad (4.1)$$

Stationary points may be local minima (x_2, x_5), maxima (x_1, x_4, x_6), or saddle points (x_5). The local optima are likely candidates for a *global optimum*. In a maximization (minimization) problem, a global optimum is the value of X that results in the largest (smallest) feasible value of $F(X)$. For the function shown in Figure 4-1, x_2 is a global minimum and x_6 is a global maximum.

If a function is bounded (i.e., it never becomes infinitely large or small) at least one of the stationary points identified by Equation 4.1 will be a global optimum. This point is found by examining all solutions to Equation 4.1 and selecting the one that yields the largest (smallest for minimization) value of $F(X)$. If the objective function has several variables, $Z = F(X_1, X_2, \ldots, X_n)$, stationary points are given by solutions to the n equations

$$\frac{\partial F}{\partial X_1} = 0, \quad \frac{\partial F}{\partial X_2} = 0, \ldots, \quad \frac{\partial F}{\partial X_n} = 0 \qquad (4.2)$$

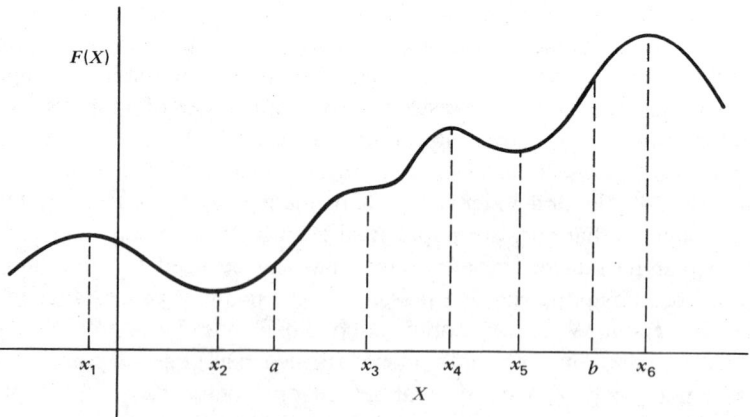

Figure 4-1 Stationary points of a function $F(X)$.

Constrained Optimization

When constraints limit the feasible values of the variables, Equations 4.1 or 4.2 do not necessarily identify local optima. Consider the optimization model

$$\text{Max } Z = F(X) \quad (4.3)$$

s.t.
$$X \geq a \quad (4.4)$$
$$X \leq b \quad (4.5)$$

where $F(X)$, a, and b are shown in Figure 4-1. Within the feasible range of $F(X)$, the stationary points indicated by Equation 4.1 are x_3, x_4, and x_5. None of these solutions is optimal, since it can be seen from Figure 4-1 that $X^* = b$.

Calculus can still be used to identify stationary points and hence local optima for constrained optimization problems. The method of Lagrange multipliers provides a means of determining such points. It is simplest to use when the constraints are equations and not inequalities. Thus the method is most readily applied to optimization models of the form

$$\text{Max } Z = F(X_1, X_2, \ldots, X_n) \quad (4.6)$$

s.t.
$$g_1(X_1, X_2, \ldots, X_n) = b_1$$
$$g_2(X_1, X_2, \ldots, X_n) = b_2$$
$$\vdots \quad (4.7)$$
$$g_m(X_1, X_2, \ldots, X_n) = b_m$$

in which the objective function and constraints are continuous and differentiable. The constraint limits $b_1, b_2, \ldots, b_m$ are constants and the decision variables $X_1, X_2, \ldots, X_n$ may be either positive or negative. It must also be assumed that solutions to the model are bounded (i.e., the optimal value of Z is not infinite).

Conditions for stationary points are derived by multiplying each constraint by a Lagrange multiplier λ_i and subtracting from the objective function. The multiplier λ_i can be envisioned as a unit penalty or shadow cost[1] incurred whenever $g_i(X_1, X_2, \ldots, X_n)$ exceeds b_i. If the net effects of these costs are subtracted from the objective function (Equation 4.6), a new objective function $H(X_1, X_2, \ldots, X_n; \lambda_1, \lambda_2, \ldots, \lambda_m)$ is obtained.

---

[1]These costs are comparable to the *dual variables* discussed in Chapter 5.

$$H(X_1, X_2, \ldots, X_n; \lambda_1, \lambda_2, \ldots, \lambda_m)$$
$$= F(X_1, X_2, \ldots, X_n) - \lambda_1[g_1(X_1, X_2, \ldots, X_n) - b_1]$$
$$- \lambda_2 [g_2(X_1, X_2, \ldots, X_n) - b_2]$$
$$\vdots$$
$$- \lambda_m [g_m(X_1, X_2, \ldots, X_n) - b_m] \quad \text{or} \quad H = F - \sum_{i=1}^{m} \lambda_i (g_i - b_i) \tag{4.8}$$

The new function H is equal to the old objective function F minus the costs of exceeding Constraints 4.7. The function contains the n original variables plus m unknown Lagrange multipliers. If the function is treated as an unconstrained objective function, stationary points are determined by setting its $n + m$ partial derivatives to zero.

$$\frac{\partial H}{\partial X_1} = 0, \quad \frac{\partial H}{\partial X_2} = 0, \ldots, \quad \frac{\partial H}{\partial X_n} = 0$$

$$\frac{\partial H}{\partial \lambda_1} = 0, \quad \frac{\partial H}{\partial \lambda_2} = 0, \ldots, \quad \frac{\partial H}{\partial \lambda_m} = 0 \tag{4.9}$$

These equations may also be written as follows.

$$\frac{\partial H}{\partial X_j} = \frac{\partial F}{\partial X_j} - \sum_{i=1}^{m} \lambda_i \frac{\partial g_i}{\partial X_j} = 0 \quad j = 1, 2, \ldots, n \tag{4.10}$$

$$\frac{\partial H}{\partial \lambda_i} = -g_i + b_i = 0 \quad i = 1, 2, \ldots, m \tag{4.11}$$

Solution of these $n + m$ equations will identify stationary points of the unconstrained function H. The solution will also be a feasible solution to the optimization model (Expressions 4.6 and 4.7) because the second set of derivatives (Equation 4.11) is identical to the original constraint set (Equations 4.7). Furthermore, when the constraints are met, the costs $\lambda_1(g_1 - b_1)$, $\lambda_2(g_2 - b_2)$, $\ldots$, and $\lambda_m(g_m - b_m)$ that are subtracted from the objective function must all be zero, and the new objective function $H(X_1, X_2, \ldots, X_n; \lambda_1, \lambda_2, \ldots, \lambda_m)$ is equivalent to the original function $F(X_1, X_2, \ldots, X_n)$. We conclude that Equations 4.10 and 4.11 are conditions for stationary point solutions to the original optimization model given by Equations 4.6 and 4.7.

The same procedure can be used when an objective function is minimized. In this case penalty costs are assessed when $g_i(X_1, X_2, \ldots, X_n)$ is *less than* b_i and costs of $\lambda_i(b_i - g_i)$ are *added* to the objective function. The new objective function is

$$H = F + \sum_{i=1}^{m} \lambda_i (b_i - g_i) \tag{4.12}$$

When partial derivatives are taken, the same necessary conditions (Equations 4.10 and 4.11) are again obtained.

Each of the stationary points determined by solutions to Equations 4.10 and 4.11 is a local optimum or saddle point. The global optimum is determined by evaluating $F(X_1, X_2, \ldots, X_n)$ at each stationary point.

EXAMPLE 4-1
Solve the following optimization model using Lagrange multipliers.

$$\text{Max } Z = 0.5X_1^2 + 20X_2X_3 + 10X_3 \quad (4.13)$$

s.t.
$$X_1 - 3X_2 + 0.5X_3 = 6 \quad (4.14)$$

$$X_2 + 2X_3 = 10 \quad (4.15) \ \square$$

The model has three variables and two constraints. The modified objective function is

$$H = 0.5X_1^2 + 20X_2X_3 + 10X_3 - \lambda_1(X_1 - 3X_2 + 0.5X_3 - 6)$$
$$- \lambda_2(X_2 + 2X_3 - 10) \quad (4.16)$$

The conditions for stationary points (Equations 4.10 and 4.11) are

$$\frac{\partial H}{\partial X_1} = X_1 - \lambda_1 = 0 \quad (4.17)$$

$$\frac{\partial H}{\partial X_2} = 20X_3 + 3\lambda_1 - \lambda_2 = 0 \quad (4.18)$$

$$\frac{\partial H}{\partial X_3} = 20X_2 + 10 - 0.5\lambda_1 - 2\lambda_2 = 0 \quad (4.19)$$

$$\frac{\partial H}{\partial \lambda_1} = -X_1 + 3X_2 - 0.5X_3 + 6 = 0 \quad (4.20)$$

$$\frac{\partial H}{\partial \lambda_2} = -X_2 - 2X_3 + 10 = 0 \quad (4.21)$$

These five equations can be reduced to two equations for X_1 and X_3. From Equations 4.17 and 4.18, $\lambda_1 = X_1$ and $\lambda_2 = 20X_3 + 3\lambda_1 = 20X_3 + 3X_1$. Equation 4.21 gives $X_2 = 10 - 2X_3$. Substituting for λ_1, λ_2, and X_2 in Equation 4.19 and 4.20, we obtain

$$6.5X_1 + 80X_3 = 210 \quad (4.19a)$$

$$X_1 + 6.5X_3 = 36 \quad (4.20a)$$

The solution to these two equations is $X_1 = 40.13$ and $X_3 = -0.64$. From Equation 4.21, $X_2 = 10 - 2X_3 = 11.27$. The objective function is $Z = 654.6$.[2]

Equations 4.17 to 4.21 have only one solution, and this solution may be either a maximum or minimum. We can select any other feasible set of variables and determine if the resulting objective function value is smaller or larger than 654.6. If the former is true the stationary point is a maximum. A larger value indicates a minimum. For example, with $X_1 = 36$, $X_2 = 10$, $X_3 = 0$, Z is 648. Thus the stationary point is a maximum and the optimal solution to the model.

The solution to the optimization model can also be illustrated graphically. If equations 4.14 and 4.15 are solved for X_3 and X_2 in terms of X_1 [i.e., $X_3 = (36 - X_1)/6.5$ and $X_2 = 10 - 2(36 - X_1)/6.5$] and these values substituted into the objective function, Z will be reduced to a function of a single variable X_1, as shown in Figure 4-2. It can be seen from the figure that the maximum value of Z is at the point identified by the Lagrange multiplier method (approximately $X_1 = 40$).

Limitations of Lagrange Multipliers

Although the approach worked well with Example 4-1, the method of Lagrange multipliers is not a very powerful technique for solving most optimization models. Equations 4.10 and 4.11 are often very difficult to solve, and many solutions are often possible. Moreover, the presence of *inequality* constraints drastically increases the required computations. For example, most realistic optimization models have nonnegativity constraints for decision variables ($X_j \geq 0$), but the solutions identified by Equations 4.10 and 4.11 may include negative values (in Example 4-1, X_3^* was -0.64). The problems caused by inequality constraints are illustrated in Example 4-2.

EXAMPLE 4-2
Solve the following optimization model using Lagrange multipliers.

$$\text{Max } Z = X^2 + 2X - Y^2 \quad (4.22)$$

$$\text{s.t.} \quad 5X + 2Y \leq 10 \quad (4.23)$$

$$X \geq 0 \quad (4.24)$$

$$Y \geq 0 \quad (4.25) \quad \square$$

Constraints 4.23 to 4.25 can be changed to equations by the introduction of three new variables S_1, S_2, and S_3.

$$5X + 2Y + S_1^2 = 10 \quad (4.23\text{a})$$

---

[2] Decision variables have been rounded to two decimal places. Without this roundoff, the value of Z is 655.6.

METHOD OF LAGRANGE MULTIPLIERS

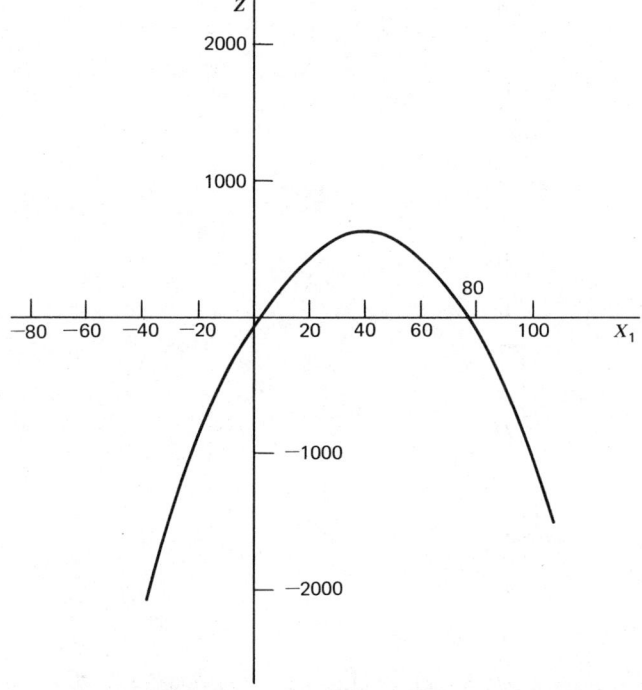

Figure 4-2 Objective Function (Equation 4.13) as a function of X_1.

$$X - S_2^2 = 0 \quad (4.24a)$$

$$Y - S_3^2 = 0 \quad (4.25a)$$

In equation 4.23a, S_1^2 is a "slack" term that is the difference between the right and left sides of Constraint 4.23. The variable is squared so that it does not have to be constrained to be nonnegative. For example, if Equation 4.23a was written as $5X + 2Y + S_1 = 10$, an additional constraint $S_1 \geq 0$ would be necessary, leading to yet another variable that would also have to be constrained, and so forth. In Equation 4.24a and 4.25a, S_2^2 and S_3^2 are "surpluses" by which X or Y can exceed zero. Equations 4.23a to 4.25a are completely equivalent to Constraints 4.23 to 4.25.

Using the three new equations, the Lagrange function $H(X, Y, S_1, S_2, S_3, \lambda_1, \lambda_2, \lambda_3)$ is given by

$$H = X^2 + 2X - Y^2 - \lambda_1(5X + 2Y + S_1^2 - 10)$$
$$- \lambda_2(X - S_2^2) - \lambda_3(Y - S_3^2) \quad (4.26)$$

One obvious effect of inequality constraints is a substantial increase in the number of variables to be considered. Stationary conditions are given by

$$\frac{\partial H}{\partial X} = 2X + 2 - 5\lambda_1 = 0 \qquad (4.27)$$

$$\frac{\partial H}{\partial Y} = -2Y - 2\lambda_1 - \lambda_3 = 0 \qquad (4.28)$$

$$\frac{\partial H}{\partial S_1} = -2\lambda_1 S_1 = 0 \qquad (4.29)$$

$$\frac{\partial H}{\partial S_2} = 2\lambda_2 S_2 = 0 \qquad (4.30)$$

$$\frac{\partial H}{\partial S_3} = 2\lambda_3 S_3 = 0 \qquad (4.31)$$

$$\frac{\partial H}{\partial \lambda_1} = -5X - 2Y - S_1^2 + 10 = 0 \qquad (4.32)$$

$$\frac{\partial H}{\partial \lambda_2} = -X + S_2^2 = 0 \qquad (4.33)$$

$$\frac{\partial H}{\partial \lambda_3} = -Y + S_3^2 = 0 \qquad (4.34)$$

Equations 4.29 to 4.31, which require $\lambda_i S_i = 0$ for $i = 1, 2, 3$, are sometimes referred to as *boundary conditions* and require either λ_i or $S_i = 0$. For example, when $S_3 = 0$, Equation 4.25a indicates that $Y = 0$. This is one of the boundaries of the feasible region. Taken together, Equations 4.29 to 4.31 imply eight different combinations of λ_i and S_i. For each of these combinations, three of the λ_i and S_i variables will be zero. The remaining five equations can be solved for the other five variables. Thus Equations 4.27 to 4.34 must be solved eight times to identify the possible candidates for an optimal solution.

Solving this optimization model by means of Lagrange multipliers would be a tedious process. Most optimization models have more constraints and variables than this simple example, and the number of solutions to be evaluated is usually so large that the method of Lagrange multipliers is rarely computationally feasible for realistic problems.

SEQUENTIAL SEARCH ALGORITHMS

Sequential search algorithms attempt to locate optimal solutions to models by iteratively evaluating alternative solutions according to some systematic set of procedures. The algorithms are designed to improve solutions successively so that each iteration produces one or more solutions that are better than those obtained in the previous iteration. There are many different ways of conducting these searches, and various sequential search algorithms are available (1, 5). The discussion in this chapter is limited to a sequential search procedure developed by Box (2). Although Box's algorithm is not necessarily typical, it illustrates some of the general features of sequential search algorithms.

Box's Algorithm

This search procedure is applied to optimization models of the form

$$\text{Max } Z = F(X_1, X_2, \ldots, X_n) \quad (4.35)$$

$$\text{s.t.} \quad g_i(X_1, X_2, \ldots, X_n) \leq \text{ or } \geq b_i, \quad i = 1, 2, \ldots, m \quad (4.36)$$

If equations are present in the constraint set, they are used to eliminate variables. Minimization problems are either converted to maximization by changing Min(Z) to Max($-Z$) or are dealt with by changing the algorithm so that an alternative with the largest Z is discarded at each iteration. Thus, in principle, the algorithm can be applied to any optimization model.

Before solutions are developed, upper and lower bounds U_j and L_j should be established for each decision variable.

$$L_j \leq X_j \leq U_j \quad j = 1, 2, \ldots, n \quad (4.37)$$

These bounds are established to prevent the selection of unrealistic values of X_j, and the values of L_j and U_j need not be exact. The algorithm works with sets of P feasible solutions where $P \geq n + 1$. At each iteration, the worst of these alternatives is replaced by a better solution. An initial feasible solution must be specified and remaining $P-1$ solutions of the first set are generated randomly. The kth solution in any set is designated by $(x_{1k}, x_{2k}, \ldots, x_{nk})$ where x_{jk} is the value of the decision variable X_j in the kth solution.

Selection of First Set of Solutions

1. An initial feasible solution $(x_{11}, x_{21}, \ldots, x_{n1})$ is specified.
2. A subsequent solution ($k = 2$) is generated with

$$x_{jk} = L_j + r_{jk}(U_j - L_j) \quad (4.38)$$

where r_{jk} is a random number between 0 and 1. The values of the variables in the solution $(x_{1k}, x_{2k}, \ldots, x_{nk})$ will thus each lie within their respective upper and lower bounds.

3. The solution is checked for feasibility. If any of Constraints 4.36 are violated, the solution is moved closer to the previously selected feasible solutions. This requires the computation of a centroid solution $(\bar{x}_1, \bar{x}_2, \ldots, \bar{x}_n)$ based on the feasible solutions already identified. Each centroid variable is given by

$$\bar{x}_j = \frac{1}{k-1} \sum_{l=1}^{k-1} x_{jl} \qquad (4.39)$$

New values of the variables for the kth solution are

$$x'_{jk} = \frac{x_{jk} + \bar{x}_j}{2} \qquad (4.40)$$

This step is repeated until all constraints are satisfied.
4. A new solution is generated by increasing k by 1 and repeating steps 2 and 3. The process terminates when P feasible alternatives are obtained.

Selection of a Better Solution

5. The objective function is computed for each alternative,

$$Z_k = F(x_{1k}, x_{2k}, \ldots, x_{nk})$$

and the alternative with the smallest Z_k (assuming we wish to maximize Z) is eliminated.
6. If the rth alternative is removed, a new solution $(x'_{1r}, x'_{2r}, \ldots, x'_{nr})$ is generated by moving in the direction of the centroid of the other solutions. The values of the centroid variables are determined by

$$\bar{x}_j = \frac{1}{P-1} \sum_{\substack{k=1 \\ k \neq r}}^{P} x_{jk} \qquad (4.41)$$

and the values of the variables in the new solution are

$$x'_{jr} = \bar{x}_j + \alpha(\bar{x}_j - x_{jr}) \qquad (4.42)$$

where α is a constant. Box recommends a value of $\alpha = 1.3$ in Equation 4.42. This produces a new solution that will fall on the other side of the centroid from the old solution. If the value of the objective function is not an improvement over the old solution, (i.e., if $Z'_r < Z_r$), a new solution is determined by moving halfway back toward the centroid.

$$x''_{jr} = \frac{x'_{jr} + \bar{x}_j}{2} \qquad (4.43)$$

7. The new solution is checked to see that it meets the upper and lower bounds U_j and L_j. Any $x'_{jk} > U_j$ is replaced by $U_j - \delta$ where δ is a small number. Similarly, any $x'_{jk} < L_j$ is replaced by $L_j + \delta$.
8. The solution is checked for feasibility as in step 3.

Iteration and Convergence on a Local Optima

9. Steps 5 to 8 are repeated, producing a new set of feasible alternatives with one replaced solution in each set. Iterations continue until a number of successive iterations produce solutions with approximately the same objective function values.

This sequential search algorithm consists of a series of simple algebraic manipulations that successively identify improved feasible solutions. The computations are sufficiently tedious that they must be done by computer or programmable calculator. Since the procedure may only converge on a local optimum, it should be repeated several times using different starting solutions. This process is essentially open ended, and the analyst must continue to repeat the process with different starting points until he or she is confident in the optimal solution.

Application

The characteristics of this search algorithm are probably best understood by working through an example. The remainder of this section demonstrates the use of the algorithm to solve the optimization model developed in Chapter 2 for Example 2-1. This model is given by

$$\text{Max } Z = 300X_1 - 1500\sqrt{X_1} + 150X_2 - 600\sqrt{X_2} \quad (4.44)$$

s.t.
$$0.9X_1 + 0.5X_2 \leq 632.5 \quad (4.45)$$

$$X_1 + X_2 \leq 1000 \quad (4.46)$$

$$X_1, X_2 \geq 0 \quad (4.47)$$

Since this is a two-dimensional model, we can illustrate the algorithm graphically. The feasible region is shown in Figure 4-3. Lower bounds for both variables are zero, and the upper bounds can be determined from the two constraints. From Constraint 4.45, when $X_2 = 0$,

$$X_1 \leq 702.8 \quad (4.48)$$

and, similarly, with $X_1 = 0$, Constraint 4.46 requires

$$X_2 \leq 1000 \quad (4.49)$$

Starting Solutions An initial solution is selected as $x_{11} = 200$ and $x_{21} = 400$. If three solutions are used in each set ($P = 3$), two additional alternatives must be produced by steps 2 to 4. A second solution ($k = 2$) is generated by Equation 4.38. Random numbers $r_{12} = 0.315$ and $r_{22} = 0.602$ were selected by a computer random number generator. The second alternative is given by

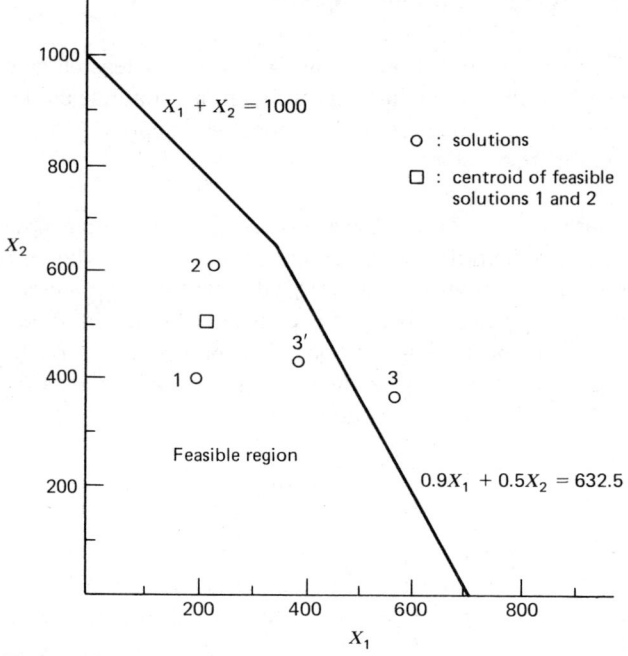

Figure 4-3 Feasible region and initial solutions for optimization model.

$$x_{12} = 0 + 0.315(702.8 - 0) = 221$$
$$x_{22} = 0 + 0.602(1000 - 0) = 602$$

where the values are rounded to the nearest integer. This solution satisfies the two constraints, so we can move on to generate a third alternative. The new random numbers were $r_{13} = 0.801$ and $r_{23} = 0.369$, which produce

$$x_{13} = 0.801(702.8) = 563$$
$$x_{23} = 0.369(1000) = 369$$

The third solution (563, 369), which is shown in Figure 4-3 with the other two solutions, is not feasible, since it violates Constraint 4.45.

$$0.9(563) + 0.5(369) = 691.2 > 632.5$$

A new alternative must be determined by step 3. The centroid of the first two solutions is given by Equation 4.39.

$$\bar{x}_1 = \frac{200 + 221}{2} = 211$$

$$\bar{x}_2 = \frac{400 + 602}{2} = 501$$

The new third solution, as calculated by Equation 4.40, is

$$\bar{x}'_{13} = \frac{563 + 211}{2} = 387$$

$$\bar{x}'_{23} = \frac{369 + 501}{2} = 435$$

This alternative, indicated by 3' in Figure 4-3, is feasible, so we now have the complete set of initial alternatives listed in Table 4-1.

Second Iteration As indicated in Table 4-1, alternative 1 has the lowest objective function value and hence should be eliminated. It is replaced by a solution determined from step 6. The centroid of the remaining solutions is calculated by Equation 4.41 as

$$\bar{x}_1 = \frac{221 + 387}{2} = 304$$

and

$$\bar{x}_2 = \frac{602 + 435}{2} = 519$$

Equation 4.42 provides a replacement (x'_{11}, x'_{21}) for the first alternative,

$$x'_{11} = 304 + 1.3(304 - 200) = 439$$

$$x'_{21} = 519 + 1.3(519 - 400) = 674$$

The new solution is shown in Figure 4-4 along with the other two alternatives. Although the new alternative improves the objective function ($Z'_1 = 185,795$), it violates both constraints. A subsequent solution (x''_{11}, x''_{21}) is generated by Equation 4.42.

TABLE 4-1 Initial Solutions for Sequential Search Algorithm

Solution	X_1	X_2	X_3
1	200	400	86,787
2	221	602	119,579
3	387	435	139,328

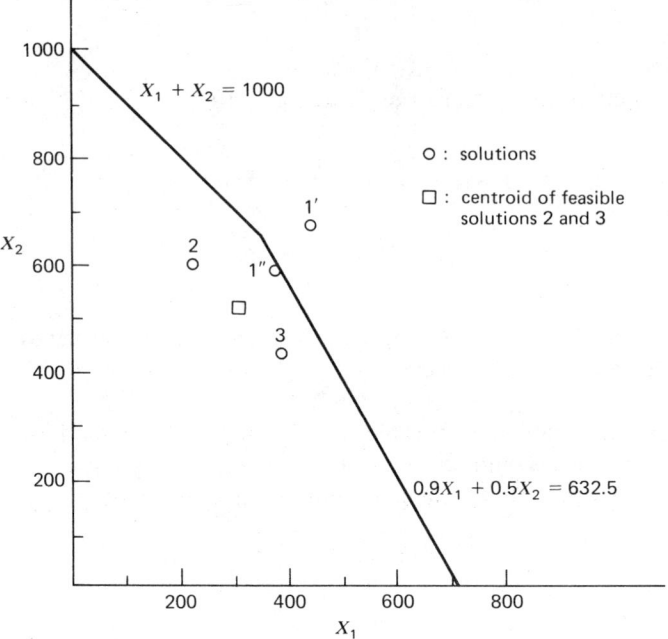

Figure 4-4 Solution set for second iteration.

$$x_{11}'' = \frac{439 + 304}{2} = 372$$

$$x_{21}'' = \frac{674 + 519}{2} = 597$$

Although this solution seems barely to violate Constraint 4.45,

$$0.9(372) + 0.5(597) = 633.3$$

this is because of round-off errors in the centroid and adjustment calculations. When more significant places are retained, $x_{11}'' = 371.6$ and $x_{21}'' = 595.5$ and both constraints are satisfied. We now have the three solutions shown in Figure 4-4, and the second iteration is complete.

Subsequent Iterations and Convergence The results of further iterations of the algorithm are summarized in Table 4-2. Each iteration replaces the worst of the three alternatives with a better solution. In adjusting variables that failed to satisfy upper or lower bounds a value of $\delta = 0.01$ was used. After 27 iterations, the algorithm has apparently converged on an optimal solution of approximately $X_1^* = 702.7$, $X_2^* = 0$, and $Z^* = 171{,}000$. This is essentially the same result obtained by the informal search procedure in Chapter 2.

TABLE 4-2 Solutions Obtained by Iterations of the Search Algorithm

	Solution 1			Solution 2			Solution 3		
Iteration	X_1^a	X_2^a	Z	X_1^a	X_2^a	Z	X_1^a	X_2^a	Z
1	200	400	86,787	221	602	119,579	387	435	139,328
2	371.6	595.5	157,251	221	602	119,579	387	435	139,328
3	371.6	595.5	157,251	430.7	487.1	157,912	387	435	139,328
4	371.6	595.5	157,251	430.7	487.1	157,912	401.3	542.4	157,729
5	473.8	409.7	158,797	430.7	487.1	157,912	401.3	542.4	157,729
6	473.8	409.7	158,797	430.7	487.1	157,912	518.5	326.2	159,488
7	473.8	409.7	158,797	581.2	213.1	161,393	518.5	326.2	159,488
8	648.7	87.5	163,924	581.2	213.1	161,393	518.5	326.2	159,488
9	648.7	87.5	163,924	581.2	213.1	161,393	658.9	75.2	165,229
10	648.7	87.5	163,924	678.3	40.7	166,695	658.9	75.2	165,229
11	675.0	48.3	166,612	678.3	40.7	166,695	658.9	75.2	165,229
12	675.0	48.3	166,612	678.3	40.7	166,695	699.8	4.6	169,662
13	695.9	11.3	168,884	678.3	40.7	166,695	699.8	4.6	169,662
14	695.9	11.3	168,884	700.3	4.0	169,802	699.8	4.6	169,662
15	701.4	2.2	170,143	700.3	4.0	169,802	699.8	4.6	169,662
16	701.4	2.2	170,143	700.3	4.0	169,802	701.6	2.1	170,189
17	701.4	2.2	170,143	702.1	1.1	170,437	701.6	2.1	170,189
18	702.0	1.4	170,360	702.1	1.1	170,437	701.6	2.1	170,189
19	702.0	1.4	170,360	702.1	1.1	170,437	702.4	0.7	170,576
20	702.6	0.2	170,790	702.1	1.1	170,437	702.4	0.7	170,576
21	702.6	0.2	170,790	702.6	0.2	170,785	702.4	0.7	170,576
22	702.6	0.2	170,790	702.6	0.2	170,785	702.7	0.1	170,869
23	702.6	0.2	170,790	702.7	0.1	170,901	702.7	0.1	170,869
24	702.7	0	170,935	702.7	0.1	170,901	702.7	0.1	170,869
25	702.7	0	170,935	702.7	0.1	170,901	702.7	0	170,995
26	702.7	0	170,935	702.8	0	170,984	702.7	0	170,995
27	702.7	0	171,000	702.8	0	170,984	702.7	0	170,995

[a]Rounded to nearest 0.1.

To confirm that this solution is a global optimum, the computations must be repeated for additional starting sets. A second series of iterations is given in Table 4-3. These results indicate one of the problems with general search algorithms. Convergence is apparently reached after 12 iterations with a solution of approximately $X_1 = 334$, $X_2 = 664$, and $Z = 156,900$. However, if the search is continued, it can be seen that by iteration 20, the solutions have changed, and by iteration 62 the algorithm has converged on the solution produced by the first set of iterations. The process of

TABLE 4-3 Sets of Solutions Produced by Different Initial Solutions

Iteration	X_1^a	X_2^a	Z	X_1^a	X_2^a	Z	X_1^a	X_2^a	Z
1	50	900	121,393	70	925	128,952	269	728	149,109
2	179.2	820.5	139,575	70	925	128,952	269	728	149,109
3	179.2	820.5	139,575	274.2	725.3	150,051	269	728	149,109
4	331.6	665.6	156,538	274.2	725.3	150,051	269	728	149,109
5	331.6	665.6	156,538	274.2	725.3	150,051	325.0	674.3	156,010
6	331.6	665.6	156,538	332.7	665.4	156,789	325.0	674.3	156,010
7	331.6	665.6	156,538	332.7	665.4	156,789	334.5	662.7	156,877
8	333.9	663.8	156,881	332.7	665.4	156,789	334.5	662.7	156,877
9	333.9	663.8	156,881	334.5	662.9	156,894	334.5	662.7	156,877
10	333.9	663.8	156,881	334.5	662.9	156,894	334.0	663.8	156,894
11	334.3	663.2	156,898	334.5	662.9	156,894	334.0	663.8	156,894
12	334.3	663.2	156,898	334.1	663.7	156,897	334.0	663.8	156,894
.									
20	335.9	660.4	156,914	336.7	659.0	156,921	335.9	660.4	156,916
.									
62	702.8	0	171,008	702.8	0	171,008	702.8	0	171,008

[a] Rounded to nearest 0.1.

selecting new starting sets and carrying out new series of iterations should probably be repeated several more times before we could be confident that a global optimum has been obtained.

Limitations of General Search Algorithms

Although sequential search algorithms such as the one demonstrated in this chapter can be applied to any optimization model, in practice the applications are often much more limited. The simple two-constraint, two-variable model solved in this section required many computations. Although the calculations were readily performed by a computer program, larger models are not so tractable. Enormous amounts of computer time are often required and, unless the iterations are repeated for a substantial number of starting sets, little confidence could be placed in the optimal solutions that are produced.

Summary

Optimization models are solved by a spectrum of methods ranging from intuitive trial-and-error approaches to the highly structured procedures of mathematical programming. Whenever possible, most systems analysts prefer to use formal algorithms to solve optimization models. Systems analysis is usually most defensible when it minimizes subjectivity and ambiguity. Although neither element is ever completely eliminated, particularly in realistic problems, optimization algorithms provide planned (and essentially mechanical) approaches to model solving that place little reliance on intuition. Moreover, many algorithms are capable of identifying exact instead of approximate optimal solutions. The most general algorithms, such as the method of Lagrange multipliers and Box's sequential search algorithm, are applicable to most types of optimization models. However, general optimization algorithms usually identify locally optimal solutions. The various local optima must be compared to obtain a global optimum. Although this characteristic of general algorithms is not a fatal drawback, the algorithms are also computationally inefficient, and the computations required for models with more than several variables and constraints are so extensive that they are seldom practical.

Mathematical programming algorithms such as those discussed in succeeding chapters are frequently the most operational means of solving optimization models. These algorithms sacrifice generality for efficiency and are limited to models with restricted mathematical properties. The trade-off is generally worthwhile, since many environmental management models can be described with optimization models that are suitable for mathematical programming.

SELECTED REFERENCES

1. Beveridge, G. S. G., and R. S. Schechter, *Optimization: Theory and Practice*, McGraw-Hill, New York, 1970, pp. 206–507.
2. Box, M. J., "A New Method of Constrained Optimization and a Comparison with Other Methods," *The Computer Journal*, Vol. 8, pp. 42–52, 1965.
3. Hadley, G., *Nonlinear and Dynamic Programming*, Addison-Wesley, Reading, Mass., 1964, pp. 53–103.
4. Hillier, F. S., and G. J. Lieberman, *Operations Research*, 2nd ed., Holden-Day, San Francisco, 1974, pp. 755–758.
5. Zahradnik, R. L., *Theory and Techniques of Optimization for Practicing Engineers*, Barnes & Noble, New York, 1971.

EXERCISES

NOTE. Exercises 4-4 and 4-5 require a computer or programmable calculator.

4-1.

Determine the stationary points of the following optimization model.

$$\text{Max } 4X_1^2 + X_2 + 6X_3^3$$
$$\text{s.t.} \quad X_1 + 3X_2 + X_3 = 10$$
$$X_2 + 2X_3 = 4$$

What is the global optimum for the model? Is it one of the stationary points?

4-2.

Solve the following optimization model using Lagrange multipliers.

$$\text{Max } 4e^{-X} - Y^2$$
$$\text{s.t.} \quad 6X - Y = 6$$
$$X \geq 0$$

4-3.

Write the conditions for the stationary points for the optimization model given by Equation 4.44 and Constraints 4.45 to 4.47. How many solutions are there to the equations for stationary points?

4-4.

Repeat the iterative calculations of the sequential search algorithm for Example 2-1 using two initial solutions different from those used in this chapter.

4-5.

One of the most important elements of a search algorithm is the procedure used at each iteration for finding an improved solution. Modify step 6 of the sequential search algorithm in the chapter in a way that you think will improve the efficiency of the search. Test your suggestion by using the modified algorithm with the initial solutions given in Tables 4-2 and 4-3 to find an optimal solution to the optimization model.

CHAPTER 5
LINEAR PROGRAMMING MODELS

The most powerful technique for solving optimization models is a set of methods known collectively as *mathematical programming*. The methods are similar to other formal optimization techniques such as those discussed in Chapter 4, since they rely on well-defined algorithms or structured sets of computations that are designed to converge on optima. However, the mathematical programming approaches in this and subsequent chapters have two major advantages over other formal optimization methods. They are highly efficient and converge on global, not local, optima. These advantages are obtained by algorithms that exploit certain mathematical properties of optimization models. Each mathematical programming method is based on a different mathematical structure and can only be applied to optimization models with the appropriate properties. The most useful methods are linear programming (LP) and dynamic programming (DP). Both LP and DP have been used for a wide range of environmental management problems, and the remainder of this book discusses the characteristics and applications of these techniques. More space will be devoted to LP than DP, since LP has several characteristics that give it wider applicability.

LP models are optimization models that can be solved by LP algorithms. The most commonly used algorithm is the simplex method. This procedure is based on the theory of simultaneous linear equations and is available as a preprogrammed or "canned" package at most computer installations. Therefore, once an LP model is formulated, it can be rapidly and easily solved by computer. An important feature of LP is that it can be used to solve very large models, even those containing thousands of variables and constraints. No other optimization method has a similar capability.

The only significant disadvantage of LP is implied by its name. It can only be used for linear optimization models. A linear mathematical function $f(X_1, X_2, \ldots, X_n)$ is one that can be written in the form

$$f(X_1, X_2, \ldots, X_n) = a_1X_1 + a_2X_2 + \ldots + a_nX_n \tag{5.1}$$

where $X_1, X_2, \ldots, X_n$ are variables and $a_1, a_2, \ldots, a_n$ are constants. This limitation of LP is far from trivial. None of the models in Chapters 2, 3, or 4 can be solved using LP. For example, the effluent constraint

$$3X - Y + 0.03Y^2 \leq 10 \tag{5.2}$$

for the wastewater management example in Chapter 2 contains a nonlinear term

($0.03Y^2$). The pesticide and municipal wastewater planning models of previous chapters both have nonlinear objective functions.

In general, any optimization model of the following form can be solved using LP.

$$\text{Max(Min)} \ Z = c_1X_1 + c_2X_2 + \ldots + c_n X_n \tag{5.3}$$

s.t.
$$a_{11}X_1 + a_{12}X_2 + \ldots + a_{1n}X_n \leq, =, \geq b_1$$
$$a_{21}X_1 + a_{22}X_2 + \ldots + a_{2n}X_n \leq, =, \geq b_2 \tag{5.4}$$
$$\vdots$$
$$a_{m1}X_1 + a_{m2}X_2 + \ldots + a_{mn}X_n \leq, =, \geq b_m$$

$$X_1 \geq 0$$
$$X_2 \geq 0 \tag{5.5}$$
$$\vdots$$
$$X_n \geq 0$$

where $c_1, c_2, \ldots, a_{11}, a_{12}, \ldots,$ and $b_1, b_2, \ldots,$ are all constants.[1]

A TWO-DIMENSIONAL LINEAR PROGRAMMING EXAMPLE

Although the optimization models developed in previous chapters were nonlinear, an alternative form of the pesticide example from Chapter 2 (Example 2-1) can be proposed that will have a linear structure.

EXAMPLE 5-1
As in Example 2-1, 1000 ha of farmland surrounding a lake is available for two crops. Each hectare of crop 1 loses 0.9 kg/yr of pesticide to the lake, and the comparable loss from crop 2 is 0.5 kg/yr. Total pesticide losses are not allowed to exceed 632.5 kg/yr. Crop returns are $300 and $150/ha for crops 1 and 2, respectively. Unlike Example 2-1, which considered economies of scale in cropping costs, it is assumed that in this example only average costs are available. These are estimated to be $160/ha for crop 1 and $50/ha for crop 2. The problem is to determine the cropping combination that maximizes farmer profits subject to a constraint on pesticide losses to the lake. □

---

[1]The nonnegativity conditions (Constraints 5.5) are a requirement for use of the simplex method. However, it will subsequently be shown that simple transformations can be used for negative variables.

A TWO-DIMENSIONAL LINEAR PROGRAMMING EXAMPLE

The decision variables for the problem are X_1 and X_2, the hectares of crops 1 and 2. Annual profits ($/yr) are $Z = (300 - 160)X_1 + (150 - 50)X_2 = 140X_1 + 100X_2$. The optimization model is

$$\text{Max } Z = 140X_1 + 100X_2 \tag{5.6}$$

s.t.
$$0.9X_1 + 0.5X_2 \leq 632.5 \tag{5.7}$$

$$X_1 + X_2 \leq 1000 \tag{5.8}$$

$$X_1 \geq 0 \tag{5.9}$$

$$X_2 \geq 0$$

Constraint 5.7 limits pesticide losses, and Constraint 5.8 is the physical limitation on available land (1000 ha). The feasible region for the model is shown in Figure 5-1.

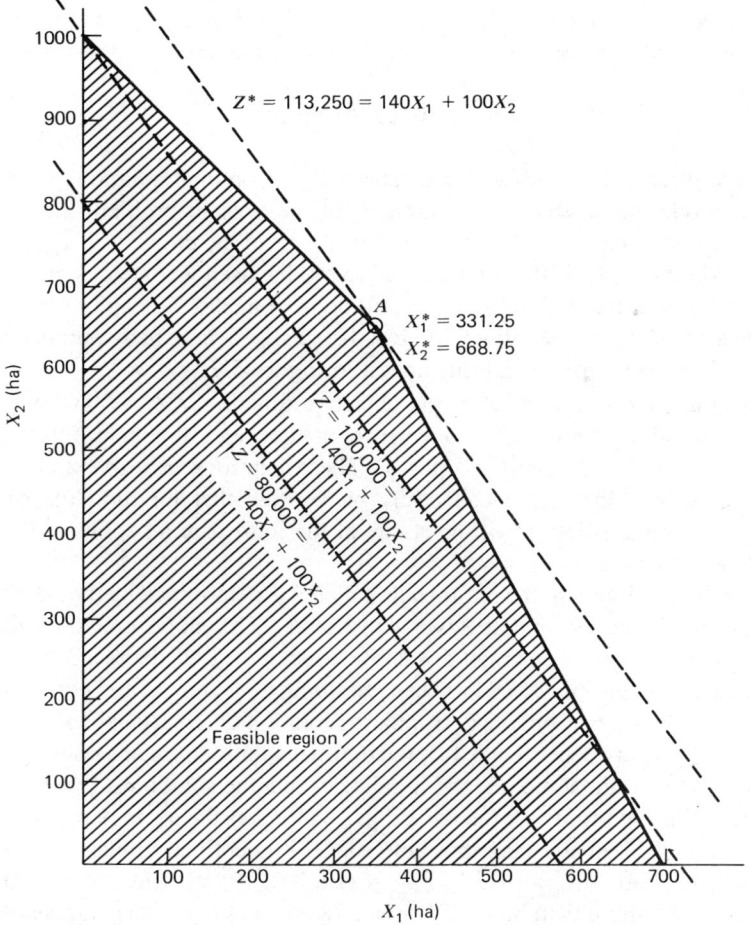

Figure 5-1 Feasible region and solution to Example 5-1.

Linear Programming Solution

The model is by definition an LP model, since the objective function and constraints are linear and the decision variables must be nonnegative. Two-dimensional (two-variable) LP models can be solved by the graphical method shown in Figure 5-1. The dashed lines are the objective function plotted for various values of Z. For example, the line $140X_1 + 100X_2 = 80,000$ is the lowest line, and $140X_1 + 100X_2 = 100,000$ is the middle line. The value of the objective function should be made as large as possible, and Z is increased as the line $Z = 140X_1 + 100X_2$ is shifted upward.

The problem is solved by finding the largest value of Z for which X_1 and X_2 are still part of the feasible region. This limit is point A in Figure 5-1, which is a *corner point* or *extreme point* of the feasible region. The objective function cannot be raised further without lifting X_1 and X_2 out of the feasible region. The solution to the optimization model is $X_1^* = 668.75$, $X_2^* = 331.25$ (or $X_1 = 669$, $X_2 = 331$, rounded to the nearest hectare), and $Z^* = \$113,250$.

The ease with which this problem was solved contrasts with the more lengthy procedures required to solve the models of the previous chapters. The optimal solution to the present model is exact and was obtained with minimal computations.

Sensitivity Analysis

Analysts are often concerned with the sensitivity of optimal solutions to the values chosen for model parameters. For example, in the present problem there might be uncertainty concerning the profits associated with one of the crops, say crop 1. If actual profits are substantially different from the $140/ha used in the objective function (Equation 5.6), will the optimal solution still be reasonable? To explore this question, the coefficient of X_1 in Equation 5.6 can be changed and new optimal solutions generated. Two such changes are illustrated in Figure 5-2.

With profits reduced to $50/ha, the objective function is $Z = 50X_1 + 100X_2$ and the optimal solution is point C. Conversely, at the much higher profit of $220/ha, $Z = 220X_1 + 100X_2$ and point B is optimal. These solutions are also extreme points of the feasible region. In fact, it can easily be verified that for *any* linear objective function, the optimal solution will be at one of the four extreme points of the feasible region, A, B, C or the origin ($X_1 = X_2 = 0$).

The optimal solution to the optimization model is determined by the relative slopes of the objective function and the two constraints. The slope of Constraint 5.7 is $-0.9/0.5 = -1.8$, and Constraint 5.8 has a slope of -1. If the respective profits of crops 1 and 2 are p_1 and p_2 (\$/ha) then, assuming p_1 and p_2 are both positive, if $p_1/p_2 > 1.8$, solution B is obtained. Similarly, solution C results when $p_1/p_2 < 1$. For any value of p_1/p_2 between 1.8 and 1.0, the optimal solution remains point A. This was the solution to the original model, and it indicates that the solution is not very sensitive to the exact values of profits for the two crops. As long as the average profits from crop 1 are from 0 to 80% greater than those of crop 2, it is optimal to plant 331 ha of crop 1 and 669 ha of crop 2 ($X_1^* = 331.25$, $X_2^* = 668.75$). If crop 1 average profits exceed those of crop 2 by more than 80%, $X_1^* = 702.78$ and $X_2^* = 0$; if they are less than crop

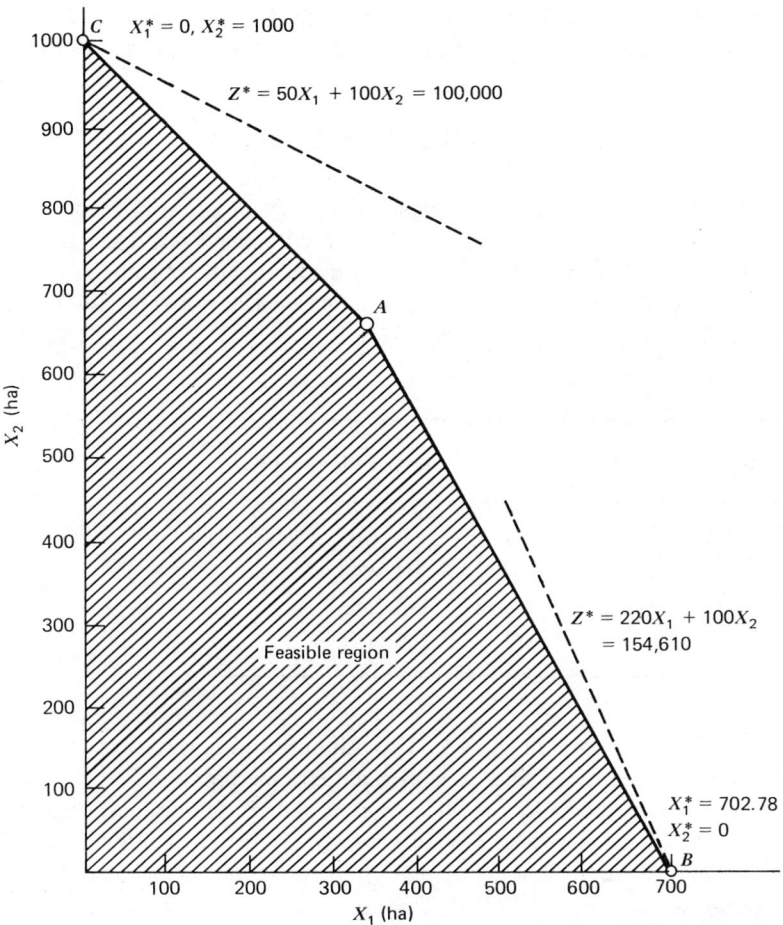

Figure 5-2 Sensitivity of optimal solutions to changes in objective function.

2, $X_1^* = 0$ and $X_2^* = 1000$. Finally, we can observe that if $p_1/p_2 = 1.8$ or 1.0, there is an infinite number of optimal solutions. In the first case, all solutions on line A-B are optimal; for the second situation, any solution on line C-A is optimal.

This type of sensitivity analysis is often a necessary part of systems analysis. The numerical values of model parameters are frequently uncertain, and it is important to know the effects that errors in parameter estimates have on optimal solutions. When solutions are sensitive to the likely ranges of errors, it may be necessary to refine data collection and analysis to obtain more confidence in optimization results. Conversely, if these possible errors do not influence the optimal solution, there may be little incentive for obtaining more accurate parameter estimates.

Sensitivity analysis has many other uses. It can be used to determine if anticipated future changes in economic conditions should change optimal decisions. Modifications of parameters other than objective function coefficients may also be important. For example, decision makers in the pesticide example might be interested in the effect that a tightening or relaxation of the pesticide loss constraint would have on farm profits.

THE SIMPLEX METHOD

The graphical solutions to the previous example suggest a more straightforward way of obtaining optimal solutions. Since such solutions will always occur at extreme points of the feasible region, a model can be solved by evaluating the objective function at all extreme points. For the objective function given by Equation 5.6, $Z = 140X_1 + 100X_2$, we obtain the following.

Extreme Point	X_1	X_2	$Z = 140X_1 + 100X_2$
Origin	0	0	0
B	702.78	0	98,389
A	331.25	668.75	113,250
C	0	1,000	100,000

The optimal solution is extreme point A. The origin from Figure 5-1 ($X_1 = 0$, $X_2 = 0$) is included for completeness, since it is also an extreme point.

The systematic examination of all extreme points is seldom an efficient way of solving LP models, particularly for models having more than two or three variables and constraints. One difficulty is that the number of extreme points can be very large. Each extreme point is an intersection of two or more constraints and, even with a moderate-sized model, the possible number of intersections is very large. Moreover, it can be difficult to identify extreme points when simple two-dimensional graphs such as Figures 5-1 and 5-2 cannot be used.

The simplex method is an algebraic procedure used to examine extreme points efficiently. It selects the extreme points that are most likely to lead to an optimal solution; that is, it iteratively searches for extreme points that improve the value of the objective function. The simplex method can be demonstrated by its application to the optimization model developed for Example 5-1 (the objective function Equation 5.6 and Constraints 5.7, 5.8, and 5.9). In practice, the simplex method is seldom used for two-dimensional models, since it is much easier to solve such problems graphically or by examining all extreme points. However, application of the simplex method to a two-dimensional example can provide a clear graphical perception of the method's several computational steps. The computational procedure for larger problems is entirely analogous but is usually so tedious that a computer is required.

The simplex method is based on the theory of simultaneous linear equations, so the first step is to rewrite all model constraints except for the nonnegativity constraints in the form of linear equations. The constraints to be modified are

$$0.9X_1 + 0.5X_2 \leq 632.5 \tag{5.7}$$

and
$$X_1 + X_2 \leq 1000 \tag{5.8}$$

To transform Constraint 5.7 into an equation (i.e., to replace "$\leq$" with "="), a *slack variable*, S_1, is defined as

$$S_1 = 632.5 - 0.9X_1 - 0.5X_2 \tag{5.10}$$

The new variable S_1 is equal to the "slack" in Constraint 5.7, or the difference between the right side, 632.5, and the left side, $0.9X_1 + 0.5X_2$. A second slack variable, S_2, can be defined for Constraint 5.8.

$$S_2 = 1000 - X_1 - X_2 \tag{5.11}$$

In order to satisfy Constraints 5.7 and 5.8, S_1 and S_2 must be nonnegative. The constraints can now be written as equations.

$$0.9X_1 + 0.5X_2 + S_1 = 632.5 \tag{5.12}$$

$$X_1 + X_2 + S_2 = 1000 \tag{5.13}$$

It is not necessary to write nonnegativity constraints such as $X_1 \geq 0$ and $S_1 \geq 0$ as equations, since the simplex method will only consider solutions with nonnegative values for all variables. With the addition of slack variables, the linear programming model can be written in the following *standard form*.

$$\text{Max } Z = 140X_1 + 100X_2 \tag{5.6}$$

s.t.
$$0.9X_1 + 0.5X_2 + S_1 = 632.5 \tag{5.12}$$

$$X_1 + X_2 + S_2 = 1000 \tag{5.13}$$

$$X_1, X_2, S_1, S_2 \geq 0 \tag{5.14}$$

Before proceeding with the simplex method, we will examine the properties of solutions to Equations 5.12 and 5.13. These two equations have four unknowns or variables. If the equations had only two unknowns, we might expect to obtain a unique solution. However, with four variables, there are an infinite number of solutions. This can be seen from the definitions of slack variables (Equations 5.10 and 5.11). We can choose arbitrary values for X_1 and X_2, say $X_1 = 200$ and $X_2 = 400$, and then solve for S_1 and S_2.

$$S_1 = 632.5 - 0.9(200) - 0.5(400) = 252.5$$

$$S_2 = 1000 - 200 - 400 = 400$$

The resulting values of X_1, X_2, S_1, and S_2 satisfy Equations 5.12 and 5.13. Since a similar result can be obtained for other values of X_1 and X_2, it can be seen that the number of possible solutions to Equations 5.12 and 5.13 are infinite. In fact, any two of the four variables can be assigned arbitrary values, and solutions can still be obtained to the equations. This result is not surprising, since it can be seen from Figure 5-1 that there are an infinite number of feasible solutions to the optimization model.

The simplex method iterates from one extreme point to another, and an initial extreme point must be selected to start the computational process. In this model a convenient initial solution is obtained by setting the decision variables to zero (i. e., $X_1 = X_2 = 0$); therefore, from Equations 5.10 and 5.11, $S_1 = 632.5$ and $S_2 = 1000$. This result is written in a *simplex tableau*.

$$Z = 0 + 140X_1 + 100X_2 \qquad (5.15)$$

$$S_1 = 632.5 - 0.9X_1 - 0.5X_2 \qquad (5.10)$$

$$S_2 = 1000 - X_1 - X_2 \qquad (5.11)$$

Equations in the tableau are written with Z and nonzero variables on the left.[2] Since the remaining variables are zero, the values of Z, S_1, and S_2 are given directly by the first column on the right side of the equations, $Z = 0$, $S_1 = 632.5$, and $S_2 = 1000$.

The next iteration of the simplex method is designed to improve the objective function by incrementing one of the variables that is currently zero. The variable selected is the one that increases the objective function most rapidly. In Equation 5.15 the coefficient of $X_1(140)$ exceeds that of $X_2(100)$, so X_1 is chosen. It remains to be determined by how much X_1 can be increased. Equation 5.10 indicates that X_1 can be raised to a maximum of $632.5/0.9 = 702.78$ if S_1 is forced to zero. Conversely, from Equation 5.11, if S_2 is zero, X_1 will equal 1000. The smaller of these two values must be chosen if the new solution is to be feasible. If the larger value is selected Equation 5.10 would give $S_1 = 632.5 - 0.9(1000) = -267.5$, which is infeasible. This can also be seen from Constraint 5.7, since $X_1 = 1000$ would violate the pesticide restriction [$0.9(1000) = 900$, which exceeds 632.5]. We conclude that the maximum feasible value of X_1 is 702.78, which requires S_1 to be zero.

Equations 5.15, 5.10, and 5.11 can be rearranged to produce a second simplex tableau. To do this, Equation 5.10 is first solved for X_1.

$$X_1 = \frac{632.5}{0.9} - \frac{S_1}{0.9} - \frac{0.5X_2}{0.9} \qquad (5.16)$$

Equation 5.16 is substituted into Equations 5.15 and 5.11 to produce

$$Z = 0 + 140\left(\frac{632.5}{0.9} - \frac{S_1}{0.9} - \frac{0.5X_2}{0.9}\right) + 100X_2 \qquad (5.17)$$

---

[2] Equations 5.15, 5.10, and 5.11 constitute one possible form of a simplex tableau. Other forms are illustrated in several of the references listed at the end of this chapter.

and

$$S_2 = 1000 - 0.9\left(\frac{632.5}{0.9} - \frac{S_1}{0.9} - \frac{0.5X_2}{0.9}\right) - X_2 \qquad (5.18)$$

These three equations are combined into a second simplex tableau.[3]

$$Z = 98{,}388.88889 - 155.55556 S_1 + 22.22222 X_2 \qquad (5.17)$$
$$X_1 = 702.77778 - 1.11111 S_1 - 0.55556 X_2 \qquad (5.16)$$
$$S_2 = 297.22222 + 1.11111 S_1 - 0.44444 X_2 \qquad (5.18)$$

Since X_2 and S_1 are zero, the new solution to the LP model can be read from the tableau as approximately $X_1 = 702.78$, $S_2 = 297.22$, and $Z = 98{,}389$. This is extreme point B in Figure 5-2.

The next tableau and extreme point are determined similarly. Since X_2 and S_1 are now zero, one of these two variables can be increased to improve the objective function. Since the coefficient of X_2 in Equation 5.17 is positive while the coefficient of S_1 is negative, it is clear that Z can be improved only by increasing X_2. From Equations 5.16 and 5.18, X_2 can be increased to either $702.77778/0.55556 \simeq 1265$, with $X_1 = 0$, or $297.22222/0.44444 \simeq 669$, with $S_2 = 0$. As before, we must select the smaller of these two values in order to obtain a feasible solution. To construct the new tableau, Equation 5.18 is solved for X_2.

$$X_2 = 668.75668 + 2.50002 S_1 - 2.25002 S_2 \qquad (5.19)$$

Substituting Equation 5.19 into Equations 5.17 and 5.16 produces

$$Z = 113{,}250.147 - 99.99957 S_1 - 50.00044 S_2 \qquad (5.20)$$
$$X_1 = 331.24332 - 2.50002 S_1 + 1.25002 S_2 \qquad (5.21)$$

With a greater number of significant figures in the computations, Equations 5.19, 5.20, and 5.21 lead to the following tableau.

$$Z = 113{,}250 - 100 S_1 - 50 S_2 \qquad (5.20\text{a})$$
$$X_1 = 331.25 - 2.50 S_1 + 1.25 S_2 \qquad (5.21\text{a})$$
$$X_2 = 668.75 + 2.50 S_1 - 2.25 S_2 \qquad (5.19\text{a})$$

---

[3] In iterative computations such as these it is necessary to carry many significant figures to prevent propagation of round-off errors. It can be verified that if all calculations are rounded to the nearest 0.1, a much different optimal solution would be obtained.

This tableau gives the solution $X_1 = 331.25$, $X_2 = 668.75$, $Z = 113{,}250$, or extreme point A. Since the coefficients of the two zero variables, S_1 and S_2, in Equation 5.20a are both negative, the objective function cannot be improved further and the optimal solution has been obtained.

For this problem the simplex method has converged on an optimal solution in three iterations. Each iteration produced an extreme point that corresponded to two nonzero and two zero variables. We noted previously that two of the variables in Equations 5.12 and 5.13 could always be given arbitrary values. From the steps of the simplex method, we have seen that each extreme point has two variables for which these arbitrary values are exactly zero.

The computational steps of the simplex method are mechanical and lend themselves well to a general computer program. Such programs are generally available at any computer facility, and there is seldom need to solve an LP problem by hand. Preprogrammed versions of the simplex method are very similar to the computational steps used in the preceding example. They differ chiefly in the methods used to generate an initial feasible solution. When all the constraint equations have slack variables, as in the example, an initial tableau is easily produced by letting the decision variables (X_1 and X_2 in the example) be zero. In other cases an initial feasible solution may not be apparent, and the available computer programs of the simplex method incorporate procedures to produce feasible solutions to any LP model. Two of these approaches are illustrated in the following section.

GENERAL CHARACTERISTICS OF LINEAR PROGRAMMING PROBLEMS

Standard Form

The constraint set of any linear model can be written as a set of simultaneous linear equations. In general, any linear optimization model can be written as

$$\text{Max } Z = c_1 X_1 + c_2 X_2 + \ldots + c_n X_n \tag{5.22}$$

s.t.
$$a_{11} X_1 + a_{12} X_2 + \ldots + a_{1n} X_n = b_1$$
$$a_{21} X_1 + a_{22} X_2 + \ldots + a_{2n} X_n = b_2$$
$$\vdots \tag{5.23}$$
$$a_{m1} X_1 + a_{m2} X_2 + \ldots + a_{mn} X_n = b_m$$

$$X_1, X_2, \ldots, X_n \geq 0 \tag{5.24}$$

where $X_1, X_2, \ldots$, are variables, $b_1, b_2, \ldots$, are nonnegative constants, and $c_1, c_2, \ldots$, and $a_{11}, a_{12}, \ldots$, are constants that may be positive or negative. Expressions 5.22 to 5.24 constitute the *standard form* of an LP model; before an optimization model is solved using the simplex method, it is usually transformed to this standard form.

A more compact and equivalent notation is

$$\text{Max } Z = \sum_{j=1}^{n} c_j X_j \qquad (5.22)$$

s.t.
$$\sum_{j=1}^{n} a_{ij} X_j = b_i \qquad i = 1, 2, \ldots, m \qquad (5.23)$$

$$X_j \geq 0 \qquad \forall j \qquad (5.24)$$

In Constraint 5.24, the symbol "$\forall$" means "for all"; that is, X_j must be nonnegative for all values of j. An LP model can also be written using matrix notation as

$$\text{Max } Z = \overline{C}\,\overline{X} \qquad (5.22)$$

s.t.
$$\overline{A}\,\overline{X} = \overline{b} \qquad (5.23)$$

$$\overline{X} = 0 \qquad (5.24)$$

where $\overline{C}$ is a 1-×-n row vector,

$$\overline{C} = [c_1, c_2, \ldots, c_n]$$

$\overline{X}$ is an n-×-1 column vector,

$$\overline{X} = \begin{bmatrix} X_1 \\ X_1 \\ \cdot \\ \cdot \\ \cdot \\ X_n \end{bmatrix}$$

$\overline{A}$ is an m-×-n matrix,

$$\overline{A} = \begin{bmatrix} a_{11} & a_{12} & \cdots & a_{1n} \\ a_{21} & a_{22} & \cdots & a_{2n} \\ \cdot & \cdot & & \cdot \\ \cdot & \cdot & & \cdot \\ \cdot & \cdot & & \cdot \\ a_{m1} & a_{m2} & \cdots & a_{mn} \end{bmatrix}$$

and $\overline{b}$ is an m-×-1 column vector,

$$\overline{b} = \begin{bmatrix} b_1 \\ b_2 \\ \cdot \\ \cdot \\ \cdot \\ b_m \end{bmatrix}$$

Transforming to the Standard Form

Since most linear optimization models are not in the standard form, various transformations are usually necessary before the simplex method can be used.

Inequality Constraints ($\leq$, $\geq$) We have already seen transformations of "less than or equal to" constraints to equations through use of slack variables. In general, if there are p "real" or decision variables in a model (such as X_1 and X_2 in Example 5-1), the inequality

$$\sum_{j=1}^{p} a_{ij}X_j \leq b_j \tag{5.25}$$

can be transformed into an equation by the definition of a nonnegative slack variable S_i.

$$S_i = b_i - \sum_{j=1}^{p} a_{ij}X_j \tag{5.26}$$

Constraint 5.25 becomes the equation

$$\sum_{j=1}^{p} a_{ij}X_j + S_i = b_i \tag{5.25a}$$

Of course, some inequalities can be in the form of "greater than or equal to" inequalities.

$$\sum_{j=1}^{p} a_{ij}X_j \geq b_i \tag{5.27}$$

In this case a nonnegative *surplus variable* is defined as the "surplus" in the left side of the constraint.

$$S_i = \sum_{j=1}^{p} a_{ij}X_j - b_i \tag{5.28}$$

Constraint 5.27 is written as

$$\sum_{j=1}^{p} a_{ij}X_j - S_i = b_i \tag{5.27a}$$

As a specific example, consider the following linear optimization model.

$$\text{Max } Z = 16X_1 + 3X_2 - 9X_3 \tag{5.29}$$

$$\text{s.t.} \quad 3X_1 + 2X_2 + X_3 \leq 16 \tag{5.30}$$

GENERAL CHARACTERISTICS OF LINEAR PROGRAMMING

$$1.5X_1 + 0.5X_2 - X_3 = 6 \quad (5.31)$$
$$4X_1 + 3X_2 - 1.5X_3 \geq 10 \quad (5.32)$$
$$X_j \geq 0 \quad \forall j$$

The three constraints can be transformed into equations.

$$3X_1 + 2X_2 + X_3 + S_1 = 16 \quad (5.30a)$$
$$1.5X_1 + 0.5X_2 - X_3 = 6 \quad (5.31)$$
$$4X_1 + 3X_2 - 1.5X_3 - S_3 = 10 \quad (5.32a)$$

In these equations, S_1 is a slack variable and S_3 is a surplus variable.

Each inequality in an optimization model requires the addition of a slack variable with coefficient $(+1)$ or a surplus variable with coefficient (-1). Slack variables are associated with "$\leq$" constraints and surplus variables with "$\geq$" constraints.

The standard form of this model in matrix notation is

$$\text{Max } \overline{C}\,\overline{X} \quad (5.22)$$
s.t.
$$\overline{A}\,\overline{X} = \overline{b} \quad (5.23)$$
$$\overline{X} \geq 0 \quad (5.24)$$

where

$$\overline{X} = \begin{bmatrix} X_1 \\ X_2 \\ X_3 \\ S_1 \\ S_3 \end{bmatrix}, \quad \overline{C} = [16, 3, -9, 0, 0]$$

$$A = \begin{bmatrix} 3 & 2 & 1 & 1 & 0 \\ 1.5 & 0.5 & -1 & 0 & 0 \\ 4 & 3 & -1.5 & 0 & -1 \end{bmatrix}$$

$$\overline{b} = \begin{bmatrix} 16 \\ 6 \\ 10 \end{bmatrix}$$

We have an LP model with five variables and three equations. The coefficients of slack and surplus variables in the objective function (c_j) are zero, while the a_{ij} coefficients for slack and surplus variables are 0, 1, or -1.

Computer programs of the simplex method usually add "artificial" variables to constraints that do not have slack variables in order to generate initial solutions. For example, the constraint equations, Expressions 5.30a, 5.31, and 5.32a, would be modified with artificial variables A_2 and A_3 to

$$3X_1 + 2X_2 + X_3 + S_1 = 16 \quad (5.30a)$$

$$1.5X_1 + 0.5X_2 - X_3 + A_2 = 6 \quad (5.31a)$$

$$4X_1 + 3X_2 - 1.5X_3 - S_3 + A_3 = 10 \quad (5.32b)$$

and initial solutions are given by $S_1 = 16$, $A_2 = 6$, and $A_3 = 10$. This procedure provides an automatic way of generating initial solutions, but it is successful only if subsequent iterations force the artificial variables to zero. Otherwise, the optimal solution obtained from the simplex method would not be a feasible solution to the original constraint equations, Expressions 5.30a, 5.31, and 5.32a.

Artificial variables will eventually be driven to zero if they are in the objective function and have large negative coefficients. Thus, the objective function of Expression 5.29 may be modified to

$$\text{Max } Z = 16X_1 + 3X_2 - 9X_3 - MA_2 - MA_3 \quad (5.29a)$$

where M is an arbitrary, very large number. Since the new terms diminish Z so drastically, any optimal solution should have $A_2 = A_3 = 0$.

An alternative approach is to solve the LP model in two phases. The first phase generates a feasible solution to the original model by means of a new objective function Z' that is the negative sum of the artificial variables. For the example, the phase one model is

$$\text{Max } Z' = -A_2 - A_3 \quad (5.29b)$$

s.t.
$$3X_1 + 2X_2 + X_3 + S_1 = 16 \quad (5.30a)$$
$$1.5X_1 + 0.5X_2 - X_3 + A_2 = 6 \quad (5.31a)$$
$$4X_1 + 3X_2 - 1.5X_3 - S_3 + A_3 = 10 \quad (5.32b)$$
$$X_1, X_2, X_3, S_1, S_3, A_2, A_3 \geq 0$$

The optimal solution to this model will have $A_2 = A_3 = 0$ and therefore be a feasible solution to the original model.

The initial simplex tableau for phase one is

$$Z' = -16 + 5.5X_1 + 3.5X_2 - 2.5X_3 - S_3 \quad (5.29c)$$
$$S_1 = 16 - 3X_1 - 2X_2 - X_3 \quad (5.30b)$$
$$A_2 = 6 - 1.5X_1 - 0.5X_2 + X_3 \quad (5.31b)$$
$$A_3 = 10 - 4X_1 - 3X_2 + 1.5X_3 + S_3 \quad (5.32c)$$

The objective function is obtained by substituting A_2 and A_3 from Equations 5.31b and 5.32c into Equation 5.29b. These substitutions produce a standard tableau with nonzero variables on the left and zero variables on the right. Subsequent iterations continue until $Z' = 0$ with $A_2 = A_3 = 0$. The associated nonzero variables provide the initial feasible solution for phase two. In this second phase, the artificial objective function Z' is replaced by its real counterpart, Equation 5.29, and the simplex iterations continue (without the artificial variables) until an optimal solution is obtained.

Minimization The goal of many linear optimization models is the minimization of an objective function.

$$\text{Min } Z = \sum_{j=1}^{n} c_j X_j \qquad (5.33)$$

Minimization problems are easily converted to maximization by multiplying the objective function by -1. *Maximizing* $\left(-\sum_{j=1}^{n} c_j X_j\right)$ is equivalent to minimizing $\sum_{j=1}^{n} c_j X_j$. The same values of X_j that make $\sum_{j=1}^{n} c_j X_j$ as small as possible will also make $\left(-\sum_{j=1}^{n} c_j X_j\right)$ as large as possible.[4]

This may be obvious, but it can be demonstrated by solving the following example graphically.

$$\text{Min } Z = 4X_1 + 2X_2 \qquad (5.34)$$

s.t.
$$X_1 + X_2 \geq 4 \qquad (5.35)$$
$$X_1 + 3X_2 \leq 9 \qquad (5.36)$$
$$X_1, X_2 \geq 0 \qquad (5.37)$$

The solution to this model is $X_1^* = 1.5$, $X_2^* = 2.5$, and $Z^* = 11$. The equivalent maximization model is

$$\text{Max }(-Z) = -4X_1 - 2X_2 \qquad (5.34\text{a})$$

s.t.
$$X_1 + X_2 \geq 4 \qquad (5.35)$$
$$X_1 + 3X_2 \leq 9 \qquad (5.36)$$
$$X_1, X_2 \geq 0 \qquad (5.37)$$

The solution is $X_1^* = 1.5$, $X_2^* = 2.5$, and $(-Z^*) = -11$ or $Z^* = 11$.

---

[4]Note that "large" negative numbers have small absolute values. For example, (-3) is larger (greater) than (-6).

Negative b_i Negative b_i are converted to positive values by multiplying the offending constraints by -1. Note, however, that this will change the direction of inequalities. For example, the constraint

$$3X_1 - 6X_2 \geq -4 \tag{5.38}$$

is equivalent to

$$-3X_1 + 6X_2 \leq 4 \tag{5.38a}$$

Negative X_j It is difficult to document physically realistic examples of decision variables that can be negative. However, if a variable X_j is encountered that is not constrained to be nonnegative, it can be replaced by the difference between two new variables,

$$X_j = Y_1 - Y_2 \tag{5.39}$$

where Y_1 and Y_2 are both required to be greater than or equal to zero. When the LP model is solved, if $Y_1^* > Y_2^*$, then X_j^* is positive; if $Y_1^* < Y_2^*$, then X_j^* is negative.

Properties of Linear Programming Solutions

The constraint set of a standard LP model

$$\sum_{j=1}^{n} a_{ij} X_j = b_i, \qquad i = 1, 2, \ldots, m \tag{5.23}$$

is a set of m simultaneous equations with n unknowns or variables. The solutions to such a set of equations have properties that are useful in linear programming. To explore these properties, let us assume that the equations are independent. Although independence has a precise mathematical meaning,[5] the term also has commonsense implications. In a set of independent equations no one of the equations can be written in terms of the others. For example, the equations

$$1.5X_1 + 3X_2 + X_3 = 12 \tag{5.40}$$

$$X_1 + 2X_2 - 4X_3 = 5 \tag{5.41}$$

$$0.5X_1 + X_2 + 5X_3 = 7 \tag{5.42}$$

---

[5] The set of equations $\overline{A}\,\overline{X} = \overline{b}$, where A is an m-×-n matrix, is independent if the rank of A is equal to m, the number of equations. The rank of a matrix is equal to the number of independent rows or columns.

GENERAL CHARACTERISTICS OF LINEAR PROGRAMMING 101

are not independent, since Equation 5.42 is Equation 5.40 minus Equation 5.41. Clearly, we would not need both equations in an optimization model.

The natures of solutions to Equations 5.23 depend on the relationships between the number of variables (n) and equations (m). If $m > n$ the equations are inconsistent[6] or overdetermined and have no feasible solution. For example, consider the equations

$$3X_1 + 2X_2 = 6 \qquad (5.43)$$

$$X_1 - 3X_2 = 2 \qquad (5.44)$$

$$-2X_1 + 7X_2 = 4 \qquad (5.45)$$

Although any pair of the three equations can be solved, it is impossible to find values of X_1 and X_2 that solve all three equations. Next consider the case $m = n$. Since the number of unknowns and equations are equal, the equations have, at most, a single or unique solution.

Neither case is particularly interesting, and they are seldom encountered in linear optimization models. Usually $n > m$ and, if at least one feasible solution exists (the equations are consistent), the equations have an infinite number of solutions with $n - m$ of the variables taking on arbitrary values. This case was demonstrated for Equations 5.12 and 5.13 in Example 5-1, and extension to larger sets of equations is straightforward. Another aspect of the example relevant to this general case was the observation that extreme points of the feasible region correspond to the $n - m$ arbitrary values being exactly zero.

Extreme point solutions to a set of linear equations are also known as *basic solutions*. Since the optimal solution to an LP problem will be a basic or extreme point solution, we can conclude that LP solutions should have $n - m$ variables equal to zero. This assumes that all m constraints are independent. If this is not the case, the number of nonzero variables will be less than the number of constraints. The general conclusion is that the optimal solution to an LP model with m constraints will have no more than m variables with nonzero values.

Before concluding this discussion of the properties of LP models, some comments on the possibilities of inconsistent and dependent equations are appropriate. Inconsistent constraints clearly frustrate the purpose of a model, since feasible solutions are impossible. When the simplex method is used to solve an LP model that has inconsistent constraints, the computer programs used will often terminate with the output "no feasible solution." This result usually indicates that the disconcerted systems analyst has either modeled the problem incorrectly or made errors in inputting data to the computer. Sometimes, however, the failure to find a feasible solution suggests a more profound difficulty. If the optimization model is a correct mathematical statement of the

---

[6]The set of equations $\overline{A}\,\overline{X} = \overline{b}$ is consistent if the rank of the m-×-$(n + 1)$ matrix $\overline{A}, \overline{b}$ is equal to the rank of $\overline{A}$.

problem and there are no input data errors, the implication of "no feasible solution" is that the problem being studied as perceived by the systems analyst cannot be solved. In this case the constraints incorporated in the model may be unrealistic. If the systems analyst is convinced that these constraints are correct there is little choice but to report to the decision maker(s) that no solution is possible. A subsequent step may then be a modification of constraints (and usually a lowering of expectations) to obtain a problem solution.

Dependent constraints cause less difficulties than inconsistent constraints. Ideally, optimization models should consist of independent constraints. However, dependent constraints may be difficult to identify, particularly for large models. Fortunately, such constraints do little harm, other than to increase the number of computations needed to obtain an optimal solution.

DUAL LINEAR PROGRAMMING MODELS

One of the characteristics of LP models that is very useful in sensitivity analysis is the existence of dual LP models. Every LP model has a parallel or dual model that can be used to generate additional information about the problem being studied. The optimization model constructed for Example 5-1 can be used to demonstrate the concept of duality. This model was

$$\text{Max } Z = 140X_1 + 100X_2 \tag{5.6}$$

$$\text{s.t.} \quad 0.9X_1 + 0.5X_2 \leq 632.5 \tag{5.7}$$

$$X_1 + X_2 \leq 1000 \tag{5.8}$$

$$X_1, X_2 \geq 0 \tag{5.9}$$

Constraint 5.7 limits pesticide losses to 632.5 kg, and Constraint 5.8 prevents total land in crops 1 (X_1) and 2 (X_2) from exceeding 1000 ha.

The rationale for a sensitivity analysis using this LP model was discussed earlier. Although much of that discussion related to uncertainty in the objective function coefficients, sensitivity analysis can be extended to the right side of the constraint set. Specifically, it can be of interest to see how solutions to the model change with variations in the allowable pesticide losses and available land. For example, we might wish to know the effect of removing some of the land from production. Similarly, the impact on farmer profits of tightening or relaxing the pesticide constraint could provide useful information to decision makers.

Since the model is two dimensional, we can easily show that changing constraint limits will shift the constraint lines (Figure 5-1) and, since the optimal solution is at the intersection of the two constraints, the optimal solution must also change. If either the allowable pesticide loss or available land is increased, optimal profits will increase. Similarly, decreases in these limits will lower optimal profits. The two constraints clearly have certain economic implications. Relaxing either constraint (increasing the right side) has a monetary *value*, indicated by the change in the optimal value of the objective function. The objective of *duality* or the analysis of dual LP models, is to quantify such values.

Specifically, we define Y_1 as the marginal value ($/kg) associated with a change in pesticide loss limits. This is equal to the increase (decrease) in Z^* that results from a unit increase (decrease) in allowable pesticide losses. Thus, if the right side of Constraint 5.7 is increased to 633.5, optimal net returns Z^* will increase by Y_1. Conversely, if the constraint limit is decreased to 631.5, Z^* will be lowered by Y_1. Similarly Y_2 is defined as the marginal value ($/ha) associated with a change in the amount of available land.

Assuming that these marginal values Y_1 and Y_2 are of interest, how can we determine what they are? One obvious procedure would be to change the appropriate constraint limits, solve the LP model for each change, and observe the new values of Z^*. There is, however, a more direct method involving a *dual LP model*. To derive this model, we must first explore the meaning of the marginal values. Constraints 5.7 and 5.8 of the LP model can be interpreted as resources that must be allocated to the two crops in order to maximize net income. Since the resources are used to provide income, they must have monetary value. When the resources are allocated optimally, their total value is

$$z = 632.5Y_1 + 1000Y_2 \qquad (5.46)$$

That is, the amount of each resource is multiplied by its associated marginal value.

We might next consider how each of the valuable resources is used by the two crops. Considering the first crop, 1.0 ha will use 0.9 kg of the pesticide allowance and 1.0 ha of the available land. Thus the total value of resources associated with 1.0 ha of crop 1 is $0.9Y_1 + 1.0Y_2$. These resources generate income. The net income from crop 1 is $140/ha (as in Equation 5.6), and it is reasonable to suggest that the value of resources used should not be less than this net income.

$$0.9Y_1 + 1.0Y_2 \geq 140 \qquad (5.47)$$

The reasons for the "$\geq$" in Constraint 5.47 are not necessarily obvious. For example, it would be equally rational to have resource value *equal* to the net return ($140/ha) derived from the resources (i.e., replace the "$\geq$" with "$=$"). This would imply a perfect efficiency in resource use. Unfortunately, we should realize that however desirable, such perfect efficiency may not always be possible for each crop. The remaining possibility ($0.9Y_1 + 1.0Y_2 \leq 140$) is even better, since it permits "something for nothing." It implies that we could extract a return from the resources that is greater than their value to us. If this occurred, we would obviously have underestimated these values.

A constraint similar to Constraint 5.47 can be derived for the resources used for crop 2. A hectare of crop 2 uses 0.5 kg of the pesticide allowance and 1.0 ha of the available land. The value of the resources used should be greater than or equal to the net income from crop 2. Therefore

$$0.5Y_1 + 1.0Y_2 \geq 100 \qquad (5.48)$$

104 LINEAR PROGRAMMING MODELS

Constraints 5.47 and 5.48 give us a good start at estimating Y_1 and Y_2, since they define the feasible values of Y_1 and Y_2. Unfortunately, such a constraint set has an infinite number of solutions. We can add some obvious nonnegativity conditions $Y_1 \geq 0$, $Y_2 \geq 0$, but we are still not much closer to obtaining specific estimates of the marginal values of the two resources. To resolve this indeterminancy, we minimize the total value of the pesticide and land resources (Equation 5.46). The result is the following LP model.

$$\text{Min } z = 632.5Y_1 + 1000Y_2 \tag{5.46}$$

$$\text{s.t.} \quad 0.9Y_1 + 1.0Y_2 \geq 140 \tag{5.47}$$

$$0.5Y_1 + 1.0Y_2 \geq 100 \tag{5.48}$$

$$Y_1, Y_2 \geq 0 \tag{5.49}$$

This model states "find the minimum total resource value such that the values of resources used to grow each crop are at least equal to the net returns associated with the crops." The optimal solution to such a model Y_1^* and Y_2^* should give us the marginal values we desire. By minimizing the total resource value, an overestimate of values is precluded. In addition, Constraints 5.47 and 5.48 prevent the marginal values from being underestimated.

The LP model specified by Expression 5.46 to 5.49 is the *dual* of the *primal* LP model given by Expressions 5.6 to 5.9. The marginal values Y_1 and Y_2 are *dual variables*. Comparison of the primal and dual models indicates some interesting juxtapositions. The coefficients of the objective function in the primal become constraint limits in the dual, and vice versa. The coefficients of the constraints have been rearranged in the dual. If we write the primal constraint coefficients as a matrix,

$$\begin{matrix} 0.9 & 0.5 \\ 1.0 & 1.0 \end{matrix}$$

the corresponding dual matrix has rows and columns transposed.

$$\begin{matrix} 0.9 & 1.0 \\ 0.5 & 1.0 \end{matrix}$$

Since the dual model is two dimensional, it can be solved graphically, as shown in Figure 5-3. The solution is $Y_1^* = \$100$, $Y_2^* = \$50$, and $z^* = \$113{,}250$. If the pesticide constraint is increased (decreased) by 1.0 kg, net farm income will be raised (lowered) by $100. This result can be confirmed by resolving the primal LP model with pesticide loss limits of 633.5 and 631.5 kg. The most startling aspect of the dual solution is that the optimal value of the dual objective function, $z^* = \$113{,}250$, is exactly the same as the optimal value of the primal objective Function (Z^*). On reflection, this result is scarcely surprising, since it indicates that the total value of the two resources (z^*) is equal to the net income derived from them (Z^*).

DUAL LINEAR PROGRAMMING MODELS

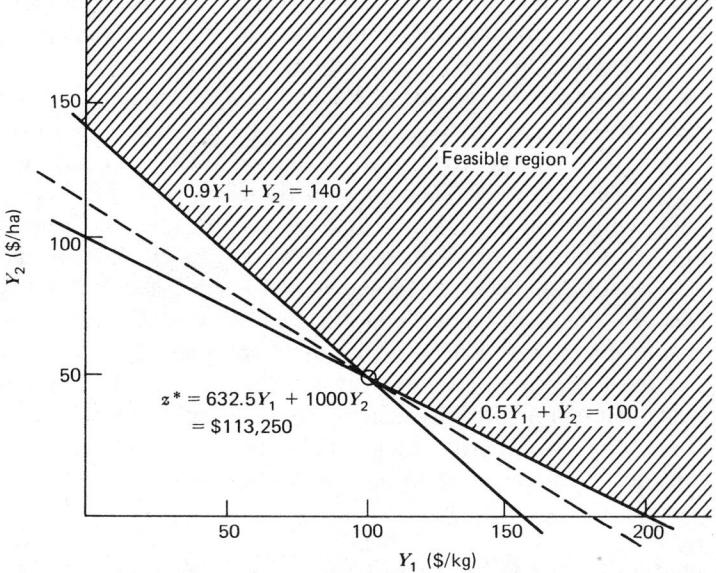

Figure 5-3 Solution to the dual LP model.

Dual variables measure the sensitivity of optimal primal solutions to changes in the right-side values of the primal constraints. Such information is frequently valuable to systems analysts and decision makers. Moreover, the optimal solution to the dual model is obtained very easily, since it is automatically generated when the primal model is solved using the simplex method! The final simplex tableau for the optimization model, Equations 5.6, 5.7, and 5.8, was

$$Z = 113{,}250 - 100S_1 - 50S_2 \quad (5.20a)$$

$$X_1 = 331.25 - 2.5S_1 + 1.25S_2 \quad (5.21a)$$

$$X_2 = 668.75 + 2.5S_1 - 2.25S_2 \quad (5.19a)$$

The slack variables S_1 and S_2 in this optimal solution are zero, indicating that both the pesticide and land resources are completely utilized. Thus $0.9X_1 + 0.5X_2 = 632.5$ and $X_1 + X_2 = 1000$. Equation 5.20a shows that if S_1 is increased, the objective function would decrease by 100 for a unit increase in S_1. With this increase, only 631.5 kg of the pesticide resource would be used. This is equivalent to changing the limit in Constraint 5.7 from 632.5 to 631.5. Therefore the coefficient of S_1 in Equation 5.20a is the negative marginal value of the pesticide resource and, since dual variables are defined as marginal values, it is evident that $(-Y_1^*) = -100$ or $Y_1^* = 100$. Similarly, $(-Y_2^*)$ is given by the coefficient of S_2 in Equation 5.20a, or $Y_2^* = 50$. These are the same optimal dual values graphically obtained in Figure 5-3.

We can conclude that the simplex method produces optimal solutions to both the dual and primal LP models. Optimal values of nonzero dual variables are given by the negatives of slack variable coefficients in the objective function in the final simplex tableau. Whenever an LP model is solved by the simplex method, solutions are also obtained to the dual of the model with no additional effort. Most computer programs of the simplex method output both primal and dual solutions.

In the previous sensitivity analysis of Example 5-1, solutions were obtained for two alternative forms of the objective function: (1) $Z = 220X_1 + 100X_2$ and (2) $Z = 50X_1 + 100X_2$ (Figure 5-2). The two associated LP models can be used to demonstrate general characteristics of dual solutions, as shown in Table 5-1. As indicated in Figure 5-2, the constraint $X_1 + X_2 \leq 1000$ is not binding for case (1) (i.e., $X_1 + X_2 = 702.78$), while the first constraint ($0.9X_1 + 0.5X_2 \leq 632.5$) is not binding for case (2). The dual LP models are also shown in Table 5-1 along with their optimal solutions. These solutions can be obtained graphically, or directly from the simplex method solution to the primal models. Each primal constraint has an associated dual variable, Y_1 for the first primal constraint and Y_2 for the second. The optimal dual solutions indicate that marginal values of nonbinding constraints are zero ($Y_2^* = 0$ for case 1 and $Y_1^* = 0$ for case 2). This is reasonable, since a unit change in the right side of such a constraint will have no effect on the optimal value of the objective function Z^*.

Generalization of Primal/Dual Linear Programming Models

The general forms of primal and dual LP models are

$$\text{Primal:} \quad \text{Max } Z = \sum_{j=1}^{n} c_j X_j \tag{5.50}$$

$$\text{s.t.} \quad \sum_{j=1}^{n} a_{ij} X_j \leq b_i \quad i = 1, 2, \ldots, m \tag{5.51}$$

$$X_j \geq 0 \quad \forall j$$

$$\text{Dual:} \quad \text{Min } z = \sum_{i=1}^{m} b_i Y_i \tag{5.52}$$

$$\text{s.t.} \quad \sum_{i=1}^{m} a_{ij} Y_i \geq c_j \quad j = 1, 2, \ldots, n \tag{5.53}$$

$$Y_i \geq 0 \quad \forall i$$

The dual variable Y_i is the marginal value[7] associated with the i th primal constraint and is equal to the marginal change in the optimal value of the objective function Z^* produced by a change in b_i.

$$Y_i = \frac{\partial Z^*}{\partial b_i} \tag{5.54}$$

---

[7] Dual variables are also sometimes referred to as *shadow prices*.

TABLE 5-1 Primal and Dual Models with Two Alternative Objective Functions

Primal	Dual
1. Max $Z = 220X_1 + 100X_2$	Min $z = 632.5Y_1 + 1000Y_2$
s.t. $\quad 0.9X_1 + 0.5X_2 \leq 632.5$	s.t. $\quad 0.9Y_1 + \geq 220$
$\quad\quad X_1 + X_2 \leq 1000$	$\quad\quad 0.5Y_1 + Y_2 \geq 100$
$Z^* = \$154{,}610$	$z^* = \$154{,}610$
$X_1^* = 702.78, \quad X_2^* = 0$	$Y_1^* = 244.44, \quad Y_2^* = 0$
2. Max $Z = 50X_1 + 100X_2$	Min $z = 632.5Y_1 + 1000Y_2$
s.t. $\quad 0.9X_1 + 0.5X_2 \leq 632.5$	s.t. $\quad 0.9Y_1 + \geq 50$
$\quad\quad X_1 + X_2 \leq 1000$	$\quad\quad 0.5Y_1 + Y_2 \geq 100$
$Z^* = 100{,}000$	$z^* = 100{,}000$
$X_1^* = 0, \quad X_2^* = 1000$	$Y_1^* = 0, \quad Y_2^* = 100$

The coefficients c_j and a_{ij} and the right side of Constraint 5.51 (b_i) are all constants. The primal has n variables and m constraints. Conversely, the dual model has m variables and n constraints.

A dual model can be derived for any LP problem. To see this, we must transform "greater than or equal to" constraints and equations in the primal to "less than or equal to" constraints. For example, consider the constraint

$$X_1 - X_2 \geq 2 \qquad (5.55)$$

The direction of the inequality is changed by multiplying by -1. Thus Constraint 5.55 is identical[8] to

$$-X_1 + X_2 \leq -2 \qquad (5.55a)$$

Similarly, an equation such as

$$3X_1 - 2X_2 + 4X_3 = 10 \qquad (5.56)$$

is equivalent to the two inequalities

---

[8] Note, however, that when the primal LP model is solved by the simplex method, the original constraint form (Constraint 5.55) must be used, since negative b_i are not permissible.

$$3X_1 - 2X_2 + 4X_3 \geq 10 \qquad (5.56a)$$
$$3X_1 - 2X_2 + 4X_3 \leq 10 \qquad (5.56b)$$

Constraint 5.56a can then be changed to a "$\leq$" constraint.

Primal and dual LP models can be written as sets of linear equations by adding slack and surplus variables.

$$\text{Primal: Max } Z = \sum_{j=1}^{n} c_j X_j \qquad (5.57)$$

s.t.
$$\sum_{j=1}^{n} a_{ij} X_j + P_i = b_i \qquad i = 1, 2, \ldots, m \qquad (5.58)$$

$$X_j, P_i \geq 0 \qquad \forall j, i$$

$$\text{Dual: Min } z = \sum_{i=1}^{m} b_i Y_i \qquad (5.59)$$

s.t.
$$\sum_{i=1}^{m} a_{ij} Y_i - D_j = c_j \qquad j = 1, 2, \ldots, n \qquad (5.60)$$

$$Y_i, D_j \geq 0 \qquad \forall i, j$$

The variables $P_1, P_2, \ldots, P_m$ are slack variables associated with the primal constraints, and $D_1, D_2, \ldots, D_n$ are surplus variables associated with the dual constraints.

These forms of the primal and dual can be used to show that the optimal values of the primal and dual objective functions, Z^* and z^*, are always equal. To see this, we first multiply each primal Constraint 5.58 by Y_i and then sum for all i.

$$\sum_i Y_i \left(\sum_j a_{ij} X_j + P_i \right) = \sum_i Y_i b_i \qquad (5.61)$$

The right side of Equation 5.60 is equal to the dual objective function z; therefore

$$\sum_i \sum_j a_{ij} Y_i X_j + \sum_i Y_i P_i = z \qquad (5.61a)$$

Similarly, each dual constraint is multiplied by X_j and all constraints are summed.

$$\sum_j X_j \left(\sum_i a_{ij} Y_i - D_j \right) = \sum_j X_j c_j \qquad (5.62)$$

Since the right side of Equation 5.62 is the primal objective function Z, the equation reduces to

$$\sum_i \sum_j a_{ij} X_j Y_i - \sum_j X_j D_j = Z \quad (5.62a)$$

Subtracting Equation 5.62a from Equation 5.61a, we obtain

$$\sum_i Y_i P_i + \sum_j X_j D_j = z - Z \quad (5.63)$$

Suppose now that the primal and dual models have been solved and optimal values of the decision variables, Y_i^*, P_i^*, X_j^*, and D_j^*, have been obtained. Can we determine what $z^* - Z^*$ is? Consider first the term $\sum_i Y_i^* P_i^*$. If, for any primal constraint i, P_i^* is greater than zero, this constraint is not binding. The associated marginal value, Y_i^*, must therefore be zero. Conversely, if the i th constraint is binding, P_i^* must be zero, and the marginal value is positive. In summary,

$$\text{If} \quad P_i^* > 0, \quad \text{then } Y_i^* = 0$$
$$P_i^* = 0, \quad \text{then } Y_i^* > 0$$

We conclude that

$$\sum_i Y_i^* P_i^* = 0 \quad (5.64)$$

and, therefore,

$$z^* - Z^* = \sum_j X_j^* D_j^* \quad (5.65)$$

The second part of the argument is to show that the right side of Equation 5.65 is identically zero. To see this, we must recognize that the *dual of the dual* LP model is, in fact, the primal model. The dual LP model (Expressions 5.52 and 5.53) can be written as

$$\text{Max}\,(-z) = -\sum_{i=1}^{m} b_i Y_i \quad (5.52a)$$

s.t.
$$-\sum_{i=1}^{m} a_{ij} Y_i \leq -c_j \quad j = 1, 2, \ldots, n \quad (5.53a)$$

$$Y_i \geq 0 \quad \forall\, i$$

The dual of this LP model is

$$\text{Min } Z = -\sum_{j=1}^{n} c_j X_j \tag{5.50a}$$

s.t.
$$-\sum_{j=1}^{n} a_{ij} X_j \geq -b_i \quad i = 1, 2, \ldots, m \tag{5.51a}$$

$$X_j \geq 0 \quad \forall j$$

However, Equation 5.50a and Constraint 5.51a are equivalent to

$$\text{Max } Z = \sum_{j=1}^{n} c_j X_j \tag{5.50}$$

s.t.
$$\sum_{j=1}^{n} a_{ij} X_j \leq b_i \quad i = 1, 2, \ldots, m \tag{5.51}$$

$$X_j \geq 0 \quad \forall j$$

which is the original form of the general primal model.

We can conclude that the original decision variables $X_1, X_2, \ldots, X_n$ are marginal values associated with the dual constraints. Thus the argument used for $Y_i^* P_i^*$ can be extended as follows.

$$\text{If} \quad D_j^* > 0, \quad \text{then } X_j^* = 0$$
$$D_j^* = 0, \quad \text{then } X_j^* > 0$$

It follows that

$$z^* - Z^* = \sum_j X_j^* D_j^* = 0 \tag{5.66}$$

Hence the result for Example 5-1 holds for dual LP models in general. Optimal values for the primal and dual objective functions, Z^* and z^*, must be equal.

APPLICATION OF LINEAR PROGRAMMING TO AIR POLLUTION CONTROL

Air pollution transport, emissions, and control technologies can often be described by linear equations and constraints. LP models can be used to analyze a variety of air quality management problems.

Air quality problems differ significantly from water quality problems, since air pollution often has more adverse effects on health and property. Except as used for drinking water, many people do not come in contact with polluted water bodies.

APPLICATION TO AIR POLLUTION CONTROL

Although the provision of safe drinking water remains a concern throughout the world, water treatment technologies are capable of rendering even severely polluted waters safe for consumption. Conversely, we must view air pollution the way fish see water pollution. People live within the atmosphere and, clean or dirty, they must breathe it. To make matters worse, many air pollutants have severe effects on human health (Table 5-2). Although it is possible to create a localized unpolluted atmosphere by air-conditioning, it is hardly feasible to protect large population segments from any exposure to polluted air. As noted in Table 5-2, air pollution also has significant effects on buildings, clothes, and crops. These property damages have been estimated to exceed billions of dollars annually in the United States.

TABLE 5-2   Major Air Pollutants

	Total Suspended Particulates (TSP)
Characteristics	Any solid or liquid particles dispersed in the atmosphere, such as dust, pollen, ash, soot, metals, and various chemicals; the particles are often classified according to size as settleable particles; aerosols: smaller than 50 microns; and fine particulates: smaller than 3 microns
Principal sources	Natural events such as forest fires, wind erosion, volcanic eruptions; stationary combustion, especially of solid fuels; construction activities; industrial processes; atmospheric chemical reactions
Principal effects	Health: directly toxic effects or aggravation of the effects of gaseous pollutants; aggravation of asthma or other respiratory or cardiorespiratory symptoms; increased cough and chest discomfort; increased mortality Other: soiling and deterioration of building materials and other surfaces; impairment of visibility; cloud formation; interference with plant photosynthesis
Controls	Cleaning of flue gases with inertial separators, fabric filters, scrubbers, or electrostatic precipitators; alternative means for solid waste reduction; improved control procedures for construction and industrial processes
	Sulfur Dioxide (SO_2)
Characteristics	A colorless gas with a pungent odor; SO_2 can oxidize to form sulfur trioxide (SO_3) which forms sulfuric acid with water
Principal sources	Combustion of sulfur-containing fossil fuels; smelting of sulfur-bearing metal ores; industrial processes; natural events such as volcanic eruptions
Principal effects	Health: aggravation of respiratory diseases including asthma, chronic bronchitis, and emphysema; reduced lung function; irritation of eyes and respiratory tract; increased mortality Other: corrosion of metal; deterioration of electrical contacts, paper, textiles, leather finishes and coatings, and building stone; formation of acid rain; leaf injury and reduced growth in plants
Controls	Use of low-sulfur fuels; removal of sulfur from fuels before use; scrubbing of flue gases with lime or catalytic conversion

TABLE 5-2 (continued)

Carbon Monoxide (CO)

Characteristics	A colorless, odorless gas with a strong chemical affinity for hemoglobin in blood
Principal sources	Incomplete combustion of fuels and other carbon-containing substances, such as in motor vehicle exhausts; natural events such as forest fires or decomposition of organic matter
Principal effects	Health: reduced tolerance for exercise; impairment of mental function; impairment of fetal development; aggravation of cardiovascular diseases Other: unknown
Controls	Automobile engine modifications (proper tuning, exhaust gas recirculation, redesign of combustion chamber); control of automobile exhaust gases (catalytic or thermal devices); improved design, operation, and maintenance of stationary furnaces (use of finely dispersed fuels, proper mixing with air, high combustion temperature)

Photochemical Oxidants (O_x)

Characteristics	Colorless, gaseous compounds that can comprise photochemical smog, (e.g., ozone (O_3), peroxyacetyl nitrate (PAN), aldehydes, and other compounds)
Principal sources	Atmospheric reactions of chemical precursors under the influence of sunlight
Principal effects	Health: aggravation of respiratory and cardiovascular illnesses; irritation of eyes and respiratory tract; impairment of cardiopulmonary function Other: deterioration of rubber, textiles and paints; impairment of visibility; leaf injury, reduced growth, and premature fruit and leaf drop in plants
Controls	Reduction of emissions of nitrogen oxides, hydrocarbons, and possibly sulfur oxides

Nitrogen Dioxide (NO_2)

Characteristics	A brownish-red gas with a pungent odor, often formed from oxidation of nitric oxide (NO)
Principal sources	Motor vehicle exhausts; high-temperature stationary combustion; atmospheric conditions
Principal effects	Health: aggravation of respiratory and cardiovascular illnesses and chronic nephritis Other: fading of paints and dyes; impairment of visibility; reduced growth and premature leaf drop in plants
Controls	Catalytic control of automobile exhaust gases; modification of automobile engines to reduce combustion temperature; scrubbing flue gases with caustic substances or urea

APPLICATION TO AIR POLLUTION CONTROL

TABLE 5-2 (continued)

	Hydrocarbons (HC)
Characteristics	Organic compounds in gaseous or particulate form (e.g., methane, ethylene, and acetylene)
Principal sources	Incomplete combustion of fuels and other carbon-containing substances, such as in motor vehicle exhausts; processing, distribution, and use of petroleum compounds such as gasoline and organic solvents; natural events such as forest fires and plant metabolism; atmospheric reactions
Principal effects	Health: suspected contribution to cancer
	Other: major precursors in the formation of photochemical oxidants through atmospheric reactions
Controls	Automobile engine modifications (proper tuning, crankcase ventilation, exhaust gas recirculation, redesign of combustion chamber); control of automobile exhaust gases (catalytic or thermal devices); improved design, operation, and maintenance of stationary furnaces (use of finely dispersed fuels, proper mixing with air, high combustion temperature); improved control procedures in processing and handling petroleum compounds

Source: Environmental Quality—The Sixth Annual Report of the Council on Environmental Quality, U.S. Government Printing Office, Washington, D.C., 1975, pp. 300–303; information compiled by Enviro Control, Inc.

Although water pollution can threaten public health and damage property, water quality concerns in developed countries are often based on aesthetics, provision of recreational opportunities, and protection of wildlife. Conversely, the rationale for air pollution control is protection of life and property. In spite of this striking difference, air and water pollution control strategies are similar. Both utilize effluent and environmental standards although, in air quality management, the standards are referred to as emission and ambient standards, respectively. Another similarity involves the transport of wastes from their point of discharge to other places in the environment. Airborne wastes are frequently discharged from high stacks well above ground level; to develop control plans, it may be necessary to estimate the effects of these emissions on ground-level pollutant concentrations. This is usually done with mathematical models that quantify the cause-and-effect relationships between air pollution emissions and air quality.

The following example illustrates an approach often used to study regional air quality problems. Although it involves only three sources and one air pollutant, it provides an introduction to more general air quality LP models. These models are subsequently presented in the final portions of this chapter.

EXAMPLE 5-2 *Air Pollution Emissions Control*

The three major sources of total suspended particulates (TSP) within a community are two coal-burning power plants and the kilns of a cement manufacturing plant. Each

114 LINEAR PROGRAMMING MODELS

tonne (1000 kg) of coal burned produces 95 kg of TSP, and each tonne of cement manufactured produces 85 kg of TSP. Cement production is 250,000 t/yr, and the two power plants burn 400,000 and 300,000 t/yr of coal, respectively. None of these three TSP sources presently has emission controls.

An environmental control agency wishes to reduce average TSP concentrations in the community's atmosphere by 80%. Methods available for TSP removal are listed in Table 5-3. Not all controls can be used at each source. Feasible controls and associated costs are given in Table 5-4. Cost ($/t) is in terms of coal or cement. □

This air pollution example requires a cost-effectiveness approach. An environmental objective is to be achieved at minimum cost. However, the environmental objective of reducing average TSP concentration by 80% is somewhat ambiguous. Since every cubic meter of the community's atmosphere cannot be monitored with TSP measuring equipment, it would seem that we can at best insure only that average TSP concentrations at certain geographic locations be diminished by 80%. This is similar to the wastewater treatment planning example of Chapter 3, for which a DO standard was to be met at all downstream sites, but the optimization model DO constraint was written for only a small number of locations. The water quality example was one dimensional, and all waste movement was in a single downstream direction. Air pollution movement is always three dimensional and, in order to monitor an ambient air quality standard adequately, waste concentrations must be measured or predicted at many sites. Although such predictions are possible, they are very difficult and often unreliable.

The uncertainties of air quality predictions are at least partial justification for the assumption of a "proportional rollback" effect; i.e., "a reduction in pollutant emissions brings about a corresponding reduction in the levels of that pollutant in the atmosphere."[9] With this assumption, air quality levels are considered only indirectly; if, for example, TSP concentrations at the various monitoring stations must be reduced an

TABLE 5-3 Emission Control Methods

Control Method	Efficiency (%)
1. Baffled settling chamber	59
2. Multiple cyclone	74
3. Long-cone cyclone	84
4. Spray scrubber	94
5. Electrostatic precipitator	97

[9]*Environmental Quality, The Eighth Annual Report of the Council on Environmental Quality,* U.S. Government Printing Office, Washington, D.C., December, 1977, p. 172.

APPLICATION TO AIR POLLUTION CONTROL

TABLE 5-4 Costs of Feasible Emission Control Methods

Control Method	Power Plant 1 ($/t)	Power Plant 2 ($/t)	Cement Factory ($/t)
Settling chamber	1.00	1.40	1.10
Multiple cyclone	a	a	1.20
Long-cone cyclone	a	a	1.50
Spray scrubber	2.00	2.20	3.00
Electrostatic precipitator	2.80	3.00	a

[a]Not feasible.

average of 80% to meet a standard, we infer an objective of reducing total TSP emissions by 80%.

The proportional rollback assumption is a useful way of avoiding the difficulties of modeling air pollution transport. Moreover, there is some empirical evidence that the assumption is valid. For example, when hydrocarbon emissions were reduced in San Francisco by 25% from 1967 to 1976, the atmospheric oxidants associated with these emissions also fell by 25%.

The objectives in the example are to reduce the total TSP emissions from the cement factory and two power plants by 80% at least cost. Emissions are controlled by selections of treatment options at each source for removing TSP from atmospheric discharges. It remains to construct and solve an optimization model to obtain an optimal control plan.

Decision variables can be defined in two ways. They can be expressed in terms of TSP emissions at each source. However, since cost data are based on the number of tonnes of coal burning or cement production controlled by a specific treatment method, a more appropriate definition is

X_{ij} = t/yr of production at source i that has emission control option j

The subscripts indicate the following.

i	Source	j	Control
1	Power plant 1	0	None
2	Power plant 2	1	Baffled settling chamber
3	Cement factory	2	Multiple cyclone
		3	Long-cone cyclone
		4	Spray scrubber
		5	Electrostatic precipitator

As usual the *null*, or "do nothing," alternative ($j = 0$) should be included in the analyses.

Since all controls are not feasible for any one source, only certain combinations of i and j are possible. Consider, for example, the variables for source 1. Since the two cyclones are not feasible for this source, the relevant variables are X_{10} (no control), X_{11} (settling), X_{14} (scrubber), and X_{15} (precipitator). The complete list of variables is given in Table 5-5.

The relationships between decision variables are dictated by mass balances and mathematical statements of the objectives. The economic objective is quantified by total annual costs ($/yr) as

$$Z = 1.0X_{11} + 2.0X_{14} + 2.8X_{15} + 1.4X_{21} + 2.2X_{24}$$
$$+ 3.0X_{25} + 1.1X_{31} + 1.2X_{32} + 1.5X_{33} + 3.0X_{34} \quad (5.67)$$

The air pollution control objective is to reduce total TSP emissions by 80%. Using the emission factors of 95 kg/tonne TSP for coal burning and 85 kg TSP per tonne of cement, current emissions are

$$\begin{aligned}
\text{Source 1:} \quad & 400{,}000\,(95) = 38{,}000{,}000 \text{ kg/yr} \\
\text{Source 2:} \quad & 300{,}000\,(95) = 28{,}500{,}000 \text{ kg/yr} \\
\text{Source 3:} \quad & 250{,}000\,(85) = 21{,}500{,}000 \text{ kg/yr} \\
& \text{Total} = 87{,}750{,}000 \text{ kg/yr}
\end{aligned}$$

This total discharge is to be reduced 80%, so maximum allowable emissions are 17,600,000 kg/yr.

Total TSP emissions are calculated from emission factors and efficiencies. For example, the annual TSP emissions from source 1 are

$$95X_{10} + 95(0.41)X_{11} + 95(0.06)X_{14} + 95(0.03)X_{15}$$
$$= 95X_{10} + 39X_{11} + 5.7X_{14} + 2.9X_{15}$$

TABLE 5-5 Decision Variables for Example 5-2

j (Control)	i (Source)		
	1	2	3
0	X_{10}	X_{20}	X_{30}
1	X_{11}	X_{21}	X_{31}
2	—	—	X_{32}
3	—	—	X_{33}
4	X_{14}	X_{24}	X_{34}
5	X_{15}	X_{25}	—

Emissions from other sources are calculated similarly, and the air pollution control objective is written as

$$95X_{10} + 39.0X_{11} + 5.7X_{14} + 2.9X_{15} + 95X_{20} + 39.0X_{21}$$
$$+ 5.7X_{24} + 2.9X_{25} + 85X_{30} + 34.9X_{31} + 22.1X_{32}$$
$$+ 13.6X_{33} + 5.1X_{34} \leq 17{,}600{,}000 \quad (5.68)$$

Since we do not have the option in this problem of changing production levels, mass balance equations should indicate that all the coal is burned and all the cement is produced. In terms of the decision variables, we have

$$X_{10} + X_{11} + X_{14} + X_{15} = 400{,}000 \quad (5.69)$$
$$X_{20} + X_{21} + X_{24} + X_{25} = 300{,}000 \quad (5.70)$$
$$X_{30} + X_{31} + X_{32} + X_{33} + X_{34} = 250{,}000 \quad (5.71)$$

The optimization model can now be written as

$$\text{Min } Z = 1.0X_{11} + 2.0X_{14} + 2.8X_{15} + 1.4X_{21} + 2.2X_{24}$$
$$+ 3.0X_{25} + 1.1X_{31} + 1.2X_{32} + 1.5X_{33} + 3.0X_{34} \quad (5.67)$$

s.t.
$$X_{10} + X_{11} + X_{14} + X_{15} = 400{,}000 \quad (5.69)$$
$$X_{20} + X_{21} + X_{24} + X_{25} = 300{,}000 \quad (5.70)$$
$$X_{30} + X_{31} + X_{32} + X_{33} + X_{34} = 250{,}000 \quad (5.71)$$
$$95X_{10} + 39.0X_{11} + 5.7X_{14} + 2.9X_{15} + 95X_{20} + 39.0X_{21}$$
$$+ 5.7X_{24} + 2.9X_{25} + 85X_{30} + 34.9X_{31} + 22.1X_{32}$$
$$+ 13.6X_{33} + 5.1X_{34} \leq 17{,}600{,}000 \quad (5.68)$$
$$X_{ij} \geq 0 \quad \forall\, i, j \quad (5.72)$$

The model has 13 decision variables. With this many variables, it would be very difficult to solve by trial and error. However, since the objective function and constraints are linear, the model is readily solved using linear programming. This was done using a computer program of the simplex method. The input coefficients for the program are listed in Table 5-6. These coefficients correspond to the standard form of an LP model (Expressions 5.22 to 5.24), and the coefficients of the objective function are all negative, since this is a minimization problem.

The optimal solution to the model, rounded to the nearest tonne is

$$X_{11}^* = 242{,}793 \text{ (settling chamber for source 1)}$$
$$X_{14}^* = 157{,}207 \text{ (scrubber for source 1)}$$
$$X_{24}^* = 300{,}000 \text{ (scrubber for source 2)}$$
$$X_{32}^* = 250{,}000 \text{ (multiple cyclone for source 3)}$$

118 LINEAR PROGRAMMING MODELS

TABLE 5-6 Coefficients for the Standard Form of the LP Model for Example 5-2

X_{10}	X_{11}	X_{14}	X_{15}	X_{20}	X_{21}	X_{24}	X_{25}	X_{30}	X_{31}	X_{32}	X_{33}	X_{34}	S_1		
0	−1	−2.0	−2.8	0	−1.4	−2.2	−3.0	0	−1.1	−1.2	−1.5	−3.0	0	=	Z
1	1	1	1	0	0	0	0	0	0	0	0	0	0	=	400,000
0	0	0	0	1	1	1	1	0	0	0	0	0	0	=	300,000
0	0	0	0	0	0	0	0	1	1	1	1	1	0	=	250,000
95.0	39.0	5.7	2.9	95.0	39.0	5.7	2.9	85.0	34.9	22.1	13.6	5.1	1	=	17,600,000

A portion of the TSP emissions from the first power plant are controlled by a settling chamber, and the remaining emissions are controlled by a scrubber. Emissions from the second power plant and the cement factory are controlled by a scrubber and multiple cyclone, respectively. Total TSP emissions are 17,600,000 kg/yr, and control costs are $Z^* = \$1,517,207/\text{yr}$.

Application of Duality

Although the solution to the LP model has provided a cost-effective emissions control plan, additional useful information can be provided from use of the simplex method. Suppose, for example, that the following is needed.

1. The quantities of coal burned (400,000 and 300,000 t/yr for sources 1 and 2, Equations 5.69 and 5.70) and cement manufactured (250,000 t/yr, Equation 5.71) are best estimates of future conditions. Either of these estimates may be in error, and the environmental control agency would like to determine the extent to which errors in these production estimates could affect the costs of the pollution control plan.
2. The emissions constraint of 17,600,000 kg/yr TSP is based on the assumption that an 80% reduction in emissions will also reduce TSP concentrations in the atmosphere by 80%. Staff members in the agency have questioned this assumption and are urging that a more stringent emissions control target be set. Conversely, the power utilities are arguing that a small relaxation of the constraint would save them substantial sums of money. The director of the agency must decide whether it would be reasonable to change the 17,600,000 kg/yr requirement. Before a decision is made, the director has requested that the costs of possible changes be evaluated.

A systems analyst must often provide much more than one or even several solutions to an environmental problem. Costs and technical data are frequently little more than rough approximations, and the level of an effluent or environmental standard is sometimes subject to political and scientific debate. The analyst should not react to this dynamic problem setting with a single static solution. Instead, the effects of changing

APPLICATION TO AIR POLLUTION CONTROL

conditions must frequently be anticipated by sensitivity analyses. Dual LP models can provide some of the required information. The agency's needs as given by the preceding points 1 and 2 can be partially met by knowledge of the marginal values associated with production requirements and the TSP emission constraint. These dual variables will indicate the cost increases or decreases associated with changes in production or maximum TSP emissions.

Before the dual of the air pollution model can be constructed, the model should first be written in the standard primal form (Expressions 5.50 and 5.51). Using the procedures outlined previously, the equivalent primal model is

$$\text{Max } (-Z) = -1.0X_{11} - 2.0X_{14} - 2.8X_{15} - 1.4X_{21} - 2.2X_{24}$$
$$- 3.0X_{25} - 1.1X_{31} - 1.2X_{32} - 1.5X_{33} - 3.0X_{34} \quad (5.67a)$$

s.t.
$$X_{10} + X_{11} + X_{14} + X_{15} \leq 400{,}000 \quad (5.69a)$$
$$-X_{10} - X_{11} - X_{14} - X_{15} \leq -400{,}000 \quad (5.69b)$$
$$X_{20} + X_{21} + X_{24} + X_{25} \leq 300{,}000 \quad (5.70a)$$
$$-X_{20} - X_{21} - X_{24} - X_{25} \leq -300{,}000 \quad (5.70b)$$
$$X_{30} + X_{31} + X_{32} + X_{33} + X_{34} \leq 250{,}000 \quad (5.71a)$$
$$-X_{30} - X_{31} - X_{32} - X_{33} - X_{34} \leq -250{,}000 \quad (5.71b)$$
$$95X_{10} + 39.0X_{11} + 5.7X_{14} + 2.9X_{15} + 95X_{20} + 39.0X_{21}$$
$$+ 5.7X_{24} + 2.9X_{25} + 85X_{30} + 34.9X_{31} + 22.1X_{32}$$
$$+ 13.6X_{33} + 5.1X_{34} \leq 17{,}600{,}000 \quad (5.68)$$
$$X_{ij} \geq 0 \quad \forall\, i, j \quad (5.72)$$

Each of the seven constraints has an associated dual variable, $Y_1, Y_2, \ldots, Y_7$. The dual model is determined somewhat more readily if the primal model is assembled in the tabular form shown in Table 5-7. The dual objective function is

$$\text{Min } z = 400{,}000Y_1 - 400{,}000Y_2 + 300{,}000Y_3 - 300{,}000Y_4$$
$$+ 250{,}000Y_5 - 250{,}000Y_6 + 17{,}600{,}000Y_7 \quad (5.73)$$

The coefficients for the first dual constraint are given by the first column in Table 5-7.

$$Y_1 - Y_2 + 95Y_7 \geq 0 \quad (5.74)$$

The second constraint is

$$Y_1 - Y_2 + 39.0Y_7 \geq -1 \quad (5.75)$$

Converting the right side to a positive number,

$$-Y_1 + Y_2 - 39.0Y_7 \leq 1 \quad (5.75a)$$

TABLE 5-7 Tabular Form of Primal LP Model for Example 5-1

X_{10}	X_{11}	X_{14}	X_{15}	X_{20}	X_{21}	X_{24}	X_{25}	X_{30}	X_{31}	X_{32}	X_{33}	X_{34}			Dual Variable
0	−1.0	−2.0	−2.8	0	−1.4	−2.2	−3.0	0	−1.1	−1.2	−1.5	−3.0	=	−Z	
1	1	1	1										≤	400,000	Y_1
−1	−1	−1	−1										≤	−400,000	Y_2
				1	1	1	1						≤	300,000	Y_3
				−1	−1	−1	−1						≤	−300,000	Y_4
								1	1	1	1	1	≤	250,000	Y_5
								−1	−1	−1	−1	−1	≤	−250,000	Y_6
95	39.0	5.7	2.9	95	39.0	5.7	2.9	85	34.9	22.1	13.6	5.1	≤	17,600,000	Y_7

The remaining constraints are derived similarly, and the complete dual LP model is

$$\text{Min } z = 400{,}000Y_1 - 400{,}000Y_2 + 300{,}000Y_3 - 300{,}000Y_4$$
$$+ 250{,}000Y_5 - 250{,}000Y_6 + 17{,}600{,}000Y_7 \quad (5.73)$$

s.t.

$$Y_1 - Y_2 \qquad\qquad\qquad + 95.0Y_7 \geq 0 \quad (5.74)$$
$$-Y_1 + Y_2 \qquad\qquad\qquad - 39.0Y_7 \leq 1.0 \quad (5.75a)$$
$$-Y_1 + Y_2 \qquad\qquad\qquad - 5.7Y_7 \leq 2.0 \quad (5.76)$$
$$-Y_1 + Y_2 \qquad\qquad\qquad - 2.9Y_7 \leq 2.8 \quad (5.77)$$
$$Y_3 - Y_4 \qquad\qquad + 95.0Y_7 \geq 0 \quad (5.78)$$
$$-Y_3 + Y_4 \qquad\qquad - 39.0Y_7 \leq 1.4 \quad (5.79)$$
$$-Y_3 + Y_4 \qquad\qquad - 5.7Y_7 \leq 2.2 \quad (5.80)$$
$$-Y_3 + Y_4 \qquad\qquad - 2.9Y_7 \leq 3.0 \quad (5.81)$$
$$Y_5 - Y_6 + 85.0Y_7 \geq 0 \quad (5.82)$$
$$-Y_5 + Y_6 - 34.9Y_7 \leq 1.1 \quad (5.83)$$
$$-Y_5 + Y_6 - 22.1Y_7 \leq 1.2 \quad (5.84)$$
$$-Y_5 + Y_6 - 13.6Y_7 \leq 1.5 \quad (5.85)$$
$$-Y_5 + Y_6 - 5.1Y_7 \leq 3.0 \quad (5.86)$$
$$-Y_1, Y_2, \ldots, Y_7 \geq 0$$

The interpretation of this dual LP model is somewhat more difficult than the case in the previous examples. Since the primal objective function was changed to a negative form (Equation 5.67a), we would expect the optimal value of the dual objective function also to be negative. Thus $z^* = -\$1,517,207 = -Z^*$. The real cost of emissions control is, of course, $Z^* = \$1,517,207$. Six of the dual variables occur everywhere in the model in pairs, and $Y_1^* - Y_2^*$, $Y_3^* - Y_4^*$, and $Y_5^* - Y_6^*$ are the marginal values (\$/t) associated with Constraints 5.69 to 5.71. These values (to the nearest \$0.01) are $Y_1^* = Y_3^* = Y_5^* = 0$, $Y_2^* = \$2.17$, $Y_4^* = \$2.37$, and $Y_6^* = \$1.86$; therefore $Y_1^* - Y_2^* = -\$2.17$, $Y_3^* - Y_4^* = -\$2.37$, and $Y_5^* - Y_6^* = -\$1.86$. For example, a unit increase in coal burning at the first power plant (Constraint 5.69), *decreases* z^* or $-Z^*$ by \$2.17. This is equivalent to a cost *increase* of \$2.17/t of coal burned. The three marginal values indicate the rates of change in emission control costs associated with increases (or decreases) in coal burning or cement production. The values are estimates of the sensitivity of control costs to production levels.

The final dual variable $Y_7^* = 0.03$ (again rounded to the nearest \$0.01) is the marginal cost (\$/kg) associated with Constraint 5.68. For example, if the TSP emission standard is raised from 17,600,000 kg/yr to 20,000,000 kg/yr, pollution control costs would be lowered by approximately[10] 0.03 (2,400,000) = \$72,000/yr.

GENERAL LINEAR PROGRAMMING MODELS FOR AIR QUALITY MANAGEMENT

Proportional Rollback Models

The previous emissions control problem is an example of a situation frequently encountered in air quality management: the reduction of total emissions within some geographic region by the installation of controls at the various sources. Although specific characteristics of sources, controls, and pollutants will vary, problems of this type can often be described by LP models that have the same basic structure. A general optimization model can be formulated that applies to many different air quality problems.

$$\text{Min } Z = \sum_{i=1}^{m} \sum_{j=1}^{n} c_{ij} X_{ij} \qquad (5.87)$$

s.t.
$$\sum_{j=1}^{n} a_{ij} X_{ij} = S_i \qquad i = 1, 2, \ldots, m \qquad (5.88)$$

$$\sum_{i=1}^{m} \sum_{j=1}^{n} b_{ijp} X_{ij} \leq A_p \qquad p = 1, 2, \ldots, q \qquad (5.89)$$

$$X_{ij} \geq 0 \qquad \forall\, i, j$$

---

[10]The estimated cost reduction is "approximate," since marginal values are based on unit changes in constraint limits. When these marginal costs are extrapolated to large increases or decreases in constraint limits, the resulting estimated total changes in the optimal value of an objective function may not be exact. Most computer programs of the simplex method determine the ranges of changes in constraint limits within which the optimal values of dual variables will stay the same.

The model includes m sources, n emission control methods, and q air pollutants. The decision variable X_{ij} is the number of units of production (e.g., t/yr of coal), with emission control j at source i.

The objective function and constraints are comparable to those in the three-source example. The objective function Z (Equation 5.87) is annual costs of emission controls, where c_{ij} is the unit cost ($/production unit) of control j at source i. Constraint 5.88 is analogous to Constraints 5.69 to 5.71 and requires that the total production requirement of S_i units be met at source i. The coefficients a_{ij} are equal to one if control j is feasible at source i and zero otherwise. The emission control objectives are given by Constraint 5.89. This constraint applies to each of q air pollutants and requires the total emissions of the pth air pollutant to be less than some maximum level A_p. The emission of pollutant p from source i with control j is b_{ijp}. If control j is not possible for source i, $b_{ijp} = 0$.

When the general model is used in a specific problem setting, the coefficients c_{ij}, a_{ij}, and b_{ijp} must be determined as well as the production requirements S_i and emission control standards A_p. When applied to an urban region, the model may have a large number of variables and constraints. For example, in an application to St. Louis, 94 sources and five air pollutants (TSP, SO_2, CO, NO_2, and HC) were considered.[11]

Air Pollution Transport Models

Proportional rollback models assume that pollutant concentrations in the atmosphere are proportional to total emissions. However, concentrations can be estimated at arbitrary locations (receptors) by means of air pollution transport models. A number of models are available, but the most commonly used is a Gaussian dispersion equation. An arbitrary air pollution source is shown in Figure 5-4. A three-dimensional coordi-

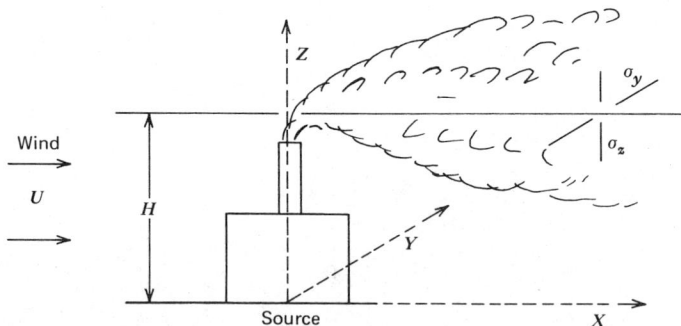

Figure 5-4 Definition diagram for air pollution dispersion model.

---

[11] R. E. Kohn, "Application of Linear Programming to a Controversy on Air Pollution Control," *Management Science*, Vol. 17, No. 10, 1971, pp. B609–B621.

nate system is defined with the origin at the pollution source. The X-coordinate is parallel to the wind direction, Z is the distance above the ground, and Y is measured perpendicular to X.

If we assume a "well-behaved" emission plume, air pollutant particles will have a Gaussian distribution about the plume centerline, which is located a distance H above the ground. For a steady-state (constant) rate of emission, we can estimate the ground-level pollutant concentration at any downwind rceptor (see Figure 5-5). This concentration is given by

$$C(x, y) = \frac{Q}{\pi U \sigma_y \sigma_z} \exp\left(\frac{-y^2}{2\sigma_y^2} - \frac{H^2}{2\sigma_z^2}\right) \quad (5.90)$$

where

$C(x, y)$ = ground-level pollutant concentration (g/m³) at point x, y
x = downwind distance from source (m)
y = crosswind distance from source (m)
U = mean wind speed (m/sec)
Q = pollutant emission rate (g/sec)
H = vertical elevation of plume center (m)
σ_z = standard deviation of plume concentration in vertical (Z) direction (m)
σ_y = standard deviation of plume concentration in horizontal (Y) direction (m)

The plume deviations σ_y and σ_z are horizontal (σ_y) and vertical (σ_z) dispersion

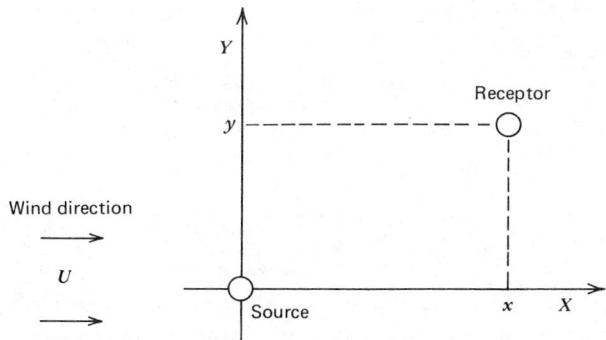

Figure 5-5 Location of a receptor (x, y) downwind of an air pollution emission.

124 LINEAR PROGRAMMING MODELS

coefficients and are functions of both meteorologic conditions and downwind distance (Figures 5-6 and 5-7 and Table 5-8).

Equation 5.90 is a useful management tool, since it establishes a cause-and-effect relationship between air pollution emissions and resulting air quality at ground level (presumably air pollution does most damage at ground levels). To use the equation, a set of meteorologic conditions must be known (wind speed U and one of the conditions A to F in Table 5-8). Also, the plume height or "effective stack height" H must be estimated. Equation 5.90 can be modified, if necessary, to account for decay of pollutants during transport by chemical reactions.

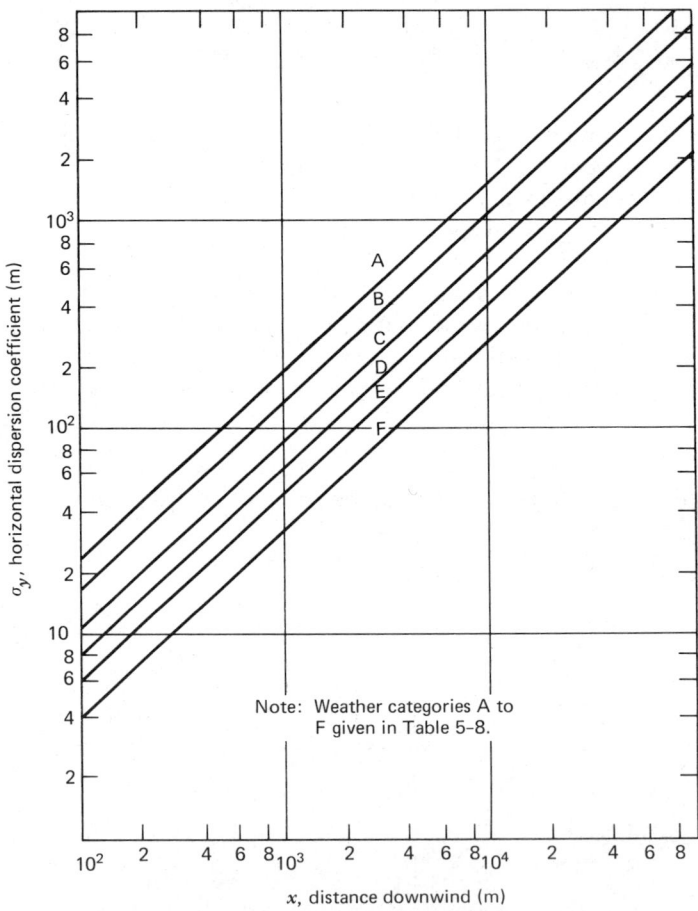

Figure 5-6 Horizontal dispersion coefficients as function of downwind distance and weather categories. (*Source.* Gifford, F. A., Jr., "Use of Routine Meteorological Observations for Estimating Atmospheric Dispersion," *Nuclear Safety,* 2(4):47–51, 1961.)

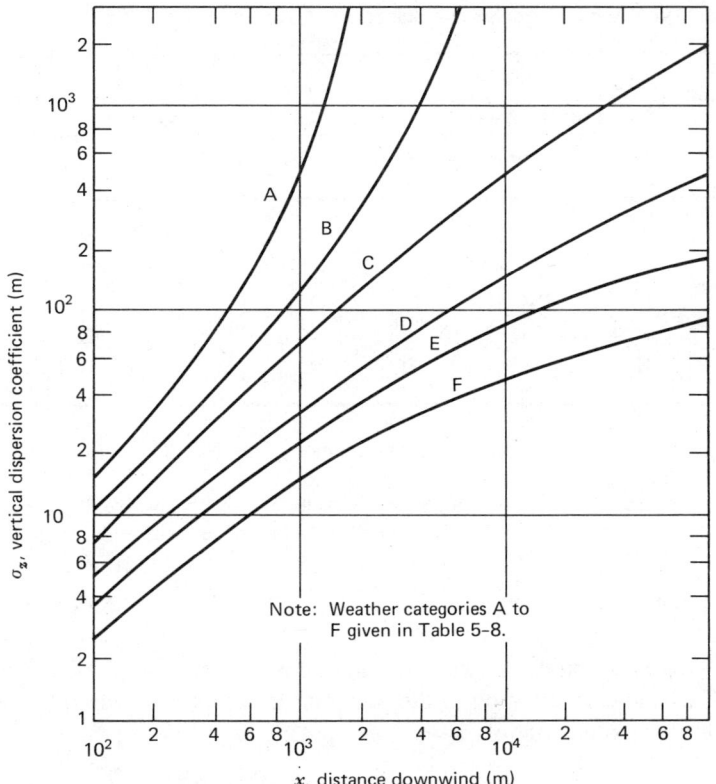

Figure 5-7 Vertical dispersion coefficients as function of downwind distance and weather categories. (*Source.* Gifford, F. A., Jr., "Use of Routine Meteorological Observations for Estimating Atmospheric Dispersion," *Nuclear Safety,* 2(4):47–51, 1961.)

When transport equations such as Equation 5.90 are incorporated into LP air quality models, the proportional rollback assumption is no longer necessary. The focus of management becomes cost-effective control of ground-level concentrations and not reduction of total emissions. Using the notation of the earlier general model (Expressions 5.87 to 5.89), emissions of pollutant p from source i with control j are $b_{ijp}X_{ij}$. If the coefficients b_{ijp} are chosen so that emissions are in g/sec, the ground-level concentration of the pollutant at some downwind location k because of the emission at source i is $t_{ik}b_{ijp}X_{ij}$. The transport factor t_{ik} is determined from Equation 5.90 as

$$t_{ik} = \frac{1}{\pi U \sigma_y \sigma_z} \exp\left(\frac{-y_{ik}^2}{2\sigma_y^2} - \frac{H_i^2}{2\sigma_z^2}\right) \qquad (5.91)$$

In this equation y_{ik} is the crosswind distance (m) between the source i and receptor k, H_i is the effective stack height (m) of source i, and the dispersion coefficients σ_y and

TABLE 5-8 Weather Categories for Selection of Dispersion Coefficients

Surface Wind Speed (m/sec)	Daytime Insolation			Nighttime Conditions	
	Strong	Moderate	Slight	≥ 4/8 Cloud Cover	≤ 3/8 Cloud Cover
<2	A	A-B	B	—	—
2	A-B	B	C	E	F
4	B	B-C	C	D	E
6	C	C-D	D	D	D
>6	C	D	D	D	D

Source. F. A. Gifford, Jr., "Use of Routine Meteorological Observations for Estimating Atmospheric Dispersion," *Nuclear Safety,* Vol. 2, No. 4, pp. 47–51, 1961.
Categories: A—extremely unstable; B—moderately unstable; C—slightly unstable; D—neutral (applicable to heavy overcast, day or night); E—slightly stable; and F—moderately stable.

σ_z (m) are functions of x_{ik}, the downwind distance (m) between source i and receptor k.

For a stationary source and receptor and known meteorologic conditions, t_{ik} is a constant. The total concentration of the pollutant at receptor k caused by m emission sources with n possible controls is

$$\sum_{i=1}^{m} \sum_{j=1}^{n} t_{ik} b_{ijp} X_{ij}$$

where t_{ik} is given by Equation 5.91 if source i is upwind of receptor k and $t_{ik} = 0$ otherwise. If C_{pk} is the air quality concentration standard (g/m³) for pollutant p at location k, the associated air quality constraint is

$$\sum_{i=1}^{m} \sum_{j=1}^{n} t_{ik} b_{ijp} X_{ij} \leq C_{pk} \qquad (5.92)$$

We can now reformulate the general air pollution control model as

$$\text{Min } Z = \sum_{i=1}^{m} \sum_{j=1}^{n} c_{ij} X_{ij} \qquad (5.87)$$

s.t.
$$\sum_{j=1}^{n} a_{ij} X_{ij} = S_i \qquad i = 1, 2, \ldots, m \qquad (5.88)$$

$$\sum_{i=1}^{m} \sum_{j=1}^{n} t_{ik} b_{ijp} X_{ij} \leq C_{pk} \qquad \begin{matrix} p = 1, 2, \ldots, q \\ k = 1, 2, \ldots, r \end{matrix} \qquad (5.92)$$

$$X_{ij} \geq 0$$

In this model,

X_{ij} = units of production at source i controlled by method j
c_{ij} = annual cost of control j at source i (\$/unit of production)
a_{ij} = 1 if control j is possible at source i and 0 otherwise
S_i = production units required at source i
b_{ijp} = emissions of pollutant p at source i if control j is used (g/sec/unit of production); $b_{ijp} = 0$ if $a_{ij} = 0$
t_{ik} = transport factor for source i and receptor k
C_{pk} = air quality standard for pollutant p at receptor k (g/m^3)

The decision variables in the model are X_{ij} and, since all remaining parameters are constants, the model is linear. This general model has m sources, n control methods, q pollutants, and r receptors or ground-level locations for which air quality standards must be met.

The two general air pollution models can be applied to a variety of air quality management problems. In any given problem the formulation of an LP model and solution by the simplex method are relatively easy. However, before a model can be solved, all of its parameters must be determined, and this is usually an extremely difficult task. The gathering of costs and emissions data is very time consuming; when pollution transport is also considered, many months of data collection and analysis may be necessary before model solutions can be generated.

Summary

Linear programming (LP) provides a powerful means of solving linear optimization models. Optimal solutions can be rapidly determined, even for large models, using readily available computer programs of the simplex method. The simplex method also provides solutions to dual LP models, and the marginal values that correspond to optimal dual variables often produce information that is useful in sensitivity analyses. A variety of environmental problems can be described by LP models. One example is air quality management; two general LP models for air pollution control were developed in this chapter. They differed substantially from the models presented in earlier chapters, since they are not specific to a given problem setting. Instead, the same general models can be applied to various geographic areas, pollutants, sources, and control technologies.

SELECTED REFERENCES

1. Burton, E. S., E. H. Pechan III, and W. Sanjour, "A Survey of Air Pollution Control Models," in R. A. Deininger (editor), *Models for Environmental Pollution Control,* Ann Arbor Science Publishers, Ann Arbor, Mich., 1973, pp. 219–235.
2. Dantzig, G. B., *Linear Programming and Extensions,* Princeton University Press, Princeton, N.J., 1963.

3. Davis, M. L., *Air Resource Management Primer*, American Society of Civil Engineers, New York, 1973.
4. Gass, S. I., *Linear Programming: Methods and Applications*, 4th ed., McGraw-Hill, New York, 1975.
5. Gustafson, S. A., and K. O. Kortanek, "On the Calculation of Optimal Long-Term Air Pollution Abatement Strategies for Multiple Source Areas," in C. A. Brebbia (editor), *Mathematical Models for Environmental Problems*, Wiley, New York, 1976, pp. 161–171.
6. Hadley, G., *Linear Programming*, Addison-Wesley, Reading, Mass., 1962.
7. Hillier, F. S., and G. J. Lieberman, *Operations Research*, 2nd ed., Holden-Day, San Francisco, 1974, Chapters 2 to 4.
8. Kohn, R. E., *A Linear Programming Model for Air Pollution Control*, MIT Press, Cambridge, Mass., 1978.
9. Sauter, G. D., "A Generic Survey of Air Quality Simulation Models," in W. R. Ott (editor), *Environmental Modeling and Simulation*, U.S. Environmental Protection Agency, Washington, D.C., 1976, pp. 30–34.
10. Teller, A., "The Use of Linear Programming to Estimate the Cost of Some Alternative Air Pollution Abatement Policies," *Proceedings*, IBM Scientific Computing Symposium, Water and Air Resource Management, International Business Machines, Inc., White Plains, N.Y., 1968, pp. 345–353.
11. Thompson, G.E., *Linear Programming*, MacMillan, New York, 1971.
12. Trijonis, J. C., "Economic Air Pollution Control Model for Los Angeles County in 1975," *Environmental Science and Technology*, Vol. 8, No. 9, 1974, pp. 811–826.

EXERCISES

NOTE. Many of the following exercises require a computer and a simplex method program.

5-1

This exercise is basically a simple variation of the wastewater management example used in Chapters 1 and 2 (Example 1-1). A metal refining factory has a capacity of 10 10^4 kg/wk, produces waste at the rate of 3 kg/kg of product, contained in wastewater at a concentration of 2 kg/m^3. The factory's waste treatment plant operates at a constant efficiency of 0.85 and has a capacity of 8 10^4m^3/wk. Wastewater is discharged into a river, and the effluent standard is 100,000 kg/wk. There is also an effluent charge of $1000/$10^4$ kg discharged. Treatment costs are $1000/$10^4$m^3, product sales price is $10,000/$10^4$ kg, and production costs are $6850/$10^4$ kg. Construct a linear optimization model that can be used to solve this wastewater problem. Solve the model graphically.

If the effluent charge is raised to $2000/10^4$ kg, by how much will the waste discharge be reduced?

5-2.

A city wishes to combine employment and environmental objectives in its use of $15 million of federal funds and $10 million in state funds. These monies are to be used to control water pollution from urban runoff by either (a) street cleaning, or (b) sewer flushing. Street cleaning generates 40 jobs/$1 million expenditure and sewer flushing produces 30 jobs/$1 million. The federal government will finance 50% of the street cleaning and 75% of the sewer flushing costs, respectively. The remaining costs will be borne by the state. Construct an LP model that can be used to determine how the city should spend the $25 million. Solve the model graphically.

5-3.

Savesome Enterprises has conducted a study of its manufacturing operations with the goal of reducing liquid and solid waste production. The plant in question produces whirlies, floomers, and arps. Net profits are $1 per whirly, $0.80 per floomer, and $1.30 per arp. These three products produce varying amounts of wastes.

Product	Liquid Wastes (m^3/unit)	Solid Wastes (kg/unit)
Whirly	2.0	1.0
Floomer	1.5	1.2
Arp	2.6	0.9

There are minimum sales commitments of 5000 whirlies/day and 3000 arps/day. Savesome has decided to limit waste production to no more than 70,000 m^3/day of liquid waste and 30,000 kg/day of solid waste.

Determine an optimal product mix for the plant using LP.

5-4.

Suppose the fixed sales commitments for the Savesome plant in Exercise 5-3 no longer have to be met.

(a) Determine an optimal product mix. Why are only two products produced?
(b) Construct the dual LP model for this problem. Solve the dual model graphically. Based on the dual solution, which waste limit (liquid or solid) has the most effect on plant profits?

5-5.

Solve the following LP model.

$$\text{Min } Z = 10X_1 + 13X_2 + 4X_3 - 7X_4$$

s.t.
$$X_1 + 2X_2 + X_3 \geq 6$$
$$0.5X_1 - X_2 + 3X_3 + 0.4X_4 \leq 10$$
$$4X_1 + 7X_2 \qquad\qquad - X_4 \geq 12$$
$$-2X_1 \qquad\qquad\qquad + 1.5X_4 \leq 7$$
$$X_1, X_2, X_3, X_4 \geq 1.0$$

5-6.

Consider the following model.

$$\text{Max } Z = 2X_1 + 12X_2$$

s.t.
$$X_1 + 2X_2 \leq 20$$
$$X_1 + X_2 \leq 13$$
$$X_1 - X_2 \geq 6$$

Write the dual of this problem. Solve the primal graphically or by using a computer program. Solve the dual. Summarize the properties of primal and dual solutions and see if your solutions have these properties. If one of the primal constraints could be relaxed, which one should be relaxed to have a maximum effect on the primal objective function?

5-7.

Reuse of treated wastewater is a viable option to disposal in water bodies. It can also be an important means of conserving community water supplies. Choking Dust, Utah, wishes to evaluate reuse options for treated sewage from its municipal sewage treatment plant (STP). Average daily flow to the STP is Q (m³). The cost of running the STP is C_T ($/m³). Three reuse options have been identified: municipal water supply, industrial water supply, and cooling water for power plants. Before wastewater can be reused in any of these options, however, additional treatment is necessary. The municipal water supply company will pay r_1 ($/m³) for the wastewater, provided it receives additional treatment at cost c_1 ($/m³). The company presently supplies W m³/day of water and estimates that wastewater could substitute for up to 30% of this supply. Additional treatment for both industrial and cooling use can be provided by a single treatment process at cost of C ($/m³). The process cannot be implemented on a small scale, however. In fact, the process is not effective for daily flows of less than E (m^3). Industry will pay r_2 ($/m^3) for the water but can use no more than I (m^3/day). Power companies can use a maximum of P_{max} (m^3/day) and will pay r_3 ($/m^3). However, they will not participate in the project unless they are guaranteed of at least P_{min} (m^3/day).

Show how LP can be used to develop a water recycling program.

5-8.

A new pesticide has been developed that is effective in controlling corn, soybean and wheat pests. As a result of field experiments, the following crop yields have been obtained.

Pesticide Application (kg/ha)	Crop Yields (kg/ha)		
	Soybeans	Wheat	Corn
0	2700	3500	5400
1.0	3800	4100	5700
2.0	4400	2700	7900

Total annual costs of production, *not including pesticide applications,* are $250, $200, and $300/ha for soybeans, wheat, and corn, respectively. Pesticide application costs are $30/ha/yr for any crops at all application rates greater than zero. Current selling prices for soybeans, wheat, and corn are $0.18, $0.15, and $0.11/kg, respectively.

Environmental authorities have, however, expressed concern over the pesticide's ecological impacts and have ruled that a farmer's *average* application rate on corn, soybeans, and wheat cannot exceed 1 kg/ha [i.e., total pesticide applied to all three crops (kg) divided by total cropped area (ha) must not exceed 1 kg/ha].

A farmer has 100 ha that can be planted to soybeans, wheat, and corn. Use a linear programming model to determine how many hectares should be planted to each crop and what the pesticide application rates should be.

5-9.

High levels of the toxic substance chlororadiated ureadicarboxyl (CRUD) have been observed in the Riley River. Environmental authorities have set a standard of 1 kg/10^{3}m^3 as the maximum allowable CRUD concentration in the river. The three major CRUD dischargers are shown in the figure. As indicated, the river has a flow of 500,000 m^3/day and a CRUD concentration of 0.2 kg/10^{3}m^3 upstream of the first discharge. The three waste sources presently discharge 1000, 1000, and 1600 kg/day of CRUD, resulting in violations of the CRUD standard in the river.

132 LINEAR PROGRAMMING MODELS

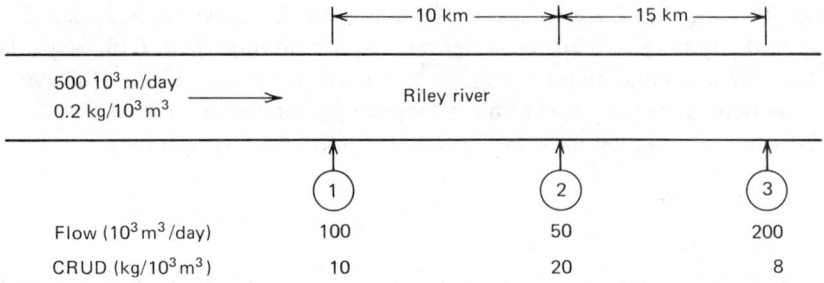

CRUD is not conserved in the river, but decays exponentially at a rate of $K = 0.03$ km^{-1}. Thus, if C_1 and C_2 are the CRUD concentrations immediately after discharges 1 and 2, respectively, the CRUD concentration at any point L km downstream of discharge 1 ($L \leq 10$) is $C_1 e^{-KL}$. Similarly, the CRUD concentration L km below discharge 2 ($L \leq 15$) is $C_2 e^{-KL}$. The cost of removing CRUD from wastewater is $\$50X/1000$ m^3 where X is the fraction of CRUD removed.

Use linear programming to determine an optimal CRUD treatment program.

5-10.

Show that Exercise 3-3 can be solved using linear programming; that is, show that the optimization model has the general form

$$\text{Max} \sum_{j=1}^{n} c_j X_j$$

s.t.

$$\sum_{j=1}^{n} a_{ij} X_j = b_i, \quad i = 1, 2, \ldots, m$$

$$X_j \geq 0 \; \forall j$$

5-11.

An air quality management plan is being developed for the purpose of controlling SO$_2$ concentrations in a city. Since the major sources of SO$_2$ emissions are stationary heating plants, it has been decided to focus on these sources and, in particular, on the use of fuel substitutions as control options. Fossil fuels differ significantly in their sulfur contents and hence in the SO$_2$ emissions produced. Three types of fuels are available for use at the m sources in the community. The required heat production at source i is R_i (Cal/day), and the heat content of fuel j when burned at source i is k_{ij} (Cal/t). The associated cost is c_{ij} (\$/t) and the SO$_2$ emission is b_{ij} (g/t). If an SO$_2$ standard of C (g/m^3) is set for each of r ground-level air pollution monitoring stations, construct an LP model that can be used to develop a cost-effective SO$_2$ control plan.

5-12.

Write the dual of the general proportional rollback LP model (Expressions 5.87, 5.88, and 5.89). Suppose the relevant decision maker wants you to explain the significance of the dual model. What would you say? Note that the decision maker is neither an economist nor engineer, and terms such as "marginal value of resources, total resource value," and the like would mean very little, so you must provide an explanation that is nontechnical and free of jargon.

CHAPTER 6
APPLICATION: MANAGEMENT OF AGRICULTURAL NONPOINT SOURCE POLLUTION[1]

The understanding of environmental systems analysis is aided by simple examples. Such examples capture the spirit of the subject but can be misleading. Actual (as opposed to hypothetical) problems are more difficult to model and solve. The intent of Chapter 3 was to illustrate the level of detail often required in the analysis of real environmental problems. The objective of this chapter is similar. A linear programming (LP) model is presented that has been used for the analysis of agricultural nonpoint source water pollution. The model incorporates many of the complexities of this type of pollution and is based on real economic, physical, and biological data. Control of nonpoint sources is important to both environmental and agricultural planning since, in many areas of the world, control of agricultural nonpoint source pollution is a necessary part of water quality management.

The use of LP to analyze agricultural nonpoint pollution is a logical extension of a history of agricultural LP applications. LP is often used to evaluate alternative farm management decisions and government agricultural policies. The technique is a standard analytical tool for the agricultural economist, and the model in this chapter introduces the application of systems analysis to agricultural planning.

NONPOINT SOURCE WATER POLLUTION

General Description

Nonpoint or diffuse source water pollution is a major water quality problem. Nonpoint source pollution is a result of drainage of precipitation waters into groundwater aquifers or surface waters such as streams and rivers. As indicated in Figure 6-1, when precipitation falls on the land surface, portions of the water may travel across the land as runoff to surface waters or percolate downward through the soil and enter a groundwater aquifer. When runoff and percolation come in contact with wastes on the land or

---

[1]Portions of this chapter were adapted from D. A. Haith and D. W. Atkinson, "A Linear Programming Model for Dairy Farm Nutrient Management," in R. C. Loehr (editor), *Food, Fertilizer and Agricultural Residues*, Ann Arbor Science Publishers, Ann Arbor, Michigan, 1977, pp. 319–337.

136 AGRICULTURAL NONPOINT SOURCE POLLUTION

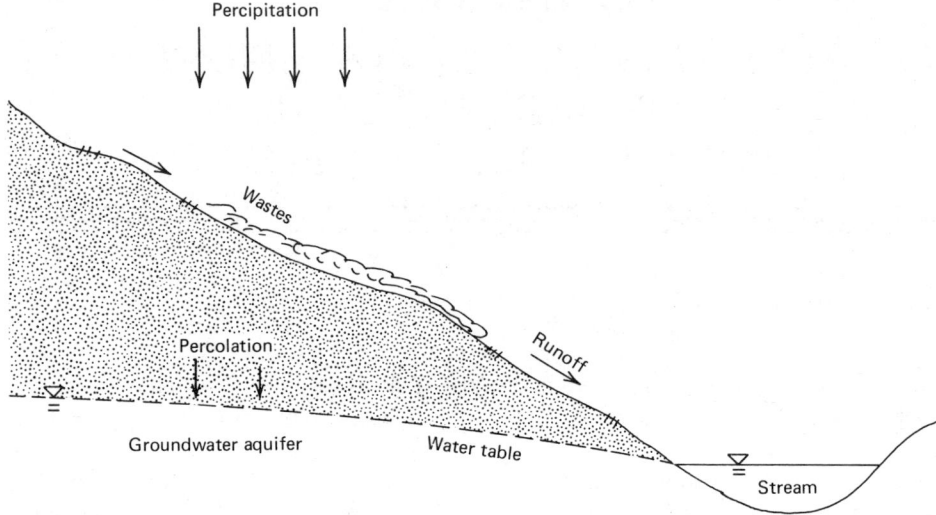

Figure 6-1 Components of nonpoint source pollution.

within the soil, some of the wastes are washed into surface or groundwater bodies. Although the wastes in Figure 6-1 are shown as a discrete pile or layer, they are more commonly dispersed as fertilizers, pesticides, heavy metals, and other toxic substances.

When contaminated with wastes, runoff and percolation are wastewaters in the same sense that the effluents from sewers and sewage treatment plants are wastewaters. However, the latter are *point sources*, since they are discharged to a river or stream at a discrete "point" or location from a pipe or channel. Conversely, polluted runoff and percolation discharges are *nonpoint* or *diffuse*, since they enter water bodies through a number of dispersed and often poorly defined drainage paths. Unless the runoff and percolation is collected by some artificial means (e.g., sewers in urban areas), it may not be possible to remove nonpoint source pollutants by means of a treatment plant. Instead, combinations of measures to reduce runoff and percolation or to limit the availability of waste substances are necessary.

Control of nonpoint source water pollution is more difficult than treatment of point sources; the former can originate in many places in the landscape, and a mixture of control measures is often needed. Nonpoint source pollution is a complex problem, and systems analysis is an important means of developing management programs for both urban and agricultural areas. Since urban runoff is generally collected in either separate storm sewers or combined sanitary and storm sewers, nonpoint source control often involves collection and subsequent partial treatment of runoff. An example of the use of systems analysis for urban problems is given in Exercise 6-3 at the end of this chapter.

Control of Agricultural Nonpoint Source Pollution

Control of agricultural nonpoint sources usually requires some adjustment of farm management decisions such as the cropping selections in the pesticide management examples of Chapters 2 and 5 (Examples 2-1 and 5-1). However, those examples were based on a simplistic view of the nonpoint source problem. Although it is sometimes possible to manage agricultural nonpoint source pollution by a simple adjustment of cropping decisions, a more realistic analysis must include an evaluation of the impact of pollution control on the entire farm enterprise. A farm is a complex system of interacting activities that compete for labor, land, and capital resources, and it can be difficult to isolate activities such as fertilizer and pesticide management from the rest of the farm operation. The imposition of environmental controls can affect farming components that are not directly related to the source of pollution. For example, banning of a specific pesticide may reduce crop yields and force reductions of livestock herds fed by the crop.

The effects of environmental regulations on agricultural production are of general concern, since the maintenance or enhancement of food and fiber production is an important social goal in most, if not all, countries. It is seldom politically feasible to implement environmental controls that severely reduce farm income. For this reason the development of plans to control agricultural nonpoint source water pollution requires assessment of the economic impacts of controls on farmers. Because of the complexities of farm systems, one of the few feasible means of making an assessment is to construct mathematical models of farms. The models are generally income-maximizing LP models of actual or representative farms. The models are manipulated by imposing selective constraints on nonpoint source pollution losses and observing the effects of these constraints on farm income. Control programs are selected that result in small income losses, or government subsidies are used to minimize reductions in income.

PROBLEM DESCRIPTION

EXAMPLE 6-1
A national planning agency must develop management programs for the control of agricultural nonpoint sources. The agency has divided agricultural enterprises into several categories, one of which is dairy farming. Agency representatives have requested a research organization to assist them in evaluating controls for nonpoint sources of nutrients (nitrogen and phosphorus) and sediment from dairy farms. Specifically, the research group has been asked to (1) develop a general model that can be used by the agency to estimate both nutrient and sediment loadings from farms and the economic impact of controls for these pollutants, and (2) demonstrate the methodology by application to representative dairy farms. □

This example illustrates a context for the systems approach that is somewhat different from the examples of the previous chapters. Systems analysis is often a research activity, with less emphasis placed on the solution of a single immediate problem than on the development of a method or model that can be used to investigate a variety of situations. The management of nonpoint source pollution from one isolated farm is of little interest to a national agency. Instead, the agency would expect that application of a model to a number of different farms would provide information that could be used to formulate a program for pollution control for dairy farms in general. This type of analysis is often used by planning and regulatory agencies to develop policies for dealing with environmental problems.

Dairy Farm Activities

A dairy farm contains many related components, but the principal ones are land, crops, and livestock. A farmer's land usually consists of several soils that differ in their suitability for crops. Because of variations in fertility, drainage, and slope, yields of a crop are not the same for all soils, and certain crops may not even be possible on a specific soil. Cropping costs also vary significantly with soil type. In selecting crops a farmer matches the needs of livestock for energy and protein with capabilities of the available soils. Crops differ in energy and protein levels and, depending on the soils on which they are grown, also have different fertilizer requirements. Certain crops are often grown in rotations; since the rotations cover several years, the farmer must make crop and soil selections with long-term needs in mind. Livestock management is the most complicated aspect of dairy farming because it involves many decisions, including feeding programs, breeding, housing, cow replacement, and maintaining animal health. Not the least of the farmer's problems is the disposal of manure. Although manure is an excellent fertilizer, it is expensive to handle and, depending on crop selections, fields may not always be available for disposal.

Nonpoint Source Pollution from Dairy Farms

Nonpoint source losses of sediment, nitrogen, and phosphorus from dairy farms are due to cropland erosion and the washing away of unused nutrients from fertilizers and manures. Eroded soil moves as sediment in runoff to streams, where it affects aquatic life and recreational and water supply uses of streams, rivers, and lakes. Erosion varies greatly with crops and management. A close-grown crop such as a grass or legume hay protects the soil surface and prevents erosion, but a row crop such as corn leaves the soil uncovered during much of the year, and frequent tillage makes soil particles susceptible to erosion.

Nitrogen and phosphorus can accelerate plant and algae growth in lakes, reservoirs, and estuaries; this leads to the eutrophication of these waters. In addition nitrogen, in the form of nitrate, can contaminate groundwaters and make them unsafe for water supply use. Since crops need nitrogen and phosphorus for growth, farmers usually supplement the natural sources of these nutrients in the soil with fertilizer and manure applications. The applied nutrients not taken up by the crop are "wastes" which, as indicated in Figure 6-1, can leave cropland through runoff and percolation. Both nitrogen and phosphorus may move with runoff in dissolved forms or in solid-phase or particulate forms associated with sediment. Dissolved nutrients are also transported by percolation.

Nonpoint source sediment, nitrogen, and phosphorus losses can seldom be eliminated from the dairy farm, but they can be reduced. Soil and water conservation practices such as contouring, terracing, and conservation tillage reduce erosion and runoff and thus reduce sediment and nutrient losses in runoff. Crop rotations of legumes and row crops reduce the need for nitrogen fertilizer applications. Crops can be selected that have low erosion rates. Fertilizer and manure applications can be controlled to provide only the nutrients needed by crops. However, any of these controls can impact on farm operations and income. A farmer cannot arbitrarily change rotations without considering the effects on livestock nutrition. Manure applications to a field can be reduced but, unless the size of the livestock herd is also reduced, the quantity of manure to be disposed of remains the same, and other fields must receive increased applications.

Limitations of the Systems Appraoch

This brief overview of dairy farming indicates that the systems analyst faces a difficult task in constructing a model for management of nonpoint source pollution. A complete model of a dairy farm would be so complicated that it could be a very awkward tool for analysis of pollution control alternatives. Data and computer requirements would likely require such extensive use of time, money, and manpower that it would be impossible to apply the model to a large number of farms. Furthermore, it is questionable whether busy agency personnel would have time to understand the characteristics of the model. Without such understanding, they might have little confidence in model output and, although the systems analyst may have constructed a very accurate model, the entire effort would be largely wasted.

This situation unfortunately occurs frequently and creates a severe credibility problem for systems analysts. Once a potential user has been exposed to a lengthy and expensive modeling project that produces little useful information, he or she is understandably reluctant to place much confidence in the systems approach. Modeling can be a fascinating intellectual exercise, and the systems analyst is sometimes so involved in the refinement of models that the essential goal of problem solving is forgotten.

The best model for a given problem is often the simplest, since it is usually comprehensible and consistent with available data. In the present case, this may mean ignoring many of the activities of a dairy farm that do not have significant environmental/economic interactions. For example, livestock manure production and nutritional requirements are important constraints on crop selection which, in turn, greatly affects sediment and nutrient losses. Conversely, timing of breeding, calf housing, and the cow culling (replacement) program are all important to a dairy farmer's success but have little impact on pollutant losses. The first set of herd activities (nutrition, manure) must be included in a model for nonpoint source management, but the second set (breeding, calves, culling) does not. Even though the model will not be an accurate mathematical description of dairy herd management, it will approximate the herd's effects on sediment and nutrient losses.

SYSTEMS ANALYSIS

Definition of System and Objectives

The primary decision maker in agricultural management problems is usually assumed to be an independent farmer, and the associated objective is maximization of net income or revenue. With pollution control constraints, an additional decision maker is a social authority that sets allowable levels of pollutant losses. This second decision maker and the associated objectives are generally artificial, however. Nonpoint source pollution is seldom regulated by effluent-type limitations. Constraint levels are manipulated to determine what farm management practices can economically reduce pollutant losses. For example, for modeling purposes we can impose a constraint on the total sediment loss from a farm and, by changing the constraint level, observe the costs of achieving reductions in sediment loss. The ultimate regulatory program is not likely to be an effluent standard on sediment. Instead, a set of management practices, with government subsidies if necessary, will be recommended or required. In the present problem, constraints are placed on erosion (and hence sediment) loss, dissolved and solid-phase nitrogen and phosphorus losses in runoff, and the total potential nitrogen loss. Therefore for modeling purposes, there are seven objectives.

1. Maximize farm net income ($/yr).
2. Limit dissolved losses of nitrogen in runoff to DN (kg/ha-yr).
3. Limit dissolved losses of phosphorus in runoff to DP (kg/ha-yr).
4. Limit solid-phase losses of nitrogen in runoff to SN (kg/ha-yr).
5. Limit solid-phase losses of phosphorus in runoff to SP (kg/ha-yr).
6. Limit total nitrogen losses from cropland to N (kg/ha-yr).
7. Limit sediment loss (erosion) from cropland to S (t/ha-yr).

Since we are concerned with *changes* in net income associated with pollution control, only variable costs and returns need be included in net income. Fixed costs associated with buildings, land, taxes, and the like, are assumed to be unrelated to pollution controls. The nutrient and sediment loss limits DN, DP, SN, SP, N and S are fixed in any one run of the LP model, but they are systematically varied in sensitivity analyses to observe effects on farm income.

The definition of the dairy farm system determines the complexity of the optimization model. To obtain a simple model, the complexity of a dairy farm must be reduced to several basic processes that determine income and pollution losses. This is much easier said than done, and the process that leads to a simple model often involves trial-and-error formulation of models of varying complexity. For this example the modeling iterations produced the simple view of the dairy farm system shown in Figure 6-2.[2] The dairy farm is reduced to a system with two primary components. The livestock component transforms nutrient inputs from crops and feed purchases into a

---

[2] The model presented in this chapter is a result of several iterations. The first and most complex model is given in D. R. Coote, D. A. Haith, and P. J. Zwerman, "Modeling the Environmental and Economic Effects of Dairy Waste Management," *Transactions of the American Society of Agricultural Engineers*, Vol. 19, No. 2, pp. 326–331, 1976. Subsequent research greatly reduced the size of this model to produce the relatively simple model presented in D. A. Haith and D. W. Atkinson, "A Linear Programming Model for Dairy Farm Nutrient Management," in R. C. Loehr (ed.), *Food, Fertilizer and Agricultural Residues*, Ann Arbor Science Publishers, Ann Arbor, Mich., 1977, pp. 319–337.

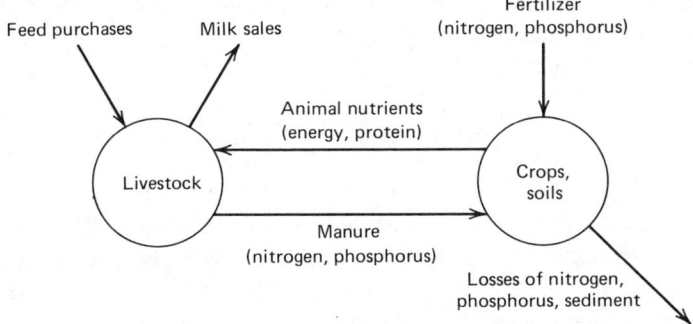

Figure 6-2 Simplified representation of a dairy farm system.

product (milk) and a waste (manure). Crops grown on the farm soils use fertilizer and manure nutrients to yield crop nutrients for livestock. The associated waste products from cropping are eroded soil (sediment) and the nitrogen and phosphorus that are unused by the crops.

Model Construction

Decision Variables The basic decisions or variables included in the model are cropland areas, manure and nitrogen fertilizer application rates and the size of milking herd.

X_{ij} = area of soil i planted to crop (or rotation) j (ha)
M_{ij} = manure spread on soil/crop X_{ij} (tonnes)
N_{ij} = fertilizer nitrogen applied to soil/crop X_{ij} (kg)
H = number of cows in the dairy herd

There are I soils and J crops, with the Jth crop, X_{iJ}, being pasture. Since only certain soil/crop combinations are feasible or reasonable on any farm, we have

$$(1 - \alpha_{ij})X_{ij} = 0 \quad \forall\, i, j \tag{6.1}$$

where $\alpha_{ij} = 1$ if the soil/crop combination (i, j) is permitted and zero otherwise. Also, cropland on each soil must be limited to the tillable area (ha), L_i, of that soil.

$$\sum_{j=1}^{J} X_{ij} \leq L_i \quad \forall\, i \tag{6.2}$$

Manure spreading may not be allowed in all cases, and

$$(1 - \beta_{ij})M_{ij} = 0 \quad \forall\, i, j \tag{6.3}$$

where $\beta_{ij} = 1$ if manure can be spread on land X_{ij}, and zero otherwise. A second constraint on manure spreading is required to assure that $M_{ij} = 0$ whenever $X_{ij} = 0$.

$$-1000 X_{ij} + M_{ij} \leq 0 \quad \forall\, i, j \tag{6.4}$$

The "1000" on the left side of Constraint 6.4 is an arbitrary large number greater than the maximum possible manure spreading rate (t/ha).

A manure mass balance is given by

$$\sum_{i=1}^{I}\sum_{j=1}^{J} M_{ij} - mH = 0 \tag{6.5}$$

where m is the amount of manure (tonnes) to be disposed of (including that of animals such as replacement heifers, which are not part of the milking herd) divided by the herd size. The herd size may be constrained to some maximum number, $H\max$, based on the available housing facilities or other considerations.

$$H \leq H\max \tag{6.6}$$

Animal Feeding Although dairy cows need many different nutrients, it is assumed that the onfarm crops are grown principally to help supply the animals' net energy and digestible protein requirements.

E = net energy requirement to be satisfied from onfarm crops (kCal/cow)
D = digestible protein requirement to be satisfied from onfarm crops (kg/cow)

These definitions imply *a priori* decisions on feed purchases (i.e., the linear programming model will not determine optimal feed purchases). The energy and protein requirements may include the needs of replacement heifers and other stock as desired. For example, if the ratio of replacement heifers to milking cows is 1:4, the nutrient requirements E and D are those of a cow plus one-quarter of the heifer requirement. Stated in another way, $E(D)$ is the total net energy (digestible protein) required from crops by all animals on the dairy farm divided by the number of cows in the milking herd.

Crop yields and nutrient contents are assumed known and specified by the following.

Y_{ij} = yield of crop (or rotation) j on soil i (units/ha)
e_{ij} = net energy content of Y_{ij} (kCal/unit)
d_{ij} = digestible protein content of Y_{ij} (kg/unit)

Net energy and protein balances for the farm are provided by

$$\sum_{i=1}^{I}\sum_{j=1}^{J} e_{ij}Y_{ij}X_{ij} - EH \geq 0 \tag{6.7}$$

and

$$\sum_{i=1}^{I}\sum_{j=1}^{J} d_{ij}Y_{ij}X_{ij} - DH \geq 0 \tag{6.8}$$

In addition, it is realistic to limit the amount of nutrients that could be supplied by pasture because of seasonal availability of pasture and its distance the from the barns,

$$\sum_{i=1}^{I} e_{iJ} Y_{iJ} X_{iJ} - \frac{ep}{100} EH \leq 0 \qquad (6.9)$$

where ep is the maximum percentage of net energy that may be supplied by pasture.

Crop Nitrogen Requirements A crop nutrient balance is constructed for nitrogen only. Potassium is not considered a potential water pollutant, and the total amount of phosphorus in the soil is generally not affected by fertilizer or manure applications. Crop needs for potassium and phosphorus are not ignored, however, since the costs of these fertilizers are included in the model's objective function.

The nitrogen requirement of crop j on soil i is specified by NR_{ij} (kg/ha). The nitrogen requirement will vary with soil fertility, and hence NR_{ij} is the requirement for the crop over and above the nitrogen provided by mineralization of soil organic matter. The nitrogen applied to the crop/soil area (i, j) is given by

$$\left(1 - \frac{nl_{ij}}{100}\right) nm M_{ij} + \left(1 - \frac{nl_{ij}}{100}\right) N_{ij}$$

where nm is the nitrogen content of the manure (kg/t) and nl_{ij} is the percent of the applied nitrogen lost to the atmosphere because of ammonia volatilization and denitrification. In order to supply the crop nitrogen requirements, we must have

$$-NR_{ij} X_{ij} + \left(1 - \frac{nl_{ij}}{100}\right) nm M_{ij} + \left(1 - \frac{nl_{ij}}{100}\right) N_{ij} \geq 0 \qquad \forall\ i, j \qquad (6.10)$$

Constraint 6.10 is a simplification of the soil nitrogen balance (Figure 6-3). It is

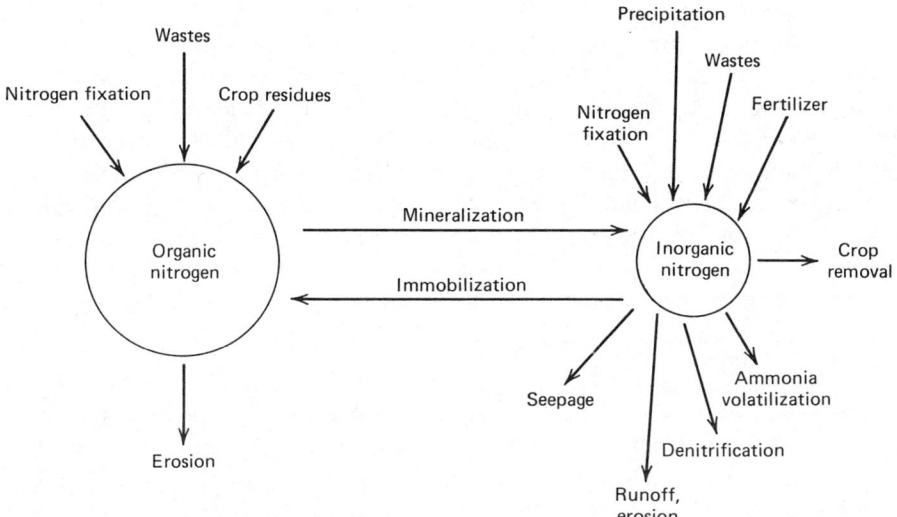

Figure 6-3 Soil nitrogen budget.

assumed that all manure nitrogen is available for crop needs and that the same percentages of manure and fertilizer nitrogen are volatilized.

Pollutant Losses The following environmental parameters must be estimated by the model for each cropped area (including pasture).

1. Total nitrogen loss: the difference between applied nitrogen and that used by crops.
2. Eroded soil.
3. Solid-phase phosphorus and nitrogen in the eroded soil.
4. Dissolved nitrogen and phosphorus in runoff.

Each loss can be restricted to a maximum average annual value per hectare. For example, the total nitrogen loss constraint is

$$-\sum_{i=1}^{I}\sum_{j=1}^{J} NR_{ij}X_{ij} + \sum_{i=1}^{I}\sum_{j=1}^{J} nmM_{ij} + \sum_{i=1}^{I}\sum_{j=1}^{J} N_{ij} \leq N \sum_{i=1}^{I} L_i \quad (6.11)$$

where N is the maximum allowable potential nitrogen loss (kg/ha). Volatilization losses are included, and it is assumed that any tillable land left idle will not produce any nitrogen losses; that is, N is multiplied by $\sum_{i=1}^{I} L_i$ instead of $\sum_{i=1}^{I}\sum_{j=1}^{J} X_{ij}$.

The erosion or soil loss constraint is

$$\sum_{i=1}^{I}\sum_{j=1}^{J} s_{ij}X_{ij} \leq S \sum_{i=1}^{I} L_i \quad (6.12)$$

where s_{ij} is the erosion (t/ha) from land area X_{ij} as determined by methods such as the Universal Soil Loss Equation (8), and S is the maximum allowable per hectare soil loss.

The two environmental constraints given by Expressions 6.11 and 6.12 are fairly obvious since, in one case (Constraint 6.11) only a simple mass balance is required and, in the other (Constraint 6.12), we can rely on a standardized soil loss equation that predicts erosion as a function of crop, soil, management practice, and geographic location. Prediction of nutrient losses in runoff is more difficult. One approach is to model the fundamental nutrient transport and biochemical reactions that take place in the soil. For example, Figure 6-3 shows the processes, inputs, and outputs that affect the soil nitrogen budget. Modeling of the budget is possible but leads to a complicated model that is expensive to run and requires data that are difficult to acquire. This does not mean that such "process-type" models are not useful[3] but, instead, that the models

---

[3] See, for example, D. C. Beyerlein and A. S. Donigian, Jr., "Modeling Soil and Water Conservation Practices," and J. D. Dean and L. A. Mulkey, "Interactive Effects of Pesticide Properties and Selected Conservation Practices on Runoff Losses," in R. C. Loehr, D. A. Haith, M. F. Walter, and C. S. Martin (eds.), *Best Management Practices for Agriculture and Silviculture*, Ann Arbor Science Publishers, Ann Arbor, Mich., 1979.

cannot be incorporated into an optimization model that is readily applicable to analysis of practices for a large number of dairy farms.

A simple procedure that is consistent with the uses of the optimization model is to multiply soil loss and runoff quantities by nutrient concentrations in the soil or runoff to estimate solid-phase and dissolved nutrient losses. The quantities of solid-phase nitrogen and phosphorus in the soil are not greatly affected by cropping, manuring, or fertilizer practices. However, these nutrients vary significantly with soil type. Constraints on solid-phase nutrient losses are

$$\sum_{i=1}^{I} \sum_{j=1}^{J} p_i s_{ij} X_{ij} \leq SP \sum_{i=1}^{I} L_i \tag{6.13}$$

and

$$\sum_{i=1}^{I} \sum_{j=1}^{J} n_i s_{ij} X_{ij} \leq SN \sum_{i=1}^{I} L_i \tag{6.14}$$

where p_i and n_i are phosphorus and nitrogen contents of soil i (kg/t). The maximum allowable solid-phase phosphorus and nitrogen losses are SP and SN (kg/ha), respectively.

Runoff losses of dissolved nitrogen and phosphorus can be estimated similarly as the product of runoff and dissolved nutrient concentrations in the runoff. These concentrations are primarily influenced by crop selection, and summer and winter concentrations are often substantially different. The appropriate constraints on dissolved losses are

$$0.1 \sum_{i=1}^{I} \sum_{j=1}^{J} (rs_{ij} ns_j + rw_{ij} nw_j) X_{ij} \leq DN \sum_{i=1}^{I} L_i \tag{6.15}$$

$$0.1 \sum_{i=1}^{I} \sum_{j=1}^{J} (rs_{ij} ps_j + rw_{ij} pw_j) X_{ij} \leq DP \sum_{i=1}^{I} L_i \tag{6.16}$$

where

rs_{ij}, rw_{ij} = summer and winter runoff (cm), respectively, from land area X_{ij}
ns_j, nw_j = dissolved nitrogen concentrations (mg/liter) in summer and winter runoff, respectively, from land planted to crop j
ps_j, pw_j = dissolved phosphorus concentrations (mg/liter) in summer and winter runoff, respectively, from land planted to crop j
DN, DP = maximum allowable losses of dissolved nitrogen and phosphorus, respectively, in runoff (kg/ha)

The constant (0.1) is a conversion factor. Summer runoff can be estimated using the U. S. Soil Conservation Service (SCS) runoff equation (5), and winter runoff can be calculated using a degree-day snowmelt equation in conjunction with the SCS equation. Phosphorus and nitrogen concentrations are average values based on field studies for the relevant crops (3).

Farm Income Since the farmer's objective is maximization of net income, Z ($/yr), the objective function for the optimization model is

$$Z = rH - \sum_{i=1}^{I} \sum_{j=1}^{J} C_{ij} X_{ij} - C_m \sum_{i=1}^{I} \sum_{j=1}^{J} M_{ij} - C_n \sum_{i=1}^{I} \sum_{j=1}^{J} N_{ij} \qquad (6.17)$$

where

r = net return per dairy cow exclusive of fixed costs, costs of farm crops, manure disposal, and nitrogen fertilizer ($)
C_{ij} = cost of cropping soil i with crop j exclusive of fixed costs and nitrogen fertilizer and manure disposal costs ($/ha)
C_m = cost of manure disposal ($/t)
C_n = cost of nitrogen fertilizer ($/kg)

Model Summary The complete model is

$$\text{Max } Z$$

subject to Constraints 6.1 to 6.16 and the usual nonnegativity restrictions on decision variables (H, X_{ij}, M_{ij}, and N_{ij}). The model is solved on an annual basis, using either average annual weather, yields, and prices data or data selected for a particular year of record. General data sources for the model are soil surveys, farm cost accounts, daily weather data, and tabulated parameters for the Universal Soil Loss Equation and the SCS runoff equation.

IMPLEMENTATION

To demonstrate the use of the LP model, it is applied in the remainder of this chapter to a representative dairy farm in Jefferson County, New York. The farm has relatively poor (unproductive) soils, gentle slopes and 124 ha of tillable land. Animal facilities can accommodate a herd size of 150 cows. Model data are first summarized, and the effects of constraints on nonpoint source nutrient and sediment losses from the farm are then presented.

Data

Soils and Crops The farm contains the four basic soil associations listed in Table 6-1. Three rotations are recommended for these soils: corn-oats-alfalfa-alfalfa (COAA),

TABLE 6-1 Soil Associations for the Jefferson County Farm

i	Soil Association	Tillable Area L_i (ha)	Phosphorus Content p_i (kg/t)	Nitrogen Content n_i (kg/t)
1.	Rockland-Panton (R/P)	26	0.90	2.0
2.	Livingston-Panton (L/P)	5	0.90	2.0
3.	Acid Sands (A/S)	9	0.12	0.8
4.	Panton-Vergennes (P/V)	84	0.94	2.2

corn-oats-grass-grass-grass (COGGG), and continuous pasture. The corn is grown for silage and the alfalfa for hay. Although the grass could be either hay or grass silage, it is assumed that all grass is silage in the present case. The possible soil/crop combinations are listed in Table 6-2. Manure may be spread on both rotations, but not pasture.

Nutrients produced from the crop rotations are given in Table 6-3. They are obtained by first multiplying average yields of a crop on a given soil (e.g., corn on Livingston-Panton soil) by nutrient contents of the crop. This is done for each year of a rotation, and the total nutrients produced by the rotation are divided by the number of years in the rotation (e.g., 4 years in the case of COAA). The maximum percentage of livestock net energy that can be satisfied by pasture on this farm is $ep = 15\%$.

Crop nitrogen requirements (NR_{ij}) are obtained similarly from a soil survey and averaged over the crop rotations (Table 6-4).

TABLE 6-2 Possible Soil/Crop Combinations, α_{ij} ($\alpha_{ij} = 1$ if Combination is Possible, $\alpha_{ij} = 0$ Otherwise)

Soil	Crop, $j=$		
	1 COAA	2 COGGG	3 Pasture
R/P	0	0	1
L/P	1	1	0
A/S	0	1	1
P/V	1	1	0

TABLE 6-3 Nutrients Produced from Cropping Options

Soil	$e_{ij} Y_{ij} / d_{ij} Y_{ij}$[a]		
	COAA	COGGG	Pasture
R/P	—	—	2900/300
L/P	5000/400	4200/220	—
A/S	—	4200/220	2900/300
P/V	6700/540	5700/300	—

[a] Averaged over rotation. The first entry is net energy (kCal/ha), and the second entry is digestible protein (kg/ha).

TABLE 6-4 Crop Nitrogen Requirements

Soil	NR_{ij} (kg/ha)		
	COAA	COGGG	Pasture
R/P	—	—	0
L/P	30	40	—
A/S	—	70	20
P/V	60	70	—

Animal Nutrition and Manure   Livestock nutrient requirements and manure production are given in Table 6-5. The net energy and digestible protein values are based on 60% of the forage requirement for cows and replacement heifers (one heifer for every four cows). Farmers in this area customarily purchase both forage and grain for their cows, and it assumed that all grain and 40% of the forage is purchased on this farm. The manure production rate includes manure from heifers during the period of time in which they are housed (9 t/heifer at 1/4 heifer/cow).

TABLE 6-5 Dairy Herd Nutrition and Manure Production

Net energy requirement, E (kCal/cow)	4000
Digestible protein requirement, D (kg/cow)	350
Manure production, m (t/cow)	19
Nitrogen content of manure, nm (kg/t)	5

Nutrient and Sediment Loss Parameters Most of the crop nitrogen is supplied by manure on the Jefferson County farm, and the nitrogen volatilization rate, nl_{ij}, is set at 35% for all i and j, corresponding to the ammonia content of the manure (ammonia is readily volatilized). Soil losses are estimated from the Universal Soil Loss Equation,

$$s_{ij} = R K_i LS_i CM_{ij} P_{ij} \qquad (6.18)$$

where R, K_i, LS_i, CM_{ij}, and P_{ij} are rainfall erosivity, soil erodability, topographic factor, cover/management factor, and practice factor, respectively (7, 8). The resulting soil losses are given in Table 6-6.

Runoff estimates, which are given in Table 6-7, are computed using the U. S. Soil Conservation Service's runoff equation,

$$Q_{ijt} = \frac{(P_t - 0.2W_{ijt})^2}{P_t + 0.8W_{ijt}} \qquad (6.19)$$

TABLE 6-6 Average Annual Soil Losses

Soil	s_{ij} (t/ha)		
	COAA	COGGG	Pasture
R/P	—	—	1.0
L/P	3.0	2.4	—
A/S	—	2.2	0.5
P/V	6.0	4.8	—

TABLE 6-7 Average Summer and Winter Runoff

Soil	rs_{ij}/rw_{ij} (cm)[a]		
	COAA	COGGG	Pasture
R/P	—	—	3.8/7.8
L/P	5.7/10.0	5.0/8.2	—
A/S	—	0.1/0.4	0/0.1
P/V	5.7/10.0	5.0/8.2	—

[a]Averaged over rotation. The first entry is summer (May to November) runoff and the second entry is winter (December to April) runoff.

where Q_{ijt} is runoff from crop/soil combination i, j on day t (cm), P_t is the precipitation (rainfall plus snowmelt) (cm) on day t, and W_{ijt} is a detention parameter, which is a tabulated function of crop, soil, and antecedent moisture conditions (3, 5, 7). Precipitation records were obtained for a typical year from the nearest weather station. The seasonal runoff values given in Table 6-7 are the sums of daily runoff during each season.

Concentrations of dissolved nitrogen and phosphorus in runoff are based on average values for individual crops (3). These concentrations, averaged over the rotations, are given in Table 6-8.

Costs and Returns Costs and returns are estimated for an arbitrary future date. Net return per cow is based on farm cost account figures, exclusive of fixed costs and costs associated with manure disposal, nitrogen fertilizer, and crop cultivation. The net return per cow is $r = \$500/\text{yr}$. Manure disposal and nitrogen fertilizer costs are $C_m = \$3/\text{t}$ and $C_n = \$0.80/\text{kg}$, respectively. Cropping costs, C_{ij}, which are also based on farm cost accounts, are given in Table 6-9.

TABLE 6-8 Dissolved Nitrogen and Phosphorus Concentrations in Runoff

Crop	Dissolved Nitrogen Concentrations (mg/liter)		Dissolved Phosphorus Concentrations (mg/liter)	
	Summer ns_j	Winter nw_j	Summer ps_j	Winter pw_j
COAA	1.8	2.5	0.23	0.25
COGG	1.6	2.6	0.22	0.24
Pasture	2.0	3.0	0.30	0.30

TABLE 6-9 Cropping Costs

Soil	C_{ij} ($/ha)		
	COAA	COGGG	Pasture
R/P	—	—	20
L/P	350	370	—
A/S	—	380	80
P/V	360	380	—

Model Summary

The LP model coefficients for the Jefferson County farm are shown in Table 6-10. Entries that are zero and slack and surplus variables are omitted from the table. Also omitted are decision variables that correspond to infeasible crop, manure, and fertilizer combinations. For example, from Table 6-2, X_{11}, X_{12}, X_{23}, X_{31}, and X_{43} are infeasible crop/soil combinations and need not be included in the model. In this application, the model has 45 variables (20 decision variables and 25 slack or surplus variables) and 26 constraints. However, as LP models go, it is not particularly large. It can be solved on most computer installations for less than $1 of computer time.

Model Solution: Impacts of Constraints on Nonpoint Source Pollutants

The effects of pollutant loss reductions on farm income are determined by solving the LP model (Table 6-10) for various values of Constraints 6.11 to 6.16, the pollutant loss constraints. Three sets of solutions are shown in Table 6-11. Only the nonzero decision variables are given in the table (rounded to the nearest integer). The initial model solution is an income-maximizing plan with no restrictions on pollutant losses. This solution indicates both the maximum income and pollutant losses that could be obtained from the farm. If these losses are acceptable, no changes in management practices are necessary. In terms of the constraint limits for sediment and nutrient losses, income is maximized provided S (sediment) ≥ 4.1 t/ha, N (total nitrogen) ≥ 76.7 kg/ha, DN (dissolved nitrogen) ≥ 2.9 kg/ha, DP (dissolved phosphorus) ≥ 0.32 kg/ha, SN (solid-phase nitrogen) ≥ 9.0 kg/ha, and SP (solid-phase phosphorus) ≥ 3.8 kg/ha. If any of these constraint limits are reduced, both management practices and income will change.

The second set of solutions shows the impact of reductions of allowable total nitrogen losses from 76.7 kg/ha to 60, 40, or 20 kg/ha. These results are obtained by setting N equal to 60, 40 or 20 kg/ha and leaving other pollutant losses unconstrained. The primary effect is to reduce herd size and hence substantially reduce farm income. This would probably be an unintended result, since the government agency would have little interest in reducing milk production. Nevertheless, cropping must be decreased in order to meet the lower nitrogen losses and, since fewer animal nutrients are produced, a smaller herd size is necessary. Although other pollutant losses were not constrained in these solutions, it can be seen that they are also reduced in comparison with the unrestricted plan. Reducing nitrogen losses thus forces management practices that also reduce losses of other pollutants.

The third set of plans is based on alternative limits on sediment or soil loss ($S = 3$, 2, and 1t/ha). The results are comparable to those produced by nitrogen restrictions except that a portion of the COAA rotation is shifted to the less erosive Livingston-Panton soil. Although not shown here, model solutions for restrictions on dissolved nitrogen and phosphorus are similar to the solutions obtained with total nitrogen constrained, and solid-phase nitrogen and phosphorus restrictions produce solutions similar to the results for sediment constraints.

TABLE 6-10 LP Model Coefficients for Jefferson County Farm

X_{13}	X_{21}	X_{22}	X_{32}	X_{33}	X_{41}	X_{42}	M_{21}	M_{22}	M_{32}	M_{41}	M_{42}
−20	−350	−370	−380	−80	−360	−380	−3.0	−3.0	−3.0	−3.0	−3.0
1											
	1	1									
			1	1							
					1	1					
	−1000						1				
		−1000						1			
			−1000						1		
				−1000						1	
					−1000						1
							1	1	1	1	1
2900	5000	4200	4200	2900	6700	5700					
300	400	220	220	300	540	300					
2900				2900							
	−30						3.25				
		−40						3.25			
			−70						3.25		
				−20							
					−60						
						−70				3.25	
											3.25
	−30	−40	−70	−20	−60	−70	5	5	5	5	5
1.0	3.0	2.4	2.2	0.5	6.0	4.8					
0.9	2.7	2.16	0.26	0.06	5.64	4.51					
2.0	6.0	4.8	1.76	0.4	13.2	10.56					
3.10	3.53	2.93	0.12	0.03	3.53	2.93					
0.35	0.38	0.31	0.01	0.00	0.38	0.31					

The net income shown in Table 6-11 is exclusive of fixed costs; when these costs are subtracted, the net income will be much lower. The model solutions can be presented as in Figure 6-4 to show the costs of reducing nonpoint source pollutant losses from the dairy farm. Costs are measured as losses in farm income. For example, if nitrogen losses are reduced from 76.7 to 60 kg/ha (22%), this costs $36,610 − 29,155 = $7455/yr in lost income. The curves for sediment and nitrogen are essentially

IMPLEMENTATION 153

TABLE 6-10 (continued)

N_{13}	N_{21}	N_{22}	N_{32}	N_{33}	N_{41}	N_{42}	H			Equation or Constraint
−0.8	−0.8	−0.8	−0.8	−0.8	−0.8	−0.8	500	=	Z	6.17
								≤	26	6.2
								≤	5	6.2
								≤	9	6.2
								≤	84	6.2
								≤	0	6.4
								≤	0	6.4
								≤	0	6.4
								≤	0	6.4
								≤	0	6.4
							−19	=	0	6.5
							1	≤	150	6.6
							−4000	≥	0	6.7
							−350	≥	0	6.8
							−600	≤	0	6.9
	0.65							≥	0	6.10
		0.65						≥	0	6.10
			0.65					≥	0	6.10
				0.65				≥	0	6.10
					0.65			≥	0	6.10
						0.65		≥	0	6.10
1	1	1	1	1	1	1		≤	124N	6.11
								≤	124S	6.12
								≤	124SP	6.13
								≤	124SN	6.14
								≤	124DN	6.15
								≤	124DP	6.16

identical and are shown as one line in the figure. The line is an example of an environmental/economic trade-off. Trade-offs must occur when objectives are incompatible. Thus we cannot reduce pollutant losses without also increasing costs (reducing income). The slope of the line in Figure 6-4 is approximately 365, indicating that we can "trade off" income for reductions in nitrogen or sediment losses at the rate of $365 for each 1% improvement (reduction) in losses.

TABLE 6-11 Solutions to Dairy Farm LP Model with Constraints on Total Nitrogen and Sediment Losses

	Plan with No Restrictions on Pollutant Losses	Plans with Total Nitrogen Loss Constrained to N (kg/ha) =			Plans with Total Sediment Loss Constrained to S (t/ha) =		
		60	40	20	3	2	1
Decisions[a]							
H, herd size	150	118	78	39	111	74	38
X_{13}, R/P pasture (ha)	26	24	16	8	23	16	8
X_{21}, L/P COAA (ha)	—	—	—	—	5	5	5
X_{33}, A/S pasture (ha)	5	—	—	—	—	—	—
X_{41}, P/V COAA (ha)	80	63	42	21	56	36	17
M_{21}/X_{21}, manure on X_{21} (t/ha)	—	—	—	—	9	9	9
M_{41}/X_{41}, manure on X_{41} (t/ha)	36	36	36	36	37	38	41
N_{33}/X_{33}, N fertilizer on X_{33} (kg/ha)	31	—	—	—	—	—	—
Impacts							
Net income (\$/yr)[b]	36,610	29,155	19,437	9,718	27,073	18,084	9,095
Sediment loss (t/ha)[c]	4.1	3.2	2.2	1.1	3.0	2.0	1.0
Total nitrogen loss (kg/ha)[c]	76.7	60	40	20	57	39	20
Runoff losses (kg/ha)[c]							
Dissolved nitrogen	2.9	2.4	1.6	0.8	2.3	1.6	0.8
Dissolved phosphorus	0.32	0.26	0.17	0.09	0.25	0.17	0.09
Solid-phase nitrogen	9.0	7.1	4.7	2.4	6.5	4.4	2.2
Solid-phase phosphorus	3.8	3.0	2.0	1.0	2.8	1.9	0.9

[a] Rounded to nearest integer.
[b] Excluding fixed costs.
[c] Averaged over 124 ha.

Figure 6-4 Effects of reductions in total nitrogen or sediment loss on farm income.

Regulatory Implications

The purpose of this modeling effort is to provide a government planning agency with information useful in developing a management program for dairy farm nonpoint sources. Based on solutions to the LP model, some specific conclusions are possible.

1. The total nitrogen loss from income-maximizing farms can be high (>75 kg/ha). Although much of this unused nitrogen is volatilized harmlessly to the atmosphere, the potential exists for significant losses of nitrogen to surface waters and aquifers.
2. Losses of sediment and nutrients in runoff are relatively low under normal (income-maximizing) conditions on this farm.
3. Reductions in sediment and nutrient losses are very expensive for this farm, since major decreases in cropped land were necessary. Thus pollution reductions could be achieved only by production cutbacks.

The next step in the analysis would be to model representative dairy farms in other regions. If the preceding observations were also seen with these farms, it should indicate to the planning agency that the costs of controlling nonpoint source pollution from dairy farms will be very high. However, this conclusion must be tempered by the limitations of the example farm that was modeled. The only management options for reducing pollution included in the model of the Jefferson County farm were fertilizer rates, manure applications, and assignment of crops to soil associations. While these decisions can and do reduce pollution, they were also quite expensive. Other management practices such as various means of soil and water conservation could be used with the crops to reduce runoff and erosion. This would provide alternative approaches to the control of dissolved and solid-phase nutrient losses associated with runoff. Soil and water conservation practices can be easily included in the LP model; this is demonstrated in Exercise 6-1 at the end of this chapter.

Summary

The application of systems analysis to environmental problems requires examinations of the problems in their totality and often leads to surprising results. The present example began with what seemed to be a fairly narrow goal: the management of nonpoint source pollution from an agricultural enterprise. However, it became apparent that the farming activities that produced pollution are integral components of a total farm system and are not readily isolated. Thus an environmental pollution problem was expanded to include animal nutrition, soil properties, crop rotations, runoff, and erosion. This may be disconcerting to the engineer or planner whose primary, if not exclusive, interest is in pollution control. Nevertheless, this broad perspective is necessary to evaluate the economic impacts of controlling nonpoint sources realistically. It is also a logical consequence of the application of systems analysis, since the systems approach is designed to consider the full complexities of environmental problems.

In addition to demonstrating a realistic LP application, the example in the chapter introduced nonpoint source pollution and agricultural planning models. Linear programming models are commonly used by government agencies to provide information needed in the development of regulatory and government assistance programs. Such LP models have the same general structure as the model in this chapter.

SELECTED REFERENCES

1. Agrawal, R. C., and E. O. Heady, *Operations Research Methods for Agricultural Decisions,* Iowa State University Press, Ames, 1972.
2. Beneke, R. R., and R. Winterboer, *Linear Programming Applications to Agriculture,* Iowa State University Press, Ames, 1973.
3. Haith, D. A., and L. J. Tubbs, "Watershed Loading Functions for Nonpoint Sources," *Journal of the Environmental Engineering Division,* American Society of Civil Engineers, Vol. 107, No. EE1, pp. 121–137, 1981.
4. Loehr, R. C., D. A. Haith, M. F. Walter, and C. S. Martin (editors), *Best Management Practices for Agriculture and Silviculture,* Ann Arbor Science Publishers, Ann Arbor, Mich., 1979.
5. Mockus, V., "Estimation of Direct Runoff from Storm Rainfall," *National Engineering Handbook*, Section 4, Hydrology, U.S. Soil Conservation Service, 1972.
6. Porter, K. S. (editor), *Nitrogen and Phosphorus: Food Production, Waste and the Environment,* Ann Arbor Science Publishers, Ann Arbor, Mich., 1975.

7. Stewart, B. A., D. A. Woolhiser, W. H. Wischmeier, J. H. Caro, and M. H. Frere, *Control of Water Pollution from Croplands,* U.S. Environmental Protection Agency, Washington, D.C., Vol. I (Report EPA - 600/2-75-026a), 1975, Vol. II (Report EPA - 600/2-75-026b), 1976.
8. Wischmeier, W. H., and D. D. Smith, *Predicting Rainfall Erosion Losses—A Guide to Conservation Planning,* Agricultural Handbook No. 537, U.S. Dept. of Agriculture Science and Education Administration, Washington, D.C., 1978.

EXERCISES

NOTE. Exercise 6-1 requires a computer and a programmed version of the simplex method.

6-1.

The discussion of regulatory implications of the modeling application to the Jefferson County farm indicated that soil and water conservation practices could be used with the crops to reduce erosion and runoff. If these practices are used with the rotation COAA, it is estimated that soil losses (s_{ij}) will be reduced 50%. Summer runoff will be reduced 30%. However, soil and water conservation practices will increase cropping costs (C_{ij}) for this rotation by 15%.
   Modify the linear programming model to account for these new alternatives and obtain a model solution for $S = 2$ t/ha, $N = 50$, $SP = 2.5$, $SN = 5$, $DN = 2$, and $DP = 0.2$ kg/ha. Note that the revised model should permit the rotation to be grown with or without the new practices; that is, let the model determine whether or not it is optimal to use soil and water conservation to reduce nutrient and sediment losses.

6-2.

Linear programming can be used to evaluate the effects of energy prices and allocations on farming practices. Modify the LP model presented in this chapter so that it can be used to investigate the effects of gasoline prices and supply limitations on a dairy farm. Assume that the only major gasoline needs are for machinery used for crop production and manure disposal. State any assumptions that are necessary and identify the additional data that would be needed to solve your model.

6-3.

One of the major sources of water pollution in urban areas is runoff. When rain falls on a city, it washes the accumulated dirt and debris from streets, parking lots, construction sites, and the like, and carries the material with the runoff water into the city's sanitary sewers or into a separate network of storm sewers. In either case, such wastes are frequently discharged, after collection, into a nearby waterway.

158 AGRICULTURAL NONPOINT SOURCE POLLUTION

A city has a storm sewer network that collects runoff from the four areas shown in the accompanying figure.

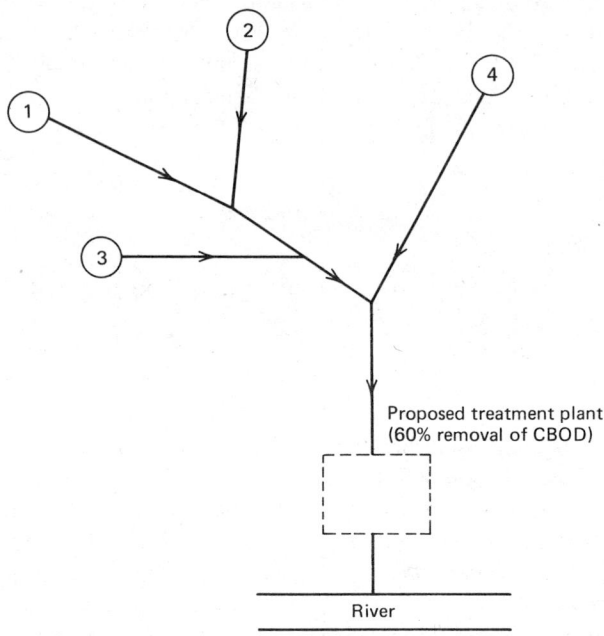

The collected runoff is presently discharged into a river without treatment. The city is correcting the problems created by the discharge by constructing the storm water treatment plant shown. The plant is to be based on the design storm, summarized as follows.

Area	Total One-Day Runoff from Area (m³)	CBOD Concentration in Runoff (kg/m³)
1	10,000	0.2
2	20,000	0.5
3	40,000	0.3
4	100,000	0.1

The runoff quantities are assumed to occur simultaneously from each area during the same 24-hr period. The existing sewers are adequate to handle these runoff quantities.

The treatment plant cost has several components. Construction costs are given by $K + c_5$ (capacity), where K is a fixed cost ($/yr), c_5 is a variable cost ($/yr-m^3/day), and "capacity" is the maximum flow (m^3/day) that can be handled by the plant. Thus, if a treatment plant is built with a capacity of 170,000 m^3/day, the construction cost is $K + 170{,}000 c_5$. The operating and maintenance (O&M) cost is $d/m^3 passing through the plant. (It is assumed that one design storm occurs each year. Although additional, smaller storms occur during the year, they do not have to be considered in this analysis.)

In order to reduce the size (and hence the construction cost) of the treatment plant, the city is considering the construction of small storage reservoirs in each runoff area. The purpose of these reservoirs is to store some portion of the runoff from the respective areas (the reservoir in each area can store runoff from its area only). This can reduce the volume of water that must be treated by the plant during the storm. The water from the reservoirs is released to the storm sewers on the day following the storm and is treated and discharged to the river during this second day. The characteristics of the reservoirs are different for each area, depending on available land excavation problems, and so forth. The total reservoir cost for area i is c_i($/m^3-yr), $i = 1, 2, 3, 4$, and the maximum reservoir size (m^3) for area i is L_i.

Effluent standards have been established for day 1 (during the storm) and day 2 (the day after the storm) for CBOD, and are 14,000 and 6000 kg, respectively. If the treatment plant is built, all runoff must pass through the plant; a by-pass will not be permitted.

Construct a linear programming model that can be used by the city to solve its urban runoff problem.

CHAPTER 7
SEPARABLE AND INTEGER PROGRAMMING

Linear programming (LP) models are optimization models with continuous decision variables and linear constraints and objective functions. However, LP methods can sometimes solve models that do not have these properties. *Separable programming* is an approach for linearizing certain nonlinear functions in optimization models. Solutions to the resulting LP models are often good approximations of the optimal solutions to the original nonlinear models. *Integer programming* is a means of solving linear optimization models containing variables that are restricted to integer values. Integer programming also provides a mechanism for handling nonlinearities such as fixed costs within an LP format.

Separable and integer programming are extremely useful optimization techniques. They extend the applications of LP to many models that would otherwise be difficult, if not impossible, to solve.

SEPARABLE PROGRAMMING

Separable programming is usually applied to optimization models with nonlinear objective functions. Such applications are emphasized in this section, which also includes an example of multiobjective planning.

Separable Objective Functions

EXAMPLE 7-1
Solve the following optimization model.

$$\text{Max } Z = 2X_1 + X_2^{1/2} - 3X_3 \quad (7.1)$$
$$\text{s.t.} \quad X_1 + 10X_2 \leq 20 \quad (7.2)$$
$$3X_1 - 2X_2 + X_3 \leq 6 \quad (7.3)$$
$$X_1, X_2, X_3 \geq 0 \quad \square$$

The objective function contains a nonlinear term ($X_2^{1/2}$), and the model cannot be solved directly by LP methods. Based on our previous experience with nonlinear models, it would seem that a solution can be obtained only by search methods. This is frustrating, since the model is *almost* linear. The constraints and most of the objective function are linear. If the single nonlinear element could be made linear, an LP model would result.

Nonlinear functions can be approximated by piecewise linear segments, as shown in Figure 7-1. In the figure, $X_2^{1/2}$ is approximated by three linear segments within the range $0 \leq X_2 \leq 2$. The upper value of this range is imposed by Constraint 7.2 (i.e., X_2 cannot be greater than $20/10 = 2$). The linear approximation to $X_2^{1/2}$ shown in Figure 7-1 is relatively accurate. If greater accuracy is desired, more segments can be added. However, it will be seen that each segment adds a variable and sometimes a constraint to the resulting LP model. The general goal of linearization is to obtain a good approximation to the nonlinear function without producing a model with excessive numbers of variables and constraints.

Several methods are available for including linearized functions in optimization models. Two of these methods are illustrated in the following discussion.

Method 1: Segment Variables A new variable can be defined for each of the linear segments. With the segments shown in Figure 7-2, the new variables x_1, x_2, and x_3 are constrained by

$$x_1 \leq 0.2 \tag{7.4}$$

$$x_2 \leq 0.6 \tag{7.5}$$

$$x_3 \leq 1.2 \tag{7.6}$$

The values on the ordinate of Figure 7-2 (0.45, 0.89, and 1.41) are given by $X_2^{1/2}$ for $X_2 = 0.2, 0.8, 2.0$. The nonlinear term in the objective function is approximated by

$$X_2^{1/2} = \alpha_1 x_1 + \alpha_2 x_2 + \alpha_3 x_3 \tag{7.7}$$

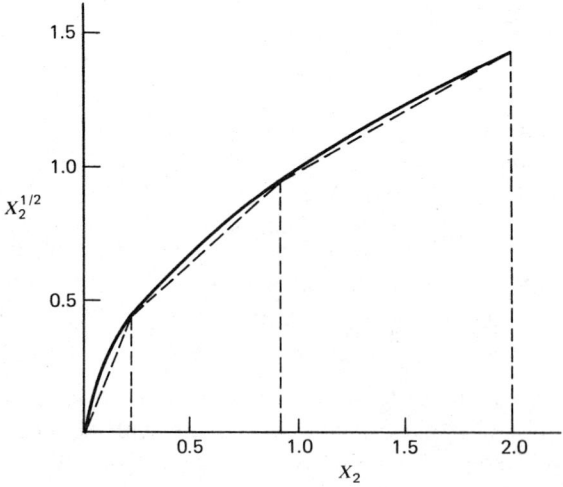

Figure 7-1. Piecewise linear approximation of $X_2^{1/2}$.

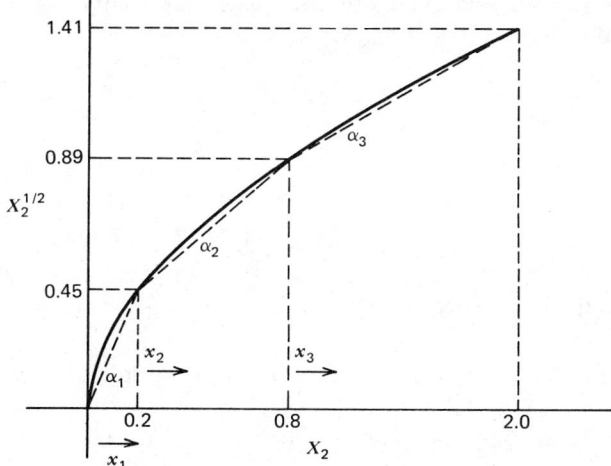

Figure 7-2. Variables and slopes for linearization of $X_2^{1/2}$.

where α_i is the slope of the ith segment. These slopes can be computed from Figure 7-2 as

$$\alpha_1 = \frac{0.45}{0.2} = 2.25$$

$$\alpha_2 = \frac{0.89 - 0.45}{0.6} = 0.73$$

$$\alpha_3 = \frac{1.41 - 0.89}{1.2} = 0.43$$

The optimization model can now be revised, using Equation 7.7 and substituting $x_1 + x_2 + x_3$ for X_2 in the constraints.

$$\text{Max } Z = 2X_1 + 2.25x_1 + 0.73x_2 + 0.43x_3 - 3X_3 \tag{7.8}$$

s.t.
$$X_1 + 10x_1 + 10x_2 + 10x_3 \le 20 \tag{7.9}$$

$$3X_1 - 2x_1 - 2x_2 - 2x_3 + X_3 \le 6 \tag{7.10}$$

$$x_1 \le 0.2 \tag{7.4}$$

$$x_2 \le 0.6 \tag{7.5}$$

$$x_3 \le 1.2 \tag{7.6}$$

$$X_1, X_3, x_1, x_2, x_3 \ge 0$$

We now have an LP model; although the number of constraints and variables have increased compared to the original model (Expressions 7.1, 7.2, and 7.3), it is possible to solve the problem using the simplex method. It is not clear, however, that a solution to this new LP model will also be a solution to the original model. For example, can an optimal solution be obtained to the LP model that has

$$x_1^* = 0, \quad x_2^* = 0, \quad x_3^* > 0$$

or

$$x_1^* > 0, \quad x_2^* = 0, \quad x_3^* > 0$$

or

$$x_1^* = 0, \quad x_2^* > 0, \quad x_3^* > 0$$

For the linearization to work, the segments of the function must fill in order. If the optimal value of the original variable X_2^* is 1.1, we must have $x_1^* = 0.2$, $x_2^* = 0.6$, and $x_3^* = 0.3$ ($x_1 + x_2 + x_3 = 1.1$) in order to approximate accurately $X_2^{1/2} = (1.1)^{1/2} = 1.05$. Thus

$$\alpha_1 x_1 + \alpha_2 x_2 + \alpha_3 x_3 = 2.25(0.2) + 0.73(0.6) + 0.43(0.3) = 1.02$$

which is a relatively good approximation to 1.05. The constraints to the LP model do not require that segments fill in order. For example, $x_1^* = 0.2$, $x_2^* = 0$, and $x_3^* = 0.9$ will also sum to $X_2^* = 1.1$ and satisfy the constraints, but the linear approximation to $X_2^{1/2}$ would be

$$2.25(0.2) + 0.43(0.9) = 0.84$$

In order to made the linearization procedure work, it would seem that additional constraints are needed to force the segments of the linearized function to fill in order; that is, if

$$x_2 > 0, \quad x_1 = 0.2$$

and if

$$x_3 > 0, \quad x_2 = 0.6$$

There is no obvious way in which such constraints could be written in a linear fashion but, fortunately, they are not needed for this problem. Any solution that does not fill the segments in order would not be optimal and hence *could not be a solution to the LP model*. This is due to the relative slopes of the three segments. For example, since $\alpha_2 < \alpha_1$, it could never be optimal to increase x_2 from zero unless x_1 is at its maximum value (0.2). It would always be better to increment x_1 by some amount Δx instead of applying the same increment to x_2. Thus $\alpha_1 \Delta x = 2.25 \Delta x$ increases the objective function by more than $\alpha_2 \Delta x = 0.73 \Delta x$. By similar reasoning, an optimal solution cannot have $x_3 > 0$ unless $x_2 = 0.6$, since $\alpha_2 > \alpha_3$. We can conclude that a solution to the LP model (Expressions 7.8 to 7.10 and 7.4 to 7.6) is approximately equivalent to the optimal solution to the original nonlinear model (Expressions 7.1 to 7.3).

The coefficients for the LP model are shown in Table 7-1. Constraint 7.6 ($x_3 \le 1.2$) has been omitted, since x_3^* is positive only when $x_1^* = 0.2$ and $x_2^* = 0.6$; therefore Constraint 7.9 will prevent x_3^* from exceeding 1.2. The model has five decision variables, four slack variables, and four constraints. Compared to the original, model size has increased substantially, but the model is now much easier to solve, since the simplex method can be used. The solution is $X_1^* = 3.13$, $x_1^* = 0.20$, $x_2^* = 0.60$, $x_3^* = 0.89$, $X_3^* = 0$, and $Z^* = 7.52$. For the original model (Expressions 7.1 to 7.3), this indicates that $X_1^* = 3.13$, $X_2^* = 1.69$, and $X_3^* = 0$. In terms of these original variables, the optimal value of the objective function is $Z^* = 2X_1^* + X_2^{*1/2} - 3X_3^* = 7.56$.

Method 2: Segment Weights The optimization model can also be linearized using a somewhat more elegant procedure that produces a smaller LP model than method 1. Justification for this second approach is more complicated than that required for the previous method. Consider the linearization of the function shown in Figure 7-3. An arbitrary point within one of these segments, say $\bar{x}$ in the second segment, can be written as a weighted combination of the values of the function argument x at the beginning and end of the segment.

$$\bar{x} = w_1 x_1 + w_2 x_2 \qquad (7.11)$$

where

$$w_1 + w_2 = 1 \qquad (7.12)$$

If, for example, $\bar{x} = x_1$, then $w_1 = 1$ and $w_2 = 0$. For $\bar{x}$ midway between x_1 and x_2, $w_1 = w_2 = 0.5$.

The linearized value of $f(X)$ at $X = \bar{x}$ is the weighted sum of $f_1(x_1)$ amd $f_2(x_2)$. To see this, we can write the approximation of $f(\bar{x})$ as

$$f(\bar{x}) \simeq f(x_1) + (\bar{x} - x_1) \frac{[f(x_2) - f(x_1)]}{x_2 - x_1} \qquad (7.13)$$

TABLE 7-1 Coefficients of Linearized Model for Example 7-1 Using Segment Variables (Method 1)

X_1	x_1	x_2	x_3	X_3	S_1	S_2	S_3	S_4		
2	2.25	0.73	0.43	−3	0	0	0	0	=	Z
1	10	10	10	0	1	0	0	0	=	20
3	−2	−2	−2	1	0	1	0	0	=	6
0	1	0	0	0	0	0	1	0	=	0.2
0	0	1	0	0	0	0	0	1	=	0.6

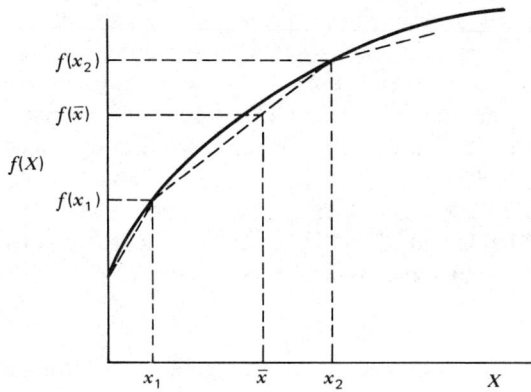

Figure 7.3. Linearization of a function $f(X)$.

The term $[f(x_2) - f(x_1)]/(x_2 - x_1)$ is the slope of the linear segment. Since $\bar{x} = w_1 x_1 + w_2 x_2$, Equation 7.13 can be written as

$$f(\bar{x}) \simeq f(x_1) + (w_1 x_1 + w_2 x_2 - x_1) \frac{[f(x_2) - f(x_1)]}{x_2 - x_1}$$

$$= f(x_1) + [(w_1 - 1)x_1 + w_2 x_2] \frac{[f(x_2) - f(x_1)]}{x_2 - x_1}$$

$$= f(x_1) + w_2(x_2 - x_1) \frac{[f(x_2) - f(x_1)]}{x_2 - x_1} \qquad (7.13a)$$

In this equation we have also used Equation 7.12 to obtain $w_1 - 1 = -w_2$. Equation 7.13a can be simplified to

$$f(\bar{x}) \simeq w_1 f(x_1) + w_2 f(x_2) \qquad (7.14)$$

Returning to the linearization of $X_2^{1/2}$, as shown in Figure 7-2, we can define four weights, w_0, w_1, w_2, and w_3, corresponding to the beginning and end points of the three segments. The function $X_2^{1/2}$ can be linearized as follows.

1. For $0 \leq X_2 \leq 0.2$ and $w_0 + w_1 = 1$,

$$X_2 = 0 w_0 + 0.2 w_1 = 0.2 w_1$$

$$X_2^{1/2} \simeq 0 w_0 + 0.45 w_1 = 0.45 w_1$$

2. For $0.2 \leq X_2 \leq 0.8$ and $w_1 + w_2 = 1$,

$$X_2 = 0.2 w_1 + 0.8 w_2$$

$$X_2^{1/2} \simeq 0.45 w_1 + 0.89 w_2$$

3. For $0.8 \leq X_2 \leq 2.0$ and $w_2 + w_3 = 1$,

$$X_2 = 0.8w_2 + 2.0w_3$$
$$X_2^{1/2} \simeq 0.89w_2 + 1.41w_3$$

These linear approximations are added to the optimization model by letting

$$X_2 = 0w_0 + 0.2w_1 + 0.8w_2 + 2.0w_3$$
$$= 0.2w_1 + 0.8w_2 + 2.0w_3 \qquad (7.15)$$

and

$$X_2^{1/2} = 0w_0 + 0.45w_1 + 0.89w_2 + 1.41w_3$$
$$= 0.45w_1 + 0.89w_2 + 1.41w_3 \qquad (7.16)$$

The resulting LP model is

$$\text{Max } Z = 2X_1 + 0.45w_1 + 0.89w_2 + 1.41w_3 - 3X_3 \qquad (7.17)$$

s.t.
$$X_1 + 2w_1 + 8w_2 + 20w_3 \leq 20 \qquad (7.18)$$
$$3X_1 - 0.4w_1 - 1.6w_2 - 4w_3 + X_3 \leq 6 \qquad (7.19)$$
$$w_0 + w_1 + w_2 + w_3 = 1 \qquad (7.20)$$
$$X_1, X_3, w_0, w_1, w_2, w_3 \geq 0$$

The new model has four additional variables (w_0, w_1, w_2, w_3) and is obviously linear. However, how do we know that its optimal solution will be consistent with the linearization processes specified by conditions 1 to 3? These conditions indicate that no more than two of the weights can be nonzero and, furthermore, the nonzero weights must be adjacent. For example, if the optimal value of X_2 is in segment two ($0.2 \leq X_2^* \leq 0.8$), only w_1 and w_2 can be nonzero. Will the LP model produce an optimal solution that has this adjacent weight property?

The answer to this question is yes, and this can be demonstrated by first showing that it is never optimal to have more than two nonzero weights, and second, that these two weights must be adjacent. To establish the first result, assume that an optimal solution exists with $X_2 = X_2^*$. The optimal weights for this solution will be those that produce a value for $X_2^{1/2} \simeq 0.45w_1 + 0.89w_2 + 1.41w_3$ that is as large as possible. This problem is equivalent to the LP model

$$\text{Max } 0.45w_1 + 0.89w_2 + 1.41w_3 \qquad (7.21)$$

s.t.
$$0.2w_1 + 0.8w_2 + 2.0w_3 = X_2^* \qquad (7.22)$$
$$w_0 + w_1 + w_2 + w_3 = 1 \qquad (7.23)$$
$$w_0, w_1, w_2, w_3 \geq 0$$

168 SEPARABLE AND INTEGER PROGRAMMING

Since this model has two constraints, we know from the discussion of LP properties in Chapter 5 that an optimal solution can have, at most, two nonzero variables. Hence no optimal solution to the complete model (Expressions 7.17 to 7.20) can have more than two nonzero weights.

To see that optimal weights must be adjacent, consider the approximations for $X_2^{1/2}$ shown in Figure 7-4. For $0.2 \leq X_2 \leq 0.8$, X_2 could be given by $0w_0 + 0.8w_2$, $0.2w_1 + 0.8w_2$, $0.2w_1 + 2.0w_3$ or $0w_0 + 2.0w_3$. The linear approximations of $X_2^{1/2}$ corresponding to these alternatives are indicated by the four diagonal dashed lines in Figure 7-4. For example, if X_2 is $0w_0 + 0.8w_2 = 0.8w_2$, $X_2^{1/2}$ is approximated by $0w_0 + 0.89w_2 = 0.89w_2$. It can be seen that for *any* value of X_2 between 0.2 and 0.8, one line, $0.45w_1 + 0.89w_2$, is always above the other three; therefore the only two weights that can be optimal for this case are w_1 and w_2. A similar argument holds for values of X_2 that fall in other segments, and we can conclude that for any optimal solution no more than two weights are nonzero, and these two weights will be adjacent.

The LP model given by Expressions 7.17 to 7.20 is shown in standard form in Table 7-2. Compared with the LP model developed by method 1 (Table 7-1), the use of segment weights produces a model with fewer variables and constraints. This is because upper bounds such as Constraints 7.4 to 7.6 for each segment are not needed in the weighting approach. The solution to the LP model in Table 7-2 is $X_1^* = 3.13$,

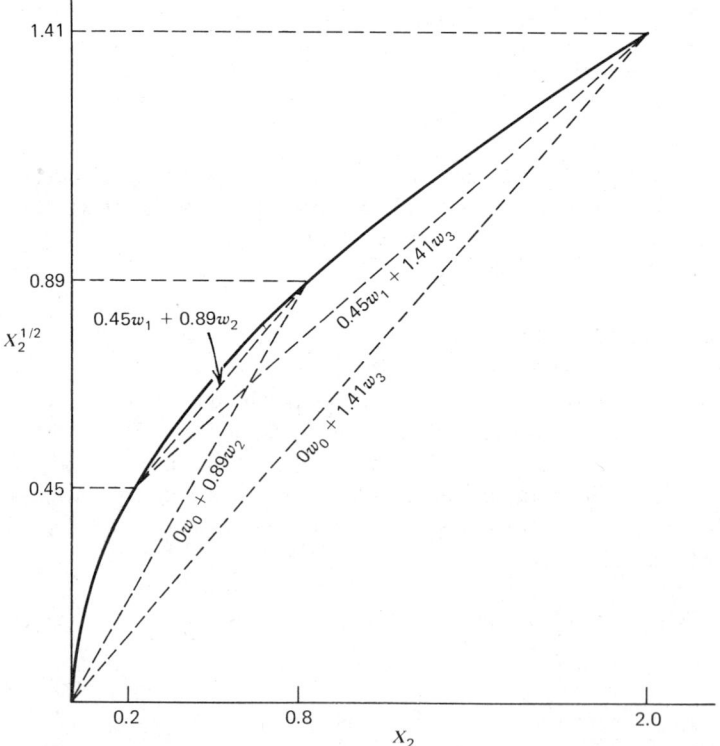

Figure 7-4. Alternative linear approximations of $X_2^{1/2}$ for $0.2 \leq X_2 \leq 0.8$.

TABLE 7-2 Coefficients of Linearized Model for Example 7-1 Using Segment Weights (Method 2)

X_1	w_0	w_1	w_2	w_3	X_3	S_1	S_2	
2	0	0.45	0.89	1.41	−3	0	0	= Z
1	0	2	8	20	0	1	0	= 20
3	0	−0.4	−1.6	−4	1	0	1	= 6
0	1	1	1	1	0	0	0	= 1

$w_2^* = 0.26$, $w_3^* = 0.74$, and $Z^* = 7.52$. This is the same solution obtained using method 1, since $X_2^* = 0.8w_2^* + 2.0w_3^* = 1.69$.

Generalized Separable Programming for Nonlinear Objective Functions

The preceding exercise is an example of separable programming. The term "separable" is taken from a property of the objective function. A function $F(X_1, X_2, \ldots, X_n)$ is said to be *separable*[1] if it can be written as

$$F(X_1, X_2, \ldots, X_n) = f_1(X_1) + f_2(X_2) + \ldots + f_n(X_n) \tag{7.24}$$

For example,

$$3X_1 - X_1^3 + 3X_2^2 - \frac{4}{X_3} + X_4 e^{X_4}$$

is a separable function, since it is the sum of four *separate* functions, each of which depends on a single decision variable. Thus

$$f_1(X_1) = 3X_1 - X_1^3$$
$$f_2(X_2) = 3X_2^2$$
$$f_3(X_3) = -\frac{4}{X_3}$$
$$f_4(X_4) = X_4 e^{X_4}$$

As a counterexample,

$$X_1 + X_2 X_3 + e^{(X_1 + X_2)}$$

is nonseparable.

---

[1] Strictly speaking, we should add the adjective *linearly* or *additive* before the word *separable*.

Any separable objective function can be linearized by either of the two methods used for Example 7-1. The linearization procedure works if the segments fill in order (method 1) or only two adjacent weights are nonzero (method 2). This condition held for the previous example, since the slopes of successive segments were *decreasing* ($\alpha_3 < \alpha_2 < \alpha_1$). This is because $X_2^{1/2}$ is a *concave* function, or a continuous function with decreasing slope. Examples of concave functions are shown in Figure 7-5. Concave functions have negative second derivatives. If the function $f_j(X_j)$ is to be maximized and is concave, the segments of the linearized approximation will fill in order or, if method 2 is used, only adjacent weights can be optimal.

The importance of maximization can be seen by changing the sign of $X_2^{1/2}$ in the objective function given by Expression 7.1. If, for example, the objective function is

$$\text{Max } Z = 2X_1 - X_2^{1/2} - 3X_3 \tag{7.1a}$$

the linearization would not have worked. The separated function to be approximated, $f_2(X_2) = -X_2^{1/2}$ can be linearized as before; using method 1 the objective function is

$$Z = 2X_1 - 2.25x_1 - 0.73x_2 - 0.43x_3 - 3X_3 \tag{7.25}$$

Since Z is being maximized, it is clearly better to increase x_3 than x_2 because this will decrease the objective function less (in an absolute sense, increase the objective function more). Considering slopes, $\alpha_1 = -2.25$, $\alpha_2 = -0.73$, and $\alpha_3 = -0.43$, it is clear that these slopes are increasing instead of decreasing ($\alpha_1 < \alpha_2 < \alpha_3$). Since the second derivative of $f_2(X_2)$

$$\frac{d^2}{dX_2^2}(-X_2^{1/2}) = \frac{X_2^{-3/2}}{4} \tag{7.26}$$

is positive, the function is nonconcave by definition.

This discussion suggests another way in which the linearization procedure could work. Suppose a linearly separable function is to be *minimized* and the separated functions $f_j(X_j)$ have *increasing slopes*. Such functions are *convex* and have positive second derivatives. Examples of convex functions are shown in Figure 7-6. When a convex function is linearized by method 1 as shown in Figure 7-7, it is clear that the slopes of successive segments are increasing ($\alpha_{j1} < \alpha_{j2} < \ldots$). When such a function is minimized, it will be optimal to make the variables with the smallest slopes as large

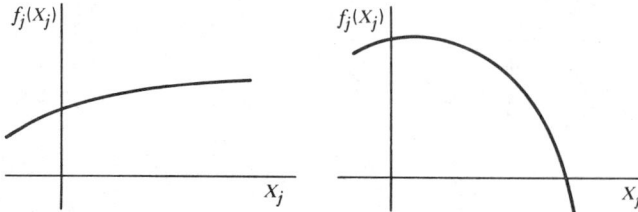

Figure 7-5. Examples of concave functions.

SEPARABLE PROGRAMMING

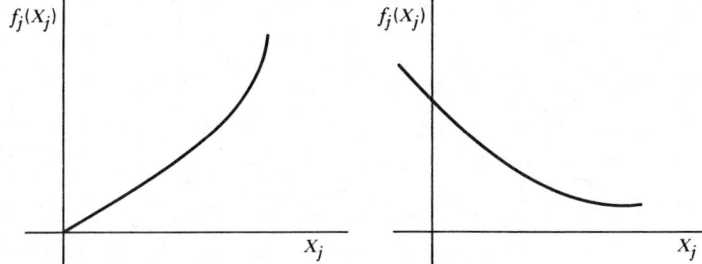

Figure 7-6. Examples of convex functions.

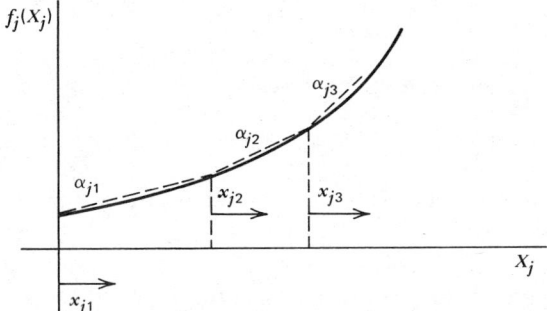

Figure 7-7. Linearization of a convex function by method 1.

as possible. It is also readily shown that when convex functions are minimized, the optimal weights for method 2 are adjacent. It follows that when convex functions are to be minimized, the LP solutions produced by separable programming will be (approximately) optimal.

We can now summarize the general characteristics of separable programming approaches to optimization models with nonlinear objective functions. The general nonlinear optimization model

$$\text{Max(Min)} \ Z = \sum_{j=1}^{n} f_j(X_j) \tag{7.28}$$

$$\text{s.t.} \quad \sum_{j=1}^{n} a_{ij} X_j = b_i \quad i = 1, 2, \ldots, m \tag{7.29}$$

$$X_j \geq 0 \quad \forall j$$

can be solved using LP if the $f_j(X_j)$ are linear or *concave* in a maximizing problem *or* the $f_j(X_j)$ are linear or *convex* in a minimizing problem.

Each nonlinear $f_j(X_j)$ is linearized with N_j segments as shown in Figure 7-8. It is only necessary to approximate $f_j(X_j)$ between the lower and upper feasible values for

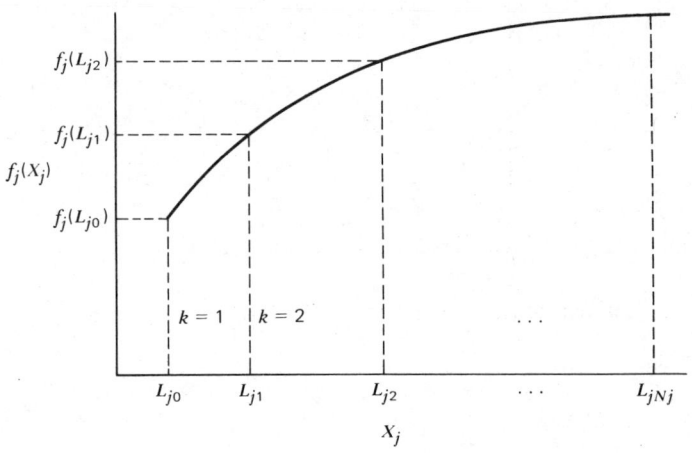

Figure 7-8. General procedure for linearizing a nonlinear function $f_j(X_j)$.

X_j (L_{j0} and L_{jN_j} in Figure 7-8). Two different methods can be used to incorporate the linearized $f_j(X_j)$ into the optimization model.

Method 1 The function $f_j(X_j)$ is approximated in the objective function as

$$f_j(X_j) = f_j(L_{j0}) + \sum_{k=1}^{N_j} \alpha_{jk} x_{jk} \tag{7.30}$$

where α_{jk} is the slope of the kth segment of $f_j(X_j)$. These slopes are given by

$$\alpha_{jk} = \frac{f_j(L_{jk}) - f_j(L_{j,k-1})}{L_{jk} - L_{j,k-1}} \tag{7.31}$$

The original variables X_j are replaced in the constraints with

$$X_j = L_{j0} + \sum_{k=1}^{N_j} x_{jk} \tag{7.32}$$

and each new variable is constrained by

$$x_{jk} \leq L_{jk} - L_{j,k-1} \tag{7.33}$$

Method 2 The function $f_j(X_j)$ is approximated in the objective function as

$$f_j(X_j) = \sum_{k=0}^{N_j} f_j(L_{jk}) w_{jk} \tag{7.34}$$

The original variables X_j are replaced in the constraints with

$$X_j = \sum_{k=0}^{N_j} L_{jk} w_{jk} \tag{7.35}$$

and the variables $w_{j0}, w_{j1}, \ldots$ are constrained by

$$\sum_{k=0}^{N_j} w_{jk} = 1 \tag{7.36}$$

An Example of Separable Programming Applied to Multiobjective Planning

EXAMPLE 7-2
A national land management agency is developing a plan for 100 km² of public land. Consistent with a general policy of multiple land uses, the agency has decided to allocate portions of the 100-km² tract to three different land uses: a wildlife sanctuary, public recreation, and commercial forestry. The government will retain title to the land, and the agency will have an annual budget of $90,000 to oversee and maintain the tract. The annual costs for the three land uses are $1000, $4000, and $5000/km² for wildlife, recreation, and forestry, respectively. Forestry also produces $7000/km² of income for the agency each year. What should the mix of land uses be for the 100 km²? It is assumed that all land in the tract is equally well suited for any of the three uses. □

Some portions of this example are readily described mathematically. If X_1, X_2, and X_3 are the areas (km²) allocated to the wildlife sanctuary, public recreation, and commercial forestry and if all 100 km² is to be included in the plan, then

$$X_1 + X_2 + X_3 = 100 \tag{7.37}$$

The budget constraint requires that total costs not exceed $90,000/yr. Noting that the cost associated with forestry is $5000 - $7000 = -$2000/km², we can write the budget constraint as

$$1000X_1 + 4000X_2 - 2000X_3 \leq 90{,}000 \tag{7.38}$$

Expressions 7.37 and 7.38 capture all the quantitative information provided in the example but do not obviously lead to the selection of an alternative. The example is open ended, since there are no quantitative statements of objectives. In terms of an optimization model, we have no objective function. Although income maximization might be inferred, this would imply that forestry is the desired land use for the tract, since it is the only option that generates income. This is hardly consistent with a policy of multiple land uses. There seem to be three qualitative objectives in this example.

1. Provide a wildlife sanctuary.
2. Provide public recreation lands.
3. Open public land to commercial forestry.

These objectives provide little basis for comparison of land use planning alternatives; before systems analysis could proceed, the agency would have to provide additional criteria for evaluating alternatives.

Public planning problems often have objectives that are quantitatively vague. Technical and financial data and constraints may be well defined, but there may be no unambiguous means of ranking feasible alternatives. This situation is not unreasonable, since public projects are intended to satisfy social needs as reflected in the decisions of its political representatives. Political decisions are usually based on a balance of many diverse interests, and it may be impossible to quantify political preferences in numerical indicators that can be used to compare alternatives. Nevertheless, commonsense generally indicates that some alternatives are better than others, and efficiency dictates that alternatives cannot be generated randomly. Instead, we would rather produce alternatives that are at least likely to be preferred by decision makers.

The usual approach to multiobjective problems, and the one used most frequently in the examples in this book, is to select a single objective for optimization and constrain the remaining objectives to certain minimum or maximum values. This is often done in environmental problems where least-cost alternatives that meet effluent or environmental standards are sought. Constraint limits may be set by law or administrative action, or they may be the best guess of the systems analyst. In any case, they can be systematically varied, and successive solutions to optimization models can indicate possible trade-offs between objectives.

Multiattribute Objective Functions The systems analyst's difficulties are minimized when all the objectives in a problem can be combined into a single objective function. For example, if the objectives can all be quantified as monetary benefits and costs, the net benefits of any alternative provides an unambiguous means of ranking alternatives. Such objective functions are sometimes referred to as "multiattribute," since they include more than one of a problem's objectives. In general, a multiattribute function should describe decision makers' preferences and need not be expressed in monetary units. The construction of such a function is an ambitious task, and it is scarcely surprising that actual applications to public planning problems are rare. We will illustrate the approach by showing how it might be applied to Example 7-2.

Multiattribute functions can have a variety of mathematical forms, but one common function is the weighted product of indicators for each separate objective (9, 14). As applied to the planning for the 100-km² tract in Example 7-2, such a function would be

$$Z = F_1^a F_2^b F_3^c \tag{7.39}$$

where $F_1(X_1)$, $F_2(X_2)$, and $F_3(X_3)$ are functions that estimate the values associated with various levels of X_1, X_2, and X_3 and a, b, and c are preference weights chosen to reflect the relative importance of the wildlife, recreation, and forestry objectives, respectively. These weights are generally chosen such that $a + b + c = 1$.

The rationale for a product form of the multiattribute objective function is twofold. Since all objectives are desirable, alternatives that provide little benefit or value with respect to one of the objectives are severely penalized. However, some objectives may be more important than others, and the coefficients a, b, and c are a means of scaling the value functions according to the relative importance of objectives.

Provided the functions and weights can be determined, the example can be described by the following optimization model.

$$\text{Max } Z = [F_1(X_1)]^a [F_2(X_2)]^b [F_3(X_3)]^c \tag{7.39}$$

s.t.
$$X_1 + X_2 + X_3 = 100 \tag{7.37}$$

$$1000X_1 + 4000X_2 - 2000X_3 \leq 90{,}000 \tag{7.38}$$

$$X_j \geq 0 \quad \forall j$$

Since the objective function given by Expression 7.39 should reflect decision makers' preferences for the various objectives, the analyst must consult with the relevant decision makers or their representatives to determine how to assign $F_j(X_j)$ values and the relative weights a, b, and c. Table 7-3 shows a possible result of these consultations. Each value function is scaled to $1 \leq F_j \leq 10$, and decision makers are asked to assign values to each of several possible levels of wildlife, recreation, or

TABLE 7-3 Decision Makers' Value Functions and Weights for the Three Objectives of Example 7-2

Wildlife Objective		Recreation Objective		Forestry Objective	
X_1 (km²)	F_1 (Value)	X_2 (km²)	F_2 (Value)	X_3 (km²)	F_3 (Value)
0	1	0	1	0	1
20	2	20	6	20	3
40	5	40	8	40	5
60	8	60	10	60	7
80	9	80	10	80	9
100	10	100	10	100	10
$a = 0.2$		$b = 0.5$		$c = 0.3$	

forestry allocations. It can be seen that the values associated with the three objectives are quite different. Decision makers evidently place a high value on provision of recreation, but only up to a certain point. Beyond $X_2 = 60$ km^2, there is no perceived improvement. Conversely, the value of forestry allocations increases much more uniformly with X_3. The weights a, b, and c reflect the decision makers' relative preferences for the three objectives. Recreation is clearly the most important objective ($b = 0.5$). The data in Table 7-3 are hypothetical and only indicate the types of results that we might obtain in this example.

Separable Programming Application With the functions and weights specified in Table 7-3, the optimization model given by Expressions 7.39, 7.37, and 7.38 can be solved to determine a set of land use allocations that best meets decision makers' preferences. The model is nonlinear and could be solved by search methods. Since the objective function is not separable, it does not seem that separable programming methods are applicable. However, it is often possible to mathematically transform functions to obtain separability. In this case, if the natural logarithm (ln) of the objective function is taken, a separable function is obtained.

$$Z' = \ln(Z) = 0.2 \ln F_1 + 0.5 \ln F_2 + 0.3 \ln F_3 \tag{7.40}$$

Since Z' is a continuously increasing function of Z, the values of F_j that maximize Z will also maximize Z'. The three functions $\ln F_1$, $\ln F_2$, and $\ln F_3$ are shown in Figure 7-9. Two of the functions, $\ln F_2$ and $\ln F_3$, are concave, but $\ln F_1$ is slightly convex in the range $20 \le X_1 \le 40$. However, all of the functions can be estimated by linear segments with decreasing slopes. Since the linear approximation to each function is concave, the general criteria for separable programming are met. The revised model is

$$\text{Max } Z' = 0.2 \ln F_1(X_1) + 0.5 \ln F_2(X_2) + 0.3 \ln F_3(X_3) \tag{7.40}$$

$$\text{s.t.} \quad X_1 + X_2 + X_3 = 100 \tag{7.37}$$

$$X_1 + 4X_2 + -2X_3 \le 90 \tag{7.38}$$

$$X_j \ge 0 \quad \forall j$$

where $F_j(X_j)$ are the functions given in Table 7-3 and Constraint 7.38 has been simplified by dividing both sides by 1000.

Using the segment weighting procedure (method 2), variables w_{jk} are defined for each function, and the linear approximations are

$$\ln F_1 \simeq 2.08 w_{11} + 2.30 w_{12} \tag{7.41}$$

$$\ln F_2 \simeq 1.79 w_{21} + 2.30 w_{22} + 2.30 w_{23} \tag{7.42}$$

$$\ln F_3 \simeq 1.10 w_{31} + 1.95 w_{32} + 2.30 w_{33} \tag{7.43}$$

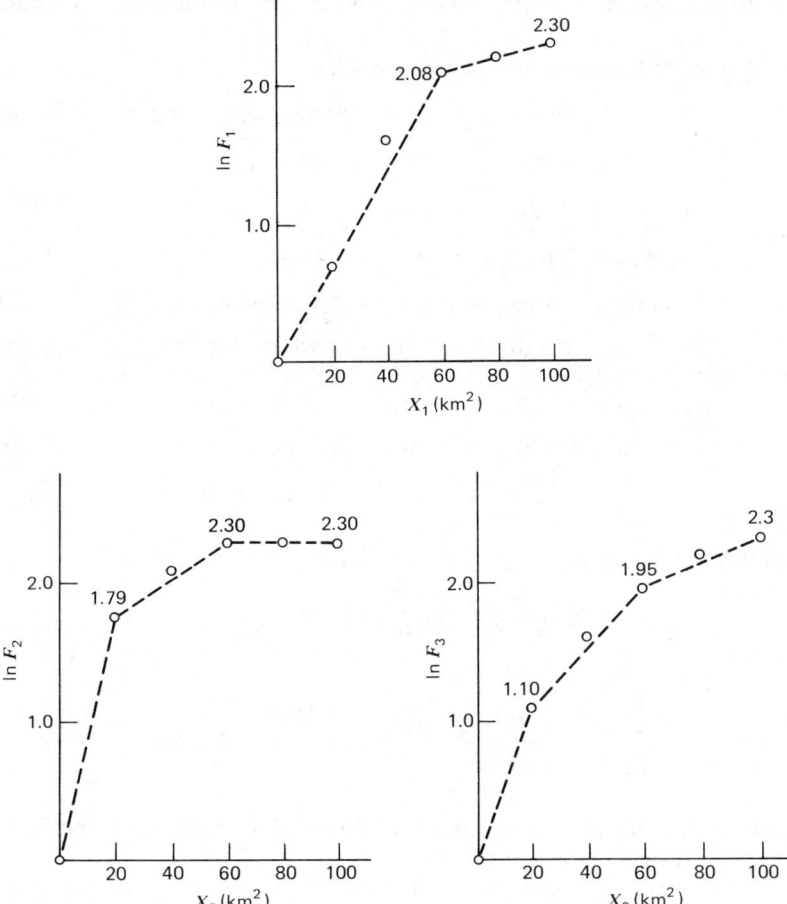

Figure 7-9. Functions ln F_j and their linear approximations.

The objective function becomes

$$Z' = 0.416w_{11} + 0.46w_{12} + 0.895w_{21} + 1.15w_{22}$$
$$+ 1.15w_{23} + 0.33w_{31} + 0.585w_{32} + 0.69w_{33} \quad (7.40a)$$

The original decision variables are given by

$$X_1 = 60w_{11} + 100w_{12} \quad (7.44)$$
$$X_2 = 20w_{21} + 60w_{22} + 100w_{23} \quad (7.45)$$
$$X_3 = 20w_{31} + 60w_{32} + 100w_{33} \quad (7.46)$$

With these substitutions, the multiobjective model now assumes the following LP form.

$$\text{Max } Z' = 0.416w_{11} + 0.46w_{12} + 0.895w_{21} + 1.15w_{22}$$
$$+ 1.15w_{23} + 0.33w_{31} + 0.585w_{32} + 0.69w_{33} \quad (7.40a)$$

s.t.
$$60w_{11} + 100w_{12} + 20w_{21} + 60w_{22}$$
$$+ 100w_{23} + 20w_{31} + 60w_{32} + 100w_{33} = 100 \quad (7.37a)$$

$$60w_{11} + 100w_{12} + 80w_{21} + 240w_{22}$$
$$+ 400w_{23} - 40w_{31} - 120w_{32} - 200w_{33} \leq 90 \quad (7.47)$$

$$w_{10} + w_{11} + w_{12} \qquad\qquad = 1 \quad (7.47)$$
$$w_{20} + w_{21} + w_{22} + w_{23} = 1 \quad (7.48)$$
$$w_{30} + w_{31} + w_{32} + w_{33} = 1 \quad (7.49)$$
$$w_{jk} \geq 0 \qquad \forall j, k$$

The solution to this LP model is

$$w_{10}^* = 0.555, \qquad w_{11}^* = 0.945$$
$$w_{21}^* = 1.00$$
$$w_{31}^* = 0.917, \qquad w_{32}^* = 0.083$$
$$(Z')^* = 1.64$$

Translating these results back to the original model (Expressions 7.39, 7.37, and 7.38) we have

$$X_1^* \text{ (wildlife)} = 0.945(60) = 56.7 \text{ km}^2$$
$$X_2^* \text{ (recreation)} = 1.00(20) = 20 \text{ km}^2$$
$$X_3^* \text{ (forestry)} = 0.917(20) + 0.083(60) = 23.3 \text{ km}^2$$
$$Z^* = e^{Z'} = 5.16$$

The optimal plan for the preference data in Table 7-3 leads to an allocation of more than 50% of the land to a wildlife sanctuary. This is in spite of the relatively low weight given the wildlife objective ($a = 0.2$) and is due to the relatively low cost of this land use and the rapid rate of increase in the value function $F_1(X_1)$ in the range $20 \leq X_1 \leq 60$.

The determination of a single optimal plan would hardly end the systems analyst's work in this example. Preferences change with time as new decision makers exert their influence and old decision makers change their minds. Often the presentation of an alternative that supposedly conforms to preferences changes the preferences. Since the preference weights a, b, and c are usually the most uncertain parameters, the analyst may anticipate variations in preferences by systematically changing the weights and solving the LP model for each set of weights. The resulting group of alternatives could then be presented to decision makers. If none of the alternatives were acceptable, further iterations would be necessary, based on revisions of the value functions $F_j(X_j)$.

When optimization models are applied to multiobjective problems, the term "optimal" is only relative. Optimization can seldom be used to produce a single "best" alternative. Instead, an optimization model becomes a mathematical means of generating alternatives that may possibly correspond to decision makers' preferences. Solutions to multiobjective problems are produced by iterative processes involving modeling, consultation with decision makers and, hopefully, convergence on an alternative that is politically feasible.

Generalized Separable Programming

When the LP approximation to a nonlinear optimization model satisfies the required conditions for optimality (segments filled in order or adjacent nonzero weighting variables), the simplex method can be used directly to solve the LP model. When these conditions are not met (e.g., when convex functions are maximized), special algorithms can be used to force the necessary properties. For example, the simplex method can be modified with a "restricted entry" procedure that limits solutions to those that fill segments in order or have adjacent weights. When this is done, the optimal solutions to the LP model are local, not global, optima. These general algorithms for separable programming are available at many computer centers and can be used with nonlinear optimization models that have separable constraints or objective functions.

INTEGER LINEAR PROGRAMMING

Noninteger decision variables have little meaning in some environmental problems. For example, a decision variable in a solid waste management problem might be the number of refuse collection trucks. Obviously, such a variable can only have an integer (0, 1, 2, . . .) value. Since LP solution procedures such as the simplex method treat variables as continuous, integer variables often create difficulties in models that would otherwise be directly solvable using LP methods. Integer LP problems can be classified as pure or mixed integer. In the former, all decision variables must be integers; in mixed integer problems there is an assortment of integer and continuous variables.

The easiest way to deal with integer restrictions on variables is to ignore them. Consider the model

$$\text{Max } Z = 5X_1 + 2.5X_2 \quad (7.50)$$

$$\text{s.t.} \quad 3X_1 + 6X_2 \le 24 \quad (7.51)$$

$$X_1 - 2X_2 \le 4 \quad (7.52)$$

$$X_1, X_2 \ge 0$$

where both X_1 and X_2 must be integers; that is, $X_j \varepsilon$ (0, 1, 2, . . .). Suppose an initial solution is obtained to the model without considering the integer nature of the variables. This optimal solution is indicated graphically in Figure 7-10, where $X_1^* = 6$, $X_2^* = 1$, and $Z^* = 32.5$. This same solution would have been obtained from the simplex method.

We can always try to solve an integer LP problem by treating variables as continuous and obtaining an optimal solution by graphical means or the simplex method. If the optimal solution has integer values for decision variables, it must be the optimal solution to the integer problem. Unfortunately, this frequently does not happen. Consider the following model, where again X_1 and X_2 must be integers.

$$\text{Max } Z = 5X_1 + 2.5X_2 \tag{7.53}$$

$$\text{s.t.} \quad 3X_1 + 7X_2 \leq 24 \tag{7.54}$$

$$X_1 - 2X_2 \leq 5 \tag{7.55}$$

$$X_1, X_2 \geq 0$$

The feasible region for the model is shown in Figure 7-11. Feasible integer solutions are also shown in the figure. If the model is solved for the continuous case, the optimal solution is point A, or $X_1^* = 6.38$, $X_2^* = 0.69$, and $Z^* = 33.6$. This solution is unsuitable, since neither X_1^* nor X_2^* are integers.

Integer solutions are often determined by rounding off noninteger values. We can round off the continuous solution to $X_1^* = 6$, $X_2^* = 1$, which would give $Z^* = 32.5$. With very large integer models this is often the only practical means of obtaining a solution. However, such an approach has drawbacks. In this case $X_1 = 6, X_2 = 1$ is not even a feasible solution to the original model because Constraint 7.54 is violated [$3(6) + 7(1) = 25$, which is greater than 24].

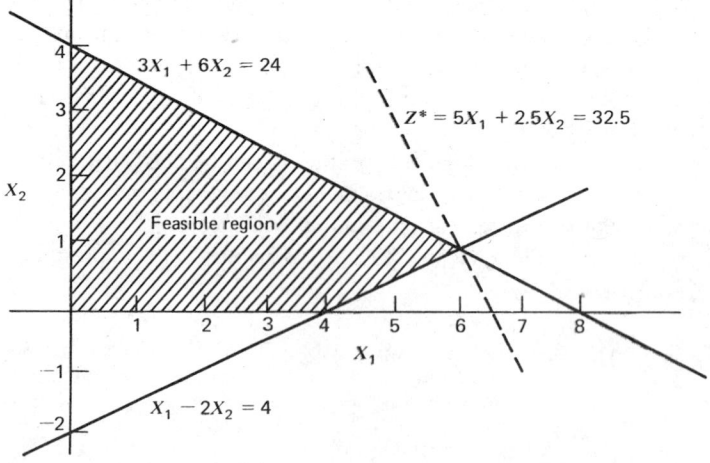

Figure 7-10. Graphical solution to an integer LP problem.

INTEGER LINEAR PROGRAMMING

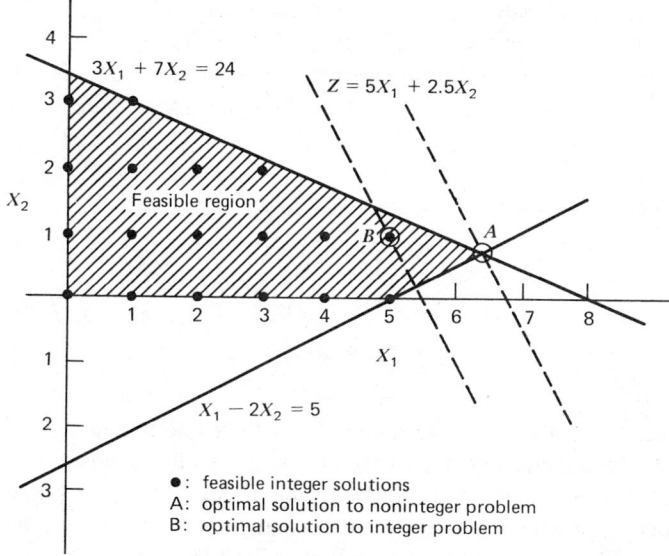

Figure 7-11. Continuous and integer solutions to an integer LP model.

An optimal integer solution can be determined graphically for this two-dimensional model. In Figure 7-11 the objective function $Z = 5X_1 + 2.5X_2$ is maximized at point B, $X_1^* = 5$, $X_2^* = 1$, and $Z^* = 27.5$. The most interesting aspect of this solution is that it is *not* an extreme point of the feasible region. Since the simplex method examines only extreme points, it is clear that the method would never find the optimal solution to this integer LP problem.

Integer Programming Algorithms

A variety of algorithms have been developed for solving integer LP problems. These algorithms are often available at computer centers and are usually based on the simplex method. A series of continuous-variable LP models is solved until the solutions converge on an optimal integer solution. Since each integer solution requires a number of continuous solutions, large integer models require a great deal of computer time. Two general procedures that can be used to solve integer LP models are *cutting plane* and *branch-and-bound* algorithms. The former adds constraints to shrink the feasible region until an integer optimal extreme point is obtained. The latter divides the feasible region into sections and finds optimal solutions for each section. Subsequent divisions are designed to isolate the portion of the feasible region containing the optimal solution.

Both cutting plane and branch-and-bound algorithms can be applied to pure or mixed integer problems, and both perform satisfactorily on small to moderate models (say less than 20 to 30 integer variables). With larger models, branch-and-bound algorithms are usually more efficient. The following discussion is limited to cutting plane methods, mainly because they are somewhat more straightforward and lend

182 SEPARABLE AND INTEGER PROGRAMMING

themselves well to an intuitive interpretation. Branch-and-bound algorithms are presented in several of the references at the end of this chapter (1, 3, 6).

A cutting plane algorithm can be demonstrated using the previous integer LP model (Expressions 7.53 to 7.55 and Figure 7-11). Adding the appropriate slack variables, the model is

$$\text{Max } Z = 5X_1 + 2.5X_2 \tag{7.53}$$

s.t.
$$3X_1 + 7X_2 + S_1 = 24 \tag{7.54}$$

$$X_1 - 2X_2 + S_2 = 5 \tag{7.55}$$

$$X_1, X_2 \; \varepsilon \; (0, 1, 2, \ldots)$$

Since the decision variables X_1 and X_2 must be integers and their coefficients in the constraints are integers, it is clear that the slack variables will also be integers. The objective of cutting planes is to add constraints to the LP model to create an optimal integer extreme point. Thus, even when the new LP model is treated as continuous, an integer solution will be obtained. This is illustrated in Figure 7-12. If two constraints, $X_1 \le 5$ and $X_1 + X_2 \le 6$ are added to the feasible region, the optimal extreme point is $X_1^* = 5$, $X_2^* = 1$, and the integer problem is solved.

The key issue in the approach is the identification of the necessary cutting plane constraints. With two-dimensional models they can be determined by graphical inspection but, for larger models, an analytical procedure is necessary. Fortunately, constraints can be determined directly from the optimal simplex tableau. For the original LP model (Expressions 7.53, 7.54, and 7.55), this tableau is

$$Z = 33.65 - 2.11S_2 - 0.96S_1 \tag{7.56}$$

$$X_2 = \frac{9}{13} + \frac{3}{13} S_2 - \frac{1}{13} S_1 \tag{7.57}$$

$$X_1 = 6\frac{5}{13} - \frac{7}{13} S_2 - \frac{2}{13} S_1 \tag{7.58}$$

This tableau can be derived by following the simplex method steps outlined in Chapter 5. Alternatively, since the optimal solution (point A in Figure 7-11) is at the intersection of Constraints 7.54 and 7.55, $S_1^* = S_2^* = 0$. These variables must be on the right side of the tableau constraints. If Equations 7.54 and 7.55 are solved for X_1 and X_2 in terms of S_1 and S_2, Equations 7.56 to 7.58, the three tableau equations, are obtained.

Consider Equation 7.58. It can be written in the following form.

$$X_1 + \left(0 + \frac{7}{13}\right)S_2 + \left(0 + \frac{2}{13}\right)S_1 = 6 + \frac{5}{13} \tag{7.58a}$$

INTEGER LINEAR PROGRAMMING

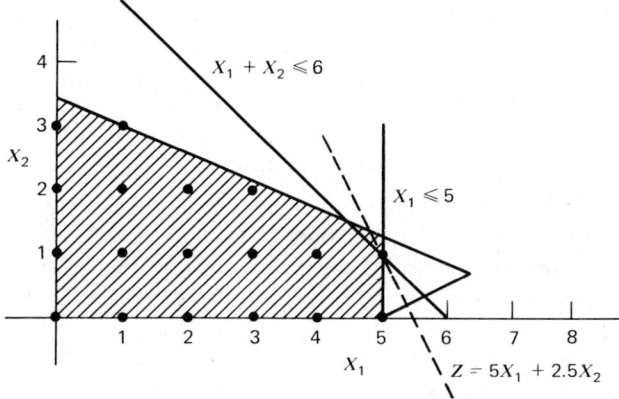

Figure 7-12. Solution to integer LP model with addition of cutting planes.

Each noninteger coefficient has been rearranged as the sum of an integer and a positive fraction. The equation can also be written as

$$\frac{7}{13} S_2 + \frac{2}{13} S_1 = \frac{5}{13} + (6 - X_1) \qquad (7.58b)$$

Since Equation 7.58b is no more than a manipulation of the LP model's original constraints, any solution to the model, including any integer solution, must satisfy it. If X_1 is an integer, this implies that

$$\frac{7}{13} S_2 + \frac{2}{13} S_1 \geq \frac{5}{13} \qquad (7.59)$$

To derive this result, we first observe that since S_1 and S_2 cannot be negative, the left side of Equation 7.58b must be nonnegative. This also implies that

$$\frac{5}{13} + (6 - X_1) \geq 0 \qquad (7.60)$$

Since the quantity $6 - X_1$ is integer valued, the right side of Constraint 7.60 can only have the values 6 5/13, 5 5/13, 4 5/13, 3 5/13, 2 5/13, 1 5/13 or 5/13. Hence Constraint 7.59 is a necessary (but not sufficient) condition for an integer solution. Subtracting a surplus variable S from the constraint, it becomes

$$\frac{7}{13} S_2 + \frac{2}{13} S_1 - S = \frac{5}{13}$$

or

$$S = -\frac{5}{13} + \frac{7}{13}S_2 + \frac{2}{13}S_1 \tag{7.59a}$$

This equation can be added directly to the optimal simplex tableau, and we can proceed to solutions of the new LP model (Expressions 7.53 to 7.55 and 7.59) by starting the simplex iterations with the new tableau given by Equations 7.56 to 7.58 and 7.59a.[2]

The effect of the new constraint on the feasible region is shown in Figure 7-13. Substituting $S_1 = 24 - 3X_1 - 7X_2$ and $S_2 = 5 - X_1 + 2X_2$ into Constraint 7.59, we obtain

$$\frac{7}{13}(5 - X_1 + 2X_2) + \frac{2}{13}(24 - 3X_1 - 7X_2) \geq \frac{5}{13}$$

or

$$35 - 7X_1 + 14X_2 + 48 - 6X_1 - 14X_2 \geq 5$$

which reduces to

$$X_1 \leq 6 \tag{7.61}$$

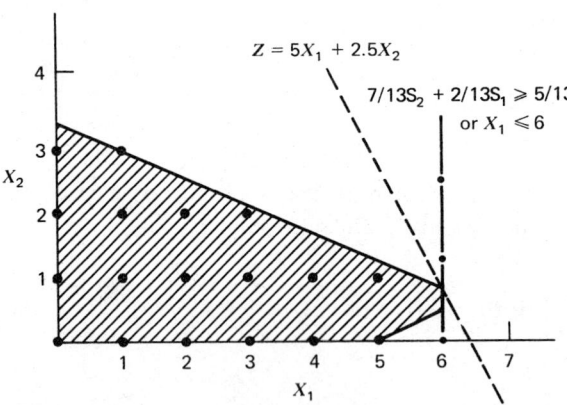

Figure 7-13. Addition of a cutting plane constraint.

---

[2] This initial tableau gives an infeasible solution, since $S = -5/13$. At this point it is necessary to switch to the associated dual LP model to obtain a feasible solution. A modification of the simplex algorithm known as the dual simplex method is used with these integer problems. The method computes both primal and dual tableau entries at each iteration.

The new LP model is

$$\text{Max } Z = 5X_1 + 2.5X_2 \tag{7.53}$$

s.t.
$$3X_1 + 7X_2 + S_1 = 24 \tag{7.54}$$
$$X_1 - 2X_2 + S_2 = 5 \tag{7.55}$$
$$X_1 + S_3 = 6 \tag{7.61}$$

The new constraint has shaved the corner from the feasible region where the old noninteger optimal solution was. With the new feasible region, the optimal solution is at the intersection of Constraints 7.54 and 7.61, which is $X_1^* = 6$, $X_2^* = 6/7$. X_2^* is not an integer, so further iterations are necessary. S_1^* and S_3^* are zero, and the equation for X_2 in the final simplex tableau can be derived by solving Equations 7.54 and 7.61 in terms of S_1 and S_3. This gives

$$X_2 = \frac{6}{7} - \frac{1}{7} S_1 + \frac{3}{7} S_3 \tag{7.62}$$

Separating integer and positive fractional components as before produces

$$X_2 + \left(0 + \frac{1}{7}\right) S_1 + \left(-1 + \frac{4}{7}\right) S_3 = \frac{6}{7}$$

or

$$\frac{1}{7} S_1 + \frac{4}{7} S_3 = \frac{6}{7} + (S_3 - X_2) \tag{7.62a}$$

Following the previous reasoning, the new cutting plane constraint is

$$\frac{1}{7} S_1 + \frac{4}{7} S_3 \geq \frac{6}{7} \tag{7.63}$$

or, when substitutions for S_1 and S_3 are made,

$$X_1 + X_2 \leq 6 \tag{7.64}$$

The new feasible region is shown in Figure 7-14. The new optimal solution, at the intersection of Constraint 7.55 and the new constraint

$$X_1 + X_2 + S_4 = 6 \tag{7.64}$$

is $X_1^* = 5\ 2/3$, $X_2^* = 1/3$.

A noninteger solution has again been obtained although, as can be seen from

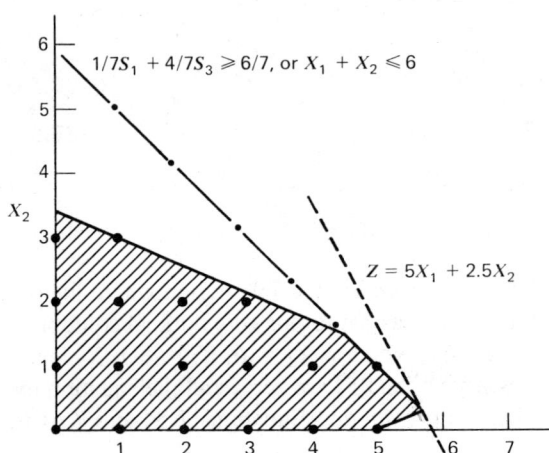

Figure 7-14. Second cutting plane constraint.

Figure 7-14, the noninteger portion of the feasible region is steadily being reduced without eliminating any feasible integer points. The equation for X_1 in the solution is

$$X_1 = 5\frac{2}{3} - \frac{1}{3}S_2 - \frac{2}{3}S_4 \tag{7.65}$$

The resulting cutting plane is

$$\frac{1}{3}S_2 + \frac{2}{3}S_4 \geq \frac{2}{3} \tag{7.66}$$

or

$$X_1 \leq 5 \tag{7.67}$$

Adding this constraint to the model produces the feasible region of Figure 7-15. An optimal integer extreme point has now been isolated; it can be seen that the objective function $Z = 5X_1 + 2.5X_2$ is now maximized at $X_1^* = 5$, $X_2^* = 1$.

The cutting plane calculations are simple algebraic operations that are readily programmed for computer. The algorithm essentially involves successive applications of the simplex method where, after each optimal solution, a new constraint is added and the newly enlarged simplex tableau is the starting point for additional iterations.

Integer LP can sometimes be used to solve models that would otherwise require a search approach. Such models may not initially contain integer variables, but they can be restructured in an integer format and subsequently solved by integer LP. One example is the "fixed charge problem." This classic systems analysis application is illustrated by a solid wastes management example in the following section.

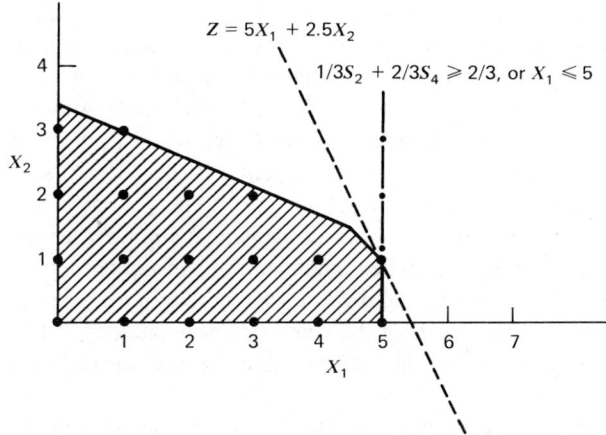

Figure 7-15. Addition of third cutting plane constraint and optimal solution to the integer LP problem.

Municipal Solid Wastes Management Example—A Fixed Charge Problem

Solid waste is a residual product from human activities that occurs as a solid as opposed to a liquid or gas. Solid wastes include agricultural manures and crop residues, mining slag, residential, commercial, and institutional garbage, abandoned automobiles, litter such as beverage cans and bottles, and dewatered sludges from wastewater treatment plants. The problems associated with solid wastes are equally varied. Garbage and other refuse accumulations can cause health and safety problems, litter and abandoned automobiles are aesthetic nuisances, mining wastes can result in drainage of acid waters to streams, and improper manure disposal often contributes nonpoint source nutrient inputs to surface and groundwaters.

Although most forms of solid waste have inherent environmental dangers, municipal solid wastes are frequently of most concern. These wastes include garbage and refuse from homes, commercial, and industrial establishments, street sweepings, and sludges. After collection, municipal solid wastes may be disposed of by incineration, landfilling, ocean dumping, and recycling. Incineration is a relatively expensive disposal alternative that can result in air pollution. Sanitary landfills involve the disposal of waste on large land surfaces. The solid waste is spread in layers on low-lying areas, with layers of earth separating layers of waste. After subsidence, landfill areas may be used for parks or other recreational activities. Buildings are sometimes constructed on sanitary landfills, but differential settling and seepage of gases such as methane often cause serious difficulties. Ocean dumping has been a common means of solid waste disposal for coastal cities but, because of uncertain effects on marine waters, the practice has been discontinued in many areas.

Recycling is in many ways the most attractive means of solid waste disposal; it treats the waste as a resource from which economic value can be derived. Various recycling options are available, many of which have long been in common use. Newspapers and other paper material are recycled in paper production, metals such as copper, aluminum, and lead are salvaged and recycled, and the organic portions of solid wastes are sometimes composted and used as a soil conditioner. The production of energy from solid waste combustion can be economically attractive when traditional energy resources are scarce. The primary difficulty with recycling is the need to sort or separate the various components of municipal solid wastes prior to recycling. Some sorting can be done at the source as, for example, when homeowners compost leaves and other organic wastes and save newspapers, bottles, and cans for subsequent return to recycling centers. In high-density urban areas, solid waste sorting requires a centralized facility within which the various components of the waste can be separated. It has proved very difficult to design large-scale sorting facilities that are economical and reliable.

The great variety of solid waste management problems suggests the need for many different types of models. Models have been used to evaluate the environmental impacts of solid waste disposal alternatives. Examples are manure disposal, acid mine drainage, waste incineration, and leaching of chemicals from sanitary landfills and sludge disposal areas. In addition, models have been developed to aid in the development of cost-effective plans for collection and disposal of municipal solid wastes. The following example illustrates this problem with a fixed charge solid waste disposal model.

EXAMPLE 7-3

Two cities wish to develop a regional disposal system for their solid wastes. Three disposal alternatives are possible: sanitary landfill, incineration, and ocean dumping. Each alternative must meet environmental or effluent standards. For example, the emissions from the waste incinerator must meet air pollution standards. The costs of meeting standards are included in the total cost of each alternative.

The waste disposal operation has two components. First, the waste must be hauled (at some cost) from each community to a disposal site (landfill, burning, or ocean dumping). Some disposal methods may be inexpensive, but they are far from the cities. Others may be quite expensive, but they are close enough for inexpensive hauling.

City 1 has a population of 40,000 and a weekly solid waste production of 700 t. City 2, with 65,000 people, generates 1200 t/wk.

Site 1, which will be an incinerator, is 15 km from city 1 and 10 km from city 2. Site 2, which is the shore embarking point for ocean dumping, is 5 and 15 km from cities 1 and 2, respectively. The sanitary landfill is 30 km from city 1 and 25 km from city 2.

The fixed and variable costs, as well as the capacity for each disposal alternative, are listed in Table 7-4.

The cost of hauling is $0.50/t/km. The problem, which is illustrated in Figure 7-16, is to determine which of the disposal alternatives should be built and operated by the cities. □

As with most problems of this type, the rationale for investigating regional systems is the presence of economies of scale. In this case the economies are manifest in fixed

TABLE 7-4 Costs and Capacities of Solid Waste Disposal Alternatives

Site	Method	Fixed Cost ($/yr)	Variable Cost ($/t)	Capacity (t/wk)
1	Incineration	200,000	12	1000
2	Ocean dumping	60,000	16	500
3	Sanitary landfill	100,000	6	1300

costs associated with construction and "start-up" of the disposal alternatives. The cost function for incineration is shown in Figure 7-17. The function is discontinuous at the origin, since the fixed cost of $200,000/yr is incurred only if the incinerator is built. The effects of fixed costs on unit or average costs are shown in Figure 7-18. Unit costs fall sharply with increased incinerator use because the fixed cost is spread out over the greater quantities incinerated. For example, at 10,000 t/yr, the unit or average cost is

$$\frac{200{,}000 + 120{,}000}{10{,}000} = \$32/t$$

At 80,000 t/yr, unit cost drops to

$$\frac{200{,}000 + 960{,}000}{80{,}000} = \$14.5/t$$

Before beginning a systems analysis of any problem, we should determine if the

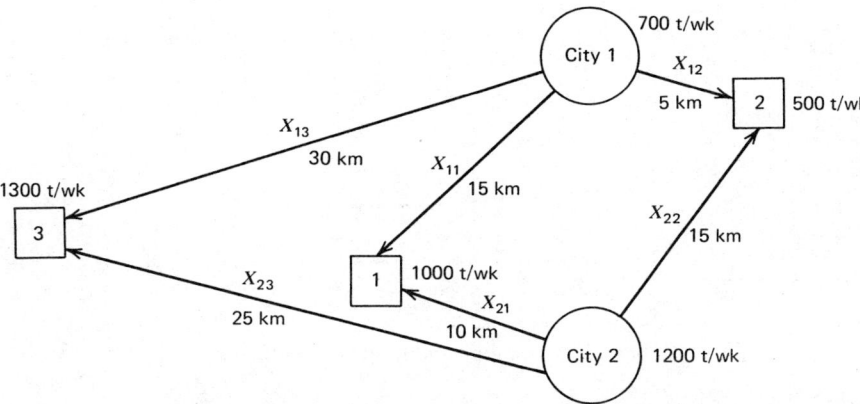

Figure 7-16. Sources and disposal alternatives for solid wastes management example.

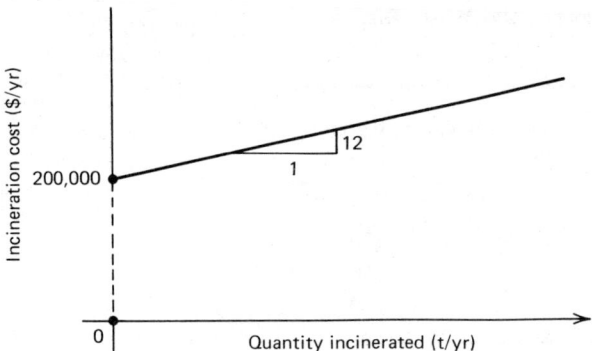

Figure 7-17. Incineration cost function.

problem is amenable to the systems approach. As suggested in Chapter 2, such problems have four general attributes.

1. Clearly defined, quantifiable objectives.
2. Describable by a reasonably tractable mathematical model.
3. Sufficient data to characterize the effects of alternate solutions.
4. No obvious best alternative.

At first glance, the objectives are clear: dispose of the two cities' solid wastes at minimum total cost. However, this presumes a regional or joint authority to operate the disposal facilities and a system of cost sharing that is mutually agreeable to the two cities. Without these administrative arrangements the economic objectives may be neither clear nor quantifiable. In fact, they may become evident only after years of political feuding.

The extent to which the problem can be modeled is usually determined only after the modeling effort is initiated. The third criterion (sufficient data) is apparently met,

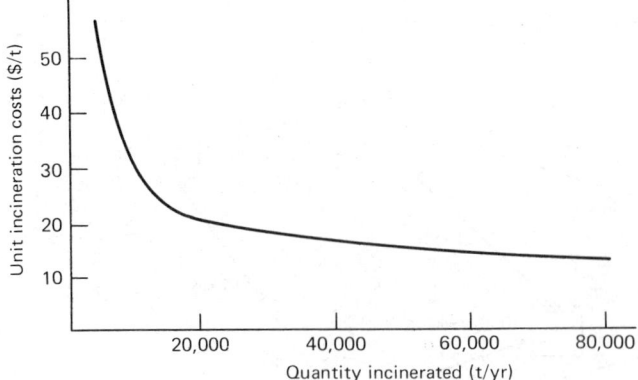

Figure 7-18. Unit incineration costs as a function of incinerator use.

since we have a complete description of solid waste production, disposal capacities, and costs associated with waste transport and disposal.

The existence of an obvious best alternative is conditional on the ingenuity of the analyst. If the analyst is clever enough to identify an optimal solution without constructing a model, a great deal of unnecessary work can be avoided. Most individuals would probably have difficulty solving this solid wastes example without using an optimization model. It is not difficult, however, to conceive of a similar problem in which the best alternative could be determined with very little effort. If the solid waste disposal facilities were already in operation so that fixed costs could be ignored, and each facility could accommodate the total solid waste production from the two cities (i.e., no capacity constraints), each city could be treated independently and a simple cost accounting procedure used to determine the least expensive disposal alternative. For example, we might first consider city 1 and calculate the cost per tonne (transportation plus disposal) of incineration, ocean dumping, and landfilling. The alternative with the cheapest cost would be selected. A similar accounting procedure would be used for city 2.

Fixed costs and capacity constraints complicate the problem and preclude this independent accounting procedure. The decisions of one city will affect the unit costs and disposal capacities available to the other city. Such interdependence is best described by an optimization model, and it seems unlikely that any but the most perceptive analyst would be able to see an obvious solution to this problem.

Definition of System and Objectives The system that describes the problem is shown in Figure 7-16. Components are the solid waste sources, cities 1 and 2, and the various disposal alternatives—incineration (1), ocean dumping (2), and sanitary landfilling (3). The boundaries of the system exclude several potential environmental problems such as the effects of ocean dumping on marine waters and of incineration on air quality. This follows from the problem statement, which presumes that relevant environmental and effluent standards are incorporated in the design and operation of disposal alternatives. These standards simplify the analysis considerably; without them it would be necessary to consider the mechanisms of pollutant transport and assimilation in the ocean and atmosphere. Similarly, the leaching of pollutants from the landfill to groundwaters would require analysis.

In the absence of environmental or effluent standards, this problem would be so complicated that it might defy rational solution by any means, including systems analysis. With the standards, we can essentially ignore environmental objectives, and what remains is a cost-effectiveness problem with two objectives.

1. Minimize total costs($/wk) of solid waste transport and disposal.
2. Dispose of the solid waste from city 1 (700 t/wk) and city 2 (1200 t/wk).

Generation and Evaluation of Alternatives (Modeling) As usual, a mathematical statement of the problem requires definition of decision variables and description of objectives, mass balances, and physical limitations such as capacities. Each of these

192 SEPARABLE AND INTEGER PROGRAMMING

three types of relationships must be written in terms of the decision variables. Two different types of factors can be controlled in the problem. The first is whether or not a particular disposal alternative is implemented. This requires a discontinuous variable; based on our knowledge of integer programming, an integer variable would be appropriate.

$$Y_j = \begin{cases} 1 & \text{if disposal method } j \text{ is used} \\ 0 & \text{otherwise} \end{cases}$$

With this type of definition, linear terms can be incorporated into the objective function to account for fixed costs. For example, the fixed cost of incinerators (\$/wk) is $200,000/52 = \$3850$, and the addition of $3850Y_1$ to an objective function will correctly reflect the fixed cost of incineration provided Y_1 is forced to be 1 when incineration is used and 0 otherwise. It remains to be seen whether constraints can be designed to limit Y_j to the desired values.

In addition to selecting disposal alternatives to implement, it is also possible to control the quantities of each city's solid waste that are incinerated, dumped in the ocean, or landfilled. A second decision variable is shown in Figure 7-16 and is defined as

X_{ij} = quantity of solid waste transported from city i to disposal location j (t/wk)

There are nine decision variables, three of which (Y_1, Y_2, Y_3) are integer.

Model construction can begin with mass balances at each city.

$$\sum_{j=1}^{3} X_{1j} = 700 \tag{7.68}$$

$$\sum_{j=1}^{3} X_{2j} = 1200 \tag{7.69}$$

Equations 7.68 and 7.69 also quantify the second objective of the systems analysis (solid waste disposal). Mass balances are similarly necessary at each disposal site. These balances are incorporated in capacity constraints at the three sites.

$$\sum_{i=1}^{2} X_{i1} \leq 1000 \tag{7.70}$$

$$\sum_{i=1}^{2} X_{i2} \leq 500 \tag{7.71}$$

$$\sum_{i=1}^{2} X_{i3} \leq 1300 \tag{7.72}$$

Quantification of annual costs Z requires us to consider fixed, transportation, and variable disposal costs. Converting to $/wk, fixed costs are $3850Y_1 + 1150Y_2 + 1920Y_3$. Transportation costs are computed by multiplying hauling costs by distance by amount hauled. For example, the transportation cost ($/wk) of hauling the solid wastes from city 1 to the incinerator are ($0.50/t) (15 km) $(X_{11}) = 7.5X_{11}$. Total transportation costs for the two cities are

City 1: $7.5X_{11} + 2.5X_{12} + 15.0X_{13}$

City 2: $5.0X_{21} + 7.5X_{22} + 12.5X_{23}$

Variable costs of disposal for incineration, ocean dumping, and landfilling are calculated as variable cost times weekly waste disposal. For the two cities, these costs are

$$12.0X_{11} + 16.0X_{12} + 6.0X_{13} + 12.0X_{21} + 16.0X_{22} + 6.0X_{23}$$

Collecting terms, the total costs of solid waste transport and disposal are

$$Z = 3850Y_1 + 1150Y_2 + 1920Y_3 + 19.5X_{11} + 18.5X_{12}$$

$$+ 21.0X_{13} + 17.0X_{21} + 23.5X_{22} + 18.5X_{23} \qquad (7.73)$$

To complete the model, it remains only to constrain the integer variables such that

$$Y_j = \begin{cases} 0 & \text{if} \quad X_{1j} + X_{2j} = 0 \\ 1 & \text{if} \quad X_{1j} + X_{2j} > 0 \end{cases} \qquad (7.74)$$

Since the other relationships between variables are linear, if the constraints on Y_j are also linear the resulting optimization model will be a mixed integer LP model that can be solved by available computer programs. One obvious constraint is a limitation on the possible values of Y_j.

$$Y_j \leq 1 \qquad \forall j \qquad (7.75)$$

Given that Y_j is an integer, Constraint 7.75 limits Y_j to be either 0 or 1. If the optimization model consisted of the objective function given by Expression 7.73 and Constraints 7.68 to 7.72 and 7.75, an optimal solution would always have $Y_j^* = 0$. This is because costs are to be minimized, and the coefficients of Y_j in the objective function are positive. Thus Y_j will be made as small as possible in any solution. How then can we force Y_j to be one when $X_{1j} + X_{2j}$ is nonzero? Consider the constraint

$$10{,}000Y_j \geq X_{1j} + X_{2j} \qquad (7.76)$$

where "10,000" is an arbitrary number at least as large as the maximum possible value of $X_{1j} + X_{2j}$. If $X_{1j} + X_{2j}$ is greater than zero, Y_j must also be greater than zero and hence equal to one in order to satisfy the constraint. Conversely, if $X_{1j} + X_{2j}$ is equal to zero, Y_j can be either zero or one. However, in order to minimize costs, Y_j must be zero, as explained previously. We conclude that Constraints 7.75 and 7.76 are equivalent to Constraint 7.74. The resulting mixed integer LP model is

$$\text{Min } Z = 3850Y_1 + 1150Y_2 + 1920Y_3 + 19.5X_{11} + 18.5X_{12}$$
$$+ 21.0X_{13} + 17.0X_{21} + 23.5X_{22} + 18.5X_{23} \quad (7.73)$$

s.t.
$$\sum_{j=1}^{3} X_{1j} = 700 \quad (7.68)$$

$$\sum_{j=1}^{3} X_{2j} = 1200 \quad (7.69)$$

$$\sum_{i=1}^{2} X_{i1} \le 1000 \quad (7.70)$$

$$\sum_{i=1}^{2} X_{i2} \le 500 \quad (7.71)$$

$$\sum_{i=1}^{2} X_{i3} \le 1300 \quad (7.72)$$

$$Y_j \le 1 \quad \forall j \quad (7.75)$$

$$\sum_{i=1}^{2} X_{ij} - 10{,}000Y_j \le 0 \quad \forall j \quad (7.76)$$

$$X_{ij} \ge 0 \quad \forall i, j$$
$$Y_j \in (0, 1, 2, \ldots) \quad \forall j$$

The optimization model can be expressed in a simpler form by combining Constraints 7.70 to 7.72 with Constraint 7.76, the special integer constraint. For example, the two constraints on ocean dumping,

$$\sum_{i=1}^{2} X_{i2} \le 500 \quad (7.71)$$

and

$$\sum_{i=1}^{2} X_{i2} \le 10{,}000Y_2 \quad (7.76)$$

are equivalent to a single constraint

$$\sum_{i=1}^{2} X_{i2} \leq 500 Y_2 \tag{7.71a}$$

Since Y_2 is either zero or one, Constraint 7.71a prevents the capacity of 500 t/wk from being exceeded. Furthermore, if $X_{12} + X_{22} > 0$, Y_2 must equal 1 to satisfy Constraint 7.71a. Constraint 7.76 can be eliminated from the model, and Constraints 7.70 to 7.72 are replaced by

$$\sum_{i=1}^{2} X_{i1} - 1000 Y_1 \leq 0 \tag{7.70a}$$

$$\sum_{i=1}^{2} X_{i2} - 500 Y_2 \leq 0 \tag{7.71a}$$

$$\sum_{i=1}^{3} X_{i3} - 1300 Y_3 \leq 0 \tag{7.72a}$$

The coefficients for this revised model are shown in Table 7-5. The optimal solution is

$$Y_1^* = 1 \quad X_{11}^* = 200 \text{ t/wk}$$
$$Y_2^* = 1 \quad X_{12}^* = 500 \text{ t/wk}$$
$$Y_3^* = 1 \quad X_{21}^* = 800 \text{ t/wk}$$
$$X_{23}^* = 400 \text{ t/wk}$$

TABLE 7-5 Coefficients for Mixed Integer Solid Wastes Disposal Example

Y_1	Y_2	Y_3	X_{11}	X_{12}	X_{13}	X_{21}	X_{22}	X_{23}		
3850	1150	1920	19.5	18.5	21.0	17.0	23.5	18.5	=	Z
			1	1	1				=	700
						1	1	1	=	1200
−1000			1			1			≤	0
	−500			1			1		≤	0
		−1300			1			1	≤	0
1									≤	1
	1								≤	1
		1							≤	1

Minimum costs are $Z^* = \$41{,}070$. This solution is also shown in Figure 7-19. All three facilities are implemented, but only one, the incinerator, is used jointly. The average cost of waste disposal for the two cities is $\$41{,}070 / 1900 = \$21.62/\text{t}$.

Linearization by Mixed Integer Methods

The mixed integer approach to fixed charge problems can be extended to other types of objective functions. In particular, it provides a method for linearizing concave cost functions and convex return functions. We have seen previously that when the former are minimized or the latter maximized, the separable programming methods presented in the first part of this chapter do not produce optimal solutions. However, an alternative approach may be used that approximates the functions by several fixed charge functions. An example of the approximations to a concave cost function, $C(X)$, is shown in Figure 7-20. Assuming the relevant range of the function is $0 \leq X \leq L_3$, it has been divided into three segments. Within any segment k, $C(X)$ can be estimated by

$$C(X) = c_k + a_k X \tag{7.77}$$

where a_k is the slope of segment k and c_k is the intercept, or fixed charge. Since the function $C(X)$ begins at the origin, $c_1 = 0$.

A mixed integer approximation to $C(X)$ over the entire range of X is obtained by defining a new variable $x_k \leq L_k$ for each segment and letting

$$C(X) \simeq a_1 x_1 + c_2 Y_2 + a_2 x_2 + c_3 Y_3 + a_3 x_3 \tag{7.78}$$

where Y_2 and Y_3 are integer variables that must be either zero or one. Equation 7.78 estimates $C(X)$ as the sum of three fixed cost functions. For the procedure to work in an LP model, no more than one of the functions must be chosen in an optimal solution,

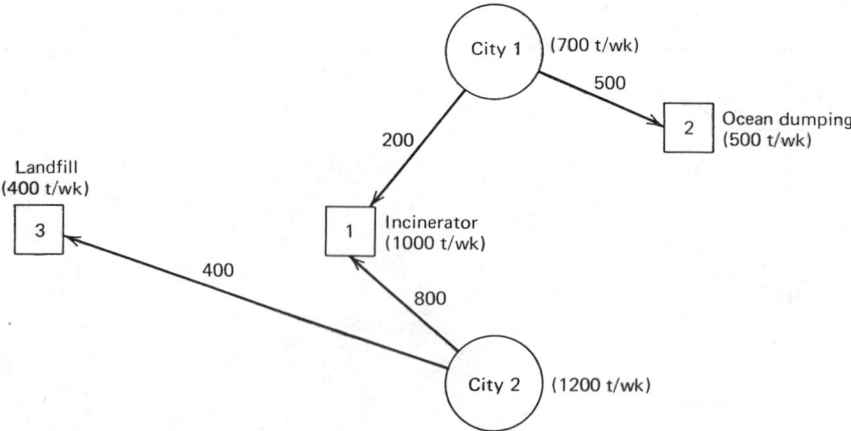

Figure 7-19. Solution to solid wastes disposal example.

and that function must correspond to the relevant range of X. If $L_{k-1} \leq X \leq L_k$, the kth function must be selected. This behavior can be forced by the addition of several constraints:

$$Y_2 + Y_3 \leq 1 \tag{7.79}$$

and

$$x_k - L_k Y_k \leq 0, \qquad k = 2, 3 \tag{7.80}$$

If the other portions of the optimization model are linear, the variable X can be replaced by

$$X = x_1 + x_2 + x_3 \tag{7.81}$$

and the resulting LP model may be solved by a mixed integer algorithm.

Constraint 7.79 will insure that no more than one of the fixed costs c_2, c_3 are selected. Constraint 7.80, which can also be written as

$$L_k Y_k \geq x_k \tag{7.80}$$

requires Y_k to be positive, and hence equal to one, whenever x_k is positive. Thus each segment variable will "bring along" its associated fixed cost. Finally, we can see from Figure 7-20 that the optimal solution must contain the appropriate cost function. If, for example, $L_1 \leq X \leq L_2$, the second cost function $c_2 Y_2 + a_2 x_2$ provides a lower cost than

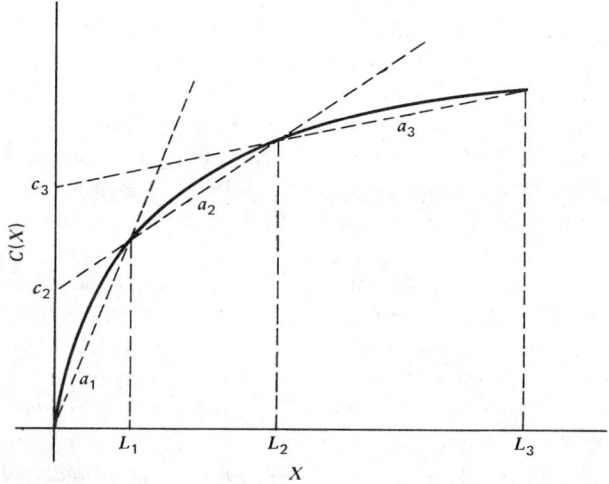

Figure 7-20. Mixed integer approximation to concave cost function.

the other two functions would within this range (L_1 to L_2). Since costs are to be minimized, the optimal LP solution must have $x_1 = x_3 = Y_3 = 0$. A similar argument applies to the remaining two segments.

In general, the procedure for linearizing a concave cost function or convex return function $C(X)$ involves replacement of $C(X)$ with fixed cost functions

$$C(X) = \sum_k (c_k Y_k + a_k x_k) \tag{7.81}$$

where Y_k are integer variables and c_k, a_k are the intercept and slope of the kth fixed charge approximation. The decision variable X is replaced by

$$X = \sum_k x_k \tag{7.82}$$

and new constraints

$$\sum_k Y_k \le 1 \tag{7.83}$$

and

$$x_k - L_k Y_k \le 0 \quad \forall\, k \tag{7.84}$$

are added to the problem. The constant L_k is the value of the decision variable $X = L_k$ at the end of the kth segment.

Summary

The mathematical programming techniques presented in this chapter greatly extend the power of LP. Separable programming is a simple technique that can make nonlinear but separable functions amenable to LP methods. The approach is most useful for separable objective functions that are concave and maximized or convex and minimized. Integer LP models have some or all of the decision variables restricted to integer values, and special algorithms have been developed to obtain the necessary integer solutions. Integer programming can also be used to linearize concave cost functions and convex return functions.

In addition to separable and integer programming techniques, this chapter also developed two general topics that are important to environmental systems analysis. One of these, multiobjective planning, has been an integral part of most of the previous examples in this book. Many of the examples have had more than one objective, but all objectives save one (the objective function) were usually included in optimization models as constraints. However, in this chapter an attempt was made to incorporate all the objectives of a land use planning problem (Example 7-2) into a single objective function that might reflect decision makers' preferences. The example also demonstrated the use of transformations to obtain a separable objective function.

A second topic, solid waste management, has been dealt with indirectly in previous examples and exercises related to agricultural wastes and sewage sludge disposal, but Example 7-3 was our first excursion into the general problems facing municipalities in their attempts to dispose of solid waste economically. The example also illustrated economies of scale because of fixed costs and the use of integer programming to model these costs.

SELECTED REFERENCES

1. Agin, N., "Optimum Seeking with Branch and Bound," *Management Science,* Vol. 13, No. 4, 1966, pp. B176–185.
2. Beale, E. M. L., "Survey of Integer Programming," *Operational Research Quarterly,* Vol. 16, No. 2, 1965, pp. 219–228.
3. Bradley, S. P., A. C. Hax, and T. L. Magnanti, *Applied Mathematical Programming,* Addison-Wesley, Reading, Mass., 1977, Chapters 9 and 13.
4. Clark, R. M., "Solid Waste Management and Models," in R. A. Deininger (editor), *Models for Environmental Pollution Control,* Ann Arbor Science Publishers, Ann Arbor, Mich., 1973, pp. 269–305.
5. Cohon, J. L., *Multiobjective Programming and Planning,* Academic Press, New York, 1978.
6. Garfinkel, R. S., and G. L. Nemhauser, *Integer Programming,* Wiley, New York, 1972.
7. Gass, S. I., *Linear Programming Methods and Applications,* 4th ed., McGraw-Hill, New York, 1975, Chapters 9 and 12.
8. Gomory, R. E., "Outline of an Algorithm for Integer Solutions to Linear Programs," *Bulletin of the American Mathematical Society,* Vol. 64, No. 5, 1958, pp. 275–278.
9. Gum, R. L., T. G. Roefs, and D. B. Kimball, "Quantifying Societal Goals: Development of a Weighting Methodology," *Water Resources Research,* Vol. 12, No. 4, 1976, pp. 617–622.
10. Hadley, G., *Nonlinear and Dynamic Programming,* Addison-Wesley, Reading, Mass., 1964, Chapters 4 and 8.
11. Haith, D. A., and D. P. Loucks, "Multiobjective Water Resources Planning," in A. K. Biswas (editor), *Systems Approach to Water Management,* McGraw-Hill, New York, 1976, pp. 365–397.
12. Hillier, F. S., and G. J. Lieberman, *Operations Research,* 2nd ed., Holden-Day, San Francisco, 1974, Chapters 17 and 18.
13. Pavoni, J. L., J. E. Heer, Jr., and D. J. Hagerty, *Handbook of Solid Waste Disposal,* Van Nostrand Reinhold, New York, 1975.
14. Stellern, M. J., E. B. Oswald, R. L. Gum, and L. M. Arthur, "Environmental Quality Possibilities (E.Q.P.): A Procedure for Evaluating Economic/Environmental Trade-offs," *Natural Resource Eco-*

nomics Division, Economics, Statistics and Cooperatives Service, U.S. Department of Agriculture, Washington, D.C., 1979.
15. Walker, W., M. Aquilina, and D. Schur, "Development and Use of a Fixed Charge Programming Model for Regional Solid Waste Planning," in W. R. Ott (editor), *Environmental Modeling and Simulation*, U.S. Environmental Protection Agency, Washington, D.C., 1976, pp. 595–599.

EXERCISES

NOTE. Most of these exercises require LP computer programs or integer LP computer programs.

7-1.

Show that when the segment weighting approach (method 2) is applied to minimization of a convex function no more than two weights will be nonzero in an optimal solution and these nonzero weights will be adjacent.

7-2.

A river flow of 40,000 m³/day is to be allocated to three uses: recreation, agriculture, and hydropower. As shown in the figure, the power plant is on the river downstream of both other uses. Thirty percent of the water diverted to agriculture returns to the river, as does 50% of the recreation allocation. The minimum diversions for agriculture and recreation are 10,000 and 6000 m³/day, respectively. The power plant has a right to 20,000 m³/day. Water allocation benefits are \$30 and \$40/10^3m³ for recreation and agriculture, respectively. Power benefits (\$/day) are $300Q^{0.3}$, where Q is the water passing through the power plant (10^3 m³/day). Determine optimal allocations using linear programming.

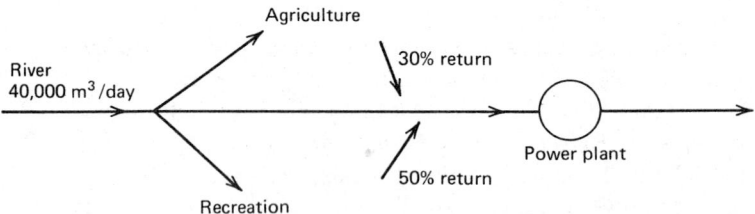

7-3.

It has been determined that runoff from 100 ha of cropland is carrying phosphorus into a small lake and contributing to the lake's eutrophication. Three crops are grown on the 100 ha. Let p_i = kg/ha/yr of phosphorus that enters the lake in runoff from crop i. Thus, if there are 30 ha of each crop, the total phosphorus entering the lake from cropland in 1 yr would be $p_1 30 + p_2 30 + p_3 30$. An environmental agency has determined that the total input of phosphorus to the lake from cropland runoff must not exceed 800 kg/yr.

The farmers using the 100 ha require minimum quantities of each crop, L_i = minimum number of ha of crop i, and obtain net returns of $R_i(X_i)$, from crop i(\$/yr), where X_i = ha of crop i. These data are summarized in the accompanying table.

Crop i	p_i (kg/ha)	L_i (ha)	$R_i(X_i)$ (\$/yr)
1	10	0	$1000 X_1^{1/2}$
2	12	15	$3000 X_2^{1/3}$
3	9	5	$1200 X_3^{1/2}$

Construct an optimization model for this problem and solve using LP.

7-4.

In Example 7-2 the segment weighting approach (method 2) to separable programming was used. Repeat the analysis using segment variables (method 1).

7-5.

A chemical manufacturing process produces toxic wastes that must be disposed of safely. The chemical is produced in a two-stage process, as shown in the figure. The intermediate output from stage 1 [X_1(kg/day)] is subsequently input to stage 2, and 0.6 kg of the final chemical product (X_2) is produced per kg of X_1 input. The production requirement for X_2 is 100 kg/day. Production costs are \$15/kg of output from stage 1 and \$20/kg of output from stage 2. However, waste disposal costs are not included in these costs.

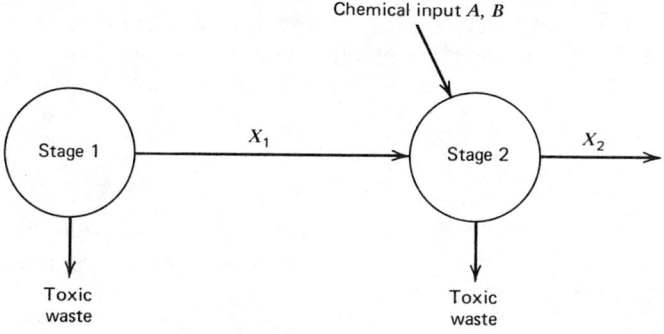

Waste production from stage 1 is 0.2 kg/kg of X_1 produced. Waste production from stage 2 depends on the quantities of two chemicals, A and B, used in the production process. When chemical A is used, 0.3 kg of waste results from each kg of chemical A used. The comparable quantity for chemical B is 0.1 kg/kg of chemical used. The two chemicals are interchangeable and may be mixed, but a total of 3 kg of the two chemicals is required for each kg of X_2 produced. An additional production cost of $0.80 is incurred for each kg of chemical B used in stage 2.

Three methods of waste disposal are available. Method 1 can be used for waste from stage 1, and method 2 is suitable for waste from stage 2. A third method can handle wastes from either or both of the two production stages. If W_j is the total waste disposed of by method j, disposal costs ($/day) are

Method 1: $40W_1^{0.3}$
Method 2: $5W_2$
Method 3: $10W_3^{0.8}$

Use linear programming to develop a cost-effective waste disposal plan.

7-6.

In the solid waste management example discussed in this chapter, no provision was made for disposal of incinerator residues and ash. These residues, which are approximately 20% by weight of the original (unburned) waste, must be disposed of by burial or ocean dumping. The distance from the incinerator to the sanitary landfill is 20 km, and the distance from the incinerator to the ocean dumping shore embarking point is 10 km. Reconstruct the optimization model to include residue and ash disposal. Solve the model.

7-7.

The air pollutant emissions control example (Example 5-2) in Chapter 5 required the selection of feasible control methods for each of three sources of TSP. The optimal solution to that problem included two control methods at source 1. For convenience of operations and monitoring, it has been decided that no more than one of the feasible control options will be installed at any source (i.e., each source must have exactly one control). Construct an integer LP model of the problem that incorporates this new requirement and solve to obtain a new cost-effective air pollution control plan.

7-8.

A farmer has 440 t of manure to dispose of. Four fields are available for disposal, but environmental regulations have specified the maximum manure application rates (t/ha)

that can be used on each field, depending on the field's proximity to water bodies. The costs of manure disposal are given by

$$K_i + c_i X_i \quad \text{if } X_i > 0$$
$$0 \quad \text{if } X_i = 0$$

where X_i is the tonnes of manure disposed of on field i. Characteristics for each field are given in the following table.

	Field			
	1	2	3	4
Size (ha)	10	4	12	20
Maximum manure application rate (t/ha)	20	30	5	10
K_i ($)	40	0	50	70
c_i ($/t)	$1.50	$2.00	$1.00	$1.30

Construct an optimization model that will determine an optimal disposal program and solve by linear programming.

7-9.

Solve the following optimization model using LP.

$$\text{Max } 4X_1^2 + 10X_2 + 30X_3^{1/2}$$

s.t.
$$3X_1 + X_2 + X_3 \leq 20$$
$$-X_1 + X_2 \geq 4$$
$$X_2 + 1.5X_3 \leq 10$$
$$X_1, X_2, X_3 \geq 0$$

CHAPTER 8
TRANSPORTATION MODELS

Transportation problems are classic systems analysis applications that can be described by linear programming (LP) models that have a very simple structure. This structure permits the use of algorithms that solve the models with fewer computations than would normally be required by the simplex method. In many cases solutions can be obtained without the use of a computer. Large transportation models must be solved by computer but, if a programmed transportation algorithm is available, solutions can be determined with significantly less computer time (and cost) than would be necessary if a more general LP program were used.

The standard form of the transportation problem is illustrated in Figure 8-1. Demands (b_j) for some "product" are to be met at n destinations. To meet demands, supplies (a_i) of the product that are available at m sources must be moved to the destinations. For example, the destinations might be retail sales outlets and the sources

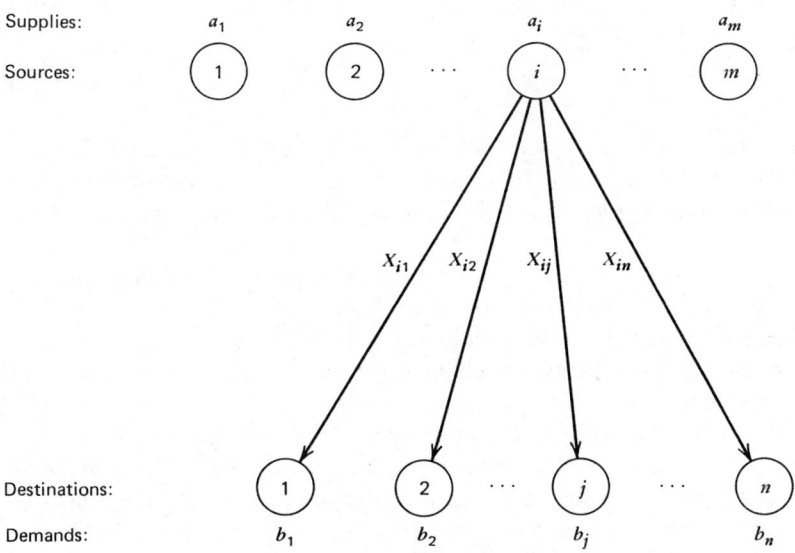

Figure 8-1. General form of a transportation problem.

factories or wholesalers. Demands and supplies are assumed to be known and in balance; that is, total demand equals total supply.

$$\sum_{j=1}^{n} b_j = \sum_{i=1}^{m} a_i \qquad (8.1)$$

The problem is to determine the quantities to be transported (hence the name "transportation problem") from each source to each destination so that all supplies are used and all demands are met at minimum cost. The decision variable is

$$X_{ij} = \text{quantity transported from source } i \text{ to destination } j$$

and the associated cost of transport is

$$c_{ij} = \text{cost of shipping one unit from source } i \text{ to destination } j$$

The problem can be described by the following optimization model.

$$\text{Min } Z = \sum_{i=1}^{m} \sum_{j=1}^{n} c_{ij} X_{ij} \qquad (8.2)$$

s.t.
$$\sum_{j=1}^{n} X_{ij} = a_i \qquad i = 1, 2, \ldots, m \qquad (8.3)$$

$$\sum_{i=1}^{m} X_{ij} = b_j \qquad j = 1, 2, \ldots, n \qquad (8.4)$$

$$X_{ij} \geq 0 \qquad \forall\, i, j \qquad (8.5)$$

Equation 8.3 states that the total quantity shipped from source i to all destinations must equal the supply at source i. Equation 8.4 is a similar mass balance at destination j and indicates that the shipments from all supply sources to the destination must equal the demand.

The optimization model contains $m \times n$ variables and $n + m$ constraints in addition to the nonnegativity constraints. The model is linear and therefore can be solved using the simplex method. The structure is much simpler than most LP models, however. The constraint coefficients are all equal to one, and the model requires no slack or surplus variables.

In most LP models, the number of nonzero variables in a basic feasible solution is equal to the number of constraints. However, in the present model, the constraints are not independent. Since total supply equals total demand, any one of the equations can be written as a combination of the remaining equations. This is readily proven algebraically but can also be shown by a simple example. Consider a transportation problem with two sources and two demands. The mass balance equations are

$$X_{11} + X_{12} = a_1 \tag{8.6}$$

$$X_{21} + X_{22} = a_2 \tag{8.7}$$

$$X_{11} + X_{21} = b_1 \tag{8.8}$$

$$X_{12} + X_{22} = b_2 \tag{8.9}$$

Any one of the equations can be obtained from the other equations. For example, Equation 8.7 is equivalent to the sum of Equations 8.8 and 8.9 minus Equation 8.6.

$$\begin{aligned} & X_{11} + X_{21} = b_1 \\ + \quad & X_{12} + X_{22} = b_2 \\ - \quad & X_{11} + X_{12} = a_1 \\ \hline & X_{21} + X_{22} = b_1 + b_2 - a_1 \end{aligned}$$

The right side, $b_1 + b_2 - a_1$, equals a_2, since $b_1 + b_2 = a_1 + a_2$. Any one equation (but no more than one) could be similarly derived from the remaining three equations. It follows that basic feasible solutions to the transportation problem have no more than $m + n - 1$ nonzero variables.

Algorithms for solving the general transportation model and a derivative model based on what is known as the "assignment problem" are presented in this chapter. The significance of these simple solution procedures to the environmental systems analyst is that problems that are not obviously transportation problems can sometimes be structured to permit the use of transportation algorithms. Thus the applicability of transportation methods goes well beyond the standard problem shown in Figure 8-1.

ALLOCATION OF ENERGY RESOURCES USING A TRANSPORTATION MODEL

EXAMPLE 8-1

A state energy agency needs a general plan for future allocation of major fossil fuels. Consumption has been divided into four sectors: residential and commercial heating (R/C), industry (I), transportation (T), and electrical power generation (E). The fossil fuels, which vary both in cost and availability, are coal (C), natural gas (N), and petroleum (P). Since the units in which these fuels are measured differ (tonnes, m^3, barrels), it is convenient to convert fuels to a common unit of heat or energy content in order to compare supplies and costs. Consumptive requirements can also be given in the same units. Table 8-1 lists available fuel quantities and expected consumption in units of 10^{11} kCal/yr.

As can be seen from the table, the state is in the fortunate position of having an excess of fuel supplies, primarily because of the large amount of coal that will be available. However, the anticipated costs of these fuels to the consumption sectors vary considerably, as indicated in Table 8-2. In general, fuels are less expensive to industrial and electricity generating users than to residential and commercial users. Natural gas is the least expensive fuel for any sector, but it is also the scarcest fuel. Transportation requirements can only be met by petroleum (essentially gasoline and diesel fuel). The problem faced by the energy agency is to allocate the fuels to consumption sectors in such fashion that total costs to users are minimized. □

Model Construction

The decision variables for this problem are the fuel allocations.

$$X_{ij} = \text{fuel of type } i \text{ allocated to sector } j \; (10^{11} \text{ kCal/yr})$$

The indices $i = 1, 2, 3$ are coal, natural gas, and petroleum and $j = 1, 2, 3, 4$ correspond to the four consumption sectors, residential/commercial, industry, trans-

TABLE 8-1 Expected Fossil Fuel Sources and Consumptive Uses

Available Fossil Fuels		Consumption	
Type	Supply, a_i (10^{11} kCal/yr)	Sector	Requirement, b_j (10^{11} kCal/yr)
Coal (C)	6.0	Residential/commercial (R/C)	1.4
Natural gas (N)	2.0	Industrial (I)	2.5
Petroleum (P)	4.0	Transportation (T)	2.0
Total	12.0	Electricity generation (E)	1.9
		Total	7.8

TABLE 8-2 Costs of Fuel Consumption, c_{ij}

Fuel	Consumption Sector (10^8/10^{11} kCal)			
	R/C	I	T	E
Coal (C)	30	24	—[a]	22
Natural gas (N)	20	18	—[a]	17
Petroleum (P)	25	23	30	21

[a]Infeasible use.

portation, and electricity. The costs, c_{ij} ($\$10^8/10^{11}$ kCal), of allocations are given in Table 8-2. The objective function of the model is minimization of annual costs, Z ($\$10^8$).

$$\text{Min } Z = \sum_{i=1}^{3} \sum_{j=1}^{4} c_{ij} X_{ij} \qquad (8.10)$$

Model constraints are based on energy balances for each fuel supply and consumption sector. The total allocation of fuel i is the sum of allocations to all sectors and must not exceed the available supply (Table 8-1).

$$\sum_{j=1}^{4} X_{ij} \leq a_i \quad \forall\, i \qquad (8.11)$$

In addition, the total allocations to each sector must match the consumption.

$$\sum_{i=1}^{3} X_{ij} = b_j \quad \forall\, j \qquad (8.12)$$

The complete model consists of Expressions 8.10, 8.11, and 8.12, nonnegativety constraints, and since transportation consumes only petroleum (Table 8-2), we have the additional constraints $X_{13} = 0$, $X_{23} = 0$.[1]

The optimization model for this energy allocation problem is obviously similar to the transportation model (Expressions 8.2 to 8.5). Apart from the fact that the energy model has little to do with transportation, the principal departures are the imbalance of total supplies and demands and the infeasibilities of certain allocations (X_{13}, X_{23}). However, these differences can be eliminated by simple artifices. Since supplies exceed requirements, we can create an artificial or dummy consumption sector $j = 5$, with a requirement just equal to the supply excess, $b_5 = 12.0 - 7.8 = 4.2$. The costs associated with allocations to this sector are all $c_{i5} = 0$. Supplies and demands are now balanced and, since all supplies can be consumed (even if only artificially), Constraint 8.11 can be written as an equation. The infeasible allocations X_{13} and X_{23} can be dealt with by assigning very large costs, say $c_{13} = c_{23} = 100$, so that the allocations will be much more expensive than the feasible alternatives.

With these modifications, we have a transportation model with three sources and five destinations.

$$\text{Min } Z = \sum_{i=1}^{3} \sum_{j=1}^{5} c_{ij} X_{ij} \qquad (8.13)$$

---

[1] Normally, these variables would just be omitted from the model.

s.t.
$$\sum_{j=1}^{5} X_{ij} = a_i \quad i = 1, 2, 3 \quad (8.14)$$

$$\sum_{i=1}^{3} X_{ij} = b_j \quad j = 1, 2, \ldots, 5 \quad (8.15)$$

$$X_{ij} \geq 0 \quad \forall\, i, j \quad (8.16)$$

Data for the model are summarized in Table 8-3.

Solution Algorithm

The solution procedure begins with an initial basic feasible solution and then proceeds to additional basic feasible solutions that improve with each iteration. Computations may be carried out in a table such as that given in Table 8-4. Each row contains allocations that sum to the supply a_i for a source, and the total allocations in column

TABLE 8-3 Data Summary for Energy Allocation Example

Source	Destination (Sector)					Supply a_i (10^{11} kCal/yr)
	1. (R/C)	2. (I)	3. (T)	4. (E)	5.[a]	
	Costs ($\$10^8/10^{11}$ kCal)					
1. (C)	30	24	100	22	0	6.0
2. (N)	20	18	100	17	0	2.0
3. (P)	25	23	30	21	0	4.0
Demand b_j (10^{11} kCal/yr)	1.4	2.5	2.0	1.9	4.2	

[a] "Dummy" destination.

TABLE 8-4 Basic Feasible Solution to Energy Allocation Model

Source, i	X_{ij} Destination, j					a_i
	1	2	3	4	5	
1	1.4	2.5	2.0	0.1	0	6.0
2	0	0	0	1.8	0.2	2.0
3	0	0	0	0	4.0	4.0
b_j	1.4	2.5	2.0	1.9	4.2	

j equal the demand b_j. The table contains $m + n - 1 = 7$ nonzero variables to represent a basic solution.

All sets of seven allocations are not basic solutions. For example, the seven allocations in Table 8-5 are feasible but do not represent a basic solution. We saw in Chapter 5 that in the iterations of the simplex method, a nonzero variable in a basic solution cannot be driven to zero without increasing one of the zero variables. However, it can be shown that X_{31} in Table 8-5 can be decreased to zero without changing any of the variables that are already zero. The result is a feasible solution with only six nonzero variables.

Nonbasic solutions to transportation models can be recognized by the presence of "closed loops" in the allocation table. Thus certain nonzero allocations in Table 8-5 can be connected by a closed loop of vertical and horizontal lines with nonzero allocations at each corner. Whenever this occurs, one of the allocations can be eliminated. Thus X_{31} can be reduced from 0.2 to 0.0. To maintain the supply balance, X_{35} is increased from 1.9 to 2.1. However, X_{15} must then be reduced to 2.1 to meet the demand at destination 5 ($b_5 = 4.2$); finally, X_{11} is increased to 1.4 to provide the proper totals for row 1 and column 1. The resulting solution (Table 8-6) is feasible but nonbasic, since there are only six positive variables. Any feasible solution with $m + n - 1$ nonzero

TABLE 8-5 Example of a Nonbasic Feasible Solution

i/j	X_{ij}					a_i
	1	2	3	4	5	
1	1.2	2.5	0	0	2.3	6.0
2	0	0	2.0	0	0	2.0
3	0.2	0	0	1.9	1.9	4.0
b_j	1.4	2.5	2.0	1.9	4.2	

TABLE 8-6 Reduction of Solution from Table 8-5 to a Solution with only Six Nonzero Variables

i/j	X_{ij}					a_i
	1	2	3	4	5	
1	1.4	2.5	0	0	2.1	6.0
2	0	0	2.0	0	0	2.0
3	0	0	0	1.9	2.1	4.0
b_j	1.4	2.5	2.0	1.9	4.2	

variables that contains a closed loop can always be reduced to a (nonbasic) solution with less than $m + n - 1$ variables.

The initial solution shown in Table 8-4 is feasible because rows and columns sum to the correct supplies and demands and basic because there are no closed loops. There are several ways of generating initial basic solutions, but the solution in Table 8-4 was determined by the "northwest corner" method. This procedure begins with the top left allocation and makes X_{11} as large as possible without exceeding a_1 or b_1. Additional allocations are made by proceeding either to the right or downward as far as possible. Since the demand at destination 1 is already met by $X_{11} = 1.4$, we must move to the right. Additional allocations of $X_{12} = 2.5$ and $X_{13} = 2.0$ are possible, thus meeting demands b_2 and b_3. Because $X_{11} + X_{12} + X_{13} = 5.9$, only $6.0 - 5.9 = 0.1$ remains to be allocated in row 1 ($X_{14} = 0.1$). We must then move down ($X_{24} = 1.8$) to meet demand $b_4 = 1.9$. The process continues to the right and down until all sources are allocated and all demands met.

The next iteration of this transportation algorithm obtains a solution that reduces costs. As with the simplex method, this improved solution is a new extreme point produced by driving one of the previous solution variables to zero and bringing a new variable into the solution.

The algorithm compares the allocation costs of variables already in the solution with the remaining variables. This is done by defining shadow costs u_i for each supply and v_j for each destination. These shadow costs apportion the costs of the nonzero allocations to their respective sources and destinations and are chosen so that for each nonzero allocation

$$c_{ij} = u_i + v_j \qquad (8.17)$$

Equation 8.17 indicates that the cost of assigning one unit to transportation route i, j must be accounted for by the shadow costs u_i and v_j.

Seven equations of the form given by Equation 8.17 can be written for the seven nonzero allocations; because there are eight shadow costs, solutions are not unique. One of the shadow costs can be assigned an arbitrary value (say $u_1 = 0$) and the remaining values determined in steps ii to viii in Table 8-7. With $u_1 = 0$, v_1 must be 30, so that $c_{11} - u_1 - v_1 = 0$. Similarly, $v_2 = 24$, $v_3 = 100$, and $v_4 = 22$. The last assignment requires $u_2 = -5$, since $c_{24} = u_2 + v_4$ or $u_2 = 17 - 22 = -5$. Hence $v_5 = 5$ and finally $u_3 = -5$.

The shadow costs u_i and v_j are used to determine which of the variables currently equal to zero should be brought into the solution. To derive the general procedure, we can first observe that $u_i(a_i - \sum_j X_{ij})$ can be added to the objective function (Z, Equation 8.2) without affecting costs, because $a_i - \sum_j X_{ij} = 0$ (Constraint 8.3). Similarly, $v_j (b_j - \sum_i X_{ij})$ can be added to Z with no effect. If comparable additions are made for each supply and demand, the objective function becomes

$$Z = \sum_i \sum_j c_{ij} X_{ij} + \sum_i u_i \left(a_i - \sum_j X_{ij} \right) + \sum_j v_j \left(b_j - \sum_i X_{ij} \right)$$

TABLE 8-7 Costs Associated with Initial Solution

	c_{ij}					
i/j	1	2	3	4	5	u_i
1	30	24	100	22		0 (i)
2				17	0	−5 (vi)
3					0	−5 (viii)
v_j	30	24	100	22	5	
	(ii)	(iii)	(iv)	(v)	(vii)	

$$= \sum_i \sum_j (c_{ij} - u_i - v_j) X_{ij} + \sum_i u_i a_i + \sum_j v_j b_j \qquad (8.18)$$

For any set of u_i and v_j, the value of Z can be decreased only by changing the values of X_{ij} because all other quantities in Equation 8.18 are fixed.

For any X_{ij} already in the solution, $c_{ij} - u_i - v_j = 0$ from Equation 8.17. For any X_{ij} not in the solution, $c_{ij} - u_i - v_j$ is either ≥ 0 or <0. If the former is the case, increasing X_{ij} would not improve Z (since Z is to be minimized). Conversely, if $c_{ij} - u_i - v_j$ is negative, the objective function would be decreased if X_{ij} is made nonzero. To minimize costs most rapidly, the variable with the *most negative* $c_{ij} - u_i - v_j$ should be selected to enter the solution. Thus, at each iteration of the algorithm, a solution can be improved by the following procedure.

1. Using the costs c_{ij} for each nonzero allocation, shadow costs u_i and v_j are computed by Equation 8.17.
2. Allocation costs $c_{ij} - u_i - v_j$ are determined for each X_{ij} that is currently zero.
3. The variable X_{ij} with the most negative $c_{ij} - u_i - v_j$ is selected to enter the solution. If none of the zero level variables have $c_{ij} - u_i - v_j < 0$, no further improvement in Z is possible, and an optimal solution has been found.

The form of the objective function given by Equation 8.18 clarifies the meaning of the shadow costs u_i and v_j. Since $c_{ij} - u_i - v_j$ is zero for any nonzero X_{ij}, the value of Z at any iteration is $\sum_i u_i a_i + \sum_j v_j b_j$. Recalling the discussion of duality in Chapter 5, we see that we have multiplied the "resource limits," or right sides of Constraints 8.3 and 8.4, by associated costs u_i and v_j. Hence u_i and v_j are the marginal costs or *dual variables* associated with each constraint. In the optimal solution, u_i is the marginal change in optimal costs produced by a unit change in supply a_i. The comparable marginal cost of demand b_j is the shadow cost or dual variable v_j.

214 TRANSPORTATION MODELS

Returning to the example, the allocation costs $c_{ij} - u_i - v_j$ are shown for each zero level variable in Table 8-8. Since the allocation costs associated with X_{33} are the most negative (-65), the next iteration (extreme point) should have $X_{33} > 0$ and set a variable formerly in the solution to zero.

The procedure for deleting and adding variables to a solution is shown in Table 8-9. When a variable is added, a series of additions to and subtractions from the old allocations are needed to satisfy supplies and demands. These adjustments are made by finding a closed loop with the new variable and the old variables. Within the loop shown in Table 8-9, an increase in the new variable (X_{33}) will force the increases (+) and reductions ($-$) indicated. Since no variable can be made negative, we locate the smallest value that is to be decreased ($X_{24} = 1.8$) and increase X_{33} to 1.8. Following the loop, each variable at a corner is alternatively increased and decreased, leading to the new solution shown in Table 8-10. This solution is feasible because supply and demand constraints are met and basic because there are seven positive variables and no closed loops.

TABLE 8-8 Allocation costs for Variables Not in the Solution

	$c_{ij} - u_i - v_j$					
i/j	1	2	3	4	5	u_i
1					-5	0
2	-5	-1	5			-5
3	0	4	-65	4		-5
v_j	30	24	100	22	5	

TABLE 8-9 Procedure for Changing a Variable in the Solution

	X_{ij}					
i/j	1	2	3	4	5	a_i
1	1.4	2.5	2.0	0.1	0	6.0
2	0	0	0	1.8	0.2	2.0
3	0	0	0	0	4.0	4.0
b_j	1.4	2.5	2.0	1.9	4.2	

ALLOCATION OF ENERGY RESOURCES 215

TABLE 8-10 New Basic Feasible Solution

i/j	X_{ij}					a_i
	1	2	3	4	5	
1	1.4	2.5	0.2	1.9	0	6.0
2	0	0	0	0	2.0	2.0
3	0	0	1.8	0	2.2	4.0
b_j	1.4	2.5	2.0	1.9	4.2	

The set of computations in Tables 8-7, 8-8, and 8-9 can be combined into a single table (Table 8-11). The principal entries are the allocations X_{ij}. Above each positive allocation is the associated cost c_{ij} used to determine shadow costs u_i and v_j. Entries above the variables that are not in the solution (i.e., equal to zero) are the allocation costs $c_{ij} - u_i - v_j$.

The general computational procedure in Table 8-11 is repeated for as many iterations as necessary to obtain an optimal solution. These iterations are shown in Tables 8-12 to 8-17 for the energy allocation example.

The optimal set of energy allocations is produced after seven iterations (Table 8-17) and is given by

$$X_{12}^* = 1.8 \qquad X_{32}^* = 0.1$$
$$X_{15}^* = 4.2 \qquad X_{33}^* = 2.0$$
$$X_{21}^* = 1.4 \qquad X_{34}^* = 1.9$$
$$X_{22}^* = 0.6$$

TABLE 8-11 Combined Operations for First Iteration

i/j	1	2	3	4	5	a_i	u_i
		−		+			
1	1.4^{30}	2.5^{24}	2.0^{100}	0.1^{22}	0^{-5}	6.0	0
					− +		
2	0^{-5}	0^{-1}	0^{5}	1.8^{17}	0.2^{0}	2.0	−5
3	0^{0}	0^{4}	0^{-65}	0^{4}	4.0^{0}	4.0	−5
			+		−		
b_j	1.4	2.5	2.0	1.9	4.2		
v_j	30	24	100	22	5		

TABLE 8-12 Iteration 2 for Energy Example

i/j	1	2	3	4	5	a_i	u_i
		−			+		
1	$1.4^{\underline{30}}$	$2.5^{\underline{24}}$	$0.2^{\underline{100}}$	$1.9^{\underline{22}}$	$0^{-\underline{70}}$	6.0	0
2	$0^{\underline{60}}$	$0^{\underline{64}}$	$0^{\underline{70}}$	$0^{\underline{65}}$	$2.0^{\underline{0}}$	2.0	−70
3	$0^{\underline{65}}$	$0^{\underline{69}}$	$1.8^{\underline{30}}$	$0^{\underline{69}}$	$2.2^{\underline{0}}$	4	−70
		+			−		
b_j	1.4	2.5	2.0	1.9	4.2		
v_j	30	24	100	22	70		

TABLE 8-13 Iteration 3 for Energy Example

i/j	1	2	3	4	5	a_i	u_i
	−				+		
1	$1.4^{\underline{30}}$	$2.5^{\underline{24}}$	$0^{\underline{70}}$	$1.9^{\underline{22}}$	$0.2^{\underline{0}}$	6.0	0
2	$0^{-\underline{10}}$	$0^{-\underline{6}}$	$0^{\underline{70}}$	$0^{-\underline{5}}$	$2.0^{\underline{0}}$	2.0	0
	+				−		
3	$0^{-\underline{5}}$	$0^{-\underline{1}}$	$2.0^{\underline{30}}$	$0^{-\underline{1}}$	$2.0^{\underline{0}}$	4.0	0
b_j	1.4	2.5	2.0	1.9	4.2		
v_j	30	24	30	22	0		

TABLE 8-14 Iteration 4 for Energy Example

i/j	1	2	3	4	5	a_i	u_i
		−			+		
1	$0^{\underline{10}}$	$2.5^{\underline{24}}$	$0^{\underline{70}}$	$1.9^{\underline{22}}$	$1.6^{\underline{0}}$	6.0	0
2	$1.4^{\underline{20}}$	$0^{-\underline{6}}$	$0^{\underline{70}}$	$0^{-\underline{5}}$	$0.6^{\underline{0}}$	2.0	0
		+			−		
3	$0^{\underline{5}}$	$0^{-\underline{1}}$	$2.0^{\underline{30}}$	$0^{-\underline{1}}$	$2.0^{\underline{0}}$	4.0	0
b_j	1.4	2.5	2.0	1.9	4.2		
v_j	20	24	30	22	0		

TABLE 8-15 Iteration 5 for Energy Example

i/j	1	2	3	4	5	a_i	u_i
			−		+		
1	0^4	1.9^{24}	0^{70}	1.9^{22}	2.2^0	6.0	0
2	1.4^{20}	0.6^{18}	0^{76}	0^1	0^6	2.0	−6
3	0^{-1}	0^{-1}	2.0^{30}	0^{-1}	2.0^0	4.0	0
			+		−		
b_j	1.4	2.5	2.0	1.9	4.2		
v_j	26	24	30	22	0		

TABLE 8-16 Iteration 6 for Energy Example

i/j	1	2	3	4	5	a_i	u_i
		−			+		
1	0^4	1.9^{24}	0^{70}	0^1	4.1^0	6.0	0
2	1.4^{20}	0.6^{18}	0^{76}	0^2	0^6	2.0	−6
3	0^{-1}	0^{-1}	2.0^{30}	1.9^{21}	0.1^0	4.0	0
	+				−		
b_j	1.4	2.5	2.0	1.9	4.2		
v_j	26	24	30	21	0		

TABLE 8-17 Final Iteration and Optimal Solution for Energy Example

i/j	1	2	3	4	5	a_i	u_i
1	0^4	1.8^{24}	0^{69}	0^0	4.2^0	6.0	0
2	1.4^{20}	0.6^{18}	0^{75}	0^1	0^6	2.0	−6
3	0^0	0.1^{23}	2.0^{30}	1.9^{21}	0^1	4.0	−1
b_j	1.4	2.5	2.0	1.9	4.2		
v_j	26	24	31	22	0		

The only coal allocation to consumption is 1.8 10^{11} kCal/yr to industry. The remaining 4.2 10^{11} kCal/yr is unused. Natural gas is allocated to residential and commercial heating (1.4 10^{11} kCal/yr) and industry (0.6 10^{11} kCal/yr). As with natural gas, petroleum supplies are completely allocated, with industry, transportation, and electricity generation receiving 0.1, 2.0, and 1.9 10^{11} kCal/yr, respectively. Total energy costs are $Z^* = 1.8(24) + 1.4(20) + 0.6(18) + 0.1(23) + 2.0(30) + 1.9(21) = \$184.2\ 10^8$/yr.

Degeneracy

The same general algorithm that has been used to solve the energy example can be applied to any transportation model. However, sometimes a condition known as degeneracy may occur. After an iteration, it may be seen that more than one variable has been eliminated; that is, the new solution has less than $m + n - 1$ positive variables. In order to proceed with subsequent iterations, the degenerate solution must be changed to a basic solution with exactly $m + n - 1$ variables. An example of degeneracy is shown in Tables 8-18 and 8-19. Table 8-18 shows an initial basic feasible solution for a transportation model with three sources and three destinations. We will assume that allocation costs indicate that variable X_{31} should enter the solution. This produces the solution shown in Table 8-19. The solution is degenerate because four variables instead of five are positive. To rectify the situation, an infinitesimal allocation is added to one of the variables, say X_{22}, that was eliminated. Since this allocation is so small, it will not perceptively affect costs, supplies, or demands. However, we now have a full set of five allocations and can continue with the next iteration.

THE ASSIGNMENT PROBLEM

The assignment problem is a special form of the transportation problem in which the demands and supplies are all equal to one. No source can be "assigned" to more than

TABLE 8-18 A Transportation Model that Produces a Degenerate Solution

i/j	1	2	3	a_i
1	2	3	0	5
2	0	1	2	3
3	0	0	1	1
b_j	2	4	3	

TABLE 8-19 A Degenerate Solution

i/j	1	2	3	a_i
1	1	4	0	5
2	0	0	3	3
3	1	0	0	1
b_j	2	4	3	

one destination. A typical example is the availability of n units (machines, groups, public facilities) that may be used in any of n locations. Each location can accommodate one unit. The problem is to assign each unit (source) to a unique location (destination) such that total assignment costs are minimized. If

$$X_{ij} = \text{number of units of source } i \text{ assigned to location } j$$

and

$$c_{ij} = \text{cost of assigning source } i \text{ to location } j$$

the optimization model for the problem is

$$\text{Min } Z = \sum_{i=1}^{n} \sum_{j=1}^{n} c_{ij} X_{ij} \qquad (8.19)$$

$$\text{s.t.} \qquad \sum_{j=1}^{n} X_{ij} = 1 \qquad \forall\, i \qquad (8.20)$$

$$\sum_{i=1}^{n} X_{ij} = 1 \qquad \forall\, j \qquad (8.21)$$

$$X_{ij} = 0 \text{ or } 1 \qquad \forall\, i, j \qquad (8.22)$$

Equations 8.20 and 8.21 insure that each source is assigned and each location receives only one assignment. The possible values for the decision variables are 0 or 1, since each source consists of a single unit. Thus $X_{ij} = 1$ if unit i is assigned to location j and 0 otherwise.

The assignment model is a version of the transportation model (Equations 8.2 to 8.5), so we might expect a basic solution to have $n + n - 1$ positive variables. This is obviously not the case. Because there are only n possible assignments, only n of the variables can be nonzero. Hence assignment models produce degenerate solutions when solved as transportation problems. The assignment model is also an integer LP model. The restriction of decision variables to integer values usually makes LP models difficult to solve because the simplex method treats variables as continuous (Chapter 7). However, the assignment model has such a simple structure that it can be readily solved without resorting to more general integer programming algorithms. In fact, the integer nature of assignment variables makes the model much easier to solve than it would otherwise be.

As is the case with transportation models, many problems can be modified to fit the general form of the assignment model. If, for example, the number of units exceeds the number of locations (or vice versa), a dummy location (or unit) can be created with associated zero costs. If an assignment is not feasible, a large cost can be assigned to it.

Recreation Planning Problem

EXAMPLE 8-2

A city's parks and recreation commission is planning an expansion of public recreation opportunities. Preliminary studies have revealed the need for three new facilities: a swimming pool, a small park, and tennis courts. Four possible locations have been identified in the city for the facilities, but costs vary among facilities and locations because of different construction needs, site conditions, and required land acquisition (Table 8-20). The commission would like to determine where the three facilities should be placed.

TABLE 8-20 Costs of Placing Recreation Facilities in Four Different Locations

Facility	Location			(10^3/yr)
	1	2	3	4
1. Swimming pool	20	40	15	30
2. Park	5	10	13	6
3. Tennis courts	8	35	16	28

□

This problem very nearly has an assignment structure and needs only the addition of a dummy facility that can be assigned to any location at zero cost. With this modification, the model is given by Expressions 8.19 to 8.22, with $n = 4$, $i = 1, 2, 3, 4$ indicating the swimming pool, park, tennis courts, and dummy facility, and $j = 1, 2, 3, 4$ corresponding to the four locations. The model can be solved with a general assignment algorithm.

A General Assignment Model Algorithm

The algorithm works directly with the problem's cost table (Table 8-21) and is based on the observation that a constant can be added to or subtracted from each cost in a row or column without changing the nature of the optimal solution. This is due to the nature of the constraints and integer variables. If, for example, a constant C is added to each cost in row 1, this merely increases the objective function for the optimal solution by the same constant, C. This is because exactly one of the allocations (X_{ij}) for the row must be equal to one and the remainder are zero. Similarly, since only one assignment per location is possible, we could add or subtract a constant to all costs in a column without affecting the solution. Clearly, this process could continue in any number of arbitrary ways. For example, the constant C could be subtracted from *all* costs in Table 8-21, thus reducing the optimal value of the objective function Z^* by $4C$.

The initial step is to select the minimum cost in each row and subtract that number from all costs in the row (Table 8-22). This identifies with entries of "0" the least costly assignments for each facility. These are location 3 for facility 1 and location 1 for facilities 2 and 3. Since facility 4 is a dummy with zero assignment costs, it could be placed anywhere.

This initial operation has failed to find an optimal solution because the zero entries do not correspond to a single assignment in each row and column. To see this, we mark possible assignments with a box, as shown in Table 8-23. This is done by finding rows or columns with single zeros.

For example, row 1 has a single zero; therefore the optimal allocation of facility 1 is $X_{13} = 1$. Since only one assignment to the third location is possible, this eliminates the possible allocation X_{43}, which also had a zero cost entry. This is indicated by crossing out the zero corresponding to the now infeasible assignment. Similarly, assignment $X_{21} = 1$ is identified, eliminating X_{31} and X_{41}. This leaves either X_{42} or X_{44} as possible assignments. Either can be selected, eliminating the other. All facilities are now assigned except for number 3. The only site remaining is location 4; because it

TABLE 8-21 Assignment Costs for Recreation Example

Facility i/j	Location			
	1	2	3	4
1	20	40	15	30
2	5	10	13	6
3	8	35	16	28
4	0	0	0	0

222 TRANSPORTATION MODELS

does not provide a least cost assignment (the entry in Table 8-23 is not zero), an optimum solution has not been reached.

The next step in this procedure is generally the subtraction of the smallest entry in each column of Table 8-23 from all entries in the column. However, since this

TABLE 8-22 Subtraction of Minimum Costs in Each Row

		Location			
Facility	i/j	1	2	3	4
1		5	25	0	15
2		0	5	8	1
3		0	27	8	20
4		0	0	0	0

TABLE 8-23 Initial Allocations for Recreation Example

		Location			
Facility	i/j	1	2	3	4
1		5	25	[0]	15
2		[0]	5	8	1
3		⊠	27	8	20
4		⊠	[0]	⊠	⊠

TABLE 8-24 Step 1—All Zeros Covered

		Location			
Facility	i/j	1	2	3	4
1		~~5~~	~~25~~	[0]	~~15~~
2		[0]	5	8	1
3		⊠	27	8	20
4		⊠	[0]	⊠	⊠

example has a dummy facility with zero costs in each column, no changes would result. Therefore we must continue to the second part of the algorithm, which attempts to identify a new zero entry by a series of subtractions and additions as follows.

1. Cover all zeros in the table with a minimum number of vertical and horizontal lines (Table 8-24). This minimum number equals the number of allocations in the current solution (three in this case).
2. Select the smallest uncovered entry and subtract it from all numbers in the table (Table 8-25).
3. To restore the former zeros, add the entry used in step 2 to each number in a covered row and column (Table 8-26). Note that this means a double addition at intersections.

These three steps produce the optimal solution shown in Table 8-26 since a single zero entry can be found for each assignment. The optimal assignments are

$$X_{13}^* = 1 \text{ (swimming pool at location 3)}$$
$$X_{24}^* = 1 \text{ (park at location 4)}$$
$$X_{31}^* = 1 \text{ (tennis courts at location 1)}$$
$$X_{42}^* = 1 \text{ (location 2 unused)}.$$

Optimal costs are $Z^* = 15 + 6 + 8 = \$29 \: 10^3/\text{yr}$. If the optimal solution had not been produced, additional iterations of the three-step procedure would have been necessary.

Summary

Transportation models (including their assignment model subset) are among the easiest LP models to solve. Algorithms exist for the models that are much more efficient than

TABLE 8-25 Step 2—Reduction of All Entries by Smallest Uncovered Entry

Facility i/j	Location			
	1	2	3	4
1	4	24	−1	14
2	−1	4	7	0
3	−1	26	7	19
4	−1	−1	−1	−1

TABLE 8-26 Step 3—Restoration of Zero Entries by Smallest Uncovered Entry

Facility i/j	Location			
	1	2	3	4
1	6	25	[0]	15
2	✗	4	7	[0]
3	[0]	26	7	19
4	1	[0]	✗	✗

the general form of the simplex method. The algorithms take advantage of the special structures of transportation problems and obtain optimal solutions by simple iterative calculations that can often be carried out by hand. A variety of problems can be described by transportation models, although they often must be restructured to match the mathematical forms of the general transportation or assignment model.

In an age of fast and relatively inexpensive digital computing, it is probably not essential for the environmental systems analyst to be familiar with transportation models. Except for the assignment problem, transportation models *can* be solved directly by the simplex method, and the analyst may use a general computer program of the simplex method to solve an LP model without even knowing that the model is a transportation problem. Programmed integer LP methods (Chapter 7) can similarly solve assignment problems. In both cases solutions will take longer and may result in greater computer costs than if transportation algorithms are used. Nevertheless, computer expenses are often a minor component of the costs of environmental systems analysis, and computing efficiency provides little motivation for studying transportation models.

The value of transportation models and algorithms is basically intrinsic. There is intellectual (and perhaps only academic) satisfaction in the ability to identify and classify a problem. Successful scientific inquiry relies on recognition of differences and similarities. All LP models are not the same, and the perceptive analyst recognizes categories of models and solutions.

A second and much more practical justification for transportation methods involves the relationship between the analyst and the computer. Although the computer is an indispensible tool of systems analysis, its role is not wholly beneficial. Particularly with LP problems, solutions are almost always generated by the computer and not the analyst. By using a canned simplex program, the analyst deals only with decisions and solutions and not with the numerical details of variable interactions. This is, of course, necessary for any but the very smallest standard LP models. However, with such a "black box" approach to problem solving, the analyst may lose understanding of the dynamics of the system being modeled. By contrast, when solutions are obtained by hand (or calculator) computations, the analyst must monitor every step of the numerical operations that produce a solution. With such a process it is hard to avoid an intimate knowledge of the problem being solved, and sometimes such knowledge can identify faulty assumptions and data or, on a more positive note, leave the systems analyst in a much better position to explain the significance of model solutions to decision makers.

The preceding argument is not an indictment of computers. Systems analysis could scarcely exist without them. However, when it is possible to generate model solutions without computers or at least without canned computer programs produced by individuals other than the program user, the systems analyst may gain additional insight into the problem being modeled. Transportation models provide an opportunity for the analyst to get his or her "hands dirty" by involvement in the details of model solutions. This is usually an opportunity of which the analyst should take advantage.

SELECTED REFERENCES

1. Aguilar, R. J., *Systems Analysis and Design in Engineering, Architecture, Construction and Planning,* Prentice-Hall, Englewood Cliffs, N.J., 1973, Chapter 8.
2. Bradley, S. P., A. C. Hax, and T. L. Magnanti, *Applied Mathematical Programming,* Addison-Wesley, Reading, Mass., 1977, Chapter 8.
3. Gass, S. I., *Linear Programming Methods and Applications,* 4th ed., McGraw-Hill, New York, 1975, Chapter 10.
4. Hadley, G., *Linear Programming,* Addison-Wesley, Reading, Mass., 1962, Chapters 9 and 10.
5. Hillier, F. S., and G. J. Lieberman, *Operations Research,* 2nd ed., Holden-Day, San Francisco, 1974, Chapter 3.
6. Vajda, S., *An Introduction to Linear Programming and the Theory of Games,* Methuen & Co., London, 1966.

EXERCISES

8-1.

Two cities are developing a joint plan for the disposal of municipal solid waste. City 1 produces 100 t/day of waste; city 2 produces 170 t/day. Three disposal sites are available for the solid wastes, but each has different capacities and costs as shown in the table. Transportation costs are $0.50/t/km.

226 TRANSPORTATION MODELS

Disposal Site	Disposal Cost ($/t)	Capacity (t/day)	Distance (km) from City 1	Distance (km) from City 2
1	12	150	15	10
2	16	70	5	15
3	6	200	30	25

Construct a transportation model that can be used to determine a joint disposal plan and solve accordingly.

8-2.

Choking Dust County has a water supply problem. The county has decided to examine the water supply requirements of the various economic sectors, the available sources of water and attempt an efficient allocation of these sources to the sectors. The preliminary analysis has determined the following.

(a) Projected water supply requirements for the various economic sectors are

Municipalities	80,000 m^3/day
Industry	170,000 m^3/day
Agriculture	160,000 m^3/day
Other	50,000 m^3/day

(b) Since only 370,000 m^3/day will be available from primary sources (surface and groundwaters), it will be necessary to develop secondary supplies if requirements are to be met. Wastewater recycling and desalination of saltwater are possible secondary sources. Recycling means the reuse of wastewater from the municipal, industrial, or agricultural sectors. The amounts of wastewater from each sector that could be reused are

Municipal	50,000 m^3/day
Agriculture	80,000 m^3/day
Industry	45,000 m^3/day

In addition, 20,000 m^3/day of desalted water would be available.

(c) Not all primary and secondary water sources can be used by each sector. Moreover, the costs of using the waters (which include transportation and necessary treatment) will vary with source and sector. The municipal sector can use only primary sources at $0.005/m^3$ or desalted water at $0.015/m^3$. Industry can recycle its own wastewater at a cost of $0.012/m^3$, use primary sources and desalted water at costs of $0.007/m^3$ and $0.010/m^3$, and municipal and agricultural wastewaters at $0.006/m^3$ and $0.010/m^3$. Agriculture can recycle its own wastewater at $0.008/m^3$ and also use primary sources and municipal wastewaters at $0.004/m^3$ and $0.006/m^3$. Finally, remaining water users (the "other" sector) may use primary sources, municipal, agricultural, and industrial wastewater, and desalted water at costs of $0.007, $0.009, $0.008, $0.010, and $0.015/m^3$.

Construct an optimization model that can be used to determine the optimal (least cost) allocation of water supplies. Solve using the transportation algorithm.

8-3.

The city parks and recreation commission is reconsidering the location of recreation facilities, since it has found out that the national government will pay all costs. Hence the commission has decided to maximize public use of the facilities and place them where they will receive the most visitors. Anticipated visitors at the four locations are as follows.

	Location			(no./yr)
Facility	1	2	3	4
Swimming pool	12,000	5,000	10,000	9,000
Park	9,000	8,000	7,000	6,000
Tennis Courts	12,000	16,000	9,000	11,000

Use an assignment model to determine where the facilities should be located.

8-4.

Three different housing and recreation developments are planned for a coastal area. There are four possible sites for the developments and, although no site is in a saltwater marsh, each site will have some effect on neighboring marshes because of drainage and shoreline changes. Saltwater marshes are among the world's most productive areas, and reductions in productivity can have serious effects on aquatic food chains. If we measure annual productivity of a marsh in kg of biomass, the productivity losses associated with the developments at various sites are as follows.

Development 1	(kg loss)	Development 2	(kg loss)	Development 3	(kg loss)
Site 1	5,000	Site 1	18,000	Site 1	14,000
Site 2	20,000	Site 2	28,000	Site 2	17,000
Site 3	6,000	Site 3	25,000	Site 3	8,000
Site 4	10,000	Site 4	21,000	Site 4	10,000

No site can accommodate more than one development. Where should the developments be located to minimize marsh productivity loss? Formulate as an LP problem and solve using an appropriate method.

CHAPTER 9
DYNAMIC PROGRAMMING MODELS

Dynamic programming (DP) is a mathematical programming procedure that can sometimes be used to solve optimization models. As with linear programming, DP can only be used for models with a certain structure. The required structure for linear programming (LP) models is implied by the name. Although certain nonlinear models can be solved by means of separable or integer programming, optimization models must ultimately be in a linear form to obtain solutions by LP. By contrast, DP is adaptable to both linear and nonlinear models. In addition, discontinuous variables and functions cause no particular difficulties with DP.

The required model structure for DP is difficult to describe in general terms because DP models can have a variety of mathematical forms. However, problems suitable for DP can usually be interpreted as *sequential allocation processes*. For example, we might allocate portions of a landfill to several different types of waste. The allocation can be "sequential," since we can first allocate parts of the landfill to the first waste, then make allocations to waste 2, and so forth, until all allocations are completed. DP problems are broken down into a sequence of decisions, each of which involves the allocation of one or more quantities, or "resources."

The most striking difference between LP and DP involves the methods used to obtain solutions. In a sense, all LP models are the same because they can be solved by standardized algorithms and computer programs that are usually based on the simplex method. Conversely, each DP model is somewhat unique, and the computations required to obtain a solution must be tailored to the characteristics of the model being solved. Generally applicable or "standard" programs for solving DP problems are of limited value. A new algorithm or computer program is usually developed for each model.

DP implies a particular way of looking at optimization models. The basic ideas of DP, while inherently simple, can nonetheless be subtle. In addition, a specialized mathematical notation has traditionally accompanied DP. The combination of subtle ideas and notation can be both intimidating and frustrating, and many individuals find that they can learn how to use DP only through working examples. This approach is encouraged in this chapter, which contains examples from land use planning, solid waste management, and air and water pollution control. To stress the simple nature of the DP approach, the first example is developed in an intuitive fashion that avoids the formalism of more general DP problems. We will subsequently build on this example by introducing the definitions and mathematical notation that constitute the traditional DP subject area.

APPLICATION OF DYNAMIC PROGRAMMING TO LAND USE PLANNING

EXAMPLE 9-1

A municipality wishes to zone 60 ha of currently vacant land. Zoning is to be in 10-ha units. Concerned with both possible tax revenues and costs of providing municipal services, the community has hired a consultant to determine net tax revenues (tax payments minus costs of municipal services) from three possible development options: light commercial, high-density residential (apartments), and recreational. Net tax revenues from these options in 10^2/yr are as follows.

Commercial	Residential	Recreational
$6A^{0.6}$	$A^{1.1}$	$50[1 - \exp(-A/15)]$

where in each case A is the quantity (ha) of land devoted to the land use. How should the municipality zone the 60 ha in order to maximize tax revenues? □

This example, while perhaps overly simple, stresses a recurring theme of municipal land use planners. Land use plans serve many purposes, but a general objective is often the "orderly development" of a community. Ideally, such development fosters a diversity of activities consistent with the community's cultural, economic, and environmental needs. However, communities must also realistically consider the costs of development options, particularly the direct costs of municipal services. This example illustrates the use of a net revenue criterion (tax payments minus service costs) in land use planning.

Decision variables for the problem are

X_i = land zoned for use i (ha), where i = 1, 2, 3 indicates commercial, residential, and recreational uses, respectively

Net tax revenues Z (10^2/yr) are to be maximized, and the resulting optimization model is

$$\text{Max } Z = 6X_1^{0.6} + X_2^{1.1} + 50(1 - e^{-X_3/15}) \qquad (9.1)$$

$$\text{s.t.} \quad X_1 + X_2 + X_3 = 60 \qquad (9.2)$$

$$X_i \in (0, 10, 20, 30, 40, 50, 60) \qquad (9.3)$$

This optimization model is simple in structure, since it contains only three variables and one constraint. In spite of the simplicity there are several features that make it difficult to solve. The decision variables are discontinuous and can have only certain integer values. The objective function is separable, but it contains a mixture of concave and convex functions, as shown in Figure 9-1. Although the model could conceivably be solved using some combination of separable and mixed integer LP, this could be difficult.

The model can be solved by a fairly simple computational process that considers various combinations of land uses. As a starting point, we will first examine the tax revenues associated with the third land use (recreation). These revenues are given in Table 9-1. The second step in the procedure is to construct a comparable table for residential land use (Table 9-2).

Suppose we ignore the first land use for the time being and consider what would happen if the entire 60 ha were allocated to residential and recreational uses. The various possible combinations of X_2 and X_3 that add up to 60 ha are shown in Table 9-3 along with the resulting tax revenues. If all 60 ha are used for residences and recreation,

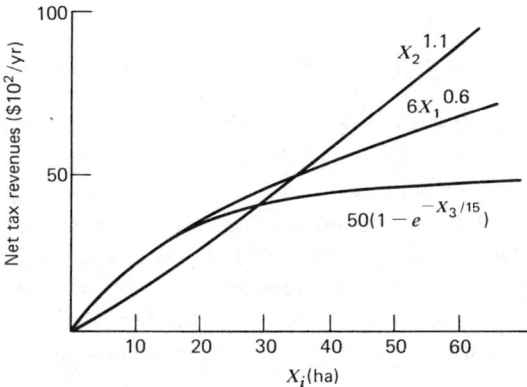

Figure 9-1. Net tax revenue functions for Example 9-1.

TABLE 9-1 Tax Revenues Associated with Recreational Land Use

X_3 (ha)	$50(1 - e^{-X_3/15})$ ($\$10^2$/yr)
0	0
10	24
20	37
30	43
40	47
50	48
60	49

TABLE 9-2 Tax Revenues Associated with Residential Land Use

X_2 (ha)	$X_2^{1.1}$ (10^2/yr)
0	0
10	13
20	27
30	42
40	58
50	74
60	90

tax revenues would be maximized with 50 ha in residential use and 10 ha devoted to recreation ($X_2 = 50$, $X_3 = 10$).

Obviously, it may not be desirable to allocate the entire 60 ha to land uses 2 and 3. If 10 ha are zoned commercially, only 50 ha will be available for the remaining two uses. In fact, the amount of land available for land uses 2 and 3 ranges from 60 to 0 ha. If we consider each of these possibilities, we obtain the land use combinations shown in Table 9-4. Depending on the amount of land allocated to the two land uses, various combinations turn out to be optimal (maximize tax revenues). For example, if 40 ha is to be allocated, the best division of land is $X_2 = 30$, $X_3 = 10$. The resulting net tax revenue from these two uses is $6600/yr. The different optimal combinations are given in Table 9-5.

The final and most important step in this computational procedure is to visualize the problem as having two stages, as indicated in Figure 9-2. The first stage is an

TABLE 9-3 Alternative Land Use Combinations for 60 ha Allocated to Land Uses 2 and 3

Total Land (ha)	X_2	X_3	$X_2^{1.1} + 50(1 - e^{-X_3/15})$ (10^2/yr)
60	0	60	0 + 49 = 49
	10	50	13 + 48 = 61
	20	40	27 + 47 = 74
	30	30	42 + 43 = 85
	40	20	58 + 37 = 95
	50	10	74 + 24 = 98
	60	0	90 + 0 = 90

TABLE 9-4 Alternative Combinations of Land Uses 2 and 3

Total Land Allocated to Uses 2 and 3 (ha)	Possible Uses		Net Revenue $X_2^{1.1} + 50(1 - e^{-X_3/15})$ (10^2/yr)
	X_2	X_3	
60	0	60	0 + 49 = 49
	10	50	13 + 48 = 61
	20	40	27 + 47 = 74
	30	30	42 + 43 = 85
	40	20	58 + 37 = 95
	50	10	74 + 24 = 98[a]
	60	0	90 + 0 = 90
50	0	50	0 + 48 = 48
	10	40	13 + 47 = 60
	20	30	27 + 43 = 70
	30	20	42 + 37 = 79
	40	10	58 + 24 = 82[a]
	50	0	74 + 0 = 74
40	0	40	0 + 47 = 47
	10	30	13 + 43 = 56
	20	20	27 + 37 = 64
	30	10	42 + 24 = 66[a]
	40	0	58 + 0 = 58
30	0	30	0 + 43 = 43
	10	20	13 + 37 = 50
	20	10	27 + 24 = 51[a]
	30	0	42 + 0 = 42
20	0	20	0 + 37 = 37[a]
	10	10	13 + 24 = 37[a]
	20	0	27 + 0 = 27
10	0	10	0 + 24 = 24[a]
	10	0	13 + 0 = 13
0	0	0	0 + 0 = 0[a]

[a] Best combinations.

allocation of land to commercial zoning. The second stage considers the best uses of the remaining $60 - X_1$ ha for residences and recreation. The second stage of the problem has already been solved, since we have determined the optimal values of X_2

234 DYNAMIC PROGRAMMING MODELS

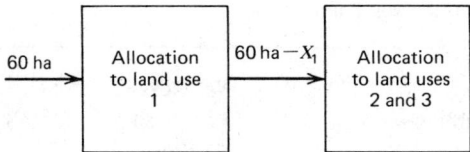

Figure 9-2. Decomposition of land use example into two stages.

TABLE 9-5 Maximum Net Tax Revenues From Land Uses 2 and 3

Land Allocated to Uses 2 and 3 (ha)	Best Allocations		Maximum Revenue ($10²/yr)
	X_2	X_3	
60	50	10	98
50	40	10	82
40	30	10	66
30	20	10	51
20	0(10)	20(10)	37
10	0	10	24
0	0	0	0

TABLE 9-6 Possible Allocations to Land Use 1 and Remaining Uses (2 and 3)

Total Land Available (ha)	X_1	Land Available to Land Uses 2 and 3 = 60 − X_1	$6X_1^{0.6}$ + Max $[X_2^{1.1} + 50(1 - e^{-X_3/15})]$[a] ($10^2$/yr)
60	0	60	0 + 98 = 98
	10	50	24 + 82 = 106
	20	40	36 + 66 = 102
	30	30	46 + 51 = 97
	40	20	55 + 37 = 92
	50	10	63 + 24 = 87
	60	0	70 + 0 = 70

[a] From Table 9-5.

and X_3 for any possible value of $60 - X_1$. These results (Table 9-5) can be combined with the possible stage 1 allocations, as shown in Table 9-6. With the completion of Table 9-6, the model is now solved. Maximum net revenues are $Z^* = \$10,600$/yr, corresponding to 10 ha of commercial zoning ($X_1^* = 10$) and 50 ha for residential and recreation use. From Table 9-5 (or Table 9-4) it can be seen that with 50 ha available, optimal allocations for these two land uses are $X_2^* = 40$, $X_3^* = 10$. The solution to the model is thus

$$Z^* = \$10,600$$
$$X_1^* = 10 \text{ ha}$$
$$X_2^* = 40 \text{ ha}$$
$$X_3^* = 10 \text{ ha}$$

These computations are an example of DP. The optimization model was solved by a sequential allocation procedure in which a resource (land) was allocated in a series of stages. The computations proceeded "backward," with the third land use being analyzed first. Letting the stages correspond to land uses, the problem solution was developed in three stages.

Stage 3 = revenues from land use 3
Stage 2 = revenues from the combination of land uses 2 and 3
Stage 1 = revenues from land use 1 and the optimal combinations of land uses 2 and 3

At any stage, only the best or optimal decisions were retained for subsequent computations.

If there had been additional land uses more stages would have been necessary. With five land uses, the five computational stages would be as follows.

Stage 5 = land use 5
Stage 4 = optimal uses 4 and 5
Stage 3 = optimal uses 3, 4, and 5
Stage 2 = optimal uses 2, 3, 4, and 5
Stage 1 = optimal uses 1, 2, 3, 4, and 5

DP is a suboptimization procedure that breaks down a problem into a series of smaller problems that are solved in a sequential and cumulative fashion.

The DP methods in Tables 9-1 to 9-6 are certainly not sophisticated. In fact, it seems that a search approach involving the enumeration of all possible alternatives has been used. However, this is not quite correct. We have not looked at all possible combinations of X_1, X_2, and X_3. At stage 2 (Table 9-4), a substantial number of suboptimal pairs of X_2 and X_3 were eliminated, and only the best were subsequently combined with X_1 (Table 9-6). A more interesting comparison between DP and direct enumeration (evaluation of all possible alternatives) involves the required amount of numerical operations. Once net revenues are computed for each land use, the evaluation of any alternative combination of X_1, X_2, and X_3 requires two additions with direct enumeration (revenues from X_1 and X_2 are added and then revenue from X_3 is added to the total). There are 28 possible combinations of X_1, X_2, and X_3 that total 60 ha. Therefore complete enumeration would require $28(2) = 56$ computations. Conversely, using DP, 28 additions were required for Table 9-4 and 7 additions were needed for Table 9-6, for a total of 35 computations. In a sense, DP has examined all possible alternatives, but it has done so in a computationally efficient manner.

The efficiency of DP becomes more dramatic with an increase in the number of stages. If a fourth land use with net tax revenues of, say, $1.4X_4$ is added to the problem, two tables similar to Table 9-4 would be required as follows.

Stage 3

Total Land Allocated to Uses 3 and 4	X_3	X_4	Net Revenue
.	.	.	.
.	.	.	.
.	.	.	.

Stage 2

Total Land Allocated to Uses 2, 3, and 4	X_2	$X_3 + X_4$	Net Revenue
.	.	.	.
.	.	.	.
.	.	.	.

Each table would require 28 additions. As before, the final table (stage 1) involves 7 additions for a total of $28 + 28 + 7 = 63$ numerical operations. By contrast, direct enumeration involves evaluation of 84 feasible alternatives, each requiring 3 additions, for a total of 252 computations.

Like other forms of mathematical programming, DP is really nothing more than a clever search strategy. As with LP, it is an iterative computational procedure that converges on an optimal solution to an optimization model.

DYNAMIC PROGRAMMING NOTATION

Although the computational steps of DP are basically simple, they require a specialized notation to express them mathematically. This notation is involved and can be confusing. However, the formalism of the notation is necessary to describe DP problems concisely. In the absence of such mathematical precision, it is nearly impossible to communicate and document the approach used in solving a particular DP problem. Some general definitions are presented in this section, and the land use example is reformulated using DP notation.

DP is a sequential allocation procedure in which one or more resources is allocated in stages 1, 2, . . . , N. In the following discussion it is assumed that a single resource is to be allocated. The following are defined.

S_t = amount of resource available for allocation at stage t; S_t is a *state variable*
X_t = amount of resource allocated to stage t; X_t is a *decision variable*
Ω_t = set of possible allocations to stage t

In the land use example stages are the three land uses, S_t is the land available for allocation to land use t (ha), and X_t is the amount of land (ha) actually allocated (zoned) to use t. The set of possible allocations is $\Omega_t = (0, 10, \ldots, 60)$, where $X_t \leq S_t$. A return function for stage t is defined as

$r_t(S_t, X_t)$ = return from stage t when S_t is available for allocation at stage t and X_t is allocated (10^2/yr)

Often, as with land use example, returns are a function only of the decision variable; that is, the return function is just $r_t(X_t)$.

A starting point in any DP solution is the construction of a diagram showing stages, state and decision variables, and return functions. The appropriate diagram for the land use example is shown in Figure 9-3. The computational procedure requires a determination of optimal decisions for each stage. Beginning with stage (land use) 3, we define

$f_3(S_3)$ = optimal return from land use 3 when S_3 is available at stage 3 (10^2/yr)

In mathematical terms, $f_3(S_3)$ must be the maximum value of $r_3(X_3)$ for a given value of S_3.

$$f_3(S_3) = \text{Max } [50(1 - e^{-X_3/15})] \qquad (9.4)$$
$$X_3 \leq S_3$$
$$X_3 \ \varepsilon \ \Omega_3$$

Equation 9.4 is an optimization model with one variable (X_3) and two constraints.

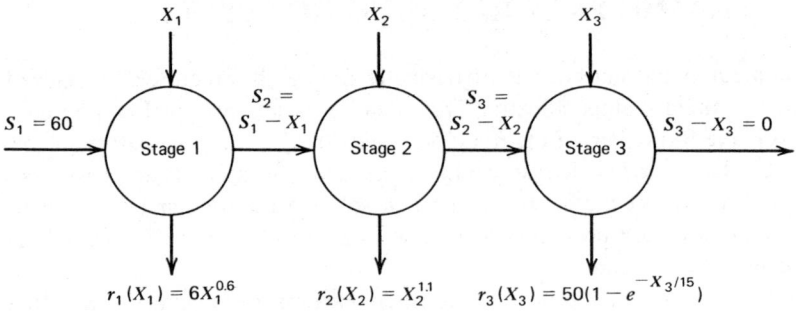

Figure 9-3. DP diagram for Example 9-1.

It can be solved provided S_3 is specified (i.e., its solution is a function of S_3). Since all land is to be used, $S_3 - X_3 = 0$ from Figure 9-3, and hence $X_3 = S_3$ for any value of S_3. Thus $f_3(S_3) = r_3(S_3) = 50(1 - e^{-S_3/15})$. Possible values of $f_3(S_3)$ are shown in Table 9-1a. Note that this table is equivalent to Table 9-1. Proceeding to stage 2, we have

$f_2(S_2)$ = optimal return from land uses 2 and 3 when S_2 is available at stage 2 ($\$10^2$/yr)

This function was given in Table 9-4 and is expressed mathematically as

$$f_2(S_2) = \text{Max } [r_2(X_2) + r_3(X_3)] \qquad (9.5)$$
$$X_2 \varepsilon \, \Omega_2, \quad X_3 \varepsilon \, \Omega_3$$
$$X_2 \leq S_2, \quad X_3 = S_2 - X_2$$

where $r_2(X_2)$ and $r_3(X_3)$ are defined in Figure 9-3. Equation 9.5 is a two-variable maximization problem. However, it can be reduced to a single-variable problem by using the results from stage 3.

$$\text{Max } [r_2(X_2) + r_3(X_3)] = \text{Max } \{r_2(X_2) + \text{Max } [r_3(X_3)]\} \qquad (9.6)$$

Since the final term on the right side of Equation 9.6 is equivalent to $f_3(S_3)$, we have

$$f_2(S_2) = \text{Max } [r_2(X_2) + f_3(S_3)] \qquad (9.7)$$

and, since $S_3 = S_2 - X_2$ (Figure 9-3), we finally obtain

$$f_2(S_2) = \text{Max } [r_2(X_2) + f_3(S_2 - X_2)] \qquad (9.8)$$
$$X_2 \leq S_2$$
$$X_2 \varepsilon \, \Omega_2$$

TABLE 9-1a   Determination of $f_3(S_3)$

S_3 (ha)	X_3	$r_3(X_3)$ (10^2/yr)	$f_3(S_3)$
60	60	49	49
50	50	48	48
40	40	47	47
30	30	43	43
20	20	37	37
10	10	24	24
0	0	0	0

Equation 9.8 is a mathematical statement of the computations shown in Table 9-4. For any fixed value of S_2, we can optimize with respect to a single variable, X_2. The equation expresses the central feature of DP. A multivariate optimization problem is broken down into stages, each of which is a smaller problem. In general, an N-stage problem can be decomposed into N smaller problems, each of which optimizes with respect to a small set of variables (often only one). Table 9-4 is duplicated as Table 9-4a, with the headings replaced by the appropriate DP notation.

Remaining stages of the DP problem are handled similarly. In the land use example only one stage remains.

$f_1(S_1)$ = optimal return from land uses 1, 2, and 3 when S_1 is available at stage 1 (10^2/yr)

$$f_1(S_1) = \text{Max}\ [r_1(X_1) + r_2(X_2) + r_3(X_3)] \tag{9.9}$$

where appropriate constraints must be placed on X_1, X_2, X_3 ($X_1 \varepsilon\ \Omega_1$, $X_2 \varepsilon\ \Omega_2$, etc). We reduce $f_1(S_1)$ to the following single-variable optimization problem.

$$f_1(S_1) = \text{Max}\ \{r_1(X_1) + \text{Max}\ [r_2(X_2) + r_3(X_3)]\}$$
$$= \text{Max}\ [r_1(X_1) + f_2(S_2)] \tag{9.10}$$

Since $S_2 = S_1 - X_1$, the final equation is

$$f_1(S_1) = \text{Max}\ [r_1(X_1) + f_2(S_1 - X_1)] \tag{9.11}$$
$$X_1 \leq S_1$$
$$X_1\ \varepsilon\ \Omega_1$$

TABLE 9-4a Determination of $f_2(S_2)$

S_2 (ha)	X_2	$S_3 = S_2 - X_2$	$r_2(X_2) + f_3(S_3)$ (10^2/yr)	$f_2(S_2)$
60	0	60	0 + 49 = 49	
	10	50	13 + 48 = 61	
	20	40	27 + 47 = 74	
	30	30	42 + 43 = 85	
	40	20	58 + 37 = 95	
	50	10	74 + 24 = 98	98
	60	0	90 + 0 = 90	
50	0	50	0 + 48 = 48	
	10	40	13 + 47 = 60	
	20	30	27 + 43 = 70	
	30	20	42 + 37 = 79	
	40	10	58 + 24 = 82	82
	50	0	74 + 0 = 74	
40	0	40	0 + 47 = 47	
	10	30	13 + 43 = 56	
	20	20	27 + 37 = 64	
	30	10	42 + 24 = 66	66
	40	0	58 + 0 = 58	
30	0	30	0 + 43 = 43	
	10	20	13 + 37 = 50	
	20	10	27 + 24 = 51	51
	30	0	42 + 0 = 42	
20	0	20	0 + 37 = 37	37
	10	10	13 + 24 = 37	37
	20	0	27 + 0 = 27	
10	0	10	0 + 24 = 24	24
	10	0	13 + 0 = 13	
0	0	0	0 + 0 = 0	0

The calculations of $f_1(S_1)$ for $S_1 = 60$ were given in Table 9-6. These results are repeated in Table 9-6a.

The optimal net tax revenue is $Z^* = f_1(60) = \$10{,}600$ and $X_1^* = 10$. From Table

TABLE 9-6a   Determination of $f_1(S_1)$

S_1 (ha)	X_1	$S_2 = S_1 - X_1$	$r_1(X_1) + f_2(S_2)$ (10^2/yr)	$f_1(S_1)$
60	0	60	0 + 98 = 98	
	10	50	24 + 82 = 106	106
	20	40	36 + 66 = 102	
	30	30	46 + 51 = 97	
	40	20	55 + 37 = 92	
	50	10	63 + 24 = 87	
	60	0	70 + 0 = 70	

9-6a, $S_2 = 50$. The optimal value of X_2^* is obtained from Table 9-4a. With $S_2 = 50$, $X_2^* = 40$, and $S_3 = 10$. From Table 9-1a, for $S_3 = 10$ we have $X_3^* = 10$.

The multistage DP computations can often be concisely summarized in a single mathematical statement or *recursive equation*. The equation for the land use example is

$$f_t(S_t) = \text{Max}\ [r_t(X_t) + f_{t+1}(S_t - X_t)] \quad (9.12)$$

$$X_t \leq S_t$$

$$X_t\ \varepsilon\ \Omega_t$$

where it is understood that for $t = 3$, $f_{t+1}(\cdot) = 0$.

Characteristics of Dynamic Programming Problems

DP is a straightforward method for solving optimization models. There are only a few essential features that must be remembered. The first and most important is the basic computational procedure. Whether done by hand or computer, the computations require a breakdown of a problem into stages and the development of a table of computations for each stage. The second aspect is the use of appropriate terminology. Stages, state variables, and recursive equations must be defined for each DP problem.

Finally, it is important to know when DP can be used. Optimization models that can be solved by DP have several common characteristics. It must be possible to visualize the model as a series of *sequential decisions*. For example, in the land use example the relevant decisions, X_1, X_2, and X_3, could be made one by one, thus facilitating the decomposition of the problem into stages. A second requirement for DP that is also necessary for decomposition is that the returns from any stage must be a function only of the decisions made at that stage and the "state of the system" at that stage. Mathematically, this usually[1] requires a separable objective function of the form

$$Z = F(S_1, S_2, \ldots, S_N, X_1, X_2, \ldots, X_N)$$
$$= r_1(S_1, X_1) + r_2(S_2, X_2) + \ldots + r_N(S_N, X_N) \tag{9.13}$$

The third and final characteristic of DP models is the presence of one or more "resources" that are to be allocated. Moreover, the number of resources to be allocated must be small. When only one resource is to be allocated, the problem is readily solved by DP. Two resources greatly increase the number of computations, since each table (such as Tables 9-1a and 9-4a) will now be three dimensional (one dimension for each resource or state variable and one dimension for the decision variable). Problems involving three or more resources and a comparable number of state variables are extremely difficult to solve. Because the computations from each stage must be saved in a multidimensional table or array, enormous amounts of computer storage are required for such problems. Even with large computers, the manipulation of the large arrays requires a very skillful use of machine storage devices. As a practical matter, optimization models that involve allocation of more than two resources are seldom solved using DP. This limitation of DP is often referred to as the "curse of dimensionality."

EXAMPLE OF PHOSPHORUS REMOVAL FROM MUNICIPAL WASTEWATERS

EXAMPLE 9-2
A city is under orders to reduce the amount of phosphorus that it discharges to a lake in its sewage. The city presently has three sewage treatment plants discharging 1000, 500, and 2000 kg/day of phosphorus into the lake and must reduce this to a *total* of 1000 kg/day for the three plants. If X_t is the *percent* of the phosphorus removed by additional treatment at plant t, the cost of such treatment (\$/yr) is given by $15X_1^2$, $10X_2^2$, and $20X_3^2$ at plants 1, 2, and 3, respectively. □

This example is a cost-effectiveness problem that is solved by determining the least cost wastewater treatment plan that meets the effluent standard for phosphorus. Treatment plant efficiencies X_t are the decision variables, and the system to be analyzed is shown in Figure 9-4.

The cost functions for phosphorus removal are convex functions of efficiencies, indicating that it becomes progressively more difficult and hence expensive to remove

---

[1] Certain other functions are also separable. For example, the function $X_1 X_2 \ldots X_N$ is also separable (although not linearly so) and can be optimized using DP. For a general discussion of separable functions, see reference 5.

increasing amounts of phosphorus. For example, it may be relatively easy to remove 30% of the effluent phosphorus at treatment plant 1. The cost of such removal is $15(30)^2 = \$13,500/\text{yr}$. To remove three times as much phosphorus, the efficiency must be $X_1 = 90\%$, and the resulting cost is $15(90)^2 = \$121,500/\text{yr}$. Thus, to increase removal by a factor of three, costs must increase ninefold.

Construction of an Optimization Model

The optimization model for this example is straightforward. The amount of phosphorus discharged into the lake from each treatment plant is shown in Figure 9-4. The total phosphorus entering the lake from all three plants must be no more than 1000 kg/day. In mathematical terms the effluent standard is

$$1000(1 - X_1/100) + 500(1 - X_2/100) + 2000(1 - X_3/100) \leq 1000 \quad (9.14)$$

Rearranging terms, we have

$$10X_1 + 5X_2 + 20X_3 \geq 2500 \quad (9.15)$$

The complete model is

$$\text{Min } Z = 15X_1^2 + 10X_2^2 + 20X_3^2 \quad (9.16)$$

s.t.

$$10X_1 + 5X_2 + 20X_3 \geq 2{,}500 \quad (9.15)$$

$$X_t \leq 100 \quad \forall\, t \quad (9.17)$$

As with the land use example, this is a fairly simple optimization model. Since the cost functions are convex, separable LP could be used to solve the model. However, the model can also be solved by DP. To see this, we must first recognize that decisions can be made sequentially, with each treatment plant being a stage. Since the objective function is separable, the "return," which is a cost in this case, for each stage is a

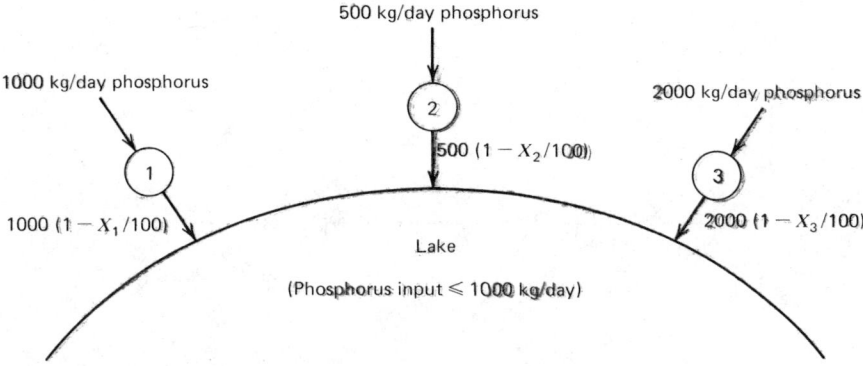

Figure 9-4. System diagram for phosphorus removal example.

244 DYNAMIC PROGRAMMING MODELS

function only of the decision (X_t) made at that stage. To determine the resource being allocated, we must examine Constraint 9.15. Although in its original form (Constraint 9.14) this constraint was in terms of daily discharge of phosphorus, the rearranged Constraint 9.15 states that "at least 2500 kg/day of phosphorus must be removed by wastewater treatment." This total removal can be considered a "resource" that must be allocated to the three treatment plants. This leads to the following definition of a state variable.

S_t = amount of phosphorus (kg/day) that remains to be removed at stage t

The relationships between stages, state and decision variables, and returns (cost functions) are shown in Figure 9-5. It may seem puzzling that the resource remaining after the third stage can be negative ($S_3 - 20X_3 \leq 0$), but this only indicates that *at least* 2500 kg/day of phosphorus must be removed. This can also be shown by writing $S_3 - 20X_3$ in terms of all the decision variables.

$$S_3 - 20X_3 = S_2 - 5X_2 - 20X_3 = S_1 - 10X_1 - 5X_2 - 20X_3$$
$$= 2500 - 10X_1 - 5X_2 - 20X_3 \leq 0$$

Transposing terms, we have

$$10X_1 + 5X_2 + 20X_3 \geq 2500 \tag{9.15}$$

Thus $S_3 - 20X_3 \leq 0$ is an alternative way of writing Constraint 9.15.

To a certain extent, the specific definition of a state variable for a DP problem is arbitrary. The state variable for this example could also be defined as follows.

S_t = amount of phosphorus (kg/day) removed prior to stage t

With this definition the DP diagram would look somewhat different. Figure 9-6 indicates that we start with $S_1 = 0$ (no previous phosphorus removal) and, at the end of stage 3, at least 2500 kg/day of phosphorus must be removed.

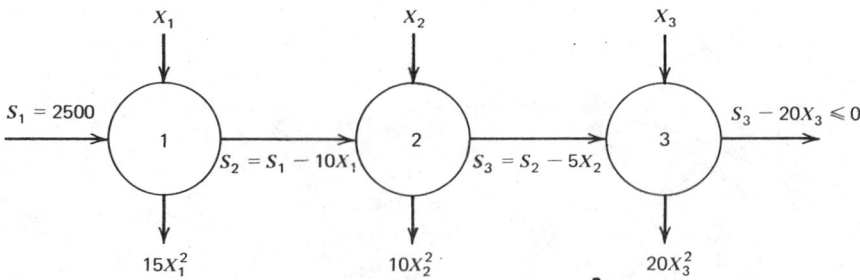

Figure 9-5. DP diagram for phosphorus removal example.

PHOSPHORUS REMOVAL FROM MUNICIPAL WASTEWATERS

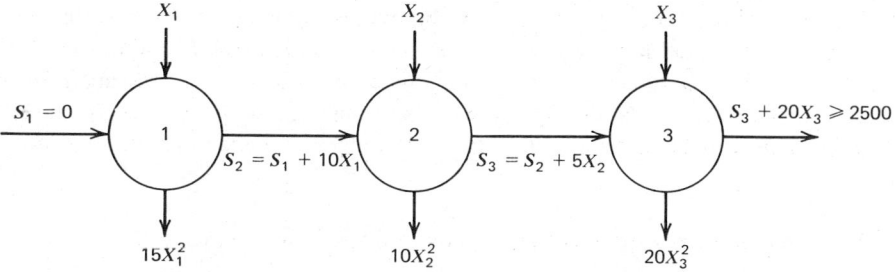

Figure 9-6. Alternative DP program for phosphorus removal example.

The optimization model can be solved with either state variable definition. If we use the definition implied by Figure 9-6, the optimal cost for any stage t is

$f_t(S_t)$ = minimum cost ($/yr) at stage t when S_t has been removed prior to stage t

The computational process requires construction of tables at each stage. These computations can be summarized mathematically as three equations starting with the last stage and proceeding backward.

Stage 3:
$$f_3(S_3) = \text{Min } (20X_3^2) \tag{9.18}$$
$$\frac{2500 - S_3}{20} \leq X_3 \leq 100$$

The conditions on X_3 are equivalent to $X_3 \leq 100$ and $S_3 + 20X_3 \geq 2500$.

Stage 2:
$$f_2(S_2) = \text{Min } [10X_2^2 + f_3(S_3)]$$
$$X_2 \leq 100$$
$$= \text{Min } [10X_2^2 + f_3(S_2 + 5X_2)] \tag{9.19}$$
$$X_2 \leq 100$$

Stage 1:
$$f_1(S_1) = \text{Min } [15X_1^2 + f_2(S_2)]$$
$$X_1 \leq 100$$
$$= \text{Min } [15X_1^2 + f_2(S_1 + 10X_1)] \tag{9.20}$$
$$X_1 \leq 100$$

Since $S_1 = 0$, the optimal (minimum) cost is given by $Z^* = f_1(0)$.

Reformulation of Model

At this point we could construct necessary tables to accompany each of the equations and obtain the optimal solution to the model. However, there are other ways by which the problem can be solved using DP. One of the interesting features of DP is that we can formulate a DP model in a variety of ways, some of which may be easier to solve than others. In setting up tables for numerical computations it is usually advantageous to make the mathematical relationships between state and decision variables as simple as possible. This can be done for the current problem by redefining the decision variables as

Y_t = amount of phosphorus (kg/day) discharged from treatment plant t

The effluent constraint is written in terms of these new variables as

$$Y_1 + Y_2 + Y_3 \leq 1000 \tag{9.21}$$

The 1000 kg/day of phosphorus discharged is the "resource" to be allocated, and an appropriate state variable is

S_t = amount of phosphorus (kg/day) discharged prior to stage t

The state variable relationship between stages (Figure 9-7) becomes

$$S_{t+1} = S_t + Y_t \tag{9.22}$$

In order to develop a complete optimization model phosphorus removal costs must be expressed in terms of the new variables. As seen in Figure 9-4, $Y_1 = 1000(1 - X_1/100)$, $Y_2 = 500(1 - X_2/100)$, and $Y_3 = 2000(1 - X_3/100)$. Solving for efficiencies and substituting into the cost functions, total removal costs are given by

$$Z = 15\left(100 - \frac{Y_1}{10}\right)^2 + 10\left(100 - \frac{Y_2}{5}\right)^2 + 20\left(100 - \frac{Y_3}{20}\right)^2 \tag{9.23}$$

A new and equivalent optimization model is

$$\text{Min } Z = 15\left(100 - \frac{Y_1}{10}\right)^2 + 10\left(100 - \frac{Y_2}{5}\right)^2 + 20\left(100 - \frac{Y_3}{20}\right)^2 \tag{9.23}$$

s.t.
$$Y_1 + Y_2 + Y_3 \leq 1000 \tag{9.21}$$
$$Y_2 \leq 500 \tag{9.24}$$
$$Y_t \geq 0 \quad \forall\, t$$

Constraint 9.24 limits phosphorus effluent from the second treatment plant to be no more than the influent. Similar constraints on discharges from the other plants, $Y_1 \leq 1000$, $Y_3 \leq 2000$, are not needed, since Constraint 9.21 limits both Y_1 and Y_3 to values that do not exceed 1000.

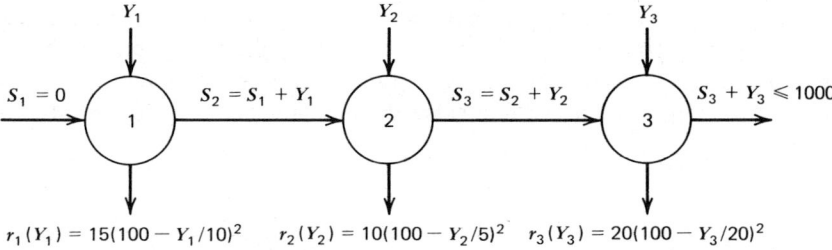

Figure 9-7. DP diagram for revised model.

Dynamic Programming Solution

The example demonstrates that optimization models for a given problem are seldom unique. The model is substantially different from the earlier version (Expressions 9.15 to 9.17), and yet both models are accurate mathematical descriptions of the phosphorus removal problem. The DP diagram for the new model is shown in Figure 9-7. An optimal cost function for each stage is

$f_t(S_t)$ = minimum cost (\$/yr) at stage t when S_t has been discharged prior to stage t

Beginning with stage 3, $f_3(S_3)$ is

$$f_3(S_3) = \text{Min} \left[20 \left(100 - \frac{Y_3}{20} \right)^2 \right] \quad (9.25)$$

$$Y_3 \leq 1000 - S_3$$

Since $f_3(S_3)$ is minimized by making Y_3 as large as possible, it will always be optimal for Y_3 to be *equal* to $1000 - S_3$. Therefore

$$f_3(S_3) = 20 \left(100 - \frac{1000 - S_3}{20} \right)^2 \quad (9.26)$$

In order to set up the tabular computations for $f_3(S_3)$, we must select the discrete values of X_3 (and hence S_3) that are to be evaluated. Unlike the land use example, the decision variables in this problem are continuous, and each can have an infinite number of values. Since we require a finite number of tabulations, it is necessary to restrict computations to a subset of possible alternatives. A typical approach is to divide the range of state and decision variables into fixed increments. For example, S_3 can be between 0 and 1000, and $f_3(S_3)$ could be evaluated for $S_3 = 0, 1, 2, \ldots, 1000$, or 0, 10, 20, \ldots, 1000, or 0, 100, 200, \ldots, 1000, or 0, 200, 400, \ldots, 1000.

Intuitively, we would suspect that the smaller the increment or *grid size* the more accurate the DP results would be. Unfortunately, decreases in grid size greatly increase storage and computation requirements (the tables are bigger and more difficult to construct). When a computer program is used for DP computations, the grid size or state and decision variable increment is sometimes an input parameter. The problem is first solved for a coarse grid and then for successively finer grids. The process stops when little improvement is seen in solutions for two successive grid sizes.

To demonstrate this process, we first solve the problem using a grid size of 200 kg/day; that is,

$$Y_t \;\varepsilon\; (0, 200, \ldots, 1000) \quad \forall \, t \tag{9.27}$$

The calculations for stage 3 are shown in Table 9-7.
The optimal (minimum) costs at stage 2 are

$$f_2(S_2) = \text{Min}\, [r_2(Y_2) + f_3(S_2 + Y_2)] \tag{9.28}$$
$$Y_2 \leq 1000 - S_2$$
$$Y_2 \leq 500$$

These computations are in Table 9-8. The final (stage 1) recursive equation is

$$f_1(S_1) = \text{Min}\, [r_1(Y_1) + f_2(S_1 + Y_1)] \tag{9.29}$$
$$Y_1 \leq 1000 - S_1$$

and the associated computations are shown in Table 9-9 for $S_1 = 0$.

Note that in computing $f_2(S_2)$ the fixed increment of 200 prevents Y_2 from reaching its maximum value of 500 kg/day. The optimal solution is $f_1(0) = \$218,000/\text{yr}$, $Y_1^* = 400$ kg/day, $Y_2^* = 200$ kg/day, and $Y_3^* = 400$ kg/day.

Tables 9-10, 9-11, and 9-12 repeat the computations for a smaller grid size. A fixed increment of 100 kg/day is used instead of 200 kg/day; that is, $Y_t \;\varepsilon\; (0, 100, \ldots, 1000)$. From Table 9-12, $Z^* = f_1(0) = \$215,000/\text{yr}$ and $Y_1^* = 400$ kg/day. This results in $S_2 = 400$, and Table 9-11 indicates that $Y_2^* = 300$ kg/day and $S_3 = 700$. Proceeding to Table 9-10, we obtain $Y_3^* = 300$ kg/day.

TABLE 9-7 Calculation of $f_3(S_3)$, Optimal Costs for Third Treatment Plant (Stage 3)

S_3 (kg/day)	Y_3	$r_3(Y_3) = f_3(S_3)$ (10^3/yr)
1000	0	200
800	200	162
600	400	128
400	600	98
200	800	72
0	1000	50

TABLE 9-8 Calculation of $f_2(S_2)$, Optimal Costs for Second and Third Treatment Plants (Stage 2)

S_2 (kg/day)	Y_2	$S_3 = S_2 + Y_2$	$r_2(Y_2) + f_3(S_3)$[a] (10^3/yr)	$f_2(S_2)$
1000	0	1000	100 + 200 = 300	300
800	0	800	100 + 162 = 262	
	200	1000	36 + 200 = 236	236
600	0	600	100 + 128 = 228	
	200	800	36 + 162 = 198	198
	400	1000	4 + 200 = 204	
400	0	400	100 + 98 = 198	
	200	600	36 + 128 = 164	164
	400	800	4 + 162 = 166	
200	0	200	100 + 72 = 172	
	200	400	36 + 98 = 134	
	400	600	4 + 128 = 132	132
0	0	0	100 + 50 = 150	
	200	200	36 + 72 = 108	
	400	400	4 + 98 = 102	102

[a] From Table 9-7

TABLE 9-9 Optimal Costs for all Three Treatment Plants (Stage 1)

S_1 (kg/day)	Y_1	$S_2 = S_1 + Y_1$	$r_1(Y_1) + f_2(S_2)$[a] (10^3/yr)	$f_1(S_1)$
0	0	0	150 + 102 = 252	
	200	200	96 + 132 = 228	
	400	400	54 + 164 = 218	218
	600	600	24 + 198 = 222	
	800	800	6 + 236 = 242	
	1000	1000	0 + 300 = 300	

[a] From Table 9-8.

TABLE 9-10 Calculation of $f_3(S_3)$ for Smaller Grid Size

S_3 (kg/day)	Y_3	$r_3(Y_3)$ ($\$10^3$/yr)
1000	0	200
900	100	181
800	200	162
700	300	145
600	400	128
500	500	113
400	600	98
300	700	85
200	800	72
100	900	61
0	1000	50

TABLE 9-11 Calculation of $f_2(S_2)$ for Smaller Grid Size

S_2 (kg/day)	Y_2	$S_3 = S_2 + Y_2$	$r_2(Y_2) + f_3(S_3)$[a] ($\$10^3$/yr)	$f_2(S_2)$
1000	0	10000	100 + 200 = 300	300
900	0	900	100 + 181 = 281	
	100	1000	64 + 200 = 264	264
800	0	800	100 + 162 = 262	
	100	900	64 + 181 = 245	
	200	1000	36 + 200 = 236	236
700	0	700	100 + 145 = 245	
	100	800	64 + 162 = 226	
	200	900	36 + 181 = 217	
	300	1000	16 + 200 = 216	216
600	0	600	100 + 128 = 228	
	100	700	64 + 145 = 209	
	200	800	36 + 162 = 198	
	300	900	16 + 181 = 197	197
	400	1000	4 + 200 = 204	

TABLE 9-11 continued.

S_2 (kg/day)	Y_2	$S_3 = S_2 + Y_2$	$r_2(Y_2) + f_3(S_3)^a$ (10^3/yr)	$f_2(S_2)$
500	0	500	100 + 113 = 213	
	100	600	64 + 128 = 192	
	200	700	36 + 145 = 181	
	300	800	16 + 162 = 178	178
	400	900	4 + 181 = 185	
	500	1000	0 + 200 = 200	
400	0	400	100 + 98 = 198	
	100	500	64 + 113 = 177	
	200	600	36 + 128 = 164	
	300	700	16 + 145 = 161	161
	400	800	4 + 162 = 166	
	500	900	0 + 181 = 181	
300	0	300	100 + 85 = 185	
	100	400	64 + 98 = 162	
	200	500	36 + 113 = 149	
	300	600	16 + 128 = 144	144
	400	700	4 + 145 = 149	
	500	800	0 + 162 = 162	
200	0	200	100 + 72 = 172	
	100	300	64 + 85 = 149	
	200	400	36 + 98 = 134	
	300	500	16 + 113 = 129	129
	400	600	4 + 128 = 132	
	500	700	0 + 145 = 145	
100	0	100	100 + 61 = 161	
	100	200	64 + 72 = 136	
	200	300	36 + 85 = 121	
	300	400	16 + 98 = 114	114
	400	500	4 + 113 = 117	
	500	600	0 + 128 = 128	
0	0	0	100 + 50 = 150	
	100	100	64 + 61 = 125	
	200	200	36 + 72 = 108	
	300	300	16 + 85 = 101	101
	400	400	4 + 98 = 102	
	500	500	0 + 113 = 113	

[a] From Table 9-10

TABLE 9-12 Calculation of $f_1(S_1)$ for Smaller Grid Size

S_1 (kg/day)	Y_1	$S_2 = S_1 + Y_1$	$r_1(Y_1) + f_2(S_2)$[a] (10^3/yr)	$f_1(S_1)$
0	0	0	150 + 101 = 251	
	100	100	122 + 114 = 236	
	200	200	96 + 129 = 225	
	300	300	74 + 144 = 218	
	400	400	54 + 161 = 215	215
	500	500	38 + 178 = 216	
	600	600	24 + 197 = 221	
	700	700	14 + 216 = 230	
	800	800	6 + 236 = 240	
	900	900	2 + 264 = 266	
	1000	1000	0 + 300 = 300	

[a] From Table 9-11.

The finer grid size has produced a relatively small improvement in the solution ($Z^* = \$215{,}000$ versus \$218,000 obtained from the coarse grid). There seems to be little advantage in repeating computations for a grid size increment of less than 100 kg/day, and we may thus consider the problem solved. In terms of the original variables, the optimal efficiencies are $X_1^* = 60\%$, $X_2^* = 40\%$, and $X_3^* = 85\%$.

Sensitivity Analysis

Certain types of sensitivity analyses are readily performed using the last-stage computations table. For example, the sensitivity of the optimal solution to changes in the effluent standard is easily determined. If the maximum allowable phosphorus discharge is lowered to 800 kg/day, the effect of this change can be determined by adding a new series of computations to Table 9-12. If we set $S_1 = 200$, this implies that 200 kg/day of the 1000 kg/day of phosphorus "resource" is not available for allocation. Letting $S_1 = 200$ is equivalent to

$$Y_1 + Y_2 + Y_3 \leq 800 \tag{9.30}$$

This is seen by expanding $S_3 + Y_3 \leq 1000$ (Figure 9-7); that is,

$$S_3 + Y_3 = S_2 + Y_2 + Y_3 = S_1 + Y_1 + Y_2 + Y_3$$
$$= 200 + Y_1 + Y_2 + Y_3 \leq 1000$$

TABLE 9-12a Stage 1 Computations for an Effluent Standard of 800 kg/day

S_1 (kg/day)	Y_1	$S_2 = S_1 + Y_1$	$r_1(Y_1) + f_2(S_2)$ ($\$10^3$/yr)	$f_1(S_1)$
200	0	200	150 + 129 = 279	
	100	300	122 + 144 = 266	
	200	400	96 + 161 = 257	
	300	500	74 + 178 = 252	
	400	600	54 + 197 = 251	251
	500	700	38 + 216 = 254	
	600	800	24 + 236 = 260	
	700	900	14 + 264 = 278	
	800	1000	6 + 300 = 306	

or

$$Y_1 + Y_2 + Y_3 \leq 800$$

The new calculations for the last stage are shown in Table 9-12a. The new optimal solution is $Z^* = f_1(200) = \$251{,}000$, $Y_1^* = 400$, $Y_2^* = 300$ (Table 9-11), and $Y_3^* = 100$ (Table 9-10). Tightening of the phosphorus standard to 800 kg/day would increase treatment costs by $36,000/yr, or 17%.

The optimal treatment alternative for any effluent standard less than 1000 kg/day can be determined by similar modifications to Table 9-12. The effects of *relaxing* the phosphorus effluent standard to some value greater than 1000 kg/day cannot be obtained so readily. Since this would increase the possible range of all state variables, the computations at each stage would have to be modified. It is advantageous to plan sensitivity analyses so that all necessary information can be generated from the last-stage computations. This can be done for the phosphorus removal problem by developing an initial solution for the largest possible effluent (3500 kg/day). In Table 9-12, S_1 could then be varied from 0 to 3500 to show the costs associated with different levels of control.

GENERALIZED ONE-DIMENSIONAL DYNAMIC PROGRAMMING

All DP problems involving a single resource or state variable are one dimensional. These problems can be described by the same general optimization model, DP diagram, and recursive equations.

Optimization Model

The general one-dimensional optimization model for DP problems is

$$\text{Max(Min) } Z = \sum_{t=1}^{N} r_t(S_t, X_t) \tag{9.31}$$

s.t.
$$S_1 \leq, =, \geq I_1 \tag{9.32}$$

$$S_{t+1} - G_t(S_t, X_t) = 0 \quad t = 1, 2, \ldots, N-1 \tag{9.33}$$

$$G_N(S_N, X_N) \leq, =, \geq I_N \tag{9.34}$$

$$X_t \in \Omega_t \quad \forall \, t \tag{9.35}$$

In this model S_t is a "resource" that is either available or has been allocated prior to stage t. The decision variable for stage t (X_t) may be either a scalar or vector quantity. In the latter case more than one type of decision is required at each stage. The "return" associated with stage t is $r_t(S_t, X_t)$. Constraint 9.32 indicates an initial condition for the first stage. The function $G_t(S_t, X_t)$ is a state transformation function that determines the value of S_{t+1}, the state variable at the end of stage t, based on S_t, the state variable prior to stage t and X_t, the decision made during the stage. Constraint 9.34 imposes a limit on the state variable at the end of the final stage (N), and Constraint 9.35 defines the possible set of values for each decision variable. The relationships between these variables and functions are shown in Figure 9-8.

Optimization models for one-dimensional DP problems are not always in the "standard" form. For example, the original model developed for the phosphorus removal example was

$$\text{Min } Z = 15X_1^2 + 10X_2^2 + 20X_3^2 \tag{9.16}$$

s.t.
$$10X_1 + 5X_2 + 20X_3 \geq 2500 \tag{9.15}$$

$$X_t \leq 100 \quad \forall \, t \tag{9.17}$$

However, using the state transformation functions shown in Figure 9-5, we can write this model as

$$\text{Min } Z = 15X_1^2 + 10X_2^2 + 20X_3^2 \tag{9.16}$$

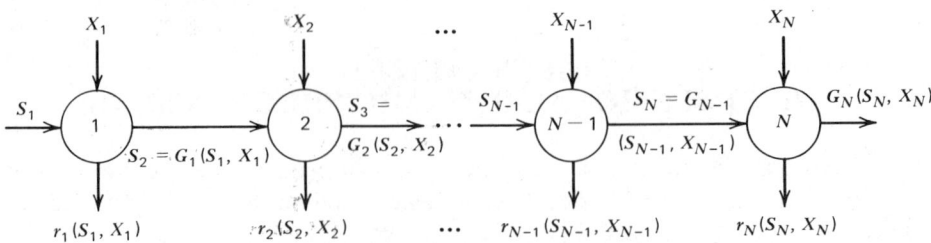

Figure 9-8. Diagram for general one-dimensional DP problems.

s.t.
$$S_1 = 2500 \tag{9.32a}$$
$$S_2 - S_1 + 10X_1 = 0 \tag{9.33a}$$
$$S_3 - S_2 + 5X_2 = 0 \tag{9.33b}$$
$$S_3 - 20X_3 \leq 0 \tag{9.34a}$$
$$X_t \leq 100 \quad \forall\, t \tag{9.17}$$

Recursive Equations

The optimal return function for stage t is defined as

$f_t(S_t)$ = optimal return at stage t; or optimal return from stages t, $t+1$, ..., N, when the state variable prior to stage t is S_t

These functions are computed as separate optimization problems for each stage.

Stage N:
$$f_N(S_N) = \text{Max(Min)}\,[r_N(S_N, X_N)] \tag{9.36}$$
$$X_N \,\varepsilon\, \Omega_N$$
$$G_N(S_N, X_N) \leq, =, \geq I_N$$

Stage $t = 1, 2, \ldots, N-1$:
$$f_t(S_t) = \text{Max(Min)}\,\{r_t(S_t, X_t) + f_{t+1}[G_t(S_t, X_t)]\} \tag{9.37}$$
$$X_t \,\varepsilon\, \Omega_t$$

The optimal value of the objective function, Z^*, is given by $Z^* = \text{Max}\, f_1(S_1)$ for $S_1 \leq, =, \geq I_1$.

INVENTORY PROBLEMS

DP is often used to solve a class of problems known collectively as "inventory" problems. These problems involve storage of quantities over time and are illustrated by the following example.

EXAMPLE 9-3 Compost Storage

An enterprising group of college students, finding themselves without summer jobs, have decided to go into the composting business during the months of May, June, July, and August. Based on their analysis of local garbage and other organic wastes, they have found that they can produce 500, 400, 300, and 300 t of compost during May, June, July, and August, respectively. Unfortunately, their market does not meet their production during each month. A market analysis reveals that they can realize the net income from compost sales each month given in Table 9-13. The maximum sales are 300, 600, 800, and 500 t in the 4 months. Since prospective sales do not match

256 DYNAMIC PROGRAMMING MODELS

TABLE 9-13 Net Income From Compost Sales

Sales (t)	Net Income (10^3)			
	May	June	July	August
0	0	0	0	0
100	1	2	2	1
200	2	3	3	2
300	3	4	4	4
400		4	5	6
500		4	6	7
600		4	8	
700			9	
800			9	

production, the students have decided to build a storage facility to store excess production from early months for later sale when demand is higher. Storage will cost money, of course, as indicated in Table 9-14. The storage facility cannot hold more than 500 t. Their problem is to determine how much to sell and store each month. □

This example involves the management of a single "resource" (compost) that, unlike the previous DP examples, is not fixed (i.e., the amount of potentially available compost changes from month to month). Cost and income quantities for the example are also completely different from those studied previously. They are not described by algebraic functions; instead, they are tabular data.

The problem is an example of an *inventory* or *storage problem*. Such problems occur whenever the supply of some product (resource, commodity, etc.) does not

TABLE 9-14 Monthly Costs of Compost Storage

Amount in Storage at Beginning of Month (t)	Storage Cost (10^3)			
	May	June	July	August
0	1	1	2	2
100	3	2	3	3
200	4	2	3	3
300	5	3	4	4
400	7	4	5	5
500	8	4	5	5

correspond in time with the demand or utilization of the product. Storage is required to match supply with demand. For example, agricultural crops may be harvested in the fall but, because demands for the crops are generally spread out during the entire year, the crops must be stored (at a cost) in the fall for subsequent sales. A second example is the operation of a reservoir for water supply. The reservoir may be on a river for which water flows during the spring are high and much greater than water supply requirements, but summer flows are too small to satisfy the water supply needs. The reservoir would store the excess river flows in the spring for subsequent use in the summer.

Common to all inventory problems is a temporal mismatch between supply and demand. The mismatch may be a simple quantity imbalance, as with the May compost production. Although 500 t of compost is produced, only 300 t can be sold during May. The imbalance may be more subtle, however. In June all the compost that is produced can be sold, but such sales may not be financially advantageous. Total income remains constant from 300 to 600 t, indicating that placing large supplies of compost on the market in June may only depress the price. If 300 t are marketed, average income from sales is $4000/300 = $13.33/t, while with sales of 600 t, the average income will fall to $4000/600 = $6.67/t. It is probably desirable to hold a portion of the June compost production in storage for subsequent sale in July or August at more favorable prices.

Assuming that the composters must return to college in September, the objectives of the problem are to sell all the compost produced at a maximum profit.

Optimization Model

Monthly production is fixed and the two quantities that can be controlled are X_t = amount (t) of compost sold during month t and S_t = amount (t) of compost in storage at the beginning of month t. The months $t = 1, 2, 3, 4$ are May to August, respectively. The storage variable S_t could be defined in other ways, such as the compost placed in storage during a month, or the compost in storage at the end of a month. However, the present definition is consistent with the data for storage costs (Table 9-14).

Mass balance relationships are required for the storage facility. In general,

$$S_{t+1} = S_t + I_t - X_t \tag{9.38}$$

where I_t is the amount of compost produced in month t. Since the storage contents must be zero at the beginning and end of the 4 months,

$$S_1 = 0 \tag{9.39}$$

and

$$S_4 + I_4 - X_4 = 0 \tag{9.40}$$

Capacity constraints are of two forms. The first limits storage contents to 500, and the second places upper limits on monthly sales.

Profits from the composting operation are equal to net sales income minus storage costs. Sales income in month t, $B_t(X_t)$, are given in Table 9-13; Table 9-14 provides storage costs for month t, $C_t(S_t)$. Profits for the month are thus $r_t(S_t, X_t) = B_t(X_t) - C_t(S_t)$.

The complete optimization model is

$$\text{Max } Z = \sum_{t=1}^{4} [B_t(X_t) - C_t(S_t)] \quad (9.41)$$

s.t.
$$S_1 = 0 \quad (9.39)$$
$$S_2 - S_1 + X_1 = 500 \quad (9.38a)$$
$$S_3 - S_2 + X_2 = 400 \quad (9.38b)$$
$$S_4 - S_3 + X_3 = 300 \quad (9.38c)$$
$$-S_4 + X_4 = 300 \quad (9.40)$$
$$S_t \leq 500 \quad \forall\, t \quad (9.42)$$
$$X_1 \in \Omega_1 \quad (9.43a)$$
$$X_2 \in \Omega_2 \quad (9.43b)$$
$$X_3 \in \Omega_3 \quad (9.43c)$$
$$X_4 \in \Omega_4 \quad (9.43d)$$

The allowable allocations, Ω_t in Constraints 9.43a to 9.43d, are $\Omega_1 = (0, 100, 200, 300)$, $\Omega_2 = (0, 100, \ldots, 600)$, $\Omega_3 = (0, 100, \ldots, 800)$, and $\Omega_4 = (0, 100, \ldots, 500)$.

Dynamic Programming Solution

The model corresponds to the standard form of a one-dimensional DP model. The stages are months, and the compost in storage at the start of the month t is the state variable S_t. The DP diagram for the example is shown in Figure 9-9. The significant differences between this diagram and previous ones for DP problems are that returns are a function of both state and decision variables and the available resource S_t is

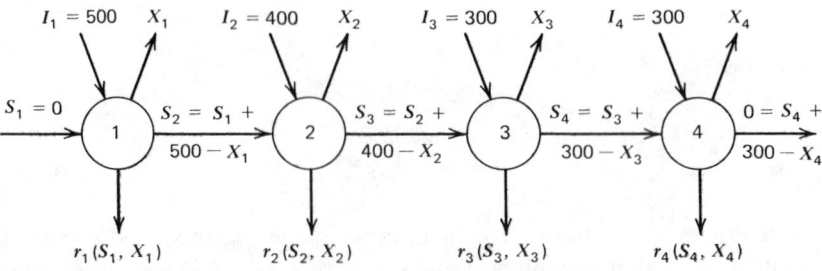

Figure 9-9. DP diagram for compost storage example.

augmented by an external supply I_t at each stage. The total amount of compost available for allocation in month t is thus $S_t + I_t$.

The optimal return function for the example is

$f_t(S_t)$ = maximum return (10^3) in remaining $4 - t + 1$ months when S_t is in storage at the beginning of month t

Starting with stage 4, we have

$$f_4(S_4) = \text{Max}\ [B_4(X_4) - C_4(S_4)] \tag{9.44}$$

$$X_4\ \varepsilon\ \Omega_4$$

From Figure 9-9, $X_4 = S_4 + 300$ and, hence,

$$f_4(S_4) = B_4(S_4 + 300) - C_4(S_4) \tag{9.45}$$

For any other stage $t \neq 4$, the general recursive equation is

$$f_t(S_t) = \text{Max}\ [B_t(X_t) - C_t(S_t) + f_{t+1}(S_t + I_t - X_t)] \tag{9.46}$$

$$X_t \leq S_t + I_t$$

$$X_t\ \varepsilon\ \Omega_t$$

The constraints on maximum values of state and decision variables can be used to minimize the number of entries in the tabular computations of $f_t(S_t)$. For example, during August (month 4), 300 t of compost will be produced and no more than 500 t can be sold. In order to dispose of all remaining compost ($S_4 + I_4 - X_4 = 0$), S_4 can be no larger than 200 t. The possible combinations of S_4 and X_4 are shown in Table 9-15, which gives the optimal return for stage 4.

In July (stage 3) maximum sales are 800 t and compost production is 300 t. The maximum value of S_3 is 500 t, the capacity of the storage facility. However, all combinations of S_3 between 0 and 500 and X_3 between 0 and 800 are not feasible. For example, if $S_3 = 500$ and $X_3 = 400$, then $S_4 = S_3 + I_3 - X_3 = 500 + 300 - 400 =$

TABLE 9-15 Optimal Returns from Stage 4

S_4 (t)	$X_4 = S_4 + 300$	$f_4(S_4) = B_4(X_4) - C_4(S_4)$ (10^3)
200	500	7 − 3 = 4
100	400	6 − 3 = 3
0	300	4 − 2 = 2

400. This would be infeasible, since the maximum value of S_4 is only 200 (Table 9-15). The feasible values for S_3, X_3, and S_4 are indicated in Table 9-16. It can be seen that for many values of S_3 there are alternative optimal decisions. For example, when $S_3 = 200$ t, sales of 300, 400, or 500 t are equally good because each results in identical returns $f_3(200) = \$5000$.

Computations for stage 2 (June) are shown in Table 9-17. As with Table 9-16, values of state and decision variables correspond to the capacity limitations of the problem. An additional consideration is the *minimum* value of S_2. Since production in May exceeds the maximum first stage sales by 200 t, there must always be at least 200 t in storage at the beginning of stage 2. Although we could compute $f_2(S_2)$ for $S_2 < 200$, there would be no point in doing so, since such values of S_2 would never occur.

Computations for the first stage (May) are shown in Table 9-18. These computations produce the optimal solution to the model. Maximum profits are $Z^* = f_1(0) = \$10,000$, and the optimal sales in May are $X_1^* = 300$ t. This results in $S_2 = 200$ t and, from Table 9-17, $X_2^* = 300$ t and $S_3 = 300$ t. Moving to Table 9-16, $X_3^* = 600$ t and $S_4 = 0$. Table 9-15 indicates that $X_4^* = 300$ t.

TABLE 9-16 Optimal Returns from Stage 3

S_3 (t)	$S_3 + 300$	X_3	$S_4 = S_3 + 300 - X_3$	$r_3(S_3, X_3) + f_4(S_4)$ (10^3)	$f_3(S_3)$
500	800	600	200	$3 + 4 = 7$	7
		700	100	$4 + 3 = 7$	7
		800	0	$4 + 2 = 6$	
400	700	500	200	$1 + 4 = 5$	
		600	100	$3 + 3 = 6$	6
		700	0	$4 + 2 = 6$	6
300	600	400	200	$1 + 4 = 5$	
		500	100	$2 + 3 = 5$	
		600	0	$4 + 2 = 6$	6
200	500	300	200	$1 + 4 = 5$	5
		400	100	$2 + 3 = 5$	5
		500	0	$3 + 2 = 5$	5
100	400	200	200	$0 + 4 = 4$	4
		300	100	$1 + 3 = 4$	4
		400	0	$2 + 2 = 4$	4
0	300	100	200	$0 + 4 = 4$	4
		200	100	$1 + 3 = 4$	4
		300	0	$2 + 2 = 4$	4

TABLE 9-17 Optimal Returns for Stage 2

S_2 (t)	$S_2 + 400$	X_2	$S_3 = S_2 + 400 - X_2$	$r_2(S_2, X_2) + f_3(S_3)$ (10^3)	$f_2(S_2)$
500	900	400	500	$0 + 7 = 7$	7
		500	400	$0 + 6 = 6$	
		600	300	$0 + 6 = 6$	
400	800	300	500	$0 + 7 = 7$	7
		400	400	$0 + 6 = 6$	
		500	300	$0 + 6 = 6$	
		600	200	$0 + 5 = 5$	
300	700	200	500	$0 + 7 = 7$	7
		300	400	$1 + 6 = 7$	7
		400	300	$1 + 6 = 7$	7
		500	200	$1 + 5 = 6$	
		600	100	$1 + 4 = 5$	
200	600	100	500	$0 + 7 = 7$	
		200	400	$1 + 6 = 7$	
		300	300	$2 + 6 = 8$	8
		400	200	$2 + 5 = 7$	
		500	100	$2 + 4 = 6$	
		600	0	$2 + 4 = 6$	

TABLE 9-18 Optimal Returns from Stage 1

S_1 (t)	$S_1 + 500$	X_1	$S_2 = S_1 + 500 - X_1$	$r_1(S_1, X_1) + f_2(S_2)$ (10^3)	$f_1(S_1)$
0	500	0	500	$-1 + 7 = 6$	
		100	400	$0 + 7 = 7$	
		200	300	$1 + 7 = 8$	
		300	200	$2 + 8 = 10$	10

Overview

The types of computations used in solving this problem have been similar to those of previous examples. However, the selection of feasible combinations of state and decision variables at any stage required a good deal more care. This was due to the *variable* nature of the resource being allocated and the capacity constraints on allocations and storage volumes. Another significant difference in this example is the tabular, discontinuous nature of cost and return functions. This feature would make the optimization model difficult, if not impossible, to solve using LP. These functions posed no problems for DP.

APPLICATION OF DYNAMIC PROGRAMMING TO AIR POLLUTANT EMISSIONS CONTROL

Air quality models can sometimes be solved by DP. As an example, consider the following modification to the total suspended particulates (TSP) emissions example described in Chapter 5.

EXAMPLE 9-4

Combined TSP emissions from three sources are to be reduced to 17,600,000 kg/yr (80% reduction). Production levels, TSP emission factors, and feasible controls are shown in Table 9-19. The only significant change from the comparable example in Chapter 5 is that in the present case *no more than one control may be used at any source* (i.e., each source must have exactly one control method). □

Pollution control alternatives of the "either/or" variety are not unusual in environmental management problems. The reasons for such restrictions are sometimes technical. It may not be structurally possible to modify existing facilities to provide for

TABLE 9-19 TSP Emissions and Control Alternatives for Example 9-4

		Source		
		1 Power Plant	2 Power Plant	3 Cement Factory
Production (t/yr)		400,000	300,000	250,000
TSP Emissions (kg/t)		95	95	85
Efficiency (%)	**Control Method**	**Costs ($/t)**		
59	Settling chamber	1.0	1.4	1.1
74	Multiple cyclone	a	a	1.2
84	Lone-cone cyclone	a	a	1.5
94	Spray scrubber	2.0	2.2	3.0
97	Electrostatic precipitator	2.8	3.0	a

a Infeasible.

more than one waste treatment process. Often, however, the restriction to one control option is based on operational reasons. Pollution control equipment can be difficult to maintain and operate properly, and highly trained personnel are usually required. By keeping the pollution control system as simple as possible, a factory or municipality may obtain more efficient and reliable waste treatment.

In the earlier LP model of this example a decision variable X_{ij} was defined as the amount of production at source i controlled by method j. With the restriction to single controls at each source, this variable would be discontinuous. For example, considering source 1, the three decision variables X_{11}, X_{14}, and X_{15} must each be equal to either zero or 400,000 t/yr. Clearly, the previous LP model (Expressions 5.67 to 5.72) is no longer appropriate, since decision variables were treated as continuous. Discontinuous decision variables always complicate LP approaches. Although such problems can sometimes be solved by integer LP (see Exercise 7-7), it is often easier to use DP. Because DP usually examines only discrete values of variables, the limitation of the variables to a small number of values may simplify DP computations.

Dynamic Programming Formulation

It may not be easy to recognize that a problem can be solved by DP. If, for example, the earlier decision variable X_{ij} is retained, the optimization model would be difficult, if not impossible, to solve using DP. To apply DP, we must interpret the problem as a sequential allocation procedure. The resource that can be allocated is the 17,600,000 kg/yr of TSP emissions. Portions of the emissions can be apportioned to each source, and the appropriate decision variable is

$$X_t = \text{emissions } (10^6 \text{ kg/yr}) \text{ of TSP by source } t$$

The value of X_t will depend on the control method for source t. It can be seen that the option of no control at any source is infeasible because the emission standard of $17.6(10)^6$ kg/yr would be violated. Without controls the emissions would be $38(10)^6$, $28.5(10)^6$, and $21.25(10)^6$ kg/yr for sources 1 to 3, any one of which would violate the TSP standard. There remain three feasible controls for sources 1 and 2 and four possibilities for source 3. Thus X_1 has three possible values. With a settling chamber, $X_1 = 0.41(95)(400,000) = 15.6(10)^6$ kg/yr. Similarly, with a scrubber or precipitator, X_1 is $2.3(10)^6$ kg/yr or $1.1(10)^6$ kg/yr. Therefore,

$$X_1 \ \varepsilon \ \Omega_1 = (15.6, 2.3, 1.1) \tag{9.47}$$

and, similarly, for the other two sources

$$X_2 \ \varepsilon \ \Omega_2 = (11.7, 1.7, 0.9) \tag{9.48}$$

$$X_3 \ \varepsilon \ \Omega_3 = (8.7, 5.5, 3.4, 1.3) \tag{9.49}$$

Since costs are not direct algebraic functions of X_t, tabular functions must be

264 DYNAMIC PROGRAMMING MODELS

developed. We define

$C_t(X_t)$ = cost (10^3/yr) of TSP emission control at source t when X_t of TSP are emitted

These costs are calculated as the expenditures required for the emission control method that produces an emission of X_t. For example, $X_1 = 1.1$ corresponds to the installation of a precipitator at a cost of $C_1(1.1) = \$1120(10)^3$/yr. The complete set of cost functions is given in Table 9-20. The optimization model for the problem is

$$\text{Min } Z = \sum_{t=1}^{3} C_t(X_t) \tag{9.50}$$

s.t.
$$\sum_{t=1}^{3} X_t \leq 17.6 \tag{9.51}$$

$$X_1 \; \varepsilon \; (15.6, \; 2.3, \; 1.1) \tag{9.47}$$

$$X_2 \; \varepsilon \; (11.7, \; 1.7, \; 0.9) \tag{9.48}$$

$$X_3 \; \varepsilon \; (8.7, \; 5.5, \; 3.4, \; 1.3) \tag{9.49}$$

The model can also be written in standard DP form by treating the sources as stages and defining a state variable as

S_t = TSP emissions (10^6 kg/yr) that can be allocated to the remaining $3 - t + 1$ sources or stages

The DP diagram for the example is shown in Figure 9-10. The final condition $S_3 - X_3 \geq 0$ allows solutions that emit less than $17.6(10)^6$ kg of TSP. Thus $S_3 - X_3 = S_2 - X_2 - X_3 = S_1 - X_1 - X_2 - X_3 = 17.6 - X_1 - X_2 - X_3 \geq 0$, or $X_1 + X_2 + X_3 \leq 17.6$. If the final condition were specified as $S_3 - X_3 = 0$, there would be no feasible solution to the problem, since no combination of allowable controls can

TABLE 9-20 Cost Functions for Example 9-4

X_1 (10^6 kg/yr)	$C_1(X_1)$ (\$$10^3$/yr)	X_2 (10^6 kg/yr)	$C_2(X_2)$ (\$$10^3$/yr)	X_3 (10^6 kg/yr)	$C_3(X_3)$ (\$$10^3$/yr)
15.6	400	11.7	420	8.7	275
2.3	800	1.7	660	5.5	300
1.1	1,120	0.9	900	3.4	375
				1.3	750

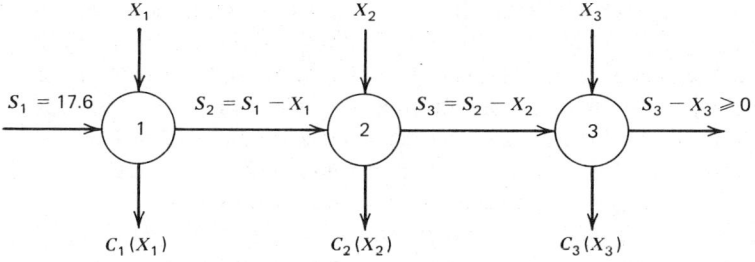

Figure 9-10. DP diagram for Example 9-4.

produce *exactly* $17.6(10)^6$ kg of TSP emissions. The DP optimization model is

$$\text{Min } Z = \sum_{t=1}^{3} C_t(X_t) \qquad (9.50)$$

s.t.
$$S_1 = 17.6 \qquad (9.52)$$
$$S_{t+1} - S_t + X_t = 0 \qquad t = 1, 2 \qquad (9.53)$$
$$S_3 - X_3 \geq 0 \qquad (9.54)$$
$$X_t \; \varepsilon \; \Omega_t \qquad \forall \, t \qquad (9.55)$$

Alternative, and equivalent, initial and final conditions for the optimization model are $S_1 \leq 17.6$ and $S_3 - X_3 = 0$. However, it is desirable to have the initial state variable S_1 *equal* to a numerical quantity, as in Equation 9.52 and Figure 9-10. When this is done, the computations for stage 1 are limited to a single value of S_1.

The optimal return function for the model is

$f_t(S_t)$ = minimum cost ($\$10^3$/yr) of remaining $3 - t + 1$ sources when S_t can be emitted by those sources

This is determined by the general recursive equation

$$f_t(S_t) = \text{Min } [C_t(X_t) + f_{t+1}(S_t - X_t)] \qquad (9.56)$$
$$X_t \leq S_t$$
$$X_t \; \varepsilon \; \Omega_t$$

where $f_{t+1}(\cdot) = 0$ for $t = 3$.

Computational Tables

This model does not have uniform fixed intervals for decision or state variables, and this requires special consideration in constructing tables of computations for $f_t(S_t)$. The results for stage 3 are shown in Table 9-21. The maximum value of S_3 is 17.6.

However, the decisions, costs and, hence, value of $f_3(S_3)$ are the same for any S_3 down to 8.7; that is, $f_3(S_3) = 275$ and $X_3^* = 8.7$ for any and all $8.7 \leq S_3 \leq 17.6$. When S_3 drops below 8.7, the largest emission alternative, $X_3 = 8.7$, must be dropped in order to maintain $S_3 - X_3 \geq 0$. In an analogous fashion, all values of S_3 can be grouped within four ranges, each of which has distinct decisions and values of $f_3(S_3)$.

The computations for $f_2(S_2)$, which are shown in Table 9-22, are shortened considerably by looking ahead to stage 1. Since $S_1 = 17.6$ and the only possible values for X_1 are 15.6, 2.3, and 1.1, it is clear that the only values of $S_2 = S_1 - X_1$ are 2.0, 15.3, and 16.5. Moreover, as shown in Table 9-22, $S_2 = 2$ is infeasible because it results in values of $S_3 = S_2 - X_2$ that are less than 1.3, the minimum possible value of S_3 (Table 9-21). It is interesting to note that the $f_2(S_2)$ calculations indicate that it is *always* optimal to use a settling chamber for source 2 ($X_2 = 11.7$), no matter what controls are used for the other sources.

Table 9-23 shows the computations for stage 1. The optimal solution is $Z^* = f_1(17.6) = \$1{,}595{,}000/\text{yr}$, $X_1^* = 2.3(10)^6$ kg/yr (scrubber), $X_2^* = 11.7(10)^6$ kg/yr (settling chamber), and $X_3^* = 3.4(10)^6$ kg/yr (long-cone cyclone). Total emissions are $2.3 + 11.7 + 3.4 = 17.4(10)^6$ kg/yr.

Extension to Multiple Pollutants

Dynamic programming is obviously a straightforward way of solving Example 9-4. This would not be the case if we were controlling more than one air pollutant. Consider

TABLE 9-21 Computations for $f_3(S_3)$

S_3 $(10^6$ kg/yr)	X_3	$S_3 - X_3$	$C_3(X_3)$ ($\$10^3$/yr)	$f_3(S_3)$
17.6	8.7	8.9	275	275
.	5.5	12.1	300	
.	3.4	14.2	375	
.	1.3	16.3	750	
8.7	8.7	0	275	
	5.5	3.2	300	
	3.4	5.3	375	
	1.3	7.4	750	
8.6–5.5	5.5	≥ 0	300	300
	3.4	≥ 0	375	
	1.3	≥ 0	750	
5.4–3.4	3.4	≥ 0	375	375
	1.3	≥ 0	750	
3.3–1.3	1.3	≥ 0	750	750

TABLE 9-22 Computations for $f_2(S_2)$

S_2 $(10^6$ kg/yr)	X_2	$S_3 = S_2 - X_2$	$C_2(X_2) + f_3(S_3)$ ($\$10^3$/yr)	$f_2(S_2)$
16.5	11.7	4.8	420 + 375 = 795	795
	1.7	14.8	660 + 275 = 935	
	0.9	15.6	900 + 275 = 1175	
15.3	11.7	3.6	420 + 375 = 795	795
	1.7	13.6	660 + 275 = 935	
	0.9	14.4	900 + 275 = 1175	
2.0	11.7	−9.7		
	1.7	0.3	Infeasible ($S_3 < 1.3$)	
	0.9	1.1		

the extension of the example to control of both total suspended particulates (TSP) and sulfur dioxide (SO_2). Let Y_t be the amount of SO_2 emitted from source t and let $\overline{X}$ and $\overline{Y}$ be the maximum total emissions of TSP and SO_2, respectively. If $C_t(X_t, Y_t)$ is the annual cost associated with emissions at stage t, the resulting optimization model is

$$\text{Min } Z = \sum_{t=1}^{3} C_t(X_t, Y_t) \tag{9.57}$$

$$\text{s.t.} \quad \sum_{t=1}^{3} X_t \leq \overline{X} \tag{9.58}$$

$$\sum_{t=1}^{3} Y_t \leq \overline{Y} \tag{9.59}$$

$$X_t, Y_t \; \varepsilon \; \Omega_t \tag{9.60}$$

Constraint 9-60 specifies allowable emission pairs (X_t, Y_t) at source t.

TABLE 9-23 Computations for $f_1(S_1)$

S_1 $(10^6$ kg/yr)	X_1	$S_2 = S_1 - X_1$	$C_1(X_1) + f_2(S_2)$ ($\$10^3$/yr)	$f_1(S_1)$
17.6	15.6	2.0	Infeasible	
	2.3	15.3	800 + 795 = 1595	1595
	1.1	16.5	1120 + 795 = 1915	

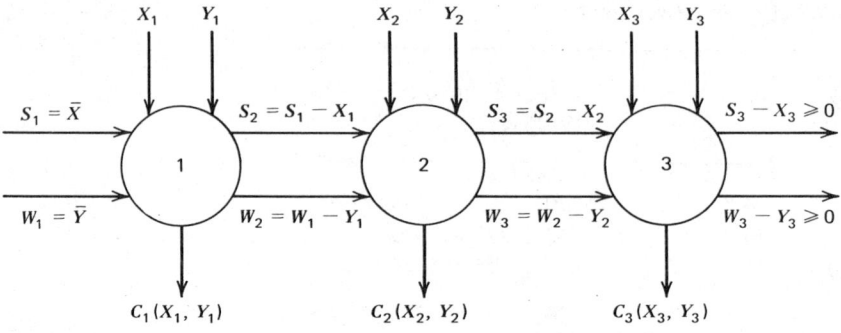

Figure 9-11. DP diagrams for extension of Example 9-4 to two air pollutants.

This optimization model involves the allocation of two resources, the allowable TSP and SO_2 levels. If we let W_t be a state variable for SO_2 emissions, the stage diagram in Figure 9-11 can be obtained. The diagram is similar to Figure 9-10, with the addition of a second set of state and decision variables. The general recursive equation is

$$f_t(S_t, W_t) = \text{Min} \, [C_t(X_t, Y_t) + f_{t+1}(S_t - X_t, W_t - Y_t)] \qquad (9.61)$$

$$X_t, Y_t \, \varepsilon \, \Omega_t$$

$$X_t \leq S_t$$

$$Y_t \leq W_t$$

The optimal return function at stage t is now a function of two variables S_t and W_t, and the optimization process is with respect to two decision variables X_t and Y_t. Although this causes no conceptual difficulties, the computation implications are enormous. The tabular computations for the single-pollutant example (Tables 9-21, 9-22, and 9-23) were two dimensional, containing all feasible combinations of S_t and X_t. Comparable tables for the two-resource case would be four dimensional, since this would include feasible combinations of S_t, W_t, X_t, and Y_t. This is the "curse of dimensionality" that was discussed earlier, and the sheer number of computations as well as the difficulty in identifying feasible computations would probably preclude the use of DP for solving the problem.

In the case of multiple pollutants, this type of air quality model must usually be solved using LP. If multiple controls are possible at each source, decision variables will be continuous and a standard LP package can be used. If some or all of the sources are restricted to controls of the "either/or" variety, decision variables will be discontinuous and integer LP is required.

FORWARD DYNAMIC PROGRAMMING

In each of the preceding examples we have carried out the computations in a "backward" direction. Calculations always began with a last stage and proceeded to the first stage, and the optimal solutions to optimization models were obtained from $f_1(S_1)$.

Such backward computations are the norm for DP problems, and many individuals seem to be comfortable with them. However, most DP problems can be solved with computations that proceed either forward or backward. To demonstrate this, Example 9-4 (with a single pollutant) is solved using forward DP.

As with backward DP, the use of forward DP permits the decomposition of an N-stage problem into N smaller problems. There are three of these sequential problems in the air pollutant emissions example. For the forward DP formulation the three problems are:

1. Optimal decision for stage 1.
2. Optimal decisions for stages 2 and 1 combined.
3. Optimal decisions for stage 3 and stages 2 and 1 combined.

Each of the subproblems is described by a return function $f_t(S_t)$ and associated recursive equation. The optimal (minimum) cost is given by $f_3(S_3)$.

State variables must be defined differently for forward DP. Suppose we attempt to solve the optimization model with the same state variable relationships used for backward DP (Figure 9-10). Forward calculations would require determination of $f_1(S_1)$, $f_2(S_2)$, and $f_3(S_3)$ in order. Optimal first stage return is

$$f_1(S_1) = \text{Min } [C_1(X_1)] \qquad (9.62)$$
$$X_1 \leq S_1$$

For the second stage,

$$f_2(S_2) = \text{Min } [C_2(X_2) + C_1(X_1)]$$
$$X_2 \leq S_2$$
$$X_1 \leq S_1$$
$$= \text{Min } \{C_2(X_2) + \text{Min } [C_1(X_1)]\} \qquad (9.63)$$
$$X_2 \leq S_2 \quad X_1 \leq S_1$$

Unfortunately, Equation 9.63 is a computational dead end. It reduces to

$$f_2(S_2) = \text{Min } [C_2(X_2) + f_1(S_1)] \qquad (9.63a)$$
$$X_2 \leq S_2$$

and there is no convenient way to eliminate S_1 from the right side; that is, the right side of Equation 9.63a is a function of X_2 and S_1 and not X_2 and S_2.

A simple way out of this diffficulty is to redefine the state variable in terms of the amount of resource *after* stage t.

S_t = amount (10^6 kg/yr) of TSP emissions remaining to be allocated after emissions at sources 1 to t

270 DYNAMIC PROGRAMMING MODELS

The resulting stage diagram is shown in Figure 9-12. The quantity S_0 in the figure is the available TSP emissions prior to stage 1. The associated optimization model is

$$\text{Min } Z = \sum_{t=1}^{3} C_t(X_t) \tag{9.64}$$

s.t.
$$S_0 \leq 17.6 \tag{9.65}$$

$$S_t - S_{t-1} + X_t = 0 \quad \forall\, t \tag{9.66}$$

$$S_3 = 0 \tag{9.67}$$

$$X_t \;\varepsilon\; \Omega_t \quad \forall\, t \tag{9.68}$$

The initial and final conditions, Equations 9.65 and 9.67, are chosen instead of the alternative $S_0 = 17.6$, $S_3 \leq 0$, so that final stage computations are needed for only a single value of S_3.

Forward Dynamic Programming Computations

The optimal (least cost) return function is

$f_t(S_t)$ = minimum cost ($\$10^3$/yr) from first t sources when S_t is available for allocation to remaining $3 - t$ sources

For stage 1 we have

$$f_1(S_1) = \text{Min } C_1(X_1) \tag{9.69}$$

$$X_1 \;\varepsilon\; \Omega_1$$

$$S_0 \leq 17.6$$

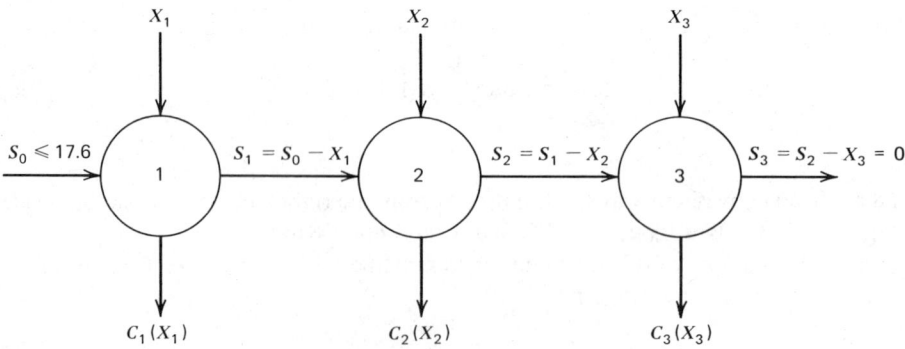

Figure 9-12. Stage diagram for solution of Example 9-4 by forward DP.

The condition $S_0 \leq 17.6$ can also be written in terms of X_1 and S_1 using the state transformation function for stage 1 ($S_1 = S_0 - X_1$). Thus

$$f_1(S_1) = \text{Min } C_1(X_1) \qquad (9.69a)$$
$$X_1 \ \varepsilon \ \Omega_1$$
$$X_1 \leq 17.6 - S_1$$

These computations are summarized in Table 9-24. Since $X_1 \ \varepsilon \ (15.6, 2.3, 1.1)$, the maximum value of S_1 is $S_1 = S_0 - X_1 = 17.6 - 1.1 = 16.5$. For $16.5 \leq S_1 \leq 15.4$, the only possible value of X_1 is 1.1 in order that $S_1 + X_1$ be no more than 17.6. Two other possible groupings are possible, $15.3 \leq S_1 \leq 2.1$ and $2.0 \leq S_1 \leq 0.0$.

The optimal return function for stage 2 is

$$f_2(S_2) = \text{Min } [C_2(X_2) + \text{Min } C_1(X_1)]$$
$$X_2 \ \varepsilon \ \Omega_2 \qquad X_1 \ \varepsilon \ \Omega_1$$
$$= \text{Min } [C_2(X_2) + f_1(S_1)] \qquad (9.70)$$
$$X_2 \ \varepsilon \ \Omega_2$$

Since $S_2 = S_1 - X_2$, we have $S_1 = S_2 + X_2$ and, hence,

$$f_2(S_2) = \text{Min } [C_2(X_2) + f_1(S_2 + X_2)] \qquad (9.71)$$
$$X_2 \ \varepsilon \ \Omega_2$$

The optimal return at stage 2 is a function only of the state and decision variables at

TABLE 9-24 Optimal Decisions for Stage 1 with Forward DP

S_1 (10^6 kg/yr)	X_1	$S_0 = S_1 + X_1$	$C_1(X_1)$ ($\$10^3$/yr)	$f_1(S_1)$
16.5–15.4	1.1	≤ 17.6	1120	1120
15.3– 2.1	1.1	≤ 17.6	1120	
	2.3	≤ 17.6	800	800
2.0– 0.0	1.1	≤ 17.6	1120	
	2.3	≤ 17.6	800	
	15.6	≤ 17.6	400	400

272   DYNAMIC PROGRAMMING MODELS

stage 2. We can extend Equation 9.71 to a general recursive equation that is applicable at any stage:

$$f_t(S_t) = \text{Min} [C_t(X_t) + f_{t-1}(S_t + X_t)] \quad (9.72)$$
$$X_t \ \varepsilon \ \Omega_t$$

where $f_{t-1}(\cdot) = 0$ for $t = 1$.

The tabular computations for stage 2 are simplified by looking ahead to stage 3. Since $S_3 = 0$ and $X_3 \ \varepsilon \ (8.7, 5.5, 3.4, 1.3)$, only four values of $S_2 = S_3 + X_3$ are possible, as shown in Table 9-25.

TABLE 9-25 Optimal Decisions for Stage 2 with Forward DP

S_2 (10^6 kg/yr)	X_2	$S_1 = S_2 + X_2$	$C_2(X_2) + f_1(S_1)$ ($\$10^3$/yr)	$f_2(S_2)$
8.7	11.7	20.4	Infeasible	
	1.7	10.4	660 + 800 = 1460	1460
	0.9	9.6	900 + 800 = 1700	
5.5	11.7	17.2	Infeasible	
	1.7	7.2	660 + 800 = 1460	1460
	0.9	6.4	900 + 800 = 1700	
3.4	11.7	15.1	420 + 800 = 1220	1220
	1.7	5.1	660 + 800 = 1460	
	0.9	4.3	900 + 800 = 1700	
1.3	11.7	13.0	420 + 800 = 1220	1220
	1.7	3.0	660 + 800 = 1460	
	0.9	2.2	900 + 800 = 1700	

TABLE 9-26 Optimal Decisions for Stage 3 with Forward DP

S_3 (10^6 kg/yr)	X_3	$S_2 = S_3 + X_3$	$C_3(X_3) + f_2(S_2)$ ($\$10^3$/yr)	$f_3(S_3)$
0	8.7	8.7	275 + 1460 = 1735	
	5.5	5.5	300 + 1460 = 1760	
	3.4	3.4	375 + 1220 = 1595	1595
	1.3	1.3	750 + 1220 = 1970	

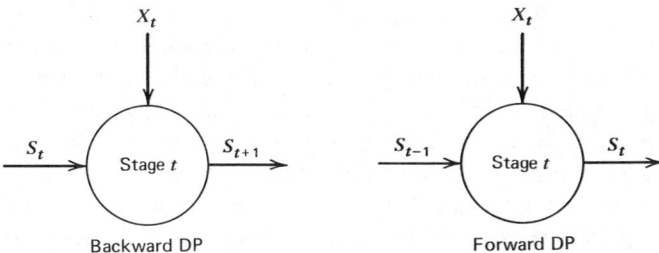

Figure 9-13. State variables for backward and forward DP.

The computations for $f_1(S_1)$ are given in Table 9-26. The optimal solution can be obtained from Tables 9-26, 9-25, and 9-24. From Table 9-26, $Z^* = f_3(0) = \$1,595,000/\text{yr}$, $X_3^* = 3.4$, and $S_2 = 3.4$. Moving to Table 9-25, we have for $S_2 = 3.4$, $X_2^* = 11.7$ and $S_1 = 15.1$. Table 9-24 indicates that $X_1^* = 2.3$ when $S_1 = 15.1$.

Summary of Forward Dynamic Programming

Most DP problems can be solved by either forward or backward calculations. The choice is usually arbitrary and depends on the preference of the systems analyst. Backward DP has been emphasized in this chapter, since it is the more traditional approach and is somewhat easier to grasp. The *only* significant difference between forward and backward DP is in the definition of state variables. The return at any stage t must be a function only of the state and decision variables at that stage in order to use DP. For this reason the state variable is defined in terms of the resource *prior* to stage t for backward DP and *after* stage t for forward DP. The alternative definitions are shown in Figure 9-13.

Summary

Problems that can be structured as sequential resource allocations can often be described by dynamic programming (DP) models. The problems may have nonlinearities, and discontinuous decision variables and objective functions and still remain solvable by DP. Solutions are obtained from a tabular computational procedure that decomposes a problem into a series of smaller subproblems or stages, each of which is solved by examining discrete values of decision variables. It is usually convenient to solve DP models "backward" (i.e., computations begin with a final stage and proceed sequentially to the first stage). To a certain extent the direction of the procedure is arbitrary, and the final example presented in the chapter was solved with both backward and forward DP.

Dynamic programming applications require a substantial level of creativity. Many optimization models are not suitable for DP and, even when they are, they must often be restructured before DP can be used. Moreover, there are usually several ways to define state variables and specify initial and final conditions. The computations are not dependent on a single standard algorithm such as the simplex method but, instead, must be organized separately for each DP model. For these reasons the solution to a DP model is never an automatic computer procedure. The systems analyst can greatly influence the efficiency of computations and the quality of an optimal solution.

There is little point in using DP to solve linear optimization models with continuous variables. Such models are more easily solved by linear programming (LP). Sometimes, however, nonlinear models can be solved by either DP or LP, and the selection of an appropriate procedure may reduce to the systems analyst's personal preference.

Although many optimization models can, in principle, be solved by DP, in actual practice the procedure is less commonly used than search methods or LP because optimization models often contain several constraints involving many variables. When DP is used for such models, each constraint may constitute a "resource" for allocation and hence require a state variable. Multistate variable problems require such extensive tables of computations that they are usually impractical even with large computer facilities.

SELECTED REFERENCES

1. Bellman, R., *Dynamic Programming*, Princeton University Press, Princeton, N.J., 1957.
2. Bradley, P., A. C. Hax, and T. L. Magnanti, *Applied Mathematical Programming*, Addison-Wesley, Reading, Mass., Chapter 11.
3. Hadley, G., *Nonlinear and Dynamic Programming*, Addison-Wesley, Reading, Mass., 1964, Chapters 10 and 11.
4. Hillier, F. S., and G. J. Lieberman, *Operations Research*, 2nd ed., Holden-Day, San Francisco, 1974, Chapter 6.
5. Nemhauser, G. L., *Introduction to Dynamic Programming*, Wiley, New York, 1966.

EXERCISES

9-1.

Solve the following optimization model using DP.

$$\text{Min } 0.25X_1^3 + 3X_2^{1.5} + 2X_2 + 1.5X_3^2 - X_3 + 16X_4 - 10X_4^{1/2}$$
$$\text{s.t.} \quad X_1 + X_2 + X_3 + X_4 \geq 20$$
$$X_i \geq 0 \quad \forall i$$

9-2.

Solve the first optimization model developed for Example 9-2 (Relationships 9.15 to 9.17) using the state transformations in Figure 9-6.

9-3.

A university has developed a new pesticide that is effective in controlling corn, soybean, and wheat pests. As a result of field experiments, the following improvements in crop yields have been obtained.

Pesticide Application (kg/ha)	Crop Yields (kg/ha)		
	Soybeans	Wheat	Corn
0	2700	3500	5400
0.5	3300	3800	5400
1.0	3800	4100	5700
1.5	4100	3500	6300
2.0	4400	2700	7900

Total annual costs of production, *not including pesticide applications,* are $250, $200, and $300/ha for soybeans, wheat, and corn, respectively. Pesticide application costs are $30/ha/yr for any crops at all application rates greater than zero.

Environmental authorities have, however, expressed concern over the pesticide's ecological impacts and have ruled that a farmer's *average* application rate on corn, soybeans, and wheat cannot exceed 1 kg/ha [i.e., total pesticide applied to all three crops (kg) divided by total cropped area (ha) must not exceed 1 kg/ha]. Current selling prices for soybeans, wheat, and corn are $0.18, $0.15 and $0.11/kg, respectively.

A farmer has decided to grow 30 ha of soybeans, 30 ha of wheat, and 30 ha of corn. Determine how much pesticide the farmer should use on each crop using DP. Assume that the farmer will not vary rates on any single crop. For example, the 30 ha of soybeans will not be divided into two portions of land each of which would have different application rates. Why is this assumption necessary?

9-4.

Solve Exercise 5-9 using DP.

9-5.

Add a fourth land use with net revenues of $1.4X_4$ to the land use planning Example 9-1 and solve the new problem by forward DP.

9-6.

The levels of two toxic substances in an industrial waste must be reduced before it can be safely disposed. The waste contains 30 and 20 kg/day of substances A and B, respectively, and these levels each must be reduced to at least 5 kg/day. To achieve these reductions, the waste can be sent through three sequential treatment operations, as shown in the figure. Several treatment processes are possible at each operation as shown in the following table.

Process	Removal (%) of A	Removal (%) of B	Cost ($/day)
Operation 1			
1	30	60	1100
2	20	30	600
3	40	70	1200
Operation 2			
1	90	10	1800
2	30	30	800
Operation 3			
1	10	20	900
2	50	0	1100
3	70	30	1400
4	0	80	1600

It is also possible to omit an entire operation if it is efficient to do so.
Determine a cost-effective treatment program using DP.

9-7.

The city of Murky Waters is going to install a new sewage treatment plant. A by-product of treatment is "sludge," an unpleasant liquid that contains much of the waste material removed from the sewage. This sludge is treated by a digestion process and then must be disposed of. You have been hired as a consultant for Murky Waters to recommend an alternative for sludge disposal. The sewage treatment plant treats 100,000 m^3/day of sewage, and 1 m^3 of sewage results in 0.003 m^3 of digested sludge. This sludge is approximately 94% water; that is, 1 m^3 of sludge contains 60 kg of solids and 970 kg of water, for a density of 1030 kg/m^3.

Your preliminary analysis has indicated three possible disposal methods: incineration, sale to farmers, and landfilling. If the sludge is dried to 40% moisture it can be burned at the city's municipal incinerator. Up to 10 m³/day can be handled by the incinerator, which is 1 km from the treatment plant. The cost of drying to 40% is $12S^{0.75}$($/day), where S is the amount of wet sludge (94% moisture) that is dried (m³/day). When dried to 60% moisture, the sludge can be sold to farmers as a soil-conditioner for $10/t (1 t = 1000 kg). Drying costs (to 60%) are $9.5S^{0.75}$($/day). The sludge must be transported to the farmlands, which are 30 km away. A maximum of 15 t/day can be sold. The city sanitary landfill is 11 km from the treatment plant. Up to 400 m³/day can be disposed of at the landfill, but sludge must be dried to 80% moisture at a cost ($/day) of $7.5S^{0.75}$.

Costs of transportation to all disposal sites are $0.50/m³/km. For example, if 10 m³/day are sent to the landfill, transportation costs are $10(11)(0.5) = $55/day$.

In solving this problem you must pay particular attention to weight-volume relationships, since drying the sludge removes water and hence reduces its weight and volume. Assume that elimination of 1 kg of water reduces sludge volume by 0.001 m³ (the density of water is 1000 kg/m³).

Determine a sludge disposal plan using DP.

9-8.

DP can sometimes be used to solve problems involving routing through a network. An example is shown in the following figure. A trip must be made through the network from node 11 to node 61. The journey is made in five stages, and the objective is to reach node 61 at minimum cost. The cost of each trip segment or arc of

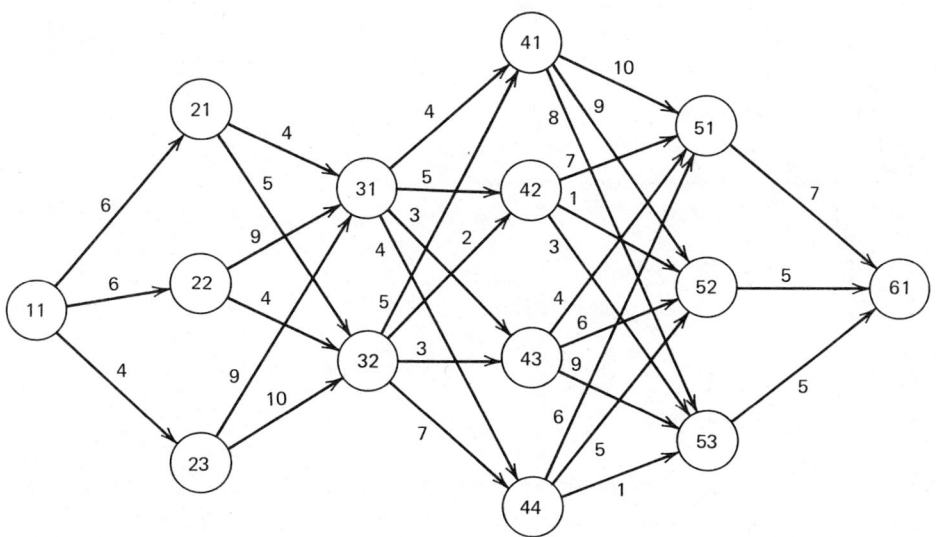

the network is shown on the figure. For example, the cost of traveling from node 21 to node 32 is 5.

Determine the optimal path through the network using DP.

9-9.

A farmer is attempting to develop an optimal manure disposal program. To do this, he has decided to divide the year into four time periods: $t = 1, 2, 3, 4$ for fall, winter, spring, and summer, and determine the best disposal rates for each period. Although 400 m^3 of manure are produced in each season, the economics of disposal differ through the year. The nutrients in the manure are not equally effective for plant growth when applied in any season, and the amounts of land available for disposal also vary. Similar variations are seen in maximum allowable application rates and disposal costs.

The nitrogen (N), phosphorus (P), and potassium (K) in the manure and their associated values to the farmer (in fertilizer savings) are

N:	3 kg/m^3,	$0.40/kg
P:	0.50 kg/m^3,	$0.40/kg
K:	2 kg/m^3,	$0.20/kg

However, the N in the manure does not all remain available to plants; depending on the time of year, portions may be volatilized or leached. If f_t is the fraction of the manure N that is applied to the land in season t and is subsequently available for growing crops, we have the following values.

t	Season	f_t, Fraction of N Remaining
1	Fall	0.3
2	Winter	0.4
3	Spring	0.6
4	Summer	0.8

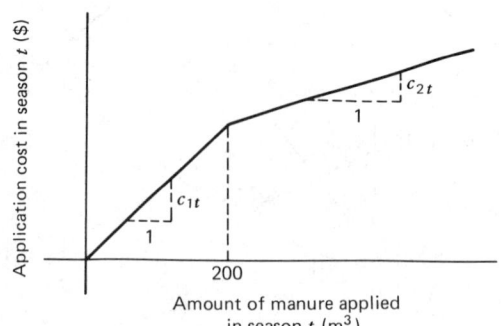

For example, if 200 m³ are applied in the fall, the nutrient value of this application is

N: 200m³(3)kg/m³(0.3)(0.40)$/kg = $ 72
P: 200m³(0.5)kg/m³(0.40)$/kg = $ 40
K: 200m³(2)kg/m³(0.20)$/kg = $ 80
$192

Costs of manure application are given in the figure. The amount of land available for manure application in season t is A_t (ha), and the maximum application rate is M_t (m³/ha). These data are summarized below.

t	Fall 1	Winter 2	Spring 3	Summer 4
A_t (ha)	60	40	40	20
M_t (m³/ha)	20	20	10	30
c_{1t} ($/m³)	0.50	0.40	0.80	1.00
c_{2t} ($/m³)	0.30	0.20	0.50	0.80

The farmer has a 600 m³ manure storage tank that must be completely emptied by the end of summer. The cost of removing the manure from storage (pumping) is $0.05/m³.
Determine an optimal manure disposal schedule for the farmer by means of DP.

9-10.

A farmer has 600 t of manure to dispose of (spread) on 30 ha of land. Three crops are possible, and manure spreading rates are 10, 40, and 20 t/ha on crops 1, 2, and 3, respectively. *If* manure is spread on a crop, the costs of spreading are;

Crop 1: $100 plus $2/t
Crop 2: $500 plus $1/t
Crop 3: $300 plus $1.5/t

Use a DP model to determine how the farmer should dispose of the manure. You may limit land increments for each crop to 5 ha.

CHAPTER 10
OPTIMIZATION OVER TIME

Whenever management objectives are achieved over long periods of time, we must be able to quantify preferences for *when* the objectives are reached. Solutions to environmental problems sometimes distribute benefits and costs far into the future, and optimization models must optimize these time streams of effects. This chapter discusses methods to compare objectives that are achieved at different future times. These techniques involve *discounting* future objectives compared to current ones and apply to many management problems in which objectives are not achieved simultaneously.

The comparison of alternative solutions to environmental problems with respect to their benefits and costs over time can be discussed at several different levels. Evaluation of the monetary consequences of alternatives requires *present value* calculations and includes the concepts of discounting and capital recovery. Monetary evaluations are straightforward, and the basic formulations are sometimes considered part of engineering economics. The engineering designation presumably refers to the purely technical nature of the calculations.

The simplicity of present value concepts masks profound theoretical and philosophical questions concerning *selections* of discount rates to use in the calculations. The issue is critical to the evaluation of publicly financed alternatives, since their relative attractivenesses are often very sensitive to changes in discount rates. The mechanics of monetary evaluations and the issues involved in selection of discount rates are discussed in this chapter. The former is of more practical importance, since discount rates for public projects are usually set by law or government policy and are seldom subject to the control of the systems analyst.

DISCOUNTING OF FUTURE OBJECTIVES

It is generally desirable to reach environmental and financial objectives as soon as possible. For example, if an environmental standard is to be met, it is better to meet it now than to wait for 10 years. Intuitively, we would feel that a delay in reaching an objective diminishes its value. Such reductions or discounting of objective values must be quantified if we are to incorporate them into optimization models. For example, we may have many air pollution control plans, each of which meets air quality standards at different times in the future with various expenditure programs. If we care when in time the standards are met and the expenses incurred, our objectives have associated time preferences that must be described mathematically in order to use systems analysis. These preferences can be quantified by discount rates, as illustrated by the following example.

EXAMPLE 10-1 Development of Wildlife Habitat

Three plans are available for development of wildlife habitat (Table 10-1). All plans produce 500 ha of comparable habitat by the end of 5 yr. The only significant difference is in the rates at which land is added. Which plan is best? □

Assuming an objective of maximizing the size of the habitat, the three plans produce identical results by the end of 5 yr. Nevertheless, if we have some preference for when the objective is met, the plans are not equivalent. We could perhaps quantify this preference by determining which plan reaches the 500 ha total first. By this criterion, plan A is inferior to the other plans. However, this conclusion is questionable, since plan A performs much better than plan B in the early years. The simple criterion of when development is completed may not capture significant differences among plans.

Time preferences can be described in a consistent fashion by discounting future achievements by greater amounts the more they are delayed. To determine an appropriate *discount rate*, we must know the extent to which the relevant decision maker (or decision makers) values the present over the future. For example, suppose we offer the decision maker a choice between 100 ha now or X ha 1 yr from now and wish to know what X must be so that the decision maker is indifferent between the two alternatives; that is

$$100 \text{ ha now} \sim X \text{ ha in 1 yr}$$

If X is say, 110 ha, the decision maker's discount rate, or annual rate of value increase, is 10%. If the 100 ha is delayed for 1 yr, it must increase by 10% to compensate for the delay. This result can also be stated as "the *present value* of 110 ha added 1 yr from

TABLE 10-1 Alternative Plans for Development of Wildlife Habitat

Plan	Land Added to the Habitat During Year (ha)						Total
	0[a]	1	2	3	4	5	
A	100	200	50	100	25	25	500
B	0	100	150	150	100	0	500
C	150	50	100	100	100	0	500

[a] Land initially part of habitat.

now is 110/1.1 = 100 ha." The delayed development has been discounted by a factor of 1/1.1.

Assuming that this perceived discount rate (10%) remains constant from year to year, we can determine present values of other future land additions. If land is not developed for 2 yr,

$$100 \text{ ha now} \sim 100(1.1)(1.1) = 121 \text{ ha in 2 yr}$$

When the 100 ha is delayed for 2 yr, an additional 21 ha is needed to compensate for the postponement. The present value of 121 ha 2 yr from now is 100 ha. In general, the present value of X ha developed t years from now is given by $X/(1.1)^t$.

Present values can be used to compare development plans. Each future land addition is equivalent to a current amount of land or present value, and the total present value of a plan can be determined. The present value of plan A is

$$100 + \frac{200}{1.1} + \frac{50}{(1.1)^2} + \frac{100}{(1.1)^3} + \frac{25}{(1.1)^4} + \frac{25}{(1.1)^5} = 431 \text{ ha}$$

Plan A is equivalent to the immediate development of 431 ha. The present value of plan B is

$$0 + \frac{100}{1.1} + \frac{150}{(1.1)^2} + \frac{150}{(1.1)^3} + \frac{100}{(1.1)^4} + \frac{0}{(1.1)^5} = 396 \text{ ha}$$

and the present value of plan C is

$$150 + \frac{50}{1.1} + \frac{100}{(1.1)^2} + \frac{100}{(1.1)^3} + \frac{100}{(1.1)^4} + \frac{0}{(1.1)^5} = 422 \text{ ha}$$

We can now compare the present value of the three plans and, since

$$\text{Plan A} \sim 431 \text{ ha now}$$
$$\text{Plan B} \sim 396 \text{ ha now}$$
$$\text{Plan C} \sim 422 \text{ ha now}$$

we conclude that plan A, which has the highest present value, is the best of the three alternatives.

The present values are, of course, dependent on the discount rate used in the computations. At a discount rate of r, expressed as a fraction, the present value of X ha t years from now is $X/(1 + r)^t$. With a discount rate of 15% ($r = 0.15$), the present values of plans A, B, and C are 404, 356, and 392 ha, respectively.

In many cases the selection of an alternative will be very sensitive to the value of the discount rate. Consider, for example, the three development plans in Table 10-2.

TABLE 10-2 Three New Development Plans

Plan	Land Added to the Habitat During Year (ha)						Total
	0	1	2	3	4	5	
A'	0	100	0	300	0	0	400
B'	0	0	50	0	100	300	450
C'	150	150	0	0	0	0	300

Based on total land developed over 5 yr, plan B' is clearly superior. However, when time preferences are taken into account, the results change significantly. Table 10-3 shows the plans' present values for four different discount rates. The rankings of the three plans change dramatically. At a discount rate of 5%, plan B' is preferred but, at rates of 10% and 15%, plan A' is superior. At the highest rate (20%), both plans are inferior to plan C'.

Discount rates provide a straightforward means of quantifying time preferences. They permit reduction of time streams of effects to present values that can then be used to compare alternative solutions to environmental problems. The procedures used in the simple example are directly applicable to more general environmental and financial objectives.

EVALUATION OF FUTURE MONETARY BENEFITS AND COSTS

Although discounting applies in principle to any objectives achieved over long periods of time, the procedure is most often used in evaluating the financial impacts of alternatives. This is partly due to the difficulties in quantifying time preferences for nonmonetary objectives but, more important, it is because the monetary consequences of

TABLE 10-3 Sensitivity of Present Values to Discount Rates

Plan	Present Value (ha), for Discount Rates of $r =$			
	0.05	0.10	0.15	0.20
A'	354	316	284	257
B'	363	296	244	204
C'	293	286	280	275

alternatives often vary dramatically over time. Since the objective functions of most optimization models are expressed in monetary units, optimal model solutions are reasonable only if they are based on realistic evaluations of time preferences. When incorporated into objective functions, time streams of monetary benefits and costs can be expressed as either present values or equivalent annual values.

Present Value Computations

Consider an alternative that produces the sequence of monetary benefits and costs shown in Figure 10-1. Benefits B_t and costs C_t are measured in current (noninflated) monetary units and are incurred at the end of year t. Initial benefits and costs are B_0 and C_0. The alternative has a useful life of N yr, and the final year's benefits B_N include any salvage value from the components of the alternative (equipment, land, buildings, etc.). The *present value* of net benefits is given by

$$\text{PVNB} = B_0 - C_0 + \sum_{t=1}^{N} \alpha_t (B_t - C_t) \tag{10.1}$$

where α_t = the present value factor, or $1/(1 + r)^t$, and r is the discount rate. In monetary evaluations, r is usually referred to as an interest rate.

If initial net benefits are zero and annual net benefits $B_t - C_t$ remain constant[1] at $B - C$,

$$\text{PVNB} = (B - C) \sum_{t=1}^{N} \alpha_t \tag{10.2}$$

The summation

$$\sum_{t=1}^{N} \alpha_t = \sum_{t=1}^{N} \frac{1}{(1+r)^t}$$

can be shown to be equal to

$$\frac{(1+r)^N - 1}{r(1+r)^N}$$

The inverse of this quantity is the capital recovery factor $f(r, N)$.

$$f(r, N) = \frac{r(1+r)^N}{(1+r)^N - 1} \tag{10.3}$$

---

[1] Constant in current monetary units ($). The actual values, expressed in future dollars, may change because of inflation. The effects of inflation on these calculations are discussed subsequently.

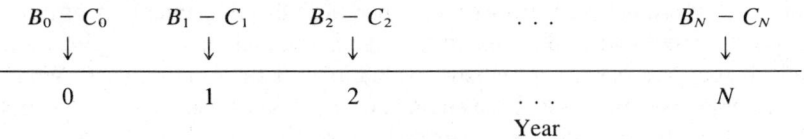

Figure 10-1. Distribution of costs and benefits over time.

Thus the present value of the sum of N equal payments $B - C$ is $(B - C)/f(r, N)$. For example, if an alternative provides $100,000/yr of net benefits for 25 yr and the discount rate is 12%, the capital recovery factor is

$$f(0.12, 25) = \frac{0.12(1.12)^{25}}{(1.12)^{25} - 1} = 0.1275$$

and the present value of these 25 yr of net benefits is $100,000/0.1275 = $784,314. Note that this is considerably less than the sum of net benefits obtained over 25 yr ($2,500,000).

Equivalent Annual Value

Although alternatives are often compared on a present value basis, equivalent annual value is also sometimes used. This involves the idea of amortization. For example, an initial construction cost C_0 may be met by borrowing and then repaying the loan over a period of N years at an interest rate of r. The required annual payment A can be inferred from Equation 10.2. The present value of the constant annual costs is $A \sum_{t=1}^{N} \alpha_t = A/f(r, N)$. This present value is the construction cost, $C_0 = A/f(r, N)$, and the equivalent annual cost is

$$A = f(r, N)C_0 \tag{10.4}$$

The capital recovery factor is thus the fraction of the initial cost that must be paid in each of N yr.

We can extend this concept and express all current and future net benefits as a single equivalent annual value. This is done by first computing the PVNB by Equation 10.2. These benefits are similar to the initial cost in Equation 10.4 and annual net benefits (ANB) are

$$\text{ANB} = f(r, N) \text{ PVNB} \tag{10.5}$$

These calculations are illustrated in the following example.

EXAMPLE 10-2

A waste treatment plant will cost $1,000,000 to construct and will result in an operating and maintenance (O&M) cost of $150,000/yr starting at the end of the first year. The plant has a life of 20 yr, and the interest rate is 7%. What will be the plant's present value cost and equivalent annual cost? The plant has no salvage value at the end of 20 yr. □

The capital recovery factor for this example is $f(0.07, 20) = 0.0944$. The present value cost is the plant's construction costs plus the present value of O&M costs.

$$\$1,000,000 + \$150,000/0.0944 = \$2,588,983$$

The equivalent annual cost can be obtained by amortizing the present value cost by the capital recovery factor.

$$\$2,588,983(0.0944) = \$244,400/\text{yr}$$

Alternatively, we could amortize the construction cost and add its annual cost to the annual O&M cost.

$$\$1,000,000(0.0944) + \$150,000 = \$244,400/\text{yr}$$

To extend the example, suppose we compare the plant to an alternative involving a phased implementation of treatment processes. This second alternative also has a 20-yr life, but it is implemented in two steps. A first process is constructed at a cost of $600,000 and operated for 10 yr with an O&M cost of $70,000/yr. At the end of 10 yr, a second process is constructed for $800,000, and the two processes have a combined O&M cost of $120,000/yr for the remaining 10 yr. This alternative has a salvage value of $150,000.

We can compute the present value of the new alternative, but the calculations are much more complicated. As a starting point, the present value of costs at year 10 is determined. This consists of a discounted salvage benefit $-\$150,000/(1.07)^{10} = -\$76,252$ plus discounted O&M costs $120,000/f(0.07, 10) = 120,000/0.1424 = \$842,697$ plus construction costs $800,000 or $1,566,445. This can be treated as a cost incurred at the end of the tenth year, and the alternative has the sequence of costs $C_0 = \$600,000$, $C_1 = C_2 = \ldots = C_9 = \$70,000$, $C_{10} = \$70,000 + \$1,566,445$. The present value at the beginning of the first year and hence the total present value cost is

$$\$600,000 + \$70,000/f(0.07, 10) + \$1,566,445/(1.07)^{10} = \$1,887,874$$

The equivalent annual cost is obtained by amortizing the present value cost over the 20-yr life of the alternative.

$$\$1,887,874\, f(0.07, 20) = \$178,215/\text{yr}$$

This second alternative is a good deal less expensive than the first treatment plant ($244,400/yr). The economies were achieved by delaying major portions of the costs until the later years of the project's life.

Effects of Inflation

Although the preceding discussion assumed noninflated costs and benefits, Equations 10.1 to 10.5 are the same with or without a general price inflation. With inflation, assume benefits and costs increase at an inflation rate r_i/yr. If, as before, $C_0, C_1, \ldots C_N$, and $B_0, B_1, \ldots, B_N$ are measured in current (noninflated) monetary units, the actual net benefits realized in each year, $NB_0, NB_1, \ldots, NB_N$ are

$$NB_0 = B_0 - C_0$$
$$NB_1 = (B_1 - C_1)(1 + r_i)$$
$$NB_2 = (B_2 - C_2)(1 + r_i)^2$$
$$\vdots \qquad \vdots$$
$$NB_N = (B_N - C_N)(1 + r_i)^N$$

The present value of these inflated net benefits is

$$\text{PVNB} = B_0 - C_0 + \sum_{t=1}^{N} \left(\frac{1 + r_i}{1 + r}\right)^t (B_t - C_t) \qquad (10.6)$$

where, as before, r is the interest rate.

An interest rate is the opportunity cost of capital. It represents a rate of earnings that lenders must receive for their investments. During inflationary periods, interest rates tend to be high, since lenders must not only obtain a return from the use of their funds but must also be compensated for the general decline in their value. If a loan of A_0 is repaid at the end of t years, the payment

$$A_t = A_0(1 + r)^t \qquad (10.7)$$

must reflect both a noninflated rate of return r_o and the inflation rate r_i, or

$$A_t = A_0(1 + r_o)^t(1 + r_i)^t = A_0(1 + r_o + r_i + r_o r_i)^t \qquad (10.7a)$$

During inflationary periods, the appropriate interest rate is $r = r_o + r_i + r_o r_i$. Applying this inflated rate to present value calculations, Equation 10.6 becomes

$$\text{PVNB} = B_0 - C_0 + \sum_{t=1}^{N} \frac{(1 + r_i)^t}{(1 + r_o)^t(1 + r_i)^t}(B_t - C_t)$$

$$= B_0 - C_0 + \sum_{t=1}^{N} \frac{B_t - C_t}{(1 + r_o)^t} \qquad (10.6a)$$

Comparing Equations 10.6 and 10.6a, we can conclude that there are two equivalent ways of accounting for inflation in present value calculations. Either (1) the actual inflated future costs and benefits are used with an interest rate r, which includes an inflation premium, or (2) costs and benefits are expressed as current monetary values and an interest rate that is free of inflation is used.

SELECTION OF DISCOUNT RATES FOR PUBLIC INVESTMENTS

When investment projects are undertaken by a private firm, they are generally based on financial objectives. The discount rates for such ventures must approximate the after-tax market rates of capital that are available to the firm. These rates may be adjusted to reflect inflation, risk, and long- or short-term funding and growth objectives, but the overall purpose of private investment is presumably individual or corporate financial well-being. The objectives of government investment are often more complicated. The many environmental projects financed wholly or partially by public monies are not designed for financial returns but instead to achieve social goals.

Although government bodies may borrow funds to pay for projects, the discount rate used to amortize construction costs and discount future monetary benefits and costs is not necessarily equal to the market interest rate. The selected discount rate must quantify social preferences for present versus future costs and benefits, and such preferences may not be accurately reflected in market rates. Nevertheless, many economists feel that when public discount rates are substantially less than the after-tax, long-term interest rates that prevail in private investment markets, private investments are sacrificed to less productive public ones.

The selection of discount rates for public projects is controversial because the rates greatly influence a project's economic viability. Consider the following example.

EXAMPLE 10-3
A public investment project produces the distribution of costs and benefits shown in Table 10-4. What effect does the discount rate selection have on the project's viability?

□

As with many public investments, the project has substantial initial costs and does not produce benefits until the later years of the project. For example, with waste treatment projects, it may be some time before the environment recovers from its previous misuse. The present value of the project's net benefits can be determined using Equation 10.1.* Table 10-5 shows that these present values decline rapidly as the discount rate is increased. At rates $r = 0.10$, 0.12, and 0.14, the net benefits are negative, indicating that costs exceed benefits and the project should not be undertaken.

As illustrated by the example, high discount rates discourage alternatives that defer benefits to the future. Conversely, alternatives that realize immediate benefits and postpone costs until future years are favored by high discount rates. Intuitively, we might feel that these results are not necessarily sound government policy, particularly

TABLE 10-4 Costs and Benefits from a Public Investment Project

Year	Costs Incurred at End of Year ($)	Benefits Produced at End of Year ($)
0	1,000,000	0
1	200,000	0
2	200,000	0
3	200,000	0
4	200,000	100,000
5	200,000	300,000
6	200,000	800,000
7	200,000	800,000
8	200,000	800,000
9	200,000	800,000
10	200,000	800,000

if society values the future beneficial effects of its current actions. There is often social and hence political pressure to keep public discount rates low; otherwise, many government projects that have popular support would not seem to be economically justified.

The selection of a discount rate to use in the monetary evaluation of public projects is not a technical decision. Since it describes social preferences, it is properly chosen by society's political representatives. Discount rates are generally set by legislative or executive decision; although the arguments of economic efficiency are often considered, the ultimate choice is a political one.

TABLE 10-5 Present Value of Net Benefits for a Public Investment Project

Discount Rate, r	Present Value of Net Benefits (10^5)
0.02	9.8
0.04	6.4
0.06	3.5
0.08	1.1
0.10	−0.9
0.12	−2.6
0.14	−4.0

CAPACITY EXPANSION PROBLEMS

The effects of discounting future costs are important in the long-term expansion of public or private facilities to meet increasing demands for a service or product. For example, as the population of a city grows, the capacities of water supply and waste treatment plants must be expanded to provide water for the increased population and to treat its wastes. A general form of the capacity expansion problem is the determination of the increase in capacity X_t in each year t that is sufficient to meet a capacity requirement P_t by the end of year t. If $C_t(S_t, X_t)$ is the cost of operating and maintaining capacity level S_t during year t and adding X_t in that year, the problem is described by an optimization model that minimizes the present value of future costs.

$$\text{Min } Z = \sum_{t=1}^{N} \alpha_t C_t(S_t, X_t) \tag{10.8}$$

s.t.
$$S_{t+1} - X_0 - \sum_{j=1}^{t} X_j = 0 \quad \forall\, t \tag{10.9}$$

$$S_t + X_t \geq P_t \quad \forall\, t \tag{10.10}$$

$$S_t, X_t \geq 0 \quad \forall\, t \tag{10.11}$$

In this model X_0 is the initial capacity, N is the length of the planning period, and α_t is the present value factor, $(1 + r)^{-t}$, with r being the discount or interest rate. It is assumed that the cost $C_t(S_t, X_t)$ is incurred at the end of year t.

In the absence of economies of scale, the solution to Expressions 10.8 to 10.11 is obvious. When costs are delayed, their present values decrease; therefore capacity additions should be delayed as long as possible. The optimal solution for this case is

$$X_1^* = P_1 - X_0$$
$$X_2^* = P_2 - P_1$$

. .

. .

. .

$$X_t^* = P_t - P_{t-1} \quad \forall\, t \neq 1$$

However, with economies of scale, it may be cheaper to add excess capacity in some years to take advantage of reduced average costs. Capacity expansion problems involve trade-offs between the advantages of economies of scale and the savings associated with delayed expenditure.

The general capacity expansion problem is readily adapted to dynamic programming (DP) by use of the state transformation function

$$S_{t+1} = S_t + X_t \tag{10.12}$$

Each year is a stage, and the DP diagram for the problem is shown in Figure 10-2. The problem is solved by backward DP using the general recursive equation

$$f_t(S_t) = \text{Min}\,[\alpha_t C_t(S_t, X_t) + f_{t+1}(S_t + X_t)] \tag{10.13}$$

$$X_t \geq P_t - S_t$$

where $f_t(S_t)$ is the minimum present value costs of expansion in years $t, t+1, t+2, \ldots, N$ when the capacity is S_t at the beginning of year t. The use of DP to solve capacity expansion problems is demonstrated in the following example.

EXAMPLE 10-4 Land Reclamation

Five hundred hectares of strip-mined land is to be restored (reclaimed) over a 5-yr period. Reclamation targets of 100, 200, 300, 400, and 500 ha have been set for years 1 to 5, respectively. The costs of restoration in any year are given in Table 10-6. The discount rate for the project is 9% ($r = 0.09$). □

If X_t is the amount of land reclaimed in year t (ha), costs of reclamation $C_t(X_t)$ from Table 10-6 exhibit economies of scale. At $X_t = 100$ ha, costs are \$4000/ha, while at $X_t = 500$ ha, the costs drop to \$3000/ha. Letting S_t be the amount of restored land

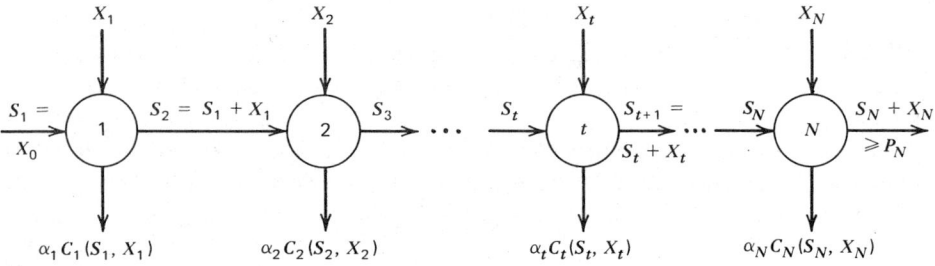

Figure 10-2. DP diagram for capacity expansion problem.

TABLE 10-6 Land Reclamation Costs

Amount of Land Reclaimed During Year (ha)	Reclamation Cost ($10³)
100	400
200	750
300	1050
400	1300
500	1500

at the beginning of the year t and assuming that costs are incurred at year's end, the optimization model is

$$\text{Min } Z = \sum_{t=1}^{5} \alpha_t C_t(X_t) \tag{10.14}$$

s.t.
$$S_1 = 0 \tag{10.15}$$
$$S_1 + X_1 \geq 100 \tag{10.16}$$
$$S_2 + X_2 \geq 200 \tag{10.17}$$
$$S_3 + X_3 \geq 300 \tag{10.18}$$
$$S_4 + X_4 \geq 400 \tag{10.19}$$
$$S_5 + X_5 \geq 500 \tag{10.20}$$
$$S_{t+1} - S_t - X_t = 0 \quad t = 1, 2, 3, 4 \tag{10.21}$$
$$S_t, X_t \geq 0 \quad \forall t \tag{10.22}$$

Since the example covers 5 yr, there are five sets of computations, as shown in Tables 10-7 to 10-11. Costs are based on increments of 100 ha, and these same

TABLE 10-7 Computations for Stage 5

S_5 (ha)	X_5	$S_5 + X_5$	$\alpha_5 C_5(X_5) = f_5(S_5)$ (10^3)
400	100	500	260
500	0	500	0

TABLE 10-8 Computations for Stage 4

S_4 (ha)	X_4	$S_5 = S_4 + X_4$	$\alpha_4 C_4(X_4) + f_5(S_5)$ (10^3)	$f_4(S_4)$
300	100	400	283 + 260 = 543	
	200	500	531 + 0 = 531	531
400	0	400	0 + 260 = 260	260
	100	500	283 + 0 = 283	
500	0	500	0 + 0 = 0	0

294 OPTIMIZATION OVER TIME

TABLE 10-9 Computations for Stage 3

S_3 (ha)	X_3	$S_4 = S_3 + X_3$	$\alpha_3 C_3(X_3) + f_4(S_4)$ (10^3)	$f_3(S_3)$
200	100	300	309 + 531 = 840	
	200	400	579 + 260 = 839	
	300	500	811 + 0 = 811	811
300	0	300	0 + 531 = 531	531
	100	400	309 + 260 = 569	
	200	500	579 + 0 = 579	
400	0	400	0 + 260 = 260	260
	100	500	309 + 0 = 309	
500	0	500	0 + 0 = 0	0

TABLE 10-10 Computations for Stage 2

S_2 (ha)	X_2	$S_3 = S_2 + X_2$	$\alpha_2 C_2(X_2) + f_3(S_3)$ (10^3)	$f_2(S_2)$
100	100	200	337 + 811 = 1148	
	200	300	631 + 531 = 1162	
	300	400	884 + 260 = 1144	
	400	500	1094 + 0 = 1094	1094
200	0	200	0 + 811 = 811	811
	100	300	337 + 531 = 868	
	200	400	631 + 260 = 891	
	300	500	884 + 0 = 884	
300	0	300	0 + 531 = 531	531
	100	400	337 + 260 = 597	
	200	500	631 + 0 = 631	
400	0	400	0 + 260 = 260	260
	100	500	337 + 0 = 337	
500	0	500	0 + 0 = 0	0

TABLE 10-11 Computations for Final Stage

S_1 (ha)	X_1	$S_2 = S_1 + X_1$	$\alpha_1 C_1(X_1) + f_2(S_2)$ ($\$10^3$)	$f_1(S_1)$
0	100	100	367 + 1094 = 1461	
	200	200	688 + 811 = 1499	
	300	300	963 + 531 = 1494	
	400	400	1193 + 260 = 1453	
	500	500	1376 + 0 = 1376	1376

increments are used in the computations. The solution is obtained from Table 10-11, which indicates that $X_1^* = 500$ ha and $f_1(0) = Z^* = \$1,376,000$. Hence $X_2^* = X_3^* = X_4^* = X_5^* = 0$, and it is optimal to undertake the entire reclamation in the first year.

Economies of scale dominated the potential cost savings of delayed capacity expansion in this example. However, as with all problems involving optimization over time, the results are influenced by the discount rate. Tables 10-7a to 10-11a repeat the

TABLE 10-7a Fifth-Stage Computations for Discount Rate of 18%

S_5 (ha)	X_5	$S_5 + X_5$	$\alpha C_5(X_5) = f_5(S_5)$ ($\$10^3$)
400	100	500	175
500	0	500	0

TABLE 10-8a Fourth-Stage Computations for Discount Rate of 18%

S_4 (ha)	X_4	$S_5 = S_4 + X_4$	$\alpha_4 C_4(X_4) + f_5(S_5)$ ($\$10^3$)	$f_4(S_4)$
300	100	400	206 + 175 = 381	381
	200	500	387 + 0 = 387	
400	0	400	0 + 175 = 175	175
	100	500	206 + 0 = 206	
500	0	500	0 + 0 = 0	0

TABLE 10-9a Third-Stage Computations for Discount Rate of 18%

S_3 (ha)	X_3	$S_4 = S_3 + X_3$	$\alpha_3 C_3(X_3) + f_4(S_4)$ ($\$10^3$)	$f_3(S_3)$
200	100	300	243 + 381 = 624	624
	200	400	456 + 175 = 631	
	300	500	639 + 0 = 639	
300	0	300	0 + 381 = 381	381
	100	400	243 + 175 = 418	
	200	500	456 + 0 = 456	
400	0	400	0 + 175 = 175	175
	100	500	243 + 0 = 243	
500	0	500	0 + 0 = 0	0

TABLE 10-10a Second-Stage Computations for Discount Rate of 18%

S_2 (ha)	X_2	$S_3 = S_2 + X_2$	$\alpha_2 C_2(X_2) + f_3(S_3)$ ($\$10^3$)	$f_2(S_2)$
100	100	200	287 + 624 = 911	911
	200	300	539 + 381 = 920	
	300	400	754 + 175 = 929	
	400	500	934 + 0 = 934	
200	0	200	0 + 624 = 624	624
	100	300	287 + 381 = 668	
	200	400	539 + 175 = 714	
	300	500	754 + 0 = 754	
300	0	300	0 + 381 = 381	381
	100	400	287 + 175 = 462	
	200	500	539 + 0 = 539	
400	0	400	0 + 175 = 175	175
	100	500	287 + 0 = 287	
500	0	500	0 + 0 = 0	0

TABLE 10-11a First-Stage Computations for Discount Rate of 18%

S_1 (ha)	X_1	$S_2 = S_1 + X_1$	$\alpha_1 C_1(X_1) + f_2(S_2)$ (10^3)	$f_1(S_1)$
0	100	100	339 + 911 = 1250	1250
	200	200	636 + 624 = 1260	
	300	300	890 + 381 = 1271	
	400	400	1102 + 175 = 1277	
	500	500	1271 + 0 = 1271	

DP computations with the discount rate doubled (18% instead of 9%). With the higher discount rate it becomes more advantageous to delay the expansion of capacity until needed. From the tables, the new solution is $Z^* = f_1(0) = \$1,250,000$, $X_1^* = X_2^* = X_3^* = X_4^* = X_5^* = 100$ ha.

Although it is not possible to generalize this simple example to all capacity expansion problems, the results demonstrate two phenomena that are often important in such problems. The first is that high discount rates discourage the addition of excess capacity. This conforms to intuition and has implications for public investment projects such as waste treatment plants. Excess capacity provides a "factor of safety" to provide for the possibility of more rapid expansion of demand than had been planned for. Without the incentive of low discount rates, it may be too expensive for communities to risk the possibility of unused capacity. The second item demonstrated by the example is the effect of the discount rate on overall project cost. Although intuition might lead us to expect that the cost of the project would increase as the discount rate rises, this is not always the case. Although the rate was doubled (from 9 to 18%) in the second set of computations, the cost of the land reclamation actually *decreased* from $1,376,000 to $1,250,000. This was because it was possible to delay costs until future years, where they would be heavily discounted. The effects of discount rates on the costs of capacity expansion are seldom obvious, since present values of costs will be influenced by the changes in demand over time and economies of scale.

Summary

This chapter presented several short examples that illustrated the use of discount rates to quantify preferences for objectives over time. The examples dealt mostly with the mechanics of present value computations. However, they also demonstrated that the selection of a discount rate can profoundly affect the nature of optimal solutions to environmental and other public planning problems. Discount rates for public investment are quantitative measures of social attitudes toward the future vis-à-vis the present; their determination should, in principle, rest with political decision makers who legitimately represent the public.

SELECTED REFERENCES

1. Aguilar, R. J., *Systems Analysis and Design in Engineering, Architecture, Construction and Planning,* Prentice-Hall, Englewood Cliffs, N. J., 1973, Chapter 2.
2. Baumol, W. J., "On the Discount Rate for Public Projects," The *Analysis and Evaluation of Public Expenditures: The PPB System Vol. I,* 91st Congress, 1st Session, Joint Committee Print, U.S. Government Printing Office, Washington, D.C., 1969, pp. 489–503.
3. Grant, E. L., W. G. Ireson, and R. S. Leavenworth, *Principles of Engineering Economy,* 6th ed., Ronald Press, New York, 1976
4. Howe, C. H., *Benefit-Cost Analysis for Water System Planning,* Water Resources Monograph No. 2, American Geophysical Union, Washington, D.C., 1971.
5. James, L. D., and R. R. Lee, *Economics of Water Resources Planning,* McGraw-Hill, New York, 1970.
6. Marglin, S. A., *Public Investment Criteria,* the M.I.T. Press, Cambridge, Mass., 1967.

EXERCISES

10-1.

Three alternative plans have been developed for the expansion of a city's water supply system over the next 15 yr. Plan A has an initial cost of $14,000,000 and O&M costs of $1,200,000/yr. There is no salvage value at the end of 15 yr. Plan B involves a phased capacity expansion. Initial cost is $10,000,000 and O&M costs are $950,000/yr in years 1 to 10. A subsequent $10,000,000 expansion is made at the end of year 10, and total O&M costs for years 11 to 15 are $2,000,000/yr. Plan B produces a salvage value of $3,000,000 at the end of year 15. Plan C is the most complicated of the three alternatives. Initial cost is $7,000,000, and subsequent expansions costing $9,000,000 and $8,000,000 are made at the end of years 5 and 10, respectively. Annual O&M costs are $500,000, $900,000, and $2,500,000 in years 1 to 5, 6 to 10, and 11 to 15, respectively. Salvage value at the end of year 15 is $4,000,000.

Compute the present value costs and equivalent annual costs for these three plans using a 5% interest rate. Show that interest rates of 10 and 15% will change the relative rankings of the three plans.

10-2.

In addition to the present value of net benefits, the benefit/cost ratio

$$\frac{B_0 + \sum_t B_t/(1+r)^t}{C_0 + \sum_t C_t/(1+r)^t}$$

is often used to compare alternative time streams of benefits and costs. Consider the following two 10-yr investment plans. Plan A has an initial cost of $1,000,000 and yearly costs and benefits of $50,000 and $250,000, respectively. The initial cost of plan B is $2,300,000, and annual costs and benefits for the 10 years are $70,000/yr and $500,000/yr, respectively.

Using a discount rate of 10%, rank the two plans using their benefit/cost ratios. Compare this ranking to that obtained using the present value of net benefits. Why are different rankings produced? Repeat the analysis with a 15% discount rate.

10-3.

Consider an investment that has no initial costs or benefits but produces constant yearly net benefits $B - C$ in perpetuity. Show that the present value net benefits are given by

$$\text{PVNB} = \frac{B - C}{r}$$

where r is the discount rate.

10-4.

A state park authority wishes to develop new park land over the next 3 yr. The state presently has 1000 ha of park and wishes to have at least 1150, 1500, and 2200 ha at the end of years 1, 2, and 3, respectively. The cost of maintaining park land is $40/ha/yr. This cost is incurred at the beginning of each year and is based on the park area at that time. The costs of development are also incurred at the beginning of the year. If Y_t = ha of park land developed during year t, the state must pay at the beginning of year t for development:

$$K_t + c_t Y_t \quad \text{if} \quad Y_t > 0$$
$$0 \quad \text{if} \quad Y_t = 0$$

The areas available for development during each year are:

Year 1 (ha)	Year 2 (ha)	Year 3 (ha)
0	0	0
200	200	200
400	400	400
600	600	600
		800

Development costs are:

Year (t)	K_t ($)	c_t ($/ha)
1	25,000	100
2	20,000	120
3	30,000	150

The appropriate interest rate is 10%.
    (a) Using DP, determine a schedule of development that minimizes the present value of costs and meets the state's target levels for park land.
    (b) Suppose the state decides that 200 ha of its current park land is really no longer suitable for use. How does this change the development schedule? By how much would costs be increased?

10-5.

Capacity expansion is being planned to meet demands in year t given by $D_0 + dt$. D_0 is the known initial demand and d is a known constant. Thus demand increases linearly with time. Initial capacity ($t = 0$) is just equal to D_0. Costs of capacity addition in year t are given by KX_t^a, where X_t is the capacity added in year t and K and a are known constants. These costs reflect economies of scale ($a < 1$) and are incurred at the end of year t. Annual operation and maintenance costs are functions of demands.

    Assume that capacity is to be added every n years. Thus an initial addition of $X_0 = nd$ is required and comparable additions are made during years $t = n, 2n, 3n, \ldots$. The appropriate discount rate is r.
    (a) Show that the present value costs of capacity expansions are given by

$$Z = K(dn)^a \frac{f(r, n)}{r}$$

        where $f(r, n)$ is the capital recovery factor. (*Note.* The series $1 + x + x^2 + x^3 + \ldots$ is equal to $1/(1 - x)$ for $x^2 < 1$.)
    (b) Show that the optimal interval n^* for capacity additions is given by the solution to the equation $ae^{rn^*} - rn^* - a = 0$. (*Note.* The present value factor $\alpha_t = 1/(1 + r)^t$ can be approximated by e^{-rt}.)

INDEX

Agricultural models, 23–28, 86–87, 135–157
Agricultural nonpoint source pollution, 24, 135–157
  controls, 26, 136, 138, 151–156
  from dairy farms, 138–139
  income effects of controls, 151–154
  prediction, 26, 144–145
  see also Nitrogen; Pesticides; Phosphorus; Runoff; Sediment
Air pollution, 110–127
  ambient standards, 113
  comparison with water pollution, 110–113
  controls, 111–113
  duality application, 118–121
  dynamic programming models, 262–273
  effects, 111–113
  emission control examples, 113–114, 202, 262
  emission standards, 113
  fuel substitution for control of, 132
  general linear programming models, 121–127
  porportional rollback, see Rollback models
  sources, 111–113
  transport, see Air pollution transport
Air pollution transport, 122–127
  dispersion coefficients, 123–125
  emission plume, 122–123
  Gaussian dispersion equation, 123
  limitations of predictive equations, 114
  in linear programming models, 125–127
  transport factor, 125
Algorithm:
  assignment, 221–223
  definition, 67
  integer linear programming, 181–187
  linear programming, see Simplex method
  optimization, 67–83
  sequential search, 74–82
  transportation, 210–218
Alternatives:
  evaluation of, 10
  generation of, 9, 179
  null, 116
  selection of, 11
Amortization, 286
Animal nutrition, 142, 148

Artificial variables, see Simplex method
Assignment models, 218–223
  algorithm, 221–223
  dummy assignments, 220
  facilities location applications, 220, 227
  general form, 219
Assimilation capacity, see Waste assimilation

Basic solution, see Linear programming
Benefit/cost analysis, 2–6
Benefit/cost ratio, 298
Benefits:
  discounting of future, 284–290
  distribution to groups, 4–5
  net, 4–6
  social, 2
Biochemical oxygen demand, 42–46
  carbonaceous, 42
  decay, 44
  mixing, 44
  nitrogenous, 42
  removal by treatment, 45–46
BOD, see Biochemical oxygen demand

Calculus, see Lagrange multipliers
Capacity expansion, 291–297, 300
  discount rate effects, 295–297
  economies of scale effects, 291, 295–297
Capital recovery factor, 285
Carbonaceous BOD, see Biochemical oxygen demand
Carbon monoxide, 112
CBOD, see Biochemical oxygen demand
Cement, emissions from manufacturing, 114
Coal:
  allocation to sectors, 207
  emissions, 114
Components, see Systems
Composting of solid wastes, 188, 255
Concave functions, 170–171
Constraints, 16, 22
Convex functions, 170–171
Corner points, see Extreme points
Cost-effectiveness, 6

Costs:
    amortization of, 286
    capital, 50
    discounting of future, 284–290
    distribution to groups, 4–5
    estimating, 50
    functions, 50
    operation and maintenance, 50
    opportunity, 5
    penalty, 69
    shadow, 69, 212–213
Crops:
    nitrogen requirement, 48, 143
    pesticide applications on, 36–37, 131, 275
    rotations, 147–150
Cyclones, multiple and long-cone, 114

Dairy farm model, 141–146
Decision makers:
    in agricultural problems, 139–140
    definition, 8
    implicit, 25
    preferences of, 8–9, 25–26, 174, 178, 282
    see also Multiobjective planning
Decision variables, 16, 22
Decomposition:
    in dynamic programming, 239
    in large optimization model, 55–59
Dilution of wastes, 24, 44, 122–123
Discount rate, 282–283
    comparison of public and private, 289
    for public investments, 289–290
    selection of, 289–290
    see also Inflation; Present value
Dissolved oxygen, 42–45
    critical conditions, 45
    equation, 44
    reaeration, 43, 45
    saturation, 42, 45
    standard, 53
Dissolved solids, 33
DO, see Dissolved oxygen
DP, see Dynamic programming
Dual linear programming models, 102–110
    air pollution application, 118–121
    derivation, 102–104, 107
    primal/dual models, 106–110
    properties, 106, 108–110
    solutions from simplex method, 105
Dual variables:
    with Lagrange multipliers, 69
    in linear programming models, 102–104, 106
    in transportation model, 213

Dynamic programming, 229–279, 291–297
    alternative models, 243–246
    computational efficiency, 235–236
    computational procedure, 230–241, 259, 265–266
    with continuous variables, 247
    diagram, 237–238, 254
    final conditions, 254
    forward computations, 268–273
    grid size effects, 247–252
    initial conditions, 254
    multiple state variable, 242, 266–268
    notation, 237–241, 254–255
    one-dimensional model, 254
    optimal return function, 237, 255
    recursive equation, 241, 255
    separability conditions, 242
    stages, 235, 237, 241, 254
    state transformation function, 254
    state variable, 237, 254

Economies of scale, 24–25, 189, 291–297
Efficiency of treatment, 7–8
Effluent charge, 5
Effluent standard, 5
Electrostatic precipitator, 114
Energy:
    allocation, 207
    effects of prices and supplies, 157
    see also Coal; Fossil fuel; Petroleum
Environmental quality standard, 5
Environmental systems analysis, 1–12
Equivalent annual value, 286
Erosion, 138, 144, 149
Eutrophication, 34–35, 138
Evapotranspiration, 47–48
Externality, 3
Extreme points, 88–90, 101, 212

Facilities location, 220, 227
Feasible region, 18
Feasible solution, 16, 22, 101–102
Fertilizer, 141–144
Fixed charge problem, 187–196
Forestry, 173
Fossil fuel:
    allocation, 207
    substitution, 132

Groundwater pollution, 49

Hydrocarbons, 113

Incineration:
　of sludge, 63, 277
　of solid waste, 187–188, 202
Inequality constraints:
　effects on Lagrange multiplier method, 72–74
　transformation to equations, 72–73, 96–97
Inflation, effects on present value computations, 288
Inflation premium, 289
Integer linear programming, 179–199
　branch-and-bound algorithm, 181
　cutting plane algorithm, 181–186
　for fixed charge problem, 192–196
　graphical solution, 180–181
　linearization by, 196–198
　mixed integer, 179
Interest rate, see Discount rate; Present value
Inventory problems, 255–262
Irrigation:
　return flows, 33
　with wastewater, see Land application of wastes

Lagrange multipliers, 68–74
　boundary conditions, 74
　conditions for local optima, 70
　general model, 69
　inequality constraints with, 72–74
　limitations of, 72–74
Land application of wastes, 47–49
　costs, 50–51
　crop irrigation, 48
　groundwater pollution from, 48–49
　limiting factors, 47–48, 53
　municipal wastewater model for, 51–53
　sludge disposal, 63, 277
　storage prior to, 47
　toxic waste disposal, 37–38
Landfills:
　for sludge disposal, 63, 277
　for solid waste, 187–188
Land reclamation, 292
Land use planning, 173–179, 230–236, 282
Linear equations:
　definition, 85
　inconsistent, 101
　independent, 100
　properties of, 91, 101
　transformation of inequalities to, 96–97
Linearization:
　by integer programming, 196–198
　in separable programming, 161–179
Linear programming, 85–133
　advantages of, 85
　air pollution applications, see Air pollution

Linear programming (Cont.):
　basic solutions, 101, 206, 219
　dual, see Dual linear programming models
　extreme points, 88–90
　feasible solutions, 101–102
　graphical solutions, 88–89, 104–105
　integer, see Integer linear programming
　matrix notation, 95, 97
　negative decision variables, 100
　simplex method, see Simplex method
　solution properties, 101
　standard form, 91, 94–95
　transformation to standard form, 96–100
LP, see Linear programming

Manure:
　disposal, 141, 202, 278–279
　nitrogen content, 143, 278
Marginal value, 103, 106
Mathematical models:
　advantages of, 13
　construction of, 13–16
　simple, need for, 139
　in systems analysis, 2
Mathematical programming, 83, 85
　see also Dynamic programming; Linear programming
Mixed integer, see Integer linear programming
Models, see Mathematical models
Multiobjective planning, 173–179
　decision maker role, 175
　generation of alternatives, 178–179
　with multiattribute function, 174–176
　use of weights, 175–176, 178

Natural gas, allocation of, 207
NBOD, see Biochemical oxygen demand
Net energy, 142
Networks, 205, 277
Nitrogen:
　balance in soil, 48, 143–144
　crop requirement, see Crops
　dioxide, 112
　dissolved, 138, 145
　mineralization of organic, 143
　nitrate, 48
　nitrification, 46
　pollution of groundwater, 48–49
　in runoff, 145
　solid-phase, 138, 145
　volatilization, 143
Nitrogenous BOD, see Biochemical oxygen demand

304 INDEX

Nonlinear programming, see Dynamic programming; Linearization; Search; Separable programming
Nonpoint source pollution, 24, 135–137
   see also Agricultural nonpoint source pollution; Urban runoff

Objective functions, 16, 22
   discontinuous, 256–258
   multiattribute, 174
Objectives, 8–9, 25–26
   discounting of future, 281–284
   multiple, 9, 151, 173–174
   qualitative, 174
   see also Multiobjective planning; Objective functions
Ocean dumping, 187–188
Oil, see Petroleum allocation
Optimal solution, 16, 22
   approximate, 16
   global, 68
   local, 68
Optimization:
   constrained, see Lagrange multipliers; Optimization model
   unconstrained, 68
Optimization model, 2, 15
   for assignment problem, 219
   for dynamic programming, 254
   general form, 22
   linear, 86
   methods of solving, 16–17
   for separable programming, 171
   for transportation problem, 206

Percolation, 47–48
Pesticides:
   application to crops, see Crops
   control of, 26
   optimization model for management, 28, 87
   pollution from, 23
   in runoff, 23
Petroleum allocation, 36, 207
Phosphorus:
   in agricultural runoff, 34, 145
   discharge to lakes, 35, 242
   dissolved, 138, 145
   removal from wastewater, 35, 242
   solid-phase, 138, 145
Photochemical oxidants, 112
Power plant emissions, 114
Preferences:
   of decision makers, see Decision makers

Preferences (Cont.):
   social, 4–5, 290
   when objectives are achieved, 281
   weighted, 175
Present value, 282–287
   computations, 285
   factor, 285
   of net benefits, 285
Protein, digestible, 142

Recreation:
   benefits, 33
   location of facilities, 220, 227
   outdoor, 173
   zoning for, 230
Recycling:
   of solid waste, 187–188
      see also Composting
   of wastewater, 47, 130, 226
Reservoirs, 33, 63, 257
Resource allocation:
   in benefit/cost analysis, 2
   in dynamic programming, 242
Rollback models:
   assumptions for, 114–115
   duality application to, 118–121
   in emissions control example, 114–117
   general form, 121
Runoff:
   agricultural, 135–136, 145, 149–150
   urban, see Urban runoff

Saddle points, 68, 71
Saltwater marsh, 227–228
Salvage value, 285–287
Sanitary landfill, see Landfills
Scrubber, 114
Search:
   Box's algorithm, 75–82
   convergence of, 80–81
   informal, 17–20, 28–31, 55–59
   limitations of, 67, 82–83
   sequential, 74–82
   starting conditions, 80–81
   strategy, 19, 28, 55
Secondary treatment, see Wastewater treatment
Sediment, 138, 155
Sensitivity analysis:
   applied to air pollution control, 118–121
   of costs, 88–90
   of discount rate, 283–284, 289–290, 295–297

INDEX 305

Sensitivity analysis (*Cont.*):
  with dual linear programming, 102–106, 118–121
  of pesticide loss constraint, 102–106
  of phosphorus effluent standard, 252–253
  of wastewater irrigation, 55–56
Separable function, 169, 242
Separable programming, 161–179
  conditions for, 169–171
  with segment variables, 162–165, 172
  with segment weights, 165–169, 172–173
  transformations to obtain separability, 176
Sequential allocation in dynamic programming, 229, 241–242
Sequential decisions, 241
Serendipity, 105
Settling chamber, 114
Sewage, *see* Wastewater treatment
Sewage farming, 42
Shadow costs, 69, 212–213
Simplex method, 90–94, 97–99
  artificial variables, 98
  initial solutions, 98
  solutions to dual model, 105
  tableau, 92
Slack variables, 73, 91, 96
Sludge disposal, 63, 276
Soil and water conservation, 26, 138, 157
Soils, 141, 147
Solid wastes:
  disposal, 187–196
  fixed costs, 189–190
  management, 187–188
  regional example, 188
  transportation, 193, 225
  see also Composting of solid wastes; Incineration; Landfills; Ocean dumping; Recycling
Standards:
  ambient, 113
  effluent, 5
  emissions, 113
  environmental quality, 5
Stationary points, 68–71
Sulfur dioxide, 111
Surplus variables, 73, 96
Systems, 1, 9
  components, 9
Systems analysis, 1–2
  amenable problems for, 22, 190–191
  by government agency, 139–140
  limitations of, 26, 139

Systems analysis (*Cont.*):
  as research activity, 137
Systems approach, 1, 20–23
  example, 6–12
  historic application, 42

Tertiary treatment, *see* Wastewater treatment
Toxic wastes:
  burial, 37–38
  food chain effects, 24
  treatment, 201–202, 275–276
Trade-offs:
  between competing resource uses, 5
  environmental/economic, 121, 151–155, 253
Transportation models, 205–228
  algorithm, 210–218
  allocation costs, 212–214
  assignment problem, *see* Assignment models
  basic solutions, 207, 210–212
  closed loops, 211, 214
  degeneracy, 218
  dual variables, 213
  dummy allocations, 209
  energy application, 207–208
  general form, 206
  northwest corner method for initial solutions, 212
  shadow costs, 212–213

Uncertainty:
  of air quality predictions, 114
  of costs, 88–90
  in model parameters, 26–27, 118
  see also Sensitivity analysis
Universal Soil Loss Equation, 144, 149
Urban runoff, 136, 157–159
  detention of, 159

Variables, definition of, 13–14, 115, 243–247, 263
  see also Decision variables: Slack variables; Surplus variables

Waste assimilation, 3, 24, 45, 122–127
Wastewater treatment:
  costs of, 50
  by filtration, 45–46
  municipal, 41–65
    model for, 51–55
  by nitrification, 46
  for phosphorus removal, 35, 242
  regional, 62, 64

Wastewater treatment (*Cont.*):
   for reuse, 47, 130, 226
   secondary, 41, 45
   tertiary, 64
Water pollution, evaluation of by benefit/cost analysis, 2–6
   see also Biochemical oxygen demand; Dissolved oxygen; Eutrophication; Groundwater pollution; Nonpoint source pollution; Pesticides; Waste assimilation; Wastewater treatment
Water supply, 130, 63, 226
Wildlife, 173, 282

Zoning, 230

U.C. BERKELEY
ENGINEERING LIBRARY